THE LONG SHADOW
OF DEFAULT

THE LONG SHADOW OF DEFAULT

BRITAIN'S UNPAID WAR DEBTS TO THE UNITED STATES, 1917–2020

DAVID JAMES GILL

Yale UNIVERSITY PRESS

New Haven and London

Published with assistance from the Louis Stern Memorial Fund.

Yale University Press books may be purchased in quantity for educational, business, or promotional use. For information, please e-mail sales.press@yale.edu (U.S. office) or sales@yaleup.co.uk (U.K. office).

Set in Sabon and Berthold City Bold type by Newgen North America, Austin, Texas
Printed in the United States of America.

Library of Congress Control Number: 2021950215
ISBN 978-0-300-24718-3 (hardcover : alk. paper)

A catalogue record for this book is available from the British Library.

This paper meets the requirements of ANSI/NISO Z39.48-1992 (Permanence of Paper).

10 9 8 7 6 5 4 3 2 1

For Thomas, Matthew, and Gemma

Contents

Illustrations and Tables

Acknowledgments

Portions of the text appear in the following article: "Rating the UK: The Britain Government's Sovereign Credit Ratings, 1976–1978," *Economic History Review* 68, no. 3 (2015). I am grateful to this journal and its publisher, Wiley-Blackwell, for allowing me to reproduce elements of my research in this book.

Many thanks to the Arts and Humanities Research Council, which funded elements of this research with a Leadership Fellowship Award (AH/P006582/1), and to the Economic History Society for a Carnevali Small Research Grant that supported an earlier pilot study. This book would not exist without the generosity of these important organizations and the many talented people working within them.

I am grateful to everyone who helped me to produce *The Long Shadow of Default*. My thanks go to Peggy Ann Brown, Fabio Capano, and Caterina Moruzzi for their research assistance and the numerous archivists who have helped me locate material for this book. I benefited from in-person or online interactions with knowledgeable and supportive staff working at the National Archives based in London and Washington, DC, the Bank of England, and the Herbert Hoover, Franklin D. Roosevelt, Harry S. Truman, Dwight D. Eisenhower, John F. Kennedy, Lyndon B. Johnson, Richard Nixon, Gerald R. Ford, and Jimmy Carter Presidential Libraries. Thank you also to the staff at the private papers held in the archives of the universities of California,

Cambridge, Kentucky, Yale, and York. Without such supportive archivists, the process of writing history would be significantly more challenging and much less rewarding.

Thank you to the many scholars who have helped me to produce this book. I am grateful to Rory Cormac, Giselle Datz, Matthew DiGiuseppe, Markus Eberhardt, Michael J. Gill, Caitlin Milazzo, Layna Mosley, Kim Oosterlinck, Patrick Shea, Cecilia Testa, and David K. Thompson for their advice and feedback on different elements of the project. Special thanks to Martin Daunton, Harold James, Duncan Needham, and Thomas Robb, who read an earlier draft of the book in its entirety. Their insightful suggestions and generous advice made my work considerably better. In much the same way, I am indebted to the two anonymous reviewers and my editor, Seth Ditchik, for their excellent feedback and valuable guidance that greatly improved the book. Thank you also to Adina Berk, Amanda Gerstenfeld, Andrew Katz, Kristy Leonard, Karen Olson, and Jeff Schier and the team at Yale University Press for their tremendous support with the project.

I presented elements of the book to a wide range of audiences between 2013 and 2019. I am grateful to the conference panelists and participants at the Economic History Society, British International Studies Association, International Studies Association, and British International History Group conferences as well as the Cambridge Financial History Seminar series. I owe a special debt of gratitude to current and former employees of the U.S. Treasury and Her Majesty's Treasury for their support and guidance throughout this project. Jerry Auten, Kathleen Cochrane, David Joy, Joan M. Kotze, Anthony Marcus, Franklin Noll, Mario Pisani, and Andy Young provided valuable insights regarding the past and present of debt management. Thanks also to the many other members of both Treasuries who attended my talks and offered useful feedback. In addition, elements of the book benefited from the insights of Lester L. Wolff and Lawrence Summers. I am grateful for their help.

My friends and colleagues in Cambridge, London, and Nottingham deserve considerable thanks for their kindness throughout the many years of researching and writing. Most important, thank you to my family for their support and patience. I dedicate this book to them.

Abbreviations

BBC	British Broadcasting Corporation
BDA	British Debts to America
BE	Bank of England Archive
BLI	British Library of Information
CAB	Cabinet file (National Archives, London)
Cmd.	Command Paper
CO	Colonial Office (National Archives, London)
FO	Foreign Office file (National Archives, London)
FRG	Federal Republic of Germany
FDRL	Franklin D. Roosevelt Presidential Library
FRUS	*Foreign Relations of the United States*
FVP	Frederick Vinson Papers (University of Kentucky Library)
GBP	British pounds
GDP	gross domestic product
HC Deb.	House of Commons debates
HHL	Herbert Hoover Presidential Library
HFP	Henry "Joe" Fowler Papers (Lyndon B. Johnson Presidential Library)
HJP	Hiram W. Johnson Papers (Bancroft Library, University of California, Berkeley)
HL Deb.	House of Lords debates
HM Treasury	His/Her Majesty's Treasury

HSTL	Harry S. Truman Presidential Library
IBRD	International Bank for Reconstruction and Development
IMF	International Monetary Fund
MP	member of Parliament (United Kingdom)
NAII	National Archives II, College Park, MD
NATO	North Atlantic Treaty Organization
PIN	Ministry of Pensions and National Insurance (National Archives, London)
PREM	Prime Minister's Office files (National Archives, London)
PSF	President's Secretary's File (FDRL)
PW	PriceWaterhouse
RG	Record Group
SBP	Stanley Baldwin Papers (Cambridge University Library)
T	HM Treasury file (National Archives, London)
USD	US dollars
WWFDC	World War Foreign Debts Commission

THE LONG SHADOW
OF DEFAULT

Introduction

SOVEREIGN DEFAULT IS a perennial feature of international history. The past century has provided plentiful examples of states that have failed to repay their debts on time or in full.[1] In the past decade alone, Greece, Argentina, Venezuela, Barbados, and Lebanon have attracted criticism from foreign investors by failing to honor their financial obligations. Many more states will face major debt crises in the wake of the economic turmoil created by the coronavirus pandemic. With millions and sometimes billions of dollars at stake in many cases, the risk of default remains a fascinating, controversial, and emotive topic. The behavior of defaulting governments angers and interests the public around the world, but most people know little about the history of such events beyond the vast sums involved. Moreover, in much of the Western world, the risk of default has appeared for many as a problem for other, typically less-developed countries; few people are aware that wealthy and powerful democracies have defaulted on their own debts in the twentieth century.[2]

This book focuses on an important but neglected episode of sovereign default involving two of the wealthiest and most powerful democracies in modern history.[3] The United Kingdom accrued considerable financial debts to the United States during the final stages of the First World War and immediate postwar period in the form of war loans.[4] On 15 June 1934, the British government unilaterally suspended payment on these U.S. loans, which totaled $4.7 billion.[5] The size of these unpaid obligations is remarkable.[6] Britain's suspension of its war debts to the United States represents one of the largest sovereign defaults of the past century.[7] Whereas many other defaulting states would go on to strike deals with some of their creditors, the United Kingdom's debts remain unpaid and outstanding. The British case therefore constitutes an historically large but also clear-cut type of sovereign default—namely, a unilateral and enduring suspension, if not outright repudiation—rather than the more cooperative and subtle forms of debt restructuring that occur more commonly today.[8]

The British government has never formally repudiated the United Kingdom's war debts to the United States, to be sure, but nor has it ever resumed payment. London has always been keen to stress that these debts were special because they had arisen as part of a cooperative wartime effort, which garnered no advantage to the recipients and were of immeasurable value to the common cause. Furthermore, as the British government has long argued, its own wartime allies owed more to the United Kingdom than it owed to the United States, but they had defaulted on their debts.[9] Notwithstanding London's initial efforts to justify this decision and its studious avoidance of the subject in the many decades that followed, Washington has never forgiven or excused this default.[10] The United States government has consistently stressed the sanctity of financial loans, noting the legal obligation into which Britain had entered as well as the later renegotiation of these obligations in 1923, and expressed its reluctance to burdening American taxpayers with foreign debts.

Despite the passage of more than a century since the end of the Great War, neither side has had the political will to resolve these outstanding obligations. Washington remains unwilling to forgive the debts, and London continues to ignore them, even as they continue to accrue interest after decades of missed payments. This political limbo is not unique to these two states. The United States continued to record the status of outstanding obligations from other war debtors dotted around the globe for decades. In 2009, the U.S. Treasury provided the latest publicly available data on these debts, revealing a long list of states that still owe tens or hundreds of millions and, in some cases, billions of dollars to the United States (Table I.1).[11]

The United Kingdom remains the largest First World War debtor to the United States but has chosen not to keep account of its unpaid

Table I.1. Indebtedness of foreign governments to the U.S. arising from World War I, 2009 (USD)

State	Agreement obligation[a]	Interest accrued	Cumulative payments		Payments received		Total outstanding
			Principal	Interest	Principal	Interest	
Armenia	11,959,917	53,996,535	32	0	0	0	65,956,420
Austria[b]	26,843,149	23,089,038	862,668	0	0	0	49,069,518
Belgium	423,587,630	691,411,606	19,157,630	33,033,643	0	0	1,062,807,963
Cuba	10,000,000	2,286,752	10,000,000	2,286,752	0	0	0
Czechoslovakia	185,071,023	362,688,842	19,829,914	304,178	0	0	527,625,773
Estonia	16,958,373	47,435,005	11	1,248,432	0	0	63,144,935
Finland	9,000,000	12,661,578	9,000,000[c]	12,661,578	0	0	0
France	4,128,326,088	9,075,648,500	226,039,588	260,036,303	0	0	12,717,898,698
Great Britain	4,933,701,642	13,762,504,853	434,181,642	1,592,803,791[i]	0	0	16,669,221,062
Greece (I)	21,163,923	3,814,037	983,923	3,143,133	0	0	20,850,904
Greece (II)[d]	13,155,921	9,746,033	4417722	9724966	151,111	177,786	8,759,266
Hungary[e]	2,051,898	3,665,641	2,051,898	3,665,641	0	0	0
Italy	2,044,870,444	1,800,256,954	37,464,319	63,365,561	0	0	3744,297,518
Latvia	7,094,654	19,931,373	9,200	752,349	0	0	26264478
Liberia	26,000	10,472	26,000	10,472	0	0	0
Lithuania	6,618,395	1,8233,083	234,783	1,003,174	0	0	2,3613,522
Nicaragua[f]	141,950	26,625	141,950	26,625	0	0	0

(continued)

Table I.1. (*continued*)

State	Agreement obligation[a]	Interest accrued	Cumulative payments		Payments received		Total outstanding
			Principal	Interest	Principal	Interest	
Poland	213,506,132[g]	599,333,563	1,287,297	21359000	0	0	790,193,397
Rumania	68,359,192	158,388,530	4,498,632[h]	292,375	0	0	221,956,715
Russia	192,601,297	885,281,689	0	8,750,312[i]	0	0	1,069,132,675
Yugoslavia	63,577,713	117,566,296	1,952,713	636,059	0	0	178,555,237
TOTAL	12,378,615,343	27,647,977,004	772,139,923	2,015,104,344	151,111	177,786	37,239,348,080

Source: U.S. Department of the Treasury and Office of Management and Budget, "U.S. Government Foreign Credit Exposure as of December 31, 2009, Part I: Summary Analysis" (data retrieved 2011, 2018), 33, table 7, data as of year-end, 31 December 2009. The U.S. Treasury has produced tables recording the indebtedness of foreign governments to the U.S. arising from World War I for decades. At the time of writing, U.S. Treasury reports containing these tables were available via British and U.S. archives, the Federal Reserve Archival System for Economic Research, and the U.S. Treasury website. Thank you to the Treasury officials and archivists who helped me to find these reports. Hereafter, all notes have been changed from numbers to italicized letters. I present the totals as provided in the published version. The totals for "Agreement obligation," "Interest accrued," "Cumulative Payments: Principal," and "Total Outstanding" vary from the sum of their respective columns by $1-$2, which likely reflects the rounding of figures. The published table also uses some curious data, including outdated spellings, such as "Rumania," and states that have since dissolved, such as Czechoslovakia. It also contains a slightly larger difference between the sum of the figures in the omitted "Principal due and unpaid" column and the total as presented in the published version. Nevertheless, these data provide a helpful insight into the status of First World War debts owed to the United States by the United Kingdom and many other states around the world. Unless otherwise stated, all U.S. Treasury data in this book are presented in their published form.

[a] Includes capitalized interest.

[b] The Federal Republic of Germany has recognized liability for securities falling due between 12 March 1938 and 8 May 1945.

[c] $8,480,090 has been made available for educational exchange programs with Finland pursuant to 22 U.S.C. 2455(e).

[d] $13,155,921 refunded by the agreement of 28 May 1964, which was ratified by Congress on 5 November 1966.

[e] Interest payment from 15 December 1932 to 15 June 1937 was paid in pengo (Hungarian currency) equivalent.

[f] The indebtedness of Nicaragua was canceled pursuant to the agreement of 14 April 1938.

[g] After deduction of claim allowance of $1,813,429.

[h] Excludes payment of $100,000 on 14 June 1940, as a token of good faith.

[i] Includes proceeds from liquidation of Russian assets in the United States.

[j] Includes donation of James Bertram's estate of $2,131,134.49 in 2002.

debts, although neither has it continued to record its own outstanding and larger credits to wartime allies.[12] Decades of inflation have gradually eroded the value of these debts, which explains why their comparative worth has reduced since default.[13] Neither the U.S. Treasury nor HM Treasury has shared any further information concerning these outstanding obligations with the public in the past ten years, but on the basis of the available data, the United Kingdom presently owes the United States approximately $18 billion.[14]

This book examines the long history of these unpaid debts. It covers a period of 103 years, from the United Kingdom's receipt of an initial loan from the United States government in 1917 through to the official status of these debts over a century later in 2020. The breadth and depth of this approach allow for one of the most detailed historical analyses of any sovereign default to date. In so doing, this book seeks to bring attention to an often-neglected episode in financial history to inform, refine, and sometimes challenge the wider study of sovereign default.[15]

RETHINKING DEFAULT

The subject of the United Kingdom's unpaid war debts to the United States was treated with considerable importance by some of the world's most influential politicians and economists. Leaders ranging from Woodrow Wilson and Franklin Roosevelt through to David Lloyd George and Winston Churchill grappled with this thorny problem prior to the Second World War. In the following decades, influential American and British policymakers such as Dean Acheson, George Ball, and Lord Halifax would go on to deal with these unpaid debts. A wide range of presidents, prime ministers, and senior officials on both sides of the Atlantic have explicitly considered the subject in their writings.[16] Leading economists such as Gustav Cassel, Irving Fisher, John Maynard Keynes, Herbert Feis, James Harvey Rogers, Frederick Leith-Ross, and George F. Warren also considered these debts in their work and advised governments on the subject.[17] Notable economists have also briefly encountered these unpaid war debts while working in the U.S. Treasury in the latter half of the twentieth century, including Paul Volcker and Lawrence Summers.[18]

Yet these unpaid debts have gradually faded from popular attention over the past century. No president or prime minister has addressed the subject directly for many decades. Leading scholars have also overlooked or downplayed this significant episode in international financial history. In an impressive analysis of government debt defaults from around the world, for example, Carmen Reinhart and Kenneth Rogoff conclude that the United Kingdom has never defaulted on external debts in the past two centuries.[19] The British default on its U.S.-backed interallied war loans therefore remains widely neglected or misunderstood by policymakers and economists today, a situation exacerbated by coverage from experts and journalists.[20]

Interest in the United Kingdom's default on its war debts to the United States has been largely limited in the study of U.S. and British history in the twentieth century.[21] None of this is to suggest that the broader "war debts problem"—namely, the thorny moral and political issues of repayment faced both by debtors and lenders in the wake of the Great War—has failed to generate some attention. Historians have ably examined the broader politics of European war debts and reparations up to the early 1930s, which naturally touch on the subject.[22] In particular, Liaquat Ahamed, Patricia Clavin, Robert Self, and Jeremy Wormell have produced valuable accounts of British war debts from creation to default.[23]

There is nevertheless good reason to return to this subject as important questions persist. Why was the United Kingdom among the last states in Europe to suspend repayment to the United States? Many other countries never sought a debt settlement with the United States, and the United Kingdom had already survived the worst of the Great Depression when it did eventually default.[24] Why states repay their debts continues to generate considerable debate among economists and political scientists, which both motivates and informs research into this question. More importantly, those studies concerning British war debts to the United States concentrate on events preceding default.[25] The history of this subject remains largely overlooked thereafter.[26] What were the consequences of British default? Scholars are aware that the Great War cast a long shadow over the twentieth century.[27] In the decades that followed the conflict, historians and economists have repeatedly stressed the enduring economic effects of the hostilities, from the destabilizing nature of reparations to the costs associated with the erosion of empires.[28] Yet the consequences of decades of missed payments on debts worth billions of dollars has received curiously little attention.

An analysis of this neglected historical episode provides valuable insights for scholars seeking to better understand the phenomenon of sovereign default. This book makes two specific contributions. The first is to examine the logic of repayment by explaining why the British government continued to repay its debts to the United States long after many other states had stopped. The second is to consider the longer-term and largely neglected consequences of the eventual default. These two insights, which are summarized in the sections below, help to inform the work of economic and political historians but also complement research produced by some social scientists, especially political scientists and international relations scholars using historical or case-study data to build or test their theories. In so doing, this book joins a small but important body of work using qualitative methods to support their explanations concerning the phenomenon of sovereign default.[29]

THE LOGIC OF REPAYMENT

Only a minority of governments fail to meet their contractual obligations to creditors every year. The central and enduring puzzle of sovereign debt is why, in the absence of a world government to enforce commitments, most states honor their obligations.[30] No one theory or approach has proven sufficient. Anomalies will always exist given the large number of examples and many types of default that exist across time and space. Social scientists' explanations for why states repay their debts tend to focus on rational assessments of economic variables—namely, that governments or key actors within them are wary of reputational harm, the risk of punishments, or economic spillover effects.[31] Cost-benefit calculations based on the economic performance of the state or actors within it provide a useful baseline in explaining why governments honor their debts, to be sure, but they can be incomplete or inappropriate in some cases.[32]

A smaller number of economists and political scientists have considered other explanations beyond rational assessments of economic variables—most importantly, domestic-political conflict and changes in state identity—to explain why states repay their debts.[33] Historians have also touched on similar themes, although typically eschewing sweeping explanations and focusing instead on specific cases. In the British case, they also highlight the importance of a mix of economic, political, and ideological drivers, which encouraged the British government to repay its debts up until 1934. British hopes for debt concessions, concerns about global economic confidence, and a desire to protect transatlantic political relations all served to discourage sovereign default.[34]

This book returns to the question of why the British government was slower than many other states to default on its war debts to the U.S. It provides fresh insights that build on the work of historians and complement the efforts of some social scientists, especially those scholars who seek to use historical cases to understand why states repay their debts despite serious economic or political challenges. I argue that reputation-based concerns helped to deter default, but in contrast to much of the existing literature, they had more to do with Britain's role as an international creditor than its being a debtor to the United States.[35] The British government was concerned that states owing money to United Kingdom—including Argentina, Australia, and Germany—might use British default as an excuse to cease repayment on their own outstanding debts.[36] A wave of defaults not only would add to the burdens of British taxpayers but could undermine the foundations of the global economy. These fears, which existed alongside the more familiar concerns already highlighted by historians, deserve more attention than they have heretofore received from scholars because they help to better explain the course of decision-making in London.

Close analysis of events also provides some support for the importance of domestic politics and national identity in decision-making. Some cabinet ministers and members of Parliament believed initially that refusal to pay would profoundly shock a large section of domestic public opinion, especially given that many British people were struggling to meet their obligations in the wake of the Great Depression. Default could thereby undermine the popularity of the government and harm its chances in future elections. As such, domestic-political interests initially deterred rather than drove default, even if cabinet concerns about public opinion eventually shifted in support of a suspension of payments. Continued repayment was politically appropriate and provided the British government with more time to gauge both reputational and domestic-political risks, which helped to prepare the country for default should a settlement with the United States prove impossible. The British government therefore recognized and respected traditions or norms of repayment not only because many ministers believed default was inappropriate or illegitimate but also because of the potential international and domestic risks involved in nonpayment.[37]

The motivations and approaches of creditors toward debtors—and their role in explaining sovereign default—tends to receive much less attention from scholars.[38] This book seeks to address this gap by focusing equal attention to the creditor in question. The United States' handling of the war debt was politically rational if not economically prudent. Washington's unwillingness to negotiate encouraged default, which cost the U.S. government tens of millions of dollars in 1934 and potentially for every year thereafter for decades to come. A small number of United States policymakers believed that hard-line tactics could encourage repayment. They were correct in their belief that the United Kingdom could afford to pay more than British representatives claimed.[39]

Yet most members of Congress were driven by short-term electoral concerns. The revision of European war debts was deeply unpopular across much of the United States. Overburdened American taxpayers remained indisposed to the reduction of foreign debts in the depths of the Depression. Few political leaders were willing to squander valuable political capital on such an unpopular issue. After Congress passed the Johnson Act, which rejected partial payments from debtor states and resulted in a further wave of international defaults, Washington could blame Europe for U.S. woes. Washington's stance also complemented, and helped to represent, an increasingly popular noninterventionist mood in the United States. This book therefore informs existing explanations of how creditors manage sovereign debt. Political concerns can evidently trump economic interests even when billions of dollars are at stake.

THE CONSEQUENCES OF DEFAULT

Scholars tend to assume dire political costs to incumbent governments following default as well as significant economic costs for the domestic economy, international trade, and reputation.[40] Many of these consequences appear to have been relatively limited with respect to the United Kingdom in the years immediately following default, with policymakers benefiting in part from the challenging economic conditions of the period.[41] The British government used the sums allocated for repayment to reverse heavy increases in taxation as well as cuts in allowances.[42] Prime Minister Stanley Baldwin went on to secure another large majority in the election of November 1935, in large part benefiting from improving economic conditions and declining levels of unemployment despite limited government efforts to promote recovery.[43] Nor did the British government's suspension of payments to the U.S. generate a domino effect of defaults. Income derived from overseas investments remained largely stable.[44] Default also failed to undermine broader transatlantic economic cooperation as both governments worked closely together on exchange-rate stabilization policies in 1935 as well as an Anglo-American Trade Agreement and Tripartite Monetary agreements of 1936.[45]

The United Kingdom was not alone in enjoying these rewards. Other major European powers such as France had already shown that suspending war-debt repayments carried limited risks, which helped to motivate British default.[46] Nevertheless, there were wider trade-offs, especially for the United Kingdom. Political scientists have shown the importance of access to credit for states with regard to international security.[47] If credit becomes more difficult to secure after nonpayment, default poses significant strategic risks for states. The British case supports these concerns. As the United States struggled through the Great Depression, the memory of these unpaid debts lingered. U.S. opinion hardened against Europe and access to U.S. finances ceased in the wake of the Johnson Act, which closed the New York securities and money markets to any government behind on its debt payments. Default consequently weakened any anti-German coalition and undermined France and the United Kingdom's ability to wage war.[48]

Many scholars assume British default to be largely irrelevant to the course of economic and political history within five to ten years of default. The existing literature sometimes erroneously claims that Britain's debts were forgiven by the U.S. in the decades that followed—noting close economic cooperation in the Second World War, further and sizeable loans in the postwar period, and the London Debt Agreement of 1953—or that they naturally expired. Yet the British government has repeatedly conceded their existence, and the U.S. Treasury has maintained detailed records of these outstanding obligations for decades.[49] Some governments evidently have long memories concerning unpaid debts, which broadly complements arguments by a small number of economists that debt markets also retain a better memory of default than commonly assumed.[50] This book provides a detailed examination of the longer-term, albeit often harder to quantify, political consequences of default in this case, encouraging a shift away from only short-term analysis.[51]

The United Kingdom's unpaid war debts to the United States cast a surprisingly long and sometimes dark shadow over policymaking on both sides of the Atlantic. British default presented a serious challenge to U.S. financial support after the Second World War. Congressional support for the rapid termination of Lend-Lease reflected, at least in part, anger at the United Kingdom's unpaid war debts. One of the main arguments by critics in Congress against the proposed Anglo-American loan that followed was that it would also not be repaid.[52] Throughout the difficult process of ratification, Congress made frequent reference to outstanding debts and the risks of future default passed onto American taxpayers.[53] Memories of British default help to explain both the restrictive and novel nature of U.S. lending to the United Kingdom during and after the Second World War.

Policymakers in Washington and London continued to discuss these war debts in the years that followed, including as a solution to the economic challenges facing the U.S. in the 1960s and 1970s. Tensions peaked in 1973 when over one hundred members of the House of Representatives sponsored a resolution that asked the U.S. Treasury to pursue the prompt repayment of these long-standing war debts. The United Kingdom remained publicly silent throughout this period. Behind the scenes, HM Treasury was preparing to deal with the issue should diplomatic pressure intensify.[54] These unpaid debts resurfaced when Treasury officials in London and Washington faced serious legal challenges to the status quo throughout the 1980s and 1990s. Much of the controversy reflected a private will, which bequeathed a multimillion-dollar donation to the United Kingdom to pay down some of its outstanding war debt to the United States. A series of protracted legal rulings followed, which ultimately led to a deposit of $2.1 million to the United States on behalf of the British government in 2002.[55]

This book's contributions to the study of sovereign default are intended to inform the work of historians and social scientists. As Noel

Maurer explains, historical research plays a key role in helping to convert "stylized facts" into "real facts, verified by data and evidence."[56] To be sure, focusing on a specific type of default in a particular historical context—in this instance a unilateral default on state-to-state war debts in the 1930s—may limit the scope for comparison to other defaults across space and time.[57] Furthermore, a focus on the course of decision-making in Washington and London, based on available archival data, will be better suited to social scientists seeking rich historical detail with which to build, test, or refine their own work.[58] Nevertheless, this case remains an important example with which many scholars should consult and contend, especially to reflect on their own assumptions about the nature of sovereign default. In one of the more cited papers concerning sovereign debt, leading economists Herschel I. Grossman and John B. Van Huyck claimed that history provides three stylized facts about default: first, that defaults are associated with identifiably bad states of the world; second, that defaults are usually partial, rather than complete; third, that sovereign states usually can borrow again soon after a default.[59] The United Kingdom's default on its war debts to the United States raises important questions about all three claims.

1   Prelude to Default, 1917–1932

THE UNITED KINGDOM survived the majority of the First World War without financial support from the United States government. Although private American investors did provide considerable amounts of credit, the U.S. Treasury only assumed the burden of sustaining the Allied effort after the United States declared war against Germany on 6 April 1917. Financial support came in the form of dollar-denominated loans. Even before the war had ended, and throughout the postwar period, Washington repeatedly rejected suggestions of revision or cancellation emanating from London and Paris. The challenges of war debts and the related issue of reparations have already attracted considerable attention from historians and economists.[1] This chapter serves as a summary of existing work to help contextualize the United Kingdom's eventual default to the United States.

Attitudes to the war debts differed on each side of the Atlantic.[2] European leaders argued that these debts were special because they had arisen as part of a cooperative wartime effort, much of which was funded by domestic sacrifices rather than foreign loans, that garnered no advantage to the recipients and were of immeasurable value to the common cause. Furthermore, they believed that the United States had benefited from the war at their expense and argued that onerous repayments would undermine economic recovery. U.S. policymakers reacted poorly to what they felt was a remarkable degree of entitlement, much of which touched on older suspicions of the European powers. They instead stressed the sanctity of commercial loans, noting the legal obligation into which Britain and Europe had entered and expressed their reluctance to burdening the United States' own taxpayers with foreign debts. Both sides also disagreed on the relationship between reparations and war debts. Britain and France sought to condition repayment of interallied war debts on German reparations, a solution that they considered just given the outcome of the war. This proposal would leave the United States largely dependent on repayment from Germany, which allowed Europe to escape its debts but saddled them to American taxpayers, who would inherit all the risks of a default. As such, the United States insisted that reparations bore no relation to war debts.

These debates continued until the United States began to pursue the collection of its debts more seriously following the creation of the World War Foreign Debt Commission in 1922. In the following year, the British government became the first debtor state to agree terms and begin repayment. Most European borrowers followed suit over the coming decade. The British government had also lent considerable sums to its allies during the war and now sought to recover these debts as well as reparations from Germany to fund its own payments. The resumption of payments was a rational effort to overcome the uncertainty afflicting European markets, secure future U.S. investment in the region, and improve trade more broadly. It also reflected growing fears of U.S. reprisals, concerns about national honor, and the failure of diplomatic efforts to secure cancellation. U.S. behavior in this period was also broadly rational. Congressional ignorance and public anger were important factors, to be sure, but cancellation or significant reductions would have contradicted U.S. national interests given ongoing competition with Europe and burdened American taxpayers, who were already struggling in the postwar recession. U.S. efforts to restructure European debts proved effective and resulted in healthy returns thereafter.[3]

The United Kingdom, like France and Germany, struggled to service its debts following the onset of the Great Depression.[4] The formation of the National Government in 1931 introduced new attitudes and approaches to economic policy. The personal and ideological complexion of the coalition government, however, meant that default was unpopular, despite lingering doubts about the rationality or fairness of continued repayment. London, working with Paris and Berlin, instead attempted to use the crisis to pressure Washington into granting a suspension of payments. As the crisis mounted, the Hoover administration grudgingly enacted a one-year moratorium to ease the international economic crisis and provide time for recovery. U.S. policymakers had envisaged a resumption of payments thereafter, but European debtors instead attempted to use this opportunity to renegotiate or cancel their debts.

In summer 1932, representatives from Britain, France, and Germany met at the Lausanne Conference and eventually reached a "gentlemen's agreement" to end reparations and war-debt payments among themselves. European leaders believed that international pressure would prompt U.S. cooperation but underestimated congressional and popular resistance in the U.S. When Washington demanded repayment later that year, London faced a difficult choice between honoring its commitments to Europe or the United States. The National Government's position was complicated by its own struggles with the economic slump as well as the precedent established on the Continent, whereby Germany began to default on U.S. loans and France expressed its intention to default on war debts. The British cabinet resisted the temptation to default in the early and more challenging stages of the Depression, however, even though it would go on to suspend repayments later in the decade despite improving conditions.[5]

THE GREAT WAR

The United Kingdom entered the Great War on 4 August 1914. The British government soon realized that it would struggle to cope with the economic demands of the conflict as money and materials grew scarce.[6] In 1914, the government sought to secure £250 million ($4.9 billion) from the public via the issuance of a war loan.[7] Although hailed as a great and patriotic success by the government and the press, the loan proved to be significantly undersubscribed. Creative accounting from the Bank of England hid this failure, which the economist and later HM Treasury official John Maynard Keynes later described as a "masterful manipulation."[8] Large-scale borrowing also generated political resistance. Trade unions and the Labour Party were increasingly critical of the enormous sums that would have to be paid back with interest by future generations.[9]

As Russia and France struggled to cope with the demands of war, the United Kingdom assumed the ever-growing burden of providing loans to its allies.[10] By early summer 1915, the British government understood that victory would require massive overseas support in the form of arms, manufactured goods, and raw materials. HM Treasury was able to raise a series of loans on the U.S. market throughout the war.[11] The U.S. public ultimately provided over $2 billion in private investments to aid the Allies, much of which went to the United Kingdom.[12] Britain also raised subsidiary loans in places like Japan, Argentina, and Canada.[13] Investment banks worked to support the financial needs of the British and French governments in this period. J. P. Morgan became the purchasing agent in the U.S. for both governments, floating loans, handling foreign exchange operations, and securing an overdraft loan.[14] The British government ultimately honored all its commercial loans and domestic debts from the war.[15]

The tremendous scale of the war meant that the United Kingdom required ever more significant sums to fund its efforts, survive successive exchange crises, and ensure vital trade. Financing its own war efforts alongside those of its allies—as well as the sheer scale of its purchasing in the United States, the rapid inflation of the cost of these vital supplies, and the growing trade deficit—presented serious economic challenges.[16] London could not necessarily expect support from Washington. Recent and unpopular trade restrictions as well as the revolution in Ireland had strained transatlantic relations throughout the latter half of 1916.[17]

President Woodrow Wilson won reelection in November 1916 on a campaign that included a commitment to neutrality. The United States nevertheless joined the Allied war effort following Germany's adoption of unrestricted submarine warfare against any vessel approaching British waters on 1 February 1917. U.S. and British representatives had begun discussions concerning financial transatlantic cooperation by March.[18] On 2 April 1917, Wilson went before Congress to request a declaration of war against Germany and urge financial support for the Allied powers. A formal declaration of war followed four days later. Congress subsequently passed the Liberty Loan Act on 24 April, which allowed the sale of war bonds to support the Allied cause. Some members of the House and Senate nevertheless expressed concern that billions of dollars of loans were hurried through Congress without any budget or any guarantee of how they would be spent.[19]

Prime Minister David Lloyd George rejoiced publicly at "the stupendous resources which this great nation will bring to the succour of the alliance."[20] The United States would subsequently provide more liberty loans to support the Allied war effort before and after the armistice, but the terms—including overall interest rates and when repayment would begin—remained unsettled and would only be agreed in a series of bilateral negotiations over the coming decade.[21] Furthermore, the U.S. had restricted advances to dollar purchases in its own markets, which benefited U.S. producers and the U.S. Treasury.[22] The British government also continued lending large sums to its European allies so that they could purchase war materials in other countries. According to Keynes's calculations in early 1919, the United Kingdom was a net creditor. It was owed £1.45 billion by its European borrowers, in contrast to debts of £800 million to the United States (Table 1.1).[23] As Lloyd George lamented, if the British government had not lent to the Allies, "we should never have incurred a halfpenny of debts to America, for the payments due to us from Europe would have been set against

Table 1.1. Loans advanced to Allies, 1919 (GBP, millions)

Loan to	By United States	By United Kingdom	By France	Total
United Kingdom	800	—	—	800
France	485	390	—	875
Italy	275	390[a]	35	700
Russia	38	520[a, b]	160	718
Belgium	56	90[c]	90	236
Serbia	4	20[c]	30	54
Romania	2	16	35	53
Greece	8	15	15	38
Portugal	—	10	—	10
Total	1,668	1,451	365	3,484

Source: CAB 104/28, Note from Keynes to Chancellor, "Treatment of Inter-Ally Debt Arising Out of the War, March 1919." Keynes considers these figures approximations. The data excludes loans raised by the United Kingdom on the market in the United States and loans raised by France on the market in the United Kingdom or from the Bank of England.

[a] After deducting loans of gold to the United Kingdom, from France (50 million), Italy (22 million), and Russia (60 million), which are returnable when the counterplans are repaid.

[b] This allows noting for interest on the debt since the Bolshevik Revolution.

[c] No interest has been charged on the advances made to these countries.

our liabilities to the United States for purchases we made from her . . . leaving us very much to the good."[24]

The total indebtedness to the United States by the official termination of the war amounted to more than $10.32 billion, of which 97 percent had been advanced to the Allies.[25] The United Kingdom was the largest debtor, with outstanding obligations to the United States of $4.28 billion acquired between April 1917 and June 1919.[26] The size of these debts was remarkable, but so too was their foreign currency denomination.[27] Total national debt—which had grown considerably, exceeding 128 percent of gross domestic product—now comprised a significant amount of foreign currency (Figure 1.1).[28] The British government was concerned about the debt burden and issues of debt sustainability.[29] Foreign debts complicated this significant challenge. Policymakers had historically accumulated sterling rather than foreign currency debt in times of crisis, which permitted it to restructure debts without a settlement and avoided the potential challenges posed by currency risk, namely, costly shifts in the exchange rate or risks to foreign currency reserves.[30] The terms of payment for these debts would now be dictated in Washington rather than London.

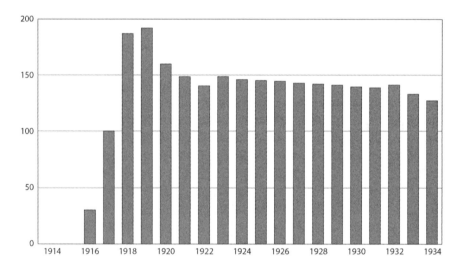

Figure 1.1. Foreign currency debt, including securities issued to overseas lenders payable in sterling, as a percentage of total national debt net [£m], 1914–1934, year ending March (Source: Wormell, *The Management of the National Debt*, appendix 3, 731–733)

Congressional objections, driven in large part by the United States' own economic burdens, meant that President Wilson had ruled out a settlement before the war had ended.[31] By late 1917, the U.S. Treasury emphasized that loans were not contributions but extensions of credit to solvent borrowers temporarily in need of dollars.[32] Secretary of the Treasury William Gibbs McAdoo certainly believed that these obligations should be honored and that any negotiations should occur bilaterally, thereby avoiding the formation of a powerful multilateral debtor bloc that could hamper U.S. economic diplomacy.[33] The United States government had initially intended for debtor states to issue long-term bonds for the advances made to them at the earliest possible time but agreed to postpone negotiations until the Paris Peace Conference, when the issue of indemnities would be discussed in more detail.[34] The treaties that ended World War I would not directly determine the level of reparations to be paid by belligerents; it was instead to be decided by a newly formed Reparations Commission. The commission's delay in reaching a final decision made it difficult for many governments to budget accordingly, which further complicated progress on resolving the outstanding war-debt issue.[35]

Informal discussions with Washington in this interim period regarding the terms of repayment created considerable resentment in London. The U.S. Treasury suggested that the British government pay interest only up to December 1921 and that thereafter repayment should resume at an interest rate of 5 percent. HM Treasury officials including Keynes saw no prospect of repaying anything before the latest date possible and, even then, not until the British government's allies had repaid the United Kingdom. The U.S. government also insisted that these debts should be marketable, thereby making the American people rather than the U.S. Treasury Europe's creditor.[36] As such, the United States was free to demand payment at any time, which was simply unaffordable.[37] Keynes had called this condition "a noose around our necks."[38] Selling to the market would also have made renegotiation far more difficult given the need to please a potentially large and diverse group of investors. Furthermore, assuming that these bonds were traded thereafter, they would exist as a visible and potentially embarrassing sign of the United Kingdom's economic performance.

Lloyd George remained in power following the general election of December 1918. The United Kingdom had suffered considerably from the war as well as the influenza pandemic that followed, which almost cost the prime minister his life.[39] Nevertheless, the coalition government comprising Conservatives and a faction of the Liberal Party persisted, having achieved a landslide victory.[40] On 10 January 1919, Austen Chamberlain replaced Bonar Law as chancellor. Chamberlain was, like his predecessor, convinced of the need for debt cancellation. In March, Keynes wrote a letter to the new chancellor, which stressed that war debts—and the reparations that the Allied powers would seek to fund them—were a "crushing burden" and "a menace to financial stability everywhere": "We shall never be able to move again, unless we can free our limbs from these paper shackles."[41] Keynes's concerns reflected more than only national interests. Other leading economists around the world, including Gustav Cassel, Irving Fisher, and Hubert D. Henderson, would also come to reach similar conclusions about the negative effects of these unpaid debts on the global economy.[42]

Freedom from these paper shackles would involve a considerable financial sacrifice from the United States (Table 1.2). Keynes argued that the United States' own good fortune—based on population, national income, financial capacity, no foreign indebtedness, and ample gold reserves—justified redistribution of the debt.[43] Such a solution held limited hope of success. As Chamberlain informed Keynes, "No doubt

Table 1.2. A proposal for mutual debt forgiveness, 1919 (GBP, millions)

	Net loss	Net gain
United States	1,668	—
United Kingdom	651	—
France	—	510
Italy	—	700
Russia	—	718
Belgium	—	236
Serbia	—	54
Romania	—	53
Greece	—	38
Portugal	—	10

Source: CAB 104/28, Note from Keynes to Chancellor, "Treatment of Inter-Ally Debt Arising out of the War, March 1919."

it would be a very good thing if the United States would propose or support a universal cancellation of debt, but . . . they show no inclination to do anything of the kind. . . . To propose the mere cancellation of debt looks as if we were trying to shift the whole burden on to America."[44]

During the Paris peace negotiations of 1919, which were disrupted by the influenza pandemic that some scholars have speculated made Wilson violently unwell, the British and French governments called a conference between the Allied powers to discuss the issue of outstanding war debts.[45] London and Paris hoped to pool these obligations and ensure either their cancellation or the substitution of Germany as the sole debtor nation.[46] Washington steadfastly refused to consider any such proposals and threatened to cut off future loans, which led Paris and London to back down.[47] From Britain's perspective, U.S. behavior was destructively self-interested and ignorant of European history. War debts hindered a return to the normal conditions of international trade that benefited all. Furthermore, Keynes explained, France had to pay more to the United States in victory than it had paid to Germany in defeat following the Franco-Prussian War of 1870–1871: "The hand of Bismarck was light compared with that of an Ally or an Associate."[48]

Wilson refused to participate in any general conference on the issue. Secretary of the Treasury Carter Glass, who had replaced McAdoo following his departure in December, advised the president not to negotiate until the financial terms of the settlement were clear. Delay also avoided the emergence of a debtor bloc or pressure for cancellation.[49] Wilson and Glass were clear that debtors should be dealt with separately and that reparations bore no relation to war debts.[50] Connecting the two issues threatened to leave the U.S. holding higher-risk reparations bonds in exchange for its lower-risk Allied bonds while leaving the Allies with no debt.[51] As Ray Baker, Wilson's press secretary at Versailles, put it, "Here was a 'joker'—so far as America was concerned—for, passed from hand to hand, these bonds would wipe out a large share of the inter-allied debts, leaving . . . America 'holding the bag.'"[52]

Historians have pondered whether a prompt settlement of war debts and reparations, alongside immediate U.S. loans to Europe, might have facilitated the economic and political reconstruction of the Continent.[53] Yet few presidents could have achieved such a settlement in the face of significant congressional resistance and growing public demands for repayment. Economic support for the Allied effort had always reflected some degree of self-interest. Sales of Liberty Loans, for instance, were driven by financial incentives as well as patriotic duty.[54] It is also debatable as to whether the U.S. held the financial power necessary to cancel or dramatically reduce war debts and fund international deficits at that time.[55] Cancellation was certainly not in the national interest of a United States engaged in financial and security competition with the United Kingdom.[56] These issues had all become far more politically sensitive by 1920 as a presidential election loomed.[57]

U.S. unwillingness to cancel or significantly reduce the war debts raised serious questions about Europe's capacity to repay. Prior to May 1919, Allied debtors had paid interest to the United States in cash, but such payments were themselves derived in part from further U.S. loans. The United Kingdom received its last U.S. loan in June 1919. The British government would therefore have to meet subsequent installments in October and November without any external support. It would struggle to secure repayment of its own debts given Europe's significant financial difficulties. This challenging situation, exacerbated by the United Kingdom's own postwar challenges, necessitated a compromise.[58]

By summer 1919, the Wilson administration had decided to extend further credits through normal business channels and proposed a deferment of interest payments for up to a maximum of three years. This decision reflected in part advice the president had received from a secret report in May, in which economic advisers to the U.S. delegation in Paris urged a temporary suspension, or "refunding of the interest," for between two and three years.[59] Glass defended this position to the House Ways and Means Committee by explaining that in the absence of normal trade levels, debtor states would not be able to secure the necessary foreign exchange credits for repayment and that payment in gold would exhaust their reserves.[60] In response to U.S. efforts, the British government agreed to postpone interest payments due from its own debtors.[61]

Between August 1919 and January 1920, the United Kingdom held debt talks with the United States. Postponing interest payments had aroused opposition in Congress, which was now paying close attention to negotiations following rumors that the United Kingdom had attempted to borrow more from the United States. The British government categorically denied these claims and stressed that its total expenditure had been financed without further borrowing since June 1919.[62] The British government nevertheless remained deeply attracted to the idea of cancellation. On 10 February 1920, Chamberlain warned of the danger of intergovernmental indebtedness to U.S. representatives in Washington but clarified that he did not intend to renew discussions on the issue following their strong resistance.[63]

On 1 March, Secretary of the Treasury David Houston, who had assumed the position following Glass's recent move to the Senate, reiterated the U.S. position to the British government. Cancellation or major reductions would never win support from Congress or the American people. Furthermore, these debts did not stand in the way of European reconstruction as they "were not a present burden on the debtor Governments, since they are not paying interest or even . . . providing in their budgets or taxes for the payment of principal or interest."[64] Such a proposal was also inherently unfair as it "does not involve mutual sacrifices on the part of the nations concerned. It simply involves a contribution mainly by the United States."[65] The United Kingdom and many other European states instead needed to raise taxes to balance their budgets and reduce expenditures, especially by accelerating the pace of disarmament.[66] In the United States, there were also broader doubts about Britain's alleged inability to repay its debts and questions about ongoing commercial rivalry. As a case in point, members of Congress noted that the British government had recently loaned money to Argentina, which subsequently transferred elements of its trade and commerce to the United Kingdom at the expense of the United States.[67]

U.S. representatives presented British officials with a tentative debt proposal on 30 April. London considered them to be "a set of humiliating political and fiscal stipulations" that made little contribution to rehabilitating Europe.[68] Repayment would resume when the exchange rate reached par, which forecasters believed could occur as early as 1922, meaning that Britain would need to make a large and sudden payment in back interest. The United States also expected the United Kingdom to draw on its own war loans to fund these repayments, thereby forcing U.S. views on Europe. Furthermore, Washington was only willing to consider cooperation if it received a "more or less pleading" request from London.[69] The United States also reiterated earlier calls to put these bonds on the open market. It was now willing to use demand obligations—namely, threatening to specify a date for full or partial payment—as a tool in negotiations.

Chamberlain resented these "intolerable pretensions" and informed the cabinet on 12 May 1920, "I would sooner pay if I could, and default if I could not, than sell my country into bondage by signing any document containing language like that."[70] Four days later, Lloyd George and Chamberlain met with Alexandre Millerand and Frédéric François-Marsal, the French premier and the minister of finance, at Lympne in Kent. Talks focused on the size and division of German reparations. British and French proposals encouraged the linkage of interallied debts and reparations as well as their parallel liquidation. The cabinet discussed the implications of the Lympne meeting on 19 and 21 May.[71] Chamberlain explained that the present terms offered by the U.S. were objectionable and would contradict the ambitions of the Lympne meeting. Yet the situation remained delicate. The chancellor noted, "we had refused in the past to say we could not pay, and he was unwilling to do so now; but we were only not in default because America had not pressed us for interest, and their abstention from doing so was occasioned entirely by the negotiations for conversion."[72] There would be no chance of remission once these bonds were marketed, however, so delay was useful. In addition, the looming U.S. presidential election made the timing unsuitable for negotiations. As such, the assembled ministers agreed to suspend further transatlantic negotiations.[73]

On 5 August, which represented a lengthy delay in responding to the United States, Lloyd George informed Wilson that France was unable to reduce its reparations claims without a reduction of Allied debts, a position that the British government considered fair, and emphasized his desire for cancellation.[74] On 3 November, Wilson replied that cancellation remained politically unacceptable in the United States. Furthermore, delay in funding the debt was "already embarrassing the United States Treasury, which will find itself compelled to begin to collect back and current interest if speedy progress is not made with the funding."[75] Lloyd George chose to ignore Wilson's threat. Only a day earlier, the Republican Warren Harding had won the presidential election. The uncertainty of Harding's position on the war debts encouraged the cabinet to adopt a cautious waiting strategy.[76]

By 30 November, however, a "private, but authoritative, source" confirmed that neither Congress nor the U.S. public would support the remission of debt and that further delay could produce "an unfortunate misunderstanding."[77] The chancellor concluded that despite such "insularity, blindness and selfishness," Britain had little choice but to resume negotiations to preserve its "dignity."[78] National honor existed alongside financial concerns. Reopening talks could help to reduce the risk of conversion and potentially improve the present offer, repayment of which would "seriously cripple" British resources.[79] Furthermore, for Chamberlain, default remained a considerable risk: "It is difficult, and perhaps impossible, to say what the effect on our internal and external credit positions would be [following default]. I believe myself that it would be little short of disastrous."[80]

On 3 December, the chancellor warned his colleagues that the stagnation of global export trade would "drown out all sensible voices" in the U.S., prompting renewed demands for payment and the sale of war bonds to individual purchasers. Chamberlain was by now convinced of the need for an arrangement with the United States and for debt remission for Europe: "Europe cannot buy for want of credit. We are suffering because Europe cannot buy. . . . We can free the credit of our Allies by remitting now the debt incurred by them to us in the common prosecution of the war on condition that each of our debtors does the same to those who are indebted to him."[81] The United Kingdom would thus honor its obligations to the United States as it forgave its own European debts, not only because this was "the right and wise thing" but because the U.S. would come to discover the situation and "ultimately be forced to cancel the debts."[82] Although such a strategy came at a high price to British taxpayers in the interim, Chamberlain concluded, "we ought to act; and in spite of the immense burden which our people are called upon to bear, I believe that such action would have their hearty approval."[83] Chamberlain was nevertheless keenly aware of the diplomatic risks involved: "If every French and Italian taxpayer is to be told by the Opposition (and perhaps by the Government) of the day that the reason why his taxes are so high is because England demands her pound of flesh, then I do not envy the task of our Foreign Secretary."[84]

Scholars might question from this point onward why the British government never chose to issue new debt on public capital markets, perhaps even at lower interest rates or as perpetuities, as they had done in the previous century with public debt. The archival evidence remains limited, but it seems reasonable to believe that British policymakers assumed that the United States would eventually cancel or reduce the debt. This waiting strategy also had the added benefit of avoiding the risks posed by public capital markets or private creditors. Nevertheless, this position was curious given that there was little evidence of the United States having forgiven debts in the past and the significant political and economic costs associated with waiting. Yet if British and French policymakers assumed that cancellation was inevitable, which is borne out in the documentary evidence, then it is understandable why they might consider their approach to be an imperfect but ultimately preferable course of action. The alternative remains an intriguing counterfactual. Dealing with individual creditors in public capital markets, rather than the U.S. Treasury and American taxpayers, could potentially have helped to depoliticize or at least moderate elements of the international war-debt imbroglio.

By December 1920, British hopes that the new Harding administration might be more accommodating faded in the light of diplomatic correspondence that it would be "less rather than more favourable" toward the United Kingdom's war debts.[85] The cabinet agreed that there was now no reason to delay coming to terms. Despite the expression of "strong views" about the selfishness of U.S. demands from cabinet ministers including the prime minister, and the dangers of passing on these costs to Britain's own European debtors and therefore further undermining trade, a majority of the cabinet felt that it was "out of the question to repudiate [the] debt, which would be tantamount to filing a petition in bankruptcy."[86] The gathered ministers consequently agreed to send representatives to Washington to secure a lengthy delay before the bonds were placed on the market. The proposed mission, however, was beset by delays within Whitehall. Congress then prevented the outgoing administration from taking any further action and negotiations were consequently postponed.[87] As such, the cabinet indefinitely postponed the mission on 7 February 1921.[88]

Why did the British government fail to act more quickly, especially considering the clear threat posed by Wilson's letter and the uncertainty surrounding the policies of the incoming administration? Lloyd George has subsequently suggested that Wilson's letter in early November had been a "put-up" job.[89] The prime minister had a vague understanding, indirectly conveyed to him, that the president needed to provide a strong response to British demands, but he could ignore the contents of the letter without danger. Lloyd George's earlier letter would be found by the incoming administration, however, encouraging Washington to negotiate with London. If this account is accurate, the prime minister had adopted a clandestine policy of "intentional delay" despite growing pressure to resume negotiations, although it remains unclear how this strategy would have led Britain to reach more favorable terms or escape repayment, as Lloyd George would later claim.[90]

THE WORLD WAR FOREIGN DEBT COMMISSION

Upon taking office in 1921, Harding made his position on domestic and international debt clear: "No civilization can survive repudiation."[91] As the U.S. economy fell into recession, Republican policymakers struggled to reconcile domestic and foreign objectives to promote the well-being of the United States.[92] U.S. banking, business, and agriculture typically recognized the interdependence of European and U.S. prosperity and frequently proposed deferring interest payments or canceling part of the debt to restore European purchasing power, encourage trade, and promote fiscal orthodoxy.[93] Outright cancellation remained unpopular, however, due to public hostility toward the burden of debt falling on the American taxpayer via increased taxation.[94] In addition, some feared that cancellation would benefit British industry and commerce at the expense of U.S. business.[95]

The Harding administration appreciated these concerns and sought to resume negotiations with the debtors on interest rates and maturity dates. Congress proved unwilling to surrender control of these foreign debts and instead proposed a five-person commission to negotiate the terms.[96] In the following months, Congress went on to stipulate that loans be repaid within twenty-five years at a minimum interest of 4.25 percent and that settlements could not be adjusted thereafter, although payments could potentially be deferred.[97] These congressional limits enjoyed bipartisan support. The Democrats approached the issue in a partisan spirit, to be sure, but the Republican Party enjoyed majorities in both houses of Congress. Both sides sought to maintain control over foreign debts due to their belief in constitutional privilege and distrust of the executive branch. Legislators were also reacting to widespread public demands for tax relief and unemployment benefits. Congress's handling of European debts served as a visible response to these domestic-political demands and trumped concerns about the expansion of U.S. trade.[98]

The Harding administration proved unwilling to engage in a bitter struggle with Congress and surrendered control of the issue.[99] The Senate passed the World War Foreign Debt Commission (WWFDC) Act on 31 January 1922. The act received the president's consent on 9 February. A commission—chaired by the new secretary of the Treasury, Andrew Mellon, and including Secretary of State Charles Evans Hughes, who would go on to become chief justice of the Supreme Court, and future president Herbert Hoover—would now handle international negotiations concerning the funding or conversion of European war-debt obligations in line with congressional guidelines.[100] As the Democratic senator Tom Watson warned, albeit with some hyperbole, this commission had "a place of tremendous power, handling the biggest debt the world ever knew. The way in which it is settled . . . will affect the destinies of the whole world for the next 25 or 50 years."[101]

The WWFDC first met on 18 April 1922 and subsequently informed London on 15 June of its desire to begin negotiations.[102] The British government had been mulling its debt strategy for the past year.[103] It had already prioritized paying off overseas obligations, and by now the only major foreign debts remaining were the war loans provided by the U.S. Treasury.[104] Ultimately, Chamberlain prepared for repayment, recognizing that the three-year postponement period was due to end around October and that failure to pay would greatly retard the process of recovery by harming British credit. As Jeremy Wormell notes, HM Treasury and the Bank of England "never contemplated repudiation," in large part because the United Kingdom was a net creditor, which drew from overseas £180 million ($860 million) in profits, "a sum which far exceeded the payments which would be made under any debt settlement."[105]

Nor could the government plead inability to pay given an expected budget surplus and reduced levels of taxation. The adequacy of gold or dollar reserves does not appear to have been a major issue.[106] HM Treasury's decision to begin repayment took place before the cabinet gave its formal approval on 16 December 1921. By now, Robert Horne had assumed the position of chancellor of the exchequer, following Chamberlain's departure for the office of Lord Privy Seal. Horne also accepted the need for repayment and was supported by most of the cabinet, albeit despite strong reservations from others including Lloyd George about unnecessarily aiding the U.S. economy. Ministers accepted that they must be at liberty to call on allied debtors for payment in cash of the interest falling due on their debts to the United Kingdom, even if securing payment was unlikely.[107]

By early 1922, the British government had decided to set aside £35 million from the budget to resume the interest payments that had previously been postponed in 1919. Horne ensured that his budget statement would include £50 million for the following year.[108] As these payments were to be funded via tax increases, they presented a serious political issue, especially given the recession of the early 1920s.[109] In early 1921, the government had found itself in a grave situation when unemployment insurance or out-of-work donations for more than a million people would run out and leave charitable contributions as their sole means of support.[110] Furthermore, the cabinet had recently decided to cut government and social expenditure to reduce the rate of taxation it believed was harming industry and preventing recovery.[111] War-debt payments therefore represented a bitter pill to swallow for the already burdened British people.[112]

On 8 June, the chancellor circulated a memorandum to cabinet ministers on how they should respond to U.S. calls for repayment. Horne warned that cooperation would mean "giving up [Britain's] strongest weapon for forcing the United States of America . . . to take part in a round-table discussion of inter-Governmental indebtedness."[113] The chancellor warned that raising the issue now would "merely drive European finance deeper into the slough and increase unemployment in the British Isles."[114] Nevertheless, Horne encouraged payment to the United States and, consequently, for European states to also resume their payments. As the chancellor explained, the government was legally bound to honor its obligations, and doing so would help to secure stability for sterling by reducing uncertainty. Repayment in dollars was also now possible. The current position of the British balance of payments allowed the government to meet its interest and sinking fund obligations without any serious exchange difficulty: "The problem is not how to find the dollars, but simply how to persuade our own people to pay the taxation involved in the transfer of dollars to the Exchequer's control."[115] Furthermore, cooperation could help win favor in the United States for a new Tariff and Shipping Subsidy Bill that would directly benefit British trade and help to offset these losses. Horne was also optimistic that once British debt had been settled, the U.S. might write down other European debts and cooperate more effectively in political and economic affairs on the Continent. As such, he concluded, "We had more to gain by the restoration of Europe than we had to lose by paying our debt to America—which we had no real chance of avoiding."[116]

The cabinet debated the issue of repayment in the following days. Ministers agreed that delay could create fresh difficulties and would slow U.S. assistance in the reconstruction of Europe. Furthermore, they stated, "however unconscionable we thought the attitude of the United States Government . . . it would be incompatible with our national honour and credit to refuse to pay, and that it was inconceivable that Great Britain would ever place herself in the humiliating position of being in fact a defaulter to America."[117] Agreement reflected, in large part, the United Kingdom's position as a creditor to much of the world, which resulted in a vested interest in the sanctity of contracts. In addition, the political and economic advantages of a prompt settlement outweighed the unlikely prospect of better terms, especially given the risk of strained relations and U.S. isolationism from European affairs.[118] The gathered ministers even accepted better treatment for other debtors than themselves in their pursuit of a "united front" against the U.S.: "if the United States would not relax her demands upon Great Britain, she might possibly be persuaded, as the result of a general settlement, to give more lenient treatment to her other debtors."[119]

The cabinet agreed to draft a dispatch to each of its European debtors. Acting Secretary of State for Foreign Affairs Arthur Balfour assumed responsibility for producing the document. The Balfour Note would set out the nature of U.S. demands and the consequent necessity of the United Kingdom exacting repayment from its European debtors. Much as the British government regretted making such demands from its wartime allies, which it considered a "wrong policy," the cabinet believed that no other course was open to it given the actions of its U.S. creditor. The gathered ministers also agreed to draft a further dispatch for transmission to Washington, which acknowledged their intention to honor the obligations but stressed that no definite proposals would be possible until the completion of debt talks with European allies. Public opinion, the ministers believed, would severely criticize any agreement that compelled the British taxpayer to satisfy the U.S. debt if they secured nothing from European debtors. Levels of taxation and unemployment were already too high, they argued, especially in comparison to countries indebted to the United Kingdom. The gathered ministers also felt that it was a good opportunity for the U.S. to learn that by demanding payment, "she would be making herself in effect the tax-gatherer and rent-collector of the civilized world."[120]

On 25 July, the cabinet returned to discuss the progress of the proposed Balfour Note. Since its last meeting, the German mark had rapidly deteriorated as the Weimar Republic struggled with hyperinflation. Failure to pay its required indemnities led France to threaten the occupation of the Ruhr.[121] Ministers questioned whether it was an opportune time to proceed. Horne thought the draft "brilliant" in its construction but "its policy profoundly wrong" in its intended result. As the minutes reveal, the chancellor argued that the critical tone of the note would cause "a controversy within the United States."[122] Furthermore, he thought the proposed strategy would lead France and other European states to put more pressure on Germany, which would become "the sole debtor," which "would make the position infinitely worse."[123] Chamberlain was "gravely anxious" and feared the effect on Anglo-American relations, especially concerning the false economy of saving money today, which "would be spent over and over again in [Britain's] subsequent loss of credit."[124]

Despite these doubts, an overwhelming majority of ministers defended the Balfour Note—and specifically the shifting of blame for the collection of debts onto the United States—as a useful way in which to gather international support for cancellation. Winston Churchill, secretary of state for the colonies, strongly supported this "righteous and a proper document, enunciating a policy of wisdom, firmness and broad justice," that held few risks for the United Kingdom: "Our attitude was not, and should not be, one of quivering fear before the United States. . . . It was absurd to suggest that they would insist on putting bonds on the market in such a way to harass us. . . . Publication would not be followed by retributive measures devised to spite us."[125] For Churchill, and much of the cabinet, the restoration of European debt payments was merely a bluff: "Our European debtors would know that they were not in fact being called upon to pay."[126] Lloyd George was disappointed by the United States' "very ignoble attitude" in that Britain was "expected to bear this unexampled burden and also to pay all [its] debts."[127] The prime minister nevertheless accepted the need for repayment because "he did not think the British Empire ought to lower its self-respect."[128] As such, the prime minister and his cabinet sought to use the Balfour Note "to wipe out international indebtedness in order to give the world a fresh start."[129]

The Balfour Note of 1 August 1922 may have been addressed to Britain's European debtors, but its intended target was the United States.[130] It accepted U.S. requests for repayment but rejected claims that the loans "were an isolated incident in which only the United States of America and Great Britain had any concern," declaring it rather "one of a connected series of transactions, in which [Britain] appears sometimes as debtor, sometimes as creditor."[131] Although the British government had thus far "silently abstained from making any demands upon their allies for repayment," it also argued that the "one-sided" solution unfairly burdened British taxpayers.[132] The Balfour Note contrasted the British debt to the United States (£850 million) with the war debts due to the United Kingdom by its allies (£2 billion) and also the reparations due from Germany, presenting an aggregate total of £3.45 billion that would be remitted if the British policy were adopted.[133]

Many U.S. policymakers reacted poorly to the tone of the Balfour Note. The British government had suggested that the debts incurred were for a great and common purpose and, by implication, criticized the United States for seeking to collect these war debts.[134] European debts thus became a problem for the American taxpayer.[135] The *Congressional Record* details members criticizing attempts to tax the American people to protect the wealth of Europe.[136] At least one senator considered Britain's attempts to "powerfully and adroitly" seek cancellation as peculiar: "She is still a great creditor nation, with investments scattered all about the world. Therefore, she is obliged to hold for the sanctity of debts between nations."[137] The Senate subsequently passed an amendment linking a proposed Bonus Bill, which would provide additional payments for veterans of the war, to interest payments from the British loan. The bill was ultimately vetoed by the president with the support of the Senate against the House. If the two issues had been legally connected, it would have been even more difficult to negotiate on this issue in the future.[138]

France reacted negatively to British demands for more money, not least when Paris was already under pressure to support a moratorium on German reparations. The Balfour Note soured diplomatic relations.[139] When London announced its intention to cooperate with Washington and collect from its own debtors, Paris faced a united front that at once required repayment and rejected the continuation of reparation payments. France's resulting isolation from its former allies, coupled with Germany's decision to cease repayment, led to the invasion of the Ruhr in the following year, which threatened to destabilize the region and economic recovery more broadly.[140]

Several historians have described the Balfour Note as disastrous given the negative responses it generated abroad, especially in the United States, but such assessments overlook or downplay its wider objectives.[141] As Anne Orde has explained, the cabinet discussions do not reveal that ministers expected to change American minds but instead sought to express resentment.[142] The prime minister had even described it as a "rebuke" in cabinet.[143] Publicizing such resentment served a useful political purpose by appeasing ministers as well as voters and, to a lesser extent, represented a bargaining counter in negotiations. As Lloyd George explained, he "did not think the immediate effect on Europe of the publication of the Despatch would be good."[144] Yet the prime minister also saw an opportunity. If he could make the U.S. see that it was "responsible for the continuance of chaos in Europe, it would be a negotiating pawn when [the British] representative went to Washington."[145] Irrespective of the prime minister's ambitious plans, growing concerns about European stability probably did help to change U.S. attitudes toward the need for a debt settlement.[146] The Balfour Note also encouraged greater resistance to compromise on the Continent. As the U.S. ambassador to London later remarked, the "Balfour Note opened the flood-gates of anti-American feelings in Europe, and will remain an ever-potent reason for non-payment."[147]

A FUNDING AGREEMENT

Lloyd George's government fell in October 1922. A significant economic downturn, and the miner strikes that followed, undermined the prime minister's popularity.[148] Many Conservatives had also been angered by the granting of independence to the Irish Free State and by progress toward limited self-government for India. Recent charges of corruption and the rising threat of war with Turkey proved too much. Lloyd George and many of his fellow ministers resigned after a majority of Conservatives voted not to continue cooperation with the Liberals.[149] The collapse of the coalition led to a new Conservative government led by Andrew Bonar Law, which went on to secure a dominant electoral victory on 15 November 1922.

The new government adhered to the existing policy of securing a settlement in the immediate future. Indeed, it passed up any opportunity for a deferment by agreeing to repay $50 million to the U.S. when the next installment fell due on 15 November.[150] In November, the cabinet agreed that Chancellor of the Exchequer Stanley Baldwin should venture to the U.S. to negotiate a settlement early in the new year. Bonar Law supported the decision, despite believing that U.S. demands were unjust, and authorized Baldwin to reach a settlement if annual payments remained below £25 million ($120 million).[151] Before leaving, Baldwin sought advice from Keynes on 18 December 1922. Keynes remained a leading intellectual figure with considerable understanding of the issue who, given concerns about economic recovery, advised against a settlement.[152]

The British mission—led by Baldwin and including the governor of the Bank of England Montagu Norman—reached New York on 4 January. "We British have always paid and will always pay our debts," Baldwin informed the gathered journalists.[153] The chancellor's negotiations with the WWFDC began shortly thereafter.[154] Baldwin did note that the U.S. had already benefited greatly from these loans as Britain had only bought U.S. goods at wartime prices, but he understood that this was "a business problem" and sought "a square deal, a settlement that will secure for America repayment to the last cent."[155] The chancellor's statement appears honestly felt. As Liaquat Ahamed reveals, Baldwin "believed strongly in settling one's debts—he was so firm an advocate of this principle that in 1919 he had anonymously donated $700,000 of his own money, a fifth of his net worth, to the government as his contribution to paying off the national debt after the war."[156]

Five days later, Harding informed the press that he expected the WWFDC to make the best settlement it could, moving beyond existing restrictions if necessary, which boded well given the inflexibility of past talks. Yet negotiations would disappoint the British delegation. By mid-January, the WWFDC recommended a settlement based on 3.5 percent interest with amortization over sixty-one years, which equated to annual payments of $187 million (£39 million).[157] Baldwin was clear that this amount was unaffordable. The WWFDC responded by offering to initially reduce interest rates for five years, but these missed payments would be appended to the principal for repayment thereafter. Baldwin understood that this limited concession would not impress the cabinet but feared that ceasing talks would undermine any hope of achieving a better settlement. As such, Baldwin sought a decision from the prime minister before he resumed talks with the commission.[158]

The prime minister was deeply unimpressed by this "ungenerous" proposal and felt it "quite impossible" to agree to such terms for only "a momentary increase of goodwill," especially when "time is on [Britain's] side in this matter."[159] Keynes concurred, noting, "[the U.S. is] just as completely at our mercy as we are at France's, and France at Germany's; it is the debtor who has the last word in these cases."[160] Bonar Law's response reflected rational concerns but also emotional resistance.[161] As Baldwin recalled, the prime minister "saw the blood of his two sons" who died in the war: "We paid in blood: they did not: you can't equate that with a cash payment."[162] Bonar Law informed the chancellor that he should now return home.

Baldwin spoke privately to Mellon, the WWFDC chairman, and stressed the need for an alternative. Mellon's highest international priority at the U.S. Treasury was to reach a settlement on these debts, but he remained keenly aware of congressional resistance to any compromise.[163] After consulting with Harding, Mellon informed Baldwin that the WWFDC would accept a reduction to 3 percent interest in the first decade, which would then rise to 3.5 percent for the remainder, equating to 3.42 percent overall. The total would therefore reach $161 million (£33.5 million) per year for the next decade before climbing to $184 million (£38.3 million) in the fifty-two years thereafter. Baldwin also expected that he might now be able to get options to pay principal as well as interest at par and to prepay the principal at any time. These concessions would help to make the bond unmarketable. Furthermore, if a settlement could be reached, Republican leaders would probably participate in some general conference that would link together debts and reparations.[164]

Baldwin believed that these were the best terms available and feared that failure to compromise would result in the return of less favorable interest rates. Agreement would also bring these lingering international tensions closer to an end and help to protect Britain's financial reputation. As he informed the cabinet, "I have little doubt that Great Britain would not regard 33 million sterling yearly as being too high a price to pay to escape appearing as a defaulter," while "the increase of 5 millions sterling in ten years' time is comparatively small and we have time to provide against it."[165] The chancellor urged the cabinet to accept and to do so swiftly. Congress would not be able to meet again until December, thereby allowing more doubt to creep into negotiations. "What is quite certain is that if we fail to settle now," he concluded, "not only American opinion but world opinion will question our willingness to pay with serious damage to our prestige."[166]

Given the Christmas recess, only a partial cabinet met to discuss this offer on 15 January 1923. The small number of ministers who were available, most of whom were junior, agreed unanimously with the prime minister that the proposed terms were "intolerably unjust" and would generate dangerous levels of hostility between the two states. Bonar Law also stressed the rising dangers of French expansion into the Ruhr and British payments in dollars to the U.S. that undermined budgetary and exchange stability.[167] Rising star Neville Chamberlain, who would soon become chancellor, noted that the prime minister had on 23 January admitted to him that he was "very worried over the American mission which had been a failure": "He considers the American attitude most unreasonable and thinks our people don't realise that if we accepted their terms it would mean £1 per head extra taxation for 60 years."[168]

Baldwin ultimately ceased talks and returned home. Both parties agreed that this outcome was an adjournment and not a breakdown. On the same day, the British press became aware of the details of negotiations. The WWFDC had insisted that nothing be written down for fear of Congress demanding access to these papers and consequently complicating bargaining. This leak meant that with general awareness of the terms, it would be difficult for the WWFDC to offer anything better.[169] Members of Congress who were opposed to the negotiations, and even some who had tentatively supported revision, now expressed anger at the secrecy of these meetings. Many took the opportunity to criticize the British government's recent decision to lend large sums to foreign countries, noting also ongoing trade and commercial rivalries, rising levels of military spending, and the existence of sufficient foreign securities to fully repay the debt.[170]

When Baldwin arrived back in the United Kingdom, his comments to the press about the difficulty of negotiations did little to improve matters and made it clear that no better deal would be forthcoming.[171] The full cabinet met on 30 January 1923, and Bonar Law remained adamantly opposed to compromise.[172] The prime minister saw the terms as unfair, especially given that Britain might not receive any further payments from Europe and would therefore carry the burden of repayment in taxation.[173] He instead proposed paying only the interest in the expectation that the U.S. would eventually change its position. He was confident that a better deal would emerge in a few years' time, which meant that "his name would be cursed if he accepted the [present] American offer."[174]

Bonar Law was eventually proven correct. Many other states, including Italy and France, secured much better terms with the United States within only a matter of years, reflecting improving economic conditions in the U.S. and a more cooperative Congress.[175] The chancellor of the exchequer nevertheless advanced a case for repayment along the lines of the existing offer.[176] He stressed that no better deal was available and dreaded ongoing interest payments that achieved no reduction to the capital of the debt. Cooperation also meant that there was a good chance to avoid making these bonds marketable, especially as the U.S. Treasury was presently in favor of retaining these debts. As the United Kingdom could redeem them at any time in gold or dollars, they were a less attractive security to the public. Furthermore, failure to reach agreement would also harm relations with the U.S., which would class Britain as "a bankrupt state."[177] Indeed, many in Congress were adamant that Britain could afford to pay and had already raised doubts about its government's commitment to repayment. The Democratic senator Kenneth McKellar referred to the deal as a form of repudiation and feared future default: "Some say she is not able to pay it. Of course, we all know she is. . . . If she is going to back out of a 5 percent interest rate, and if she is not willing to pay 4¼ percent, how do we know she is going to pay the 3 percent when the time rolls around?"[178]

A protracted and inconclusive discussion followed, in which the cabinet, many of whose members were not present two weeks earlier, favored the case made by the chancellor. Before the next cabinet meeting,

Baldwin and others spoke with Bonar Law and found him willing to accept cooperation. This change reflected sustained pressure from his colleagues who feared a destabilizing crisis for the new government.[179] This shift in position was also aided by a visit earlier that morning from former chancellor Reginald McKenna, who had stressed that City opinion was now overwhelming in favor of a settlement.[180] The cabinet consequently accepted the terms in principle but asked that the bonds not be marketed for a period of ten years and prepared a telegram to inform Washington of the government's new position.[181]

Talks between the two governments resumed swiftly. By early February, both sides had agreed on the major points of a settlement. The WWFDC remained unwilling to change stance on the terms previously suggested or a commitment to marketability, but its willingness to accept an option of immediate repayment meant that these bonds were unmarketable in practice. The commission informed the president that it had been impossible to keep to the terms of the original funding act but defended the proposed settlement: "It is a business settlement fully preserving the integrity of the obligations, and it represents the first great step in the readjustment of the intergovernmental obligations growing out of the war."[182]

On 7 February, Harding assured Congress that the debt commission had "driven a hard bargain with Great Britain" and celebrated "the first clearing of the war-clouded skies in a debt-burdened world, and the sincere commitment of one great nation to validate its financial pledges."[183] The House of Representatives passed the bill on 9 February by a vote of 271 to 2, with 146 abstaining. Many representatives expressed their dissatisfaction with the agreement's lack of collateral and were concerned about the risks of default. The Democratic representative James Collier was greeted with applause when he warned that it "would not be worth the paper they are written on if England repudiated them": "There is only one court in which those bonds, if a default should be made, could be enforced, and that is not a court of law—it is a court of force—and I for one would never refer to that court for these debts or the debts of any other country."[184]

The bill passed the Senate by 70 to 13 votes on 16 February.[185] The Democratic senator James Reed defended the agreement: "If the doubt exists, it will exist just as much after Great Britain signs a bond to substitute for her present written obligation. . . . I say, for the credit of the British nation and the British people, that they have the reputation of paying their debts."[186] The Republican Thomas Sterling noted the agreement's "splendid effect," as it would inspire the United States' "other foreign debtors" to enter similar agreements.[187] Yet there was resistance on both sides of the aisle. The Democrat Kenneth McKellar expressed his opposition to an agreement that reduced the debt, describing it as "especially unfair to the American taxpayer, already overburdened."[188] The Republican Robert La Follette warned of the longer-term risks, leaving "for two generations the United States . . . tied fast to European affairs by financial bonds, which all experience has shown are stronger even than the ties of blood."[189]

The passage of the bill, which became law in March, represents a clear example of the Republican administration seeking to reconcile conflicting domestic and international pressures bearing on the debt issue.[190] External factors had been important in changing U.S. attitudes, not least growing economic and political troubles in Europe, highlighted by the invasion of the Ruhr and the growing cost to U.S. export markets.[191] Whereas the United States had remained on the gold standard, the United Kingdom did not during World War I. Mellon was keen to settle the debts to remove political obstacles to future U.S. efforts to stabilize and rehabilitate the economies of Europe and thus their return to the gold standard, which he believed would benefit the U.S. economy.[192] Furthermore, many policymakers feared the emergence of a Franco-German détente that would press for debt cancellation in the absence of a deal.[193] The reaction in Congress and the press proved largely favorable as the agreement appeared to facilitate U.S. exports without unduly burdening the American people.[194] In contrast, there was dismay on the Continent. The French government feared that it would be forced to honor the Balfour Note, which only highlighted the need for Germany to pay its reparations.[195]

Both parties signed the Anglo-American debt settlement on 18 June 1923. In the preceding months, British representatives had done their best to improve the terms of the deal, often with some success.[196] The British government sought to weaken or dilute nonnegotiable parts of the agreement. It succeeded in making any future bonds derived from these debts unattractive to private investors by including provisions to pay in bonds and prepay the principal at will. The British government also refused to undertake various duties that would facilitate the marketing of the bonds or to be tied to any fixed arrangement for their amortization, leaving the terms "as vague and unhelpful as

Table 1.3. Settlement of indebtedness of the United Kingdom of Great Britain and Ireland to the United States, 1923 (USD)

Total amount of indebtedness to be funded is 4,600,000,000, which has been computed as follows:		
Principal amount of demand obligations to be funded		4,074,818,358.44
Interest accrued thereon from 15 April and 15 May, 1919, respectively, to 15 December, 1922, at the rate of 4 ¼ per cent per annum	629,836,106.99	
Less—Payments made by Great Britain on 16 October and 15 November, 1922, on account of interest, with interest thereon at 4 ¼ per cent per annum from said dates, respectively, to 15 December, 1922	<u>100,526,379.69</u>	<u>529,309,727.30</u>
Total principal and interest accrued and unpaid, as of 15 December 1922		4,604,128,085.74
Paid in cash by Great Britain, 15 March 1923		<u>4,128,085.74</u>
Total indebtedness to be funded into bonds of Great Britain		4,600,000,000.00

Source: CAB 104/28, P. J. Grigg, 'History of the American War Debt' (1934), 106. See also Annual Report of the Secretary of the Treasury on the State of the Finances for the Fiscal Year Ended June 30, 1923 (Washington: Government Printing Office, 1924), pp. 257-67.

possible . . . in order to create difficulties, should the time for conversion ever come."[197]

Ultimately, the United Kingdom agreed to repay $4.6 billion to the United States (Table 1.3). This figure represented all British war loans and unpaid accrued interest. Interest repayments would involve a payment of $161 million for the first decade, rising to $184 million for the remaining fifty-two years. Payments in gold would occur on 15 June and 15 December every year for the next sixty-two years. Annual installments on the principal would increase from $23 million in 1923–1924 to $175 million by 1983–1984.[198]

The British government was satisfied with the outcome initially. The terms equated to a reduction of 28 percent of the original total.[199] The Treasury's Controller of Finance Otto Niemeyer considered it "an amazing achievement in the circ[um]s[tances] to have got off so cheap": "we sh[oul]d have been out of our wits to refuse."[200] In addition, London's willingness to compromise helped to avoid any sanctions or reprisals. In contrast, when Paris excluded foreign debts in its annual balance sheet for 1924, Washington adopted a ban on U.S. loans to France until debt-funding negotiations resumed.[201]

Restructuring these debts represented a change to the original terms of repayment. Nevertheless, as Baldwin would later explain, agreement was based on the assumption that "the British government did not desire to repudiate its formal obligations by an open default."[202] The successful resolution of this long-standing problem helped to defend Britain's international reputation for financial probity, meaning that London need not surrender more ground to New York as the world's banker and could secure fresh financial support for the overvalued pound.[203] Such efforts were especially important given that the British balance of payments suffered from an increasingly large trade deficit with the United States that was coupled with a decline in dollar incomes on the invisible account, largely via the sale of dollar securities during the war and the shifting of many financial services from London to New York.[204]

The U.S.-UK settlement helped Britain to reach settlements with its wartime allies—often negotiating with both the U.S. and debtor countries in parallel—that, in turn, provided sufficient income to cover most of its own war debts. In this sense, the settlement was reasonable and provided Britain with significant savings in comparison to the original agreement.[205] Cooperation also encouraged unofficial U.S. cooperation via the Dawes Plan of 1924, which helped to end Allied occupation of the Ruhr and provided a staggered payment plan for Germany's war reparations.[206] The Dawes Plan was the first of several credit events in which Germany renegotiated—and technically defaulted—on its external debts with international approval. Beginning in 1924, Germany began to borrow heavily from the United States to drive economic recovery. Under the Dawes Plan, Germany met its obligations almost in full, benefiting from an influx of foreign loans that at least equaled the amount paid in reparations.[207] These loans created a more stable system of international payments, which enabled the peaceful transfer of reparations to the Allies, who, in turn, repaid their war debts to the United States.[208]

Political changes on both sides of the Atlantic failed to disrupt the status quo. President John Calvin Coolidge took office in August 1923 following Harding's sudden death. Coolidge won his own election

comfortably in the following year. He did not support debt cancella-
tions, as evidenced by his State of the Union address in December.[209]
The president warned, "Unless money that is borrowed is repaid,
credit cannot be secured in time of necessity."[210] Yet he was willing
to make concessions regarding interest rates and terms of repayment.
Coolidge reasoned that if foreign governments did not pay their debts,
the American people would have to do so. As a consequence, although
he had little interest in Europe and opposed cancellation, he was pragmatic: "I do not favour the cancellation of this debt, but I see no objection to adjusting it in accordance with the principles adopted for the
British debt."[211]

The general election of 6 December 1923 produced a hung Parliament, with Ramsay MacDonald forming the first Labour government
with support from the Liberal Party. Following a vote of no confidence
in October of the following year, the Conservatives defeated the Labour minority government in another general election. Baldwin returned as prime minister, with Churchill assuming the chancellorship.
Under their leadership, Britain returned to the gold standard in 1925,
which was as much a moral as an economic policy.[212] This return had
been the objective of the government since the Cunliffe Committee of
1918 but was only now possible as the uncertainties that had bedeviled
the exchanges and affected sterling began to reduce.[213] Yet, as Barry
Eichengreen puts it, "war debts and reparations hung like a dark cloud
over all international negotiations, contaminating efforts to redesign
and manage the gold standard system cooperatively" and eventually
helped to undermine its effectiveness.[214]

The United Kingdom remained in recession, suffering from an overvalued currency and high levels of unemployment.[215] The British government's decision to force down prices to go back onto gold only raised
the real burden of debt.[216] Foreign indebtedness therefore continued to
carry a high price.[217] Churchill went on to charge the U.S. with greedily
draining Europe of its meager capital via war-debt repayments, a problem exacerbated by tariffs that were largely unsympathetic to British
commercial interests.[218] These tensions eventually escalated into a series
of heated exchanges between Mellon and Churchill in the summer of
1927.[219] Coolidge ended further debate and rebuked Mellon, stressing
that "the less talk went on about debts, the better it was."[220] Although
the funding agreement had reduced the total amount of debt, the bur-

den of Britain's large repayments still weighed heavily on the government. Accordingly, it still sought to encourage the "natural evolution of American thought" toward cancellation.[221] HM Treasury hoped to use the issue of reparations to secure a substantial revision or cancellation when the Dawes reparations plan eventually foundered.[222]

Rising tensions also reflected the comparative limitations of Britain's settlement with the United States when contrasted with the terms achieved by the other great powers of Europe. The WWFDC had applied the same terms to its next eight settlements, but in the coming years the commission became freer to consider debtors' capacity to pay.[223] By the mid-1920s, the U.S. national debt was being retired more quickly than anticipated, taxes had been reduced, and prosperity protected many groups from the tax impact of debt cancellation. As such, Congress became less resistant to negotiation.[224] None of these subsequent settlements canceled any of the principal, to be sure, but variables rates of interest were significant given the sums involved. Britain was scheduled to pay 82 percent of its total debts, in contrast to 50 percent for France and 32 percent for Italy, which equated to differences of hundreds of millions of dollars.[225] Although the British government could not have foreseen the United States' decision to offer more favorable terms to other European states, these differences generated lingering resentment.[226] British newspapers and politicians would come to criticize the debt settlement, with some describing it as a "disastrous bargain" and "the most tragic and the most bungled transaction ever concluded by a British statesman," in part because of the greater leniency that the United States would show Italy and France.[227] For many observers, the deal was simply unfair. As Lloyd George would write after the agreement had been reached, "A cold shiver ran down the back of England when it was announced officially that the British government had agreed to pay."[228]

By May 1926, the United States had completed thirteen debt settlements, which covered more than 97 percent of the outstanding total, and the WWFDC dissolved the following year.[229] European debtors would now need to repay approximately $22 billion over sixty-two years.[230] Mellon confidently predicted that all war debts to the United States would be discharged by 1988.[231] Britain had simultaneously negotiated revisions to its own funding settlements in this period.[232] The contrast in revised terms was stark. British funding settlements collected only

37 percent of outstanding war debts, in contrast to the U.S. average of 60 percent. The French debt to Britain reduced to 42.6 percent of the total advanced, for instance, while Italy's fell to 15.5 percent.[233]

Several accounts explain this difference with reference to Churchill's impatience and incompetence.[234] Yet, even before Churchill began negotiations, the cabinet and prime minister had stressed their willingness to accept a worse deal than other European states to improve international trade.[235] Britain was also selective in its debt negotiations. Consultations with British dominions on original advances as well as postwar reconstruction loans enjoyed no such reductions and ensured a full return with interest at 6 percent.[236] Furthermore, the British government expected the existing system of reparations and war debts to eventually falter, a reasonable assumption given the many states involved and the lengthy duration of repayment.

The troubles of intergovernmental indebtedness returned toward the end of the decade. Despite the efforts made by the Dawes Plan, Germany was struggling to fulfill its reparations obligations. In September 1928, the United States appointed an independent committee of experts led by Owen Young, a member of the Dawes committee and the head of General Electric, "to reconcile Allied demands for money with German reluctance to pay," while "protecting America's position on war debts."[237] The major European powers subsequently organized a conference to arrive at a final settlement of reparations.[238] The agreed plan reduced reparation payments and divided annual repayments into unconditional and postponable parts financed by a consortium of U.S. investment banks.[239] In so doing, it helped to alleviate many of the problems Germany had suffered, including reparations, and helped the country return to prosperity and international confidence.[240]

The U.S. officially sat on the sidelines but was concerned that European leaders would drive the conference toward eliminating war-debt payments. The United Kingdom and France did not do so directly but had sought German annuities sufficiently large to cover ongoing war-debt repayments. If Germany was unable or unwilling to meet these demands, the United States would face renewed pressure to concede a debt reduction. Yet Coolidge and his successor, Herbert Hoover, understood that Congress would never allow Europe to coerce the United States into a settlement. As such, successive administrations continued to deny any connection between war debts and reparations.[241] The

Young Plan was formally adopted in 1930.[242] The onset of the Great Depression, however, would fatally undermine its ambitions and return the issue of war debts and reparations to the center of international politics.[243]

DEBT MORATORIUM

On 4 March 1929, Herbert Hoover assumed the presidency of the United States. He enjoyed a booming economy and widespread support following a landslide victory. Hoover had served as commerce secretary under Coolidge and as a member of the WWFDC. He was therefore familiar with the technical and political elements of the problem that would soon confront him.[244] Prior to 1922, Hoover had seriously considered the cancellation of all debts or the termination of interest payments but swiftly came to appreciate the strength of congressional resistance.[245] Europe would repay the United States, he came to argue, given sufficient pressure. Cancellation or default should be "avoided at all costs" given their negative impact on international credit and national stability, but he was pragmatic; revision or reexamination of these debts could improve the chance of repayment and help to avoid a united front against U.S. efforts at collection.[246]

Hoover resumed talks on the subject with a new British government. The general election of 30 May 1929 had resulted in a hung Parliament. MacDonald's Labour Party secured the most seats but failed to gain an overall majority. In early October, MacDonald traveled to the United States to meet with Hoover. The two leaders discussed war debts, and the president warned that "the Balfour note, even if the road were otherwise clear, made it futile for him to grant any concessions."[247] Hoover subsequently proposed to MacDonald that Britain should consider selling Bermuda, British Honduras, and Trinidad in exchange for "a credit upon the war debt which would go a long way to settle that issue." The prime minister "did not rise to the idea at all," which Hoover believed proved that "he did not take the payment of the debt very seriously."[248]

The course of the war-debts saga was profoundly altered by the Wall Street crash and the later onset of the global phenomenon known as the Great Depression.[249] While 1929 marked a U.S. stock market collapse, most of the world, and particularly European countries, still maintained considerable financial stability.[250] Repayments continued throughout 1930, but the status quo was no longer sustainable as the global crisis mounted. The decline in GDP during the Great Depression, and to a lesser extent the rise of protectionism largely in the wake of the U.S. Smoot-Hawley tariff of 1930, which raised duties on hundreds of imported goods to record levels, undermined global trade and made it harder for many states to earn dollars to service their debts to the United States.[251]

The economic challenges significantly intensified and spread around the globe in 1931, which followed Latin American as well as central and eastern European debt, currency, and banking crises.[252] Banking crises affected the United Kingdom and France much less severely than the United States or Germany.[253] On 6 June 1931, Germany could no longer manage its reparations obligations, leading to renewed calls from European powers for all-round cancellation.[254] Financial difficulties in Europe also exacerbated the recession in the United States.[255] The president reacted by warily authorizing a one-year moratorium on war-debt repayments.[256] Hoover's willingness to entertain international solutions to spur recovery, including war-debt reduction, contrasted with his resistance to domestic intervention.[257] Mellon had repeatedly warned Hoover to refrain from government intervention in the Depression. The secretary of the Treasury believed that economic recessions, as evidenced by events in 1873 and 1907, were a necessary part of the business cycle.[258]

Hoover never supported outright cancellation, which he believed would burden U.S. taxpayers and punish American investors.[259] This position is often contrasted with the work of economists such as Harold Moulton and Leo Pasvolsky, who argued that liquidation would have benefited both creditor and debtor states by fostering conditions that would improve trade.[260] Irving Fisher had also long been critical of the war debts, saying, "One of the most threatening aspects of the present depression is the staggering burden of international debts left by the World War."[261] He continued that these debts were "a formidable obstacle to recovery not only because they operate, as all debts do, to intensify depressions, but also because they are so largely political in nature and incite to political unrest."[262] In January 1932, Fisher attended a meeting of monetary experts at the University of Chicago and organized a telegram urging the president to cancel interallied debts, among other policy proposals, including a rise in the federal budget deficit and the reduction of tariffs. Thirty-two prominent economists from Chicago, Wisconsin, and Harvard universities signed the statement.[263] Yet Hoover's position on the war debts remained unchanged. Politicians and economists approached the issue with different objectives and assumptions.

Canceling war debts and reparations may well have made longer-term economic sense, but the immediate political rewards were far more questionable. A significant improvement in trade and business activity would have benefited Americans more than ongoing repayment would have, to be sure, but cancellation may only have had a limited impact on global trade during the Depression, and any rewards would have taken time to emerge.[264] Even though these large debts held considerable psychological value as an obstacle to international cooperation, they were dwarfed by the many other structural and policy difficulties that beset the global economy.[265] As Hoover had noted, the total annual payments amount to less than 7 percent of U.S. imports or exports prior to the Depression.[266] These conclusions are supported to some extent by the failure of the subsequent debt moratorium to effect major economic change. Considering the counterfactual in this case—namely, outright cancellation or significant reduction—it seems reasonable to believe that cancellation would have increased the burden on U.S. taxpayers.[267]

The president "took the plunge" on 19 June 1931, having secured the support of his cabinet—including Mellon, Secretary of State Henry Stimson, and Undersecretary of the Treasury Ogden Mills—for a plan to postpone all interallied debts repayments for one year, which assumed that these European debtors also ceased claims for German reparations in the same period.[268] Mellon had initially objected to solving Europe's problems, but he soon rallied behind Hoover as the situation on the Continent deteriorated.[269] Twelve days later, the president made his decision public knowledge. Keynes may also have indirectly informed Hoover's decision. Chairman of the Federal Reserve Eugene Meyer took Keynes into his confidence when the British economist visited the United States in June. Following private discussions about the collapse of the German economy, Meyer now suggested to Hoover that reparations be cut in half, three days before he declared the moratorium.[270]

Hoover had attempted to secure bipartisan support before announcing the moratorium. He did not call Congress in session and seek ratification, however, but instead sought approval from congressional leaders and ranking members of committees in both houses and both parties.[271] Hoover managed to secure the support of what he termed "a large majority" of Congress, but some members of Congress would subsequently question the legality and constitutionality of the process.[272] Congressional resistance helps to explain why this solution was so limited. The moratorium generated an initially positive psychological effect across the U.S. and European economies.[273] Yet it was ultimately an inadequate effort that offered no long-term solution to the economic woes of the period. The president rejected the idea of government-guaranteed loans to European states and refused to cancel the war debts.[274] Hoover was keenly aware of congressional resistance to a settlement, especially in the current political climate. The Republican senator Hiram Johnson was one of the fiercest critics of the moratorium, and his position reflected popular opinion on the subject. It was, he believed, a device to place unpaid war debts on the shoulders of the American taxpayer and for foreign governments to evade repayment: "How marvelous it would be if our banks would say to our own people who are in the red," Johnson remarked, "We grant you a moratorium."[275]

The British government and press responded favorably to the moratorium but erroneously assumed that Hoover's actions augured a reconsideration of the war-debts problem.[276] As MacDonald noted in his diary, "suspension ought to mean that we shall not make the mistake of resuming."[277] During the election campaign in October, he allegedly suggested that the moratorium "ended all foreign debts": "and never again will our people—those of the English nation or those of any other country in Europe—be troubled with the payment of the debts."[278] These expectations, as well as the growing international crisis, help to explain why the British cabinet agreed to the Hoover proposal on 24 June, which necessitated the suspension of all installments from its own debtors, thereby accepting losses of more than £11 million.[279]

In contrast to the United Kingdom and the United States, France was pleased but unmoved.[280] It defended its "absolute right" to German reparations, for both international security and financial stability.[281] This position threatened to undermine any moratorium but also meant that Britain would appear foolish for making such a sacrifice. As such, London and Washington both applied considerable pressure on Paris.[282] Such efforts proved unsuccessful initially, and the crisis consequently worsened. The president finally forced France's hand by issuing a joint statement that put international pressure on France, which he correctly predicted "would be impossible for them to answer before the world."[283] As Kenneth Mouré puts it, French acceptance was "tardy and unwilling."[284] On 6 July 1931, Hoover publicly announced the moratorium, which began retrospectively on 1 July and would function for twelve months.

By August 1931, the minority Labour government had collapsed in the absence of agreement on proposals for reducing public expenditure, which many in the cabinet believed essential to avert a run on gold, defend the pound, and balance the budget. MacDonald offered his resignation to King George V but was persuaded to form a new government drawing on the talents of members from all parties. There followed a landslide victory for the National Government in the general election of October 1931. MacDonald led the new government, with members from other parties assuming key cabinet roles. Conservatives Neville Chamberlain and Stanley Baldwin took the chancellorship and lord president of the council. Liberals such as John Simon and Walter Runciman became secretary of state for foreign affairs and president of the board of trade. The new government introduced new attitudes and approaches to economic policy, not least Britain's departure from the gold standard, and held office until the onset of the Second World War.[285]

The interwar gold standard—if understood as the United Kingdom's return to the gold standard in 1925 and its departure in 1931—had lasted little more than six years. Whether viewed as an unavoidable consequence of the financial and political turmoil of the summer or as part of a longer-term trend, this decision and the accompanying devaluation of sterling had been reluctant. Many factors had discouraged the British government, including the impact of exchange-rate alterations on war-debt repayments. The United Kingdom's obligations to the United States were denominated in dollars, but the larger debts owed to the United Kingdom were denominated in sterling. As Alec Cairncross and Barry Eichengreen note, "Devaluation would therefore raise the sterling value of debt payments to the United States while leaving unchanged sterling receipts arising from interallied payments," which explains why this "matter was of real concern to Treasury officials."[286] Nevertheless, concerns about the effect on war debts appears to have had relatively limited bearing on the decision to devalue the pound, which reflected the urgency of the situation and a growing belief that the British government would soon reach a settlement with the United States or suspend repayment. As a subsequent cabinet note concluded, "Something must be arranged about our debt if a definite default is not to be forced on us. . . . In the present financial and political situation, His Majesty's Government are not in a position to pay in respect of their war debt to the United States of America more than they themselves are paid."[287]

The onset of the Great Depression had made it harder for the British government to service its debts. Meeting the costs of each installment added to the difficulties of a country already making considerable sacrifices. The growing burden of taxation had been accompanied by rigorous control of expenditure and cuts in allowances of all kinds.[288] Unemployment had grown considerably by 1931—just as it had in the United States—and the British government had implemented further austerity measures, including cuts in employment benefits and the introduction of the means test.[289] In addition, the economic situation had encouraged the British government to enact a series of tariff measures leading to the creation of a general tariff in February of the following year, which represented a noteworthy shift away from the long-standing doctrine of free trade.[290] The state of the economy was evidently a serious concern, but nonpayment remained a political choice for the government.[291] Repudiation of foreign debt remained anathema, especially given that financial orthodoxy and economic conservatism were the dominant features of Britain's strategy to cope with the economic slump.[292] The personal and ideological complexion of the government meant that default remained unacceptable despite lingering doubts about the rationality or fairness of resumed payments in the following year.

The British government therefore continued to seek a settlement of some kind. London, working with Paris and Berlin, attempted to use the present crisis to pressure Washington into granting a suspension of payments. In response to the terms of the moratorium, the prime minister informed the president on 16 December that the "no cancel-

lation" clause would "inevitably lead to an impasse."[293] In the absence
of any reparations, France would not pay its debt to the United Kingdom, which in turn would struggle to meet its obligations to the United
States. These challenges would add yet more pressure on the economy
and sterling. Only three months earlier, the United Kingdom had suspended the gold standard, unwilling to shoulder the increasing costs of
defending the exchange rate.[294] Chamberlain advised the cabinet in December that it was up to the British government to take the initiative if
it desired a change to the war-debt settlement, stressing that something
had to be done about British war debts to the United States to avoid a
default.[295] The cabinet subsequently agreed that the forthcoming budget should forgo any further payment of war debts.[296]

Washington was aware of the difficulties facing European debtors.
On 10 December, Hoover had warned Congress that as the new year
approached, an unidentified number of indebted governments might
be unable to meet further payments until their economies recovered,
and he urged "further temporary adjustments," including the reformation of the WWFDC.[297] Many Republicans and Democrats agreed
that it was better to help debtors recover than to accept unavoidable
defaults, as there was no other way to collect the debts short of war.
Furthermore, refusing to support the moratorium would harm rather
than help the average American and would contradict a majority view
from earlier in the year.[298]

Yet Congress refused any extension or revival of a debt commission.
During the ratification process, a final clause was added to the moratorium prohibiting both proposals.[299] As Hoover recalled, "Congress
not only refused but rapped my knuckles by including in their moratorium ratification."[300] Hoover's moratorium suffered from the growing unpopularity of the administration. Rising deficits and high levels
of unemployment, alongside the widely reported failures of the Farm
Board and Prohibition policies, undermined the president's position.
Congress had by now begun to express serious reservations about the
moratorium. In the House and the Senate, Democrats and even some
Republicans criticized its unconstitutional nature. Many suggested that
Hoover's speech heralded the scaling down or cancellation of the war
debts, which came at the expense of American taxpayers and business-
people who were standing by their contracts without asking for any
reduction.[301]

THE LAUSANNE CONFERENCE

By late 1931, the United States began to fear a united front comprising Britain and France pursuing debt cancellation in the depths of the Depression. These fears were heightened by the looming international conference on reparations, which was planned to take place in Lausanne, Switzerland, in the following year.[302] The British cabinet did desire improved relations with France, especially with regard to the forthcoming conference, but cooperation was strained by different attitudes toward German reparations and how best to work with the United States.[303] Whereas Paris sought to exploit events as a lever to force debt revision, London was also keen to preserve its special position with Washington.[304]

When the cabinet met in January 1932, Simon explained that Britain's solution based on the cancellation of war debts and reparations would mean that "Germany would gain enormously; France would lose materially; America would lose heavily; but Britain would remain unaffected (assuming payments by the Dominions continue) so far as the balance of receipts and payments is concerned."[305] The secretary of state understood that the government's position would "provoke the criticism that it is easy to urge sacrifice on others when you do not join in yourself."[306] Yet he believed the United Kingdom had already paid far more than anyone else, on much less generous terms, and that something had to be done to escape the spiral of debts that undermined recovery. As Chamberlain wrote in private, "Any reparations settlement or adjustment must be accompanied by a corresponding settlement or adjustment of war debts. . . . Hoover knows it but darent [sic] say so. Unless he says so France darent [sic] move and so we are all locked in a suicidal embrace which will probably drown the lot of us!"[307]

The British government decided to adopt a two-step negotiating strategy in 1932.[308] The European powers would agree to settle the issue of reparations and would consequently address the war-debt issue with the United States, in the expectation that they could then force the hand of their creditor. This was a high-risk plan, which threatened to leave Britain in a difficult position if the U.S. chose not to cooperate, but few viable alternatives existed. In addition, the French government initially resisted and instead stressed its unconditional right to reparations.[309] The prime minister, chancellor, and foreign secretary met to discuss the plan on 19 January. There followed a full cabinet discussion on the next day. The gathered ministers agreed to focus on a reparations settlement rather than getting "mixed up with the French" concerning war debts and then "to trust . . . making a settlement afterwards with the United States."[310]

In advance of the conference, Anglo-French discussions continued throughout the spring of 1932. Despite the United Kingdom's differences from France and ongoing concerns about the state of relations with the United States, a united European front remained desirable. Most of the cabinet, with a few notable exceptions including MacDonald, believed that cooperation with France and other European powers would yield some benefits against the United States.[311] The British government's "united front" position was weakened by MacDonald's decision to leak the content of these cabinet debates directly to Stimson and Hoover, presumably to stave off conflict with the United States.[312]

The Lausanne Conference took place in Switzerland from 16 June to 9 July 1932. This gathering of representatives from Germany, France, and the United Kingdom managed to reach a financial agreement on the cancellation of outstanding reparations and war debts, albeit only after three weeks of negotiation. Prior to the conference, the cabinet had agreed to begin with a general declaration stating that all-round cancellation would benefit the world.[313] The chancellor understood that in the absence of payments from Europe, British default on its war loans to the United States would prove difficult to avoid. Nevertheless, he believed that this outcome was distinct from repudiation and hoped that the success of European cooperation would encourage the United States toward a settlement, an assumption aided by unofficial hints of future deferrals from U.S. sources.[314] As Chamberlain recognized, however, it "was impossible to . . . conclude a complete and final settlement at Lausanne because America was not represented": "We must proceed stage by stage."[315]

Chamberlain's introductory speech warned that existing debt was "disastrous to the whole economic fabric of civilisation" but reminded the attendees of the British government's generosity regarding the collection of its own war debts (Figure 1.2) and its readiness "to take [its] share in a general wiping of the slate, provided that all other

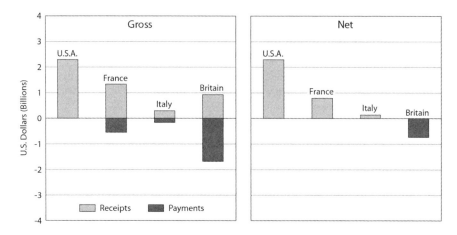

Figure 1.2. Total reparations and war-debts receipts and payments, 1932 ($ billion) (Source: CAB 104/28, American War Debt, History to the Conclusion of the Settlement of 1923, Annex II)

Governments concerned would do the same."[316] Germany proved helpful and conciliatory to these ambitions, but France remained difficult. Chamberlain found that Prime Minister Édouard Herriot of France was only willing to scale down Germany's payments, seemingly due to concerns about the United States eventually seeking the resumption of debt repayments. On 8 July, after further and difficult negotiations, Herriot and Chamberlain reached an agreement that "a new order was about to begin," thereby helping Germany but agreeing to French demands for compensation of three billion gold marks in bonds.[317]

This settlement was not yet ratified but represented a momentous occasion for the major European powers.[318] The Lausanne Conference effectively ended reparation payments, which the British government believed would provide a potential way out of the war-debts issue.[319] Indeed, it had previously been keen to keep dominion war debts separate from the moratorium and interallied war debts more broadly. Now, however, the chancellor of the exchequer confirmed at Lausanne that if there were a general cancellation of reparation and war debts, then payments on principal or interest due from the dominions should be postponed. The British government would continue to honor this stance thereafter.[320]

Yet British policymakers were under few illusions regarding the cancellation of war debts. Success still depended on securing U.S. support. Having come to a settlement, Chamberlain now advised patience, allowing world opinion to pressure the United States to capitulate.[321] This position was aided by unofficial hints from unnamed U.S. sources that, if the European powers did not draw attention to this controversial issue during the presidential elections, Hoover could defer the next debt payment due on 15 December until the conclusion of a negotiated settlement.[322]

Following the conclusion of the conference, the creditor powers reached a private "gentleman's agreement," postponing ratification until reaching a "satisfactory settlement" with the United States.[323] If London was unable to reach a satisfactory settlement with Washington, it would not ratify the Lausanne agreement.[324] As Chamberlain informed Simon, this approach allowed the British government to avoid criticisms of "the smuggest hypocrisy" after "stern lectures to its Irish and Balkan debtors on the sanctity of debts" and to avoid suggestions of a default that "would make Englishmen blush for generations."[325] Chamberlain believed that this agreement would help to compel the United States to accept the need for a "clean slate," using the period of nonpayment "to educate public opinion in the USA and hence to facilitate ultimate cancellation by consent."[326] The chief economic adviser to the British government Frederick Leith-Ross was less optimistic. He considered the agreement to be "a convenient formula" that had not resolved the war-debt issue and merely delayed an answer to the question of whether the United Kingdom should resume payments to the United States when the Hoover moratorium expired at the end of the year.[327]

Hoover remained publicly opposed to any remission or cancellation of European war debts, a cautious position that reflected the looming presidential elections and the largely negative reaction that such a policy change could produce in Congress and the press.[328] As such, Herriot's reference to the "gentleman's agreement" in a public speech only days later and its subsequent mention in an English newspaper undermined any hope of a settlement. On 12 July, the British cabinet agreed to provide an explanation of events, appreciating the "unfortunate effect" of these revelations on U.S. opinion.[329] In the ensuing Parliamentary debates, the "secret diplomacy" was criticized, but the prime minister defended such efforts by stressing the risks of failing to achieve a settlement.[330]

Hoover described the news as "a Hell of a thing" and feared that "they are trying to 'gang us' in order to fasten the sole responsibility and burden for all inter-governmental debts upon the American tax-payer."[331] Stimson, who had lauded the "magnificent" agreement and was keen on maintaining good relations, was nevertheless frustrated by the efforts of "some stupid ass in the British Treasury" to present the U.S. "with *a fait accompli* and cancel debts."[332] Ogden Mills, now sec-retary of the Treasury, was also unimpressed. He had always favored a middle road but was frustrated by Britain's and France's failure to heed his advice about not upsetting U.S. opinion.[333] Hoover subsequently declared his ignorance of recent events and stressed that the country would never be "pressed into any line of action . . . by a combination [of its debtors] either open or implied."[334]

The president maintained his opposition to cancellation but went on to raise the idea of trading war debts in exchange for the expansion of U.S. agriculture markets. Hoover was, as others in the administra-tion put it privately, urgently trying "to find some way out."[335] The British government declined this proposal due in part to its commit-ment to the imperial preference system—namely, its existing commer-cial and trade arrangements between the dominions and colonies of the British Empire—evidenced most clearly by the preferential trade agreements negotiated with the dominions at the Imperial Economic Conference held in Ottawa in the summer of 1932. As Frank Trent-mann explains, these agreements "put the final nail in the coffin of Free trade."[336] Britain's stance had many causes, but it was in part motivated by the Smoot-Hawley tariff legislation of 1930, which had raised im-port duties to protect U.S. businesses and farmers but prompted many states to retaliate by raising their own tariffs on U.S. exports. In ad-dition, Keynes had also advocated tariffs in part to support Britain's role as a global creditor. He argued that they would "allow Britain both to pay for additional imports which expansion would suck in and to finance loans to foreign debtor countries," helping to challenge "the spirit of contractionism and fear."[337] The unwinding of free trade, which would harm U.S. exports, therefore further complicated trans-atlantic negotiations.[338]

London also rejected trading the war debts for other concessions because of its own principles concerning any debt settlement and because it also held hope of political change in Washington. The Democratic Party's presidential candidate in 1932, Franklin Delano Roosevelt, opposed cancellation but had criticized Republicans who were "demanding payment and at the same time making payment impossible" by supporting a high-tariff policy.[339] In August, Roosevelt signaled to London that he sought revision of the debt on "specially favourable terms," although he would remain silent on the issue during the campaign.[340] In this period of uncertainty, the British government chose to keep a low profile. MacDonald and Simon agreed, "the best thing is to leave the U.S. government alone at present, for things are working out our way if we keep quiet."[341] London now looked toward Washington to solve the war-debt issue. Such optimism would soon be disappointed.

2   Final Payments,
1932–1933

IN LATE 1932, the British government seriously considered the possibility of defaulting on its war debts to the United States. The United Kingdom would need to make considerable sacrifices to meet its repayment schedule, and other European states including France already looked likely to default.[1] Progress toward nonpayment was nevertheless reluctant and gradual. A series of cabinet discussions from November 1932 to December 1933 reveals a general unwillingness to leave these debts unpaid.[2] This fourteen-month period included three repayments—one full payment in 1932 followed by two partial payments or what were then termed "token" installments in 1933—before suspension took place in 1934.

Decision-making in London was informed by recent events in Washington. Following Franklin Roosevelt's dominant electoral victory, the British government held out hope for a new settlement and refocused its efforts on persuading the incoming administration to reduce or cancel these war debts.[3] Roosevelt was receptive to requests for negotiations and proved willing to recognize partial or token payments.[4] He also spoke optimistically about securing a debt settlement in the future. Nevertheless, the president repeatedly proved unwilling to challenge Congress on the issue of revision or cancellation, reflecting his prioritization of domestic-political support for his New Deal reforms and doubts about the alleged difficulty of repayment.[5] Washington's position left London in a state of uncertainty, but a majority of the cabinet remained unwilling to repudiate or suspend repayments despite the significant costs involved.

This chapter addresses an important question. Why did the United Kingdom not default on its debts to the United States earlier, rather than making three additional payments? Major powers such as France—alongside smaller economies like Belgium, Estonia, Greece, Hungary, and Poland—chose to cease repayment in 1932 rather than 1934 (Table 2.1). All of these states faced smaller debts than the United Kingdom, and some enjoyed stronger financial positions or larger gold reserves.[6] Economists and political scientists have offered several explanations for why states repay their debts, which tend to focus on rational

Table 2.1. Default status of select borrowers at year end and amounts due ($, 30 June to 31 December 1932)

Country	Interest	Principal	Total
	Non-Default		
Czechoslovakia	—	1,500,000.00	1,500,000.00
Finland	128,235.00	58,000.00	186,235.00
Great Britain	65,550,000.00	30,000,000.00	95,550,000.00
Italy	1,245,437.00	—	1,245,437.00
Latvia	102,652.12	46,200.00	148,852.12
Total			98,630,524.12
	Default		
Belgium	2,125,000.00	—	2,125,000.00
Estonia	245,370.00	111,000.00	356,370.00
France	19,261,432.00	—	19,261,432.00
Greece	217,920.00	357,000.00	574,920.00
Hungary	28,444.35	12,285.00	40,729.35
Lithuania	92,386.01	—	92,386.01
Poland	3,070,980.00	1,357,000.00	4,427,980.00
Total			26,878,817.36
	Overall		
			125,509,341.48

Sources: U.S. Treasury Department, *Annual Report* (1932), 37; CAB 104/28, P. J. Grigg, "History of the American War Debt, to the Conclusion of Settlement of 1923" (1934).

assessments of economic costs—namely, reputational harm, the risk of punishments, and spillover effects within the state.[7] A smaller number of social scientists have also concentrated on domestic politics, institutional constraints, and state identity to help explain such outcomes.[8] Historians such as Robert Self and Patricia Clavin have touched on elements of these themes when focusing on the British case, arguing convincingly that a mix of economic, political, and ideological factors informed decision-making in London. They identify a wide collection of influences but focus their attention on hopes for debt concessions, concerns about global economic confidence, and a desire to protect transatlantic relations.[9]

This chapter supports and refines the work of some social scientists and historians by highlighting the importance of two other factors inhibiting default that have been neglected or downplayed in the existing literature. The first concerns Britain's role as an international creditor, which the extant literature has ignored or downplayed, especially with regard to its importance and frequency in the decision-making process.[10] There was considerable fear that states owing money to the United Kingdom—namely, Argentina, Australia, and Germany—might use British default as an excuse to cease repayment on their own outstanding debts.[11] These examples were representative of the United Kingdom's position as a creditor to much of the world, drawing sums from overseas that exceeded payments to the United States, which naturally encouraged a commitment to the sanctity of debt contracts.[12] A wave of defaults not only added to the burdens of British taxpayers but undermined the foundations of the global economy. This risk, which former chancellor of the exchequer Robert Horne called "contagious," ultimately proved exaggerated.[13] Nevertheless such fears were widely held, both in the government and on the opposition benches, which was understandable given that the United Kingdom was the world's second-largest international lender, after the United States.[14] Many Americans, including President Herbert Hoover, were also anxious about the contagious nature of default.[15] Claims about the importance of reputation in explaining sovereign default are therefore still relevant, but they largely reflected concerns about existing lending rather than future borrowing.

The second factor concerned the impact of domestic-political considerations on decision-making, which scholars typically neglect or simplify as only encouraging default.[16] Despite a significant majority in the House of Commons, some cabinet ministers and members of Parliament believed that refusal to pay would profoundly shock a large section of public opinion, especially given that many people were struggling to meet their own obligations in the wake of the Great Depression. Default would thereby undermine the popularity of the government and harm its chances in future elections. This insight lends some credence to explanations for repayment based on domestic politics or state identity. Continued repayment was not only politically appropriate but provided the British government with more time to manage reputational and political risks and prepare the country for default if no settlement could be reached. Overall, the British government recognized and chose to observe traditions or norms of repayment initially because many ministers believed default was unacceptable or unfair and because of the perceived international and domestic risks involved in nonpayment.[17]

FINAL FULL REPAYMENT

President Herbert Hoover suffered a humbling defeat to Franklin Roosevelt as the results of the presidential election emerged on 8 November 1932. The Great Depression had dominated the campaign.[18] Voters overwhelmingly rejected the Hoover administration as the country struggled with record levels of unemployment, which affected almost a quarter of the working population, while the government ran ever-larger deficits and accumulated rising levels of debt.[19] Hoover would enjoy little consolation from abroad. Two days after the election result, the British ambassador to the U.S. Ronald Lindsay dropped what Secretary of State Henry Stimson would describe as a "bombshell about the debt settlement."[20] Britain had requested a delay in paying the next installment of its war debts following the agreements reached at Lausanne.[21] The Hoover administration would receive similar messages from France, Poland, Greece, Belgium, Italy, and Czechoslovakia in the coming days. Stimson and Treasury Secretary Ogden Mills eventually convinced Hoover to invite Roosevelt to help craft a bipartisan response to this European debt challenge during the interregnum. The president dispatched a telegram to the president-elect that warned of the seriousness of the situation, not least the fear that any default could precipitate "a tidal wave" of further defaults on public and private debts within the United States itself, and suggested a meeting at the White House.[22]

Roosevelt had previously accused the U.S. government of greed on the issue of war debts but upon declaring his candidacy began to adopt political positions more akin to those of Hoover, including claims that rising expenditures on armaments proved that European debtors could manage repayment.[23] The president-elect and his key economic advisers—Raymond Moley and Rexford Tugwell—were nevertheless wary of the president's invitation. They viewed such talks as dangerous given the risks of being tied into any agreements that might constrain their political freedom in office and of being associated with Hoover's unsuccessful efforts to tackle the Depression.[24]

Negotiations would also be problematic given the incoming administration's still-unsettled position on the importance of the war debts. Hoover believed his government had adopted all the domestic policies necessary for recovery but was willing to entertain international solutions, principally war-debt reduction. The Roosevelt administration was more divided on the issue. Some advisers stressed the importance of international approaches, but others, including Moley and Tugwell, were committed to prioritizing domestic recovery programs.[25] Moley warned that the war-debt issue represented "a perilous division in his triumphant party."[26] Nevertheless, Roosevelt and many of his advisers were conscious of the popular criticism they might receive by declining a meeting with Hoover, especially on such an important topic, and agreed to attend. Moley and Tugwell subsequently began preparations for the talks and promptly concluded that "the debt problem was more political than economic."[27] They believed that cancellation was electorally unacceptable and advised Roosevelt against cooperation with Hoover.[28] As Tugwell later put it, "Cancellation was political dynamite. We mustn't touch it off."[29]

The talks took place on 22 November. Hoover stressed the need to discuss the idea with European debtors, citing the risks posed to foreign relations and the "dangers to the world of having a process of default signified by such a gigantic action," and urged the reformation of a foreign debt commission.[30] The president-elect remained noncommittal, and Moley soon began to negotiate on his behalf. The president directed himself to educating what he saw as a "very ignorant"

yet "well-meaning young man," which was fitting as Moley would describe Hoover as "the best informed individual in the country on the
question of the debts."[31] Hoover and Stimson's subsequent accounts
of the meeting suggests that an agreement to cooperate had emerged,
whereas Roosevelt and Moley denied any such outcome.[32] The ambi-
guity of these talks, however, was soon addressed. On the following
day, Roosevelt issued a press statement that stressed that responsibility
for policy lay with the current president and expressed his preference
for the use of established diplomatic channels. According to Moley,
"this statement and the formulas it presented were to be the new Administration's policy throughout the year that followed Roosevelt's inauguration."[33] At the core of the president-elect's thinking was a belief
that the issue of the war debts, whether paid or not, would never in
any serious way hinder recovery at home or abroad.[34] Cooperation
with the United Kingdom was therefore preferable rather than essential; congressional and public support for Roosevelt's new policies was
far more important.

None of this is to deny that economists who would come to work
closely with Roosevelt recognized the potential value of reducing the
war debts. James Harvey Rogers—who had been mentored by Irving
Fisher while at Yale University—and George F. Warren both supported
a reduction or cancellation of the debt.[35] Oliver Sprague, a professor of
economics at Harvard who had known Roosevelt as an undergraduate,
agreed with these sentiments. Sprague, who was now serving as economic adviser to the Bank of England but would soon become financial and executive assistant to the secretary of the Treasury, had urged
American bankers and Treasury officials that the United Kingdom's
war debts should be reduced. His audiences were often sympathetic
but, much like Roosevelt, accepted that prevailing political realities
prohibited such concessions.[36]

By late November, there was still no definitive U.S. response to the
British government's request for a delay in paying the next installment.
Hoover's meeting with Roosevelt had highlighted the outgoing administration's rising fear of mass repudiation and ongoing uncertainty
surrounding repayment.[37] As Hoover would ask U.S. ambassador to
the United Kingdom Andrew Mellon in the coming weeks, "Do you
think they are going to default then?"[38] The president was right to be
concerned. Chancellor of the Exchequer Neville Chamberlain had for

some time believed that "no payment whatever will be made on December 15."[39] As Self reveals, however, he would soon undergo a Damascene conversion. Following a meeting with the governor of the Bank of England, Montagu Norman, on 27 November, the chancellor learned that Mills wanted to help the British government, privately offering detailed advice on how to secure a two-year suspension, thereby raising hopes of future compromise.[40] Norman would also warn Chamberlain that a suspension of payments would prompt other debtors to default on their debts to the United Kingdom. This particular concern would come to exert considerable influence over British policymaking in the coming weeks and months.[41]

Senior members of the British cabinet met to discuss the war-debts problem on the evening of 28 November 1932. The prime minister stated that there was little chance of obtaining a remission of the semi-annual payment of $95.5 million (£27.7 million) due on 15 December—an installment comprising $30 million principal and $65.5 million interest—especially in the uncertainty of the presidential transition period. Congress was due to meet on 5 December and, given other concerns, was unlikely to vote in favor of suspension in time. As such, the prime minister wished to know whether the gathered ministers "favour default or not."[42]

After a lengthy debate, the cabinet met again the following evening and agreed that if the United States did not permit a remission, the United Kingdom should pay the installment but also present a note to its creditor setting forth the facts and arguments in support of a request for a suspension. If the note held good prospects of acceptance, the British government would then seek to ascertain whether this option would be available to other debtors. Clarity on this matter was important because differentiation might upset the Lausanne agreement reached earlier that year, in which Britain, France, and Germany reached a "gentleman's agreement" to reduce reparations and war-debt payments among themselves with the expectation that the United States would follow their lead.[43] The cabinet's decision to honor the agreement reached at Lausanne was costly because it meant that the United Kingdom received no more income from its European debtors despite continuing payments to the United States (Figure 2.1).

The content of the cabinet debate over these two days reveals that repayment was a difficult decision. Default remained a tempting option

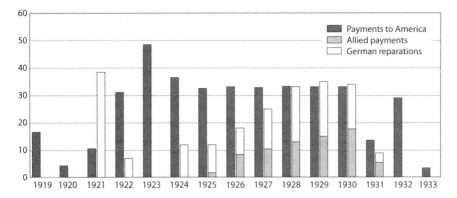

Figure 2.1. Summary of British receipts and payments, 1919–1934 (£ million).
Allied payments comprised France, Italy, Romania, Portugal, Greece, and Serbia.
(Source: T 236/736, "Summary of Receipts and Payments, 1919–1934" [1948])

for the cabinet given the costs of the installments and the demanding economic environment.[44] The war debts remained remarkably stubborn. By November 1932, the British government had provided payments totaling more than $1.9 billion toward the original advances of $4.28 billion.[45] Despite these efforts, the nominal amount of the debt still outstanding stood at more than $4.5 billion due to accumulated interest. Meeting these costs added to the burden of a country already making considerable sacrifices. High levels of taxation and unemployment had been accompanied by rigorous control of expenditure and cuts in allowances of all kinds.[46] The state of the economy was a serious concern, but it was not yet determinative with regard to foreign debt repayment. Default remained a political choice. The chancellor was clear that there were sufficient funds available to continue repayment in the short term. The debate concerned willingness rather than ability to pay. Chamberlain was clear: "There was no warrant for the statement made in the Press that we were unable to pay. We could pay. The question was whether we should."[47]

The budgetary position was only part of the problem of intergovernmental debt. The revenues of the United Kingdom were in sterling, whereas debt payments to the United States required dollars or gold. Transferring amounts of this magnitude risked the rapid erosion of British dollar reserves and a sharp depreciation of sterling against the dollar. When the British government made its 15 December payment, it turned over one-seventh of its gold reserve, which some ministers believed to be unsustainable.[48] Reserves could potentially have been replenished through further sacrifices or by mobilizing foreign holdings of U.S. assets—as policymakers in the Roosevelt administration believed, the transfer problem was "appreciable but not determinative"—but the gathered ministers appear to have disregarded these alternatives.[49] The chancellor accepted that payment in gold could have an injurious effect on the economy and sterling, especially as the United Kingdom could not count on receiving anything from its own debtors abroad, whether in foreign countries or the dominions. Nevertheless, Chamberlain still thought payment necessary. Although it was possible that the present situation would be repeated in June the following year, the chancellor believed that both sides would by then have entered discussions for a final settlement.[50]

Several ministers questioned the effectiveness of continued repayment. Secretary of State for War Douglas Hogg said that they could not go on making these payments indefinitely. Hogg and President of the Board of Trade Walter Runciman doubted that payment of this installment would help them in the future, especially as it would be awkward for Roosevelt not to be paid in June if Hoover had been paid in December. Runciman noted that payment would be possible in gold, but it would reduce national reserves by up to a fifth, which might not be sufficient backing for future credit issuances in London.[51] Secretary of State for Foreign Affairs John Simon agreed with a final payment, however, stressing the loss of any potential concessions on the debt from the United States after default. He hoped that payment would be made in such a manner "to give the impression of a last despairing effort in order to effect payment."[52] Baldwin also supported the chancellor's line. Payment now did not mean a perpetuation of payments. Baldwin reasoned that, when the new president took office, negotiations should resume, which would provide an opportunity for the government to make its case.

There were also compelling domestic reasons to avoid default for some members of the cabinet. Chamberlain noted that Norman had previously warned him that refusal to pay would cause a profound shock to a large section of public opinion in the United Kingdom. Secretary of State for Dominion Affairs James Henry Thomas emphasized that while the mass of the people would not understand the details, the result of default would be "a tremendous propaganda" to get rid of the National Government.[53] Minister of Health Edward Hilton Young stressed the importance of payment from the point of view of the sanctity not only of public debts but also of private debts. "Everywhere people were struggling to meet their obligations," he explained, and the "effect of a conspicuous default by the government would be very serious on these people. It would affect the whole standard of probity in debts."[54] Baldwin also believed it would be "a tremendous shock to the vast majority of the working classes" if they realized that the government was able to pay and did not.[55] These concerns might appear exaggerated but were pertinent. It is worth noting that many British citizens were in prison for unpaid debts at that time.[56]

The political significance that these ministers attached to default is nevertheless questionable. Repudiation of foreign debt would have been anathema to the government and much of the public, especially given that financial orthodoxy and economic conservatism were the dominant features of its strategy to cope with the economic slump.[57] Yet the recent decision to leave the gold standard and the bond-conversion operation that had run earlier in the year, which led to a reduction in the rate of interest paid on a large proportion of public debt, had carried far greater risks and represented more significant economic changes.[58] Concerns about political challenges are also puzzling. Labour did experience an impressive recovery in local elections and by-elections after 1931, but the National Government nevertheless enjoyed a large majority and faced a generally weakened opposition.[59]

The United Kingdom's relations with the United States played an important but subtle role in deterring default. There was little mention in the cabinet minutes about fear of reprisals or the costs of future borrowing. Members of the cabinet were instead anxious that noncompliance might prejudice future negotiations or even undermine hopes of future concessions, which remained the government's central ambition.[60] Even if the minutes downplayed the costs to Anglo-American relations, the gathered ministers surely recognized the potential harm to diplomatic relations. As Herbert Feis, economic adviser to the State Department, had warned Lindsay during these cabinet discussions, British default would "engender lasting bitterness which would complicate and possibly defeat all hopes of cooperation on matters of world importance," from arms control to economic stability.[61] There were also geostrategic dimensions to consider even if only distantly at that time. The Foreign Office believed that "good Anglo-American relations" were "one of the most effective restraints on Germany in Europe."[62]

One of the most powerful reasons against default, which would re-occur repeatedly in cabinet discussions over the coming months, concerned the wider international repercussions of such a decision. Chamberlain recalled Norman's "definite view that [British] default . . . would be followed by default by three countries that owed [Britain] money—Australia, Argentina and Germany": "The result would be that these three countries would follow our lead and jump at a plausible excuse for doing so."[63] Simon similarly questioned how the government was to conduct itself in matters of default toward such countries as Chile, Greece, Austria, Russia, and the Irish Free State. More broadly, Baldwin believed that "repudiation might bring the world within sight of the end of capitalism." He remarked, "Our word was unique in the world."[64] If Britain broke its word, it would set a dangerous example, and the effect on public and private debts throughout the world would, he felt, be "very serious."[65] Concerns about the sanctity of debt contracts therefore reflected the United Kingdom's position as a creditor to much of the world, drawing sums from overseas that exceeded payments to the United States, as well as the observance of norms concerning the illegitimacy of default.[66] These anxieties had probably been exacerbated by the reduction in income from foreign governments over the preceding year.[67] Strong beliefs about the international dangers of unpaid debts also appear to have been felt by much of the cabinet and were shared by many politicians in opposition parties.[68] Such views were shared by economists and widely reported in the national press. *The Times*, for example, quoted Gustav Cassel's warning that "many of her [Britain's] debtors would be only too willing to follow her example if such a wealthy nation were to tread the path of default."[69]

For all these reasons, a majority of the cabinet agreed that the United Kingdom should continue to repay the United States. The gathered ministers all stressed, however, that the next installment due on 15 December was intended as a final payment. London should therefore notify Washington of this assumption and stress that any further payment would depend on the resumption of negotiations. Much of the cabinet now argued that Britain ought to make a strong claim on several countries to pay the United Kingdom, especially France, which was in a better position to pay. France enjoyed the second-largest gold hoard in the world and behaved, as the financial journalist André Kostolany put it, like "an old miser."[70] Nevertheless, the chancellor believed that the government of Prime Minister Édouard Herriot would not survive if it attempted to make a payment. Many cabinet ministers were keen to avoid antagonizing Paris due to a shared commitment to the agreements reached at the Lausanne Conference as well the potential impact that any divisions might have on the World Disarmament Conference scheduled for early in the new year. Failure to present a united front could further imperil the international economy and European security.[71]

On the following morning of 29 November, the members of the cabinet resumed discussions. Although no decision had been taken in the evening, the trend of the discussion had been in favor of payment being made on 15 December if Congress refused suspension. Early in the meeting, the chancellor reported that he had received information from an authoritative source that both Hoover and Roosevelt had agreed to a reexamination of the war-debt situation.[72] The administration was unlikely to give the same terms to its debtors on the Continent, however, if they defaulted. Different agreements could undermine the Lausanne agreement, to which the chancellor attached the utmost importance, and risked making relations with European powers very difficult. The chancellor stressed that they should not accept any agreement unless the proposal was also available to debtors on the Continent. This uncompromising position raised serious difficulties, especially given the risk of a leak to the press. Critics, they feared, would claim that the British government had refused a favorable offer in the interests of France, rather than seeing such actions as an attempt to defend the Lausanne agreement and European policy more broadly. Nevertheless, the cabinet ultimately supported the chancellor's position.[73]

The British government subsequently informed the Hoover administration of the urgent need for a revision of the debts, stressing the economic rather than political case for change, and argued for an end to differentiation between Britain and France to protect the terms of the Lausanne agreement.[74] The president and his advisers were disappointed by this message and believed that they would be unable to persuade Congress to consent to a postponement of French debt. In an attempt to overcome this stalemate, Hoover sent Mellon to London to warn the government against defaulting, but it soon became clear that neither side was willing to negotiate.[75] As Stimson recalls, "matters slid toward an impasse of default from Europe and public resentment at home."[76] The Hoover administration would soon come to believe that Britain would not default, however, following MacDonald's curious decision to divulge to U.S. officials that his government would pay in full if its request for a postponement failed.[77] The Hoover administration eventually provided a response on 7 December that challenged the economic and political logic of British claims and stressed the limited prospect of Congress accepting any proposal for a postponement of the December payment.[78]

Later that same day, the cabinet met to discuss Hoover's latest statements. In the circumstances, the gathered ministers considered three possible courses. First, Chamberlain proposed to pay in gold and in full but accompanied by an explanation that this decision was "exceptional and abnormal" and was made only because there had not been time for adequate discussion between London and Washington. Second, Chief Economic Adviser Frederick Leith-Ross advocated a suspension of the principal of the payment for two years. Third, the Foreign Office supported a counterproposal with half the payment in gold and the remainder in bonds. The chancellor argued against both alternatives to his plan. Seeking a suspension was likely to involve Congress, he believed, which would only be satisfied by full payment. Making a counterproposal would be humiliating and would contradict the government's recent arguments, which were based not on inability to pay but on the serious reactions that payment would have on the world economy. The chancellor's proposal for full payment ultimately met with the unanimous approval of the cabinet.[79]

Chamberlain subsequently stressed the "exceptional and abnormal" nature of payment in a formal note to the Hoover administration on 11 December. Concerned by the conditions now attached to payment and well aware of the risks of a poor reaction in the United States, Stimson issued a formal reply emphasizing that receipt of this payment did not constitute an endorsement of any such condition.[80] The publication of the U.S. note on 12 December created "a great to-do" in Washington and "a general chorus of approval from the Hill" concerning Hoover's unyielding response.[81]

The decision to continue repayment came at significant cost. On 13 December, the chancellor informed the cabinet that he proposed to pay out of revenue, which would involve an increase in the budget deficit.[82] He added that if the British government made a final agreement with the United States, it should have a right to call on its debtors to pay a proportionate share, including the payment it was now making. The cabinet then discussed the forthcoming debate in Parliament. Runciman expressed his hope that the chancellor would not belittle the very heavy burden placed on the country and the taxpayer by this latest payment. The president of the Board of Trade was anxious that it should not be thought, either at home or abroad, that the cabinet had made this payment easily. Thomas expressed the hope, however, that care would be taken not to go too far in this direction. There were signs of an improvement in trade, and it was most undesirable to damp them down by arousing suspicions of extra taxation.[83]

The chancellor went into considerable detail to justify his decision in the House of Commons on 14 December. He was clear that this payment was expensive and involved the loss of a huge quantity of gold. Such losses were manageable in this instance, but he warned that further payments would be difficult to sustain.[84] The government's ability to meet these costs as well as concerns about the repercussions and inappropriateness of nonpayment, however, explained its hesitation to default. As Chamberlain informed the House, "A default by the British Government, on a sum which they could not truthfully say they were unable to pay, would have resounded all round the world. It might have been taken as a justification for other debtors to follow their example, and, further than that, a default at that time and in those circumstances would have administered a shock to the moral sense of our people which might have had a very profound effect upon our whole conception of the meaning of obligations, public or private, with consequences that one could only guess at."[85] The British government's motivations for repayment were evidently driven by a mix of material and ideational concerns, as evidenced privately in cabinet and then publicly in the Commons, which differed from many social scientists' focus on reputational harm, the risk of punishments, or spillover effects within the state.[86] The available archival data reduce confidence in these explanations in this instance.[87] Private cabinet minutes as well as subsequent public announcements instead suggest that the British government's decision to honor its debts, and thereby continue working toward a debt settlement with the United States, was motivated by domestic-political concerns, repayment traditions or norms, diplomatic anxieties, and the risk of consequent defaults by the United Kingdom's own debtors.

The opposition largely supported the British government's decision. The Labour politician and leader of the Socialist League Stafford Cripps admitted, "We also agree with the action which has been taken by His Majesty's Government in making this payment. . . . We had the gold; we had the means of transmitting the money without doing any serious damage to our exchange, and it seems to us that, in view of those circumstances, this Government . . . could not possibly have put forward any valid excuse."[88] The issue of the next installment generated little debate on the day or in the coming months. As opposition members subsequently admitted, "If the House has said little on this matter hitherto it was not because feeling was not deep, but because we felt that Debate would not be helpful and that representations would not assist the ultimate settlement of these delicate negotiations."[89]

Political support for repayment at this stage was strong, and the government also enjoyed the backing of John Maynard Keynes. Keynes agreed that the cabinet "should agree to pay what is now demanded, so as to give America time for reconsideration," but he warned that national sentiment "will not continue to acquiesce in what we know with conviction to be utterly wrong" and warned of the "evil consequences" of continued payment.[90] For the time being, national sentiment appeared largely supportive. There had been some apprehension about the possible effect on the City of London of an announcement concerning another payment, but it was actually reassured by the decision to pay.[91] Much of the national and local press also reported favorably on the decision to make one last payment. *The Economist* described the decision as "entirely justified," and *The Times* celebrated Chamberlain's efforts as "deserv[ing of] all the congratulations which he has received"; some regional newspapers ran headlines such as "No Alternative" and "We Cannot Default."[92] There remained a strong distaste for nonpayment in the press, including published letters from the public, which would remain clearly visible over the next eighteen months.[93]

The United Kingdom's position contrasted starkly with that of France. London had encouraged Paris to make a payment in December. French public opinion had hardened against repayment, however, and many French politicians had become hostile to the idea of further installments. The government's resolution to pay was defeated, and Herriot consequently resigned. French politicians deliberately prolonged the consequent ministerial crisis beyond 15 December, thereby allowing default to occur in the absence of any specific governmental responsibility.[94] Stimson lauded Herriot's bravery for insisting on payment despite public and parliamentary opposition: "he is much bigger today than anyone on our side of the Atlantic."[95] Many other states would follow France's lead into default, which cost the United States more than $26 million in missed payments (see Table 2.1).

The Hoover administration received the news of British payment with relief.[96] Congress had debated the British government's ability to pay and found little sympathy for default, especially given what it considered to be comparatively high levels of military spending and unemployment benefit.[97] The president could now end his term without the embarrassment of a default from his largest debtor and benefited from the receipt of more than $98 million from European states by the end of the year, albeit the vast majority coming from the United Kingdom. Yet the threat of repudiation lingered and encouraged a thoughtful response. Hoover made another attempt to work with Roosevelt in mid-December, encouraged by Stimson and Mills to share his knowledge and avoid a further setback to recovery, but the president-elect politely refused.[98] Roosevelt was probably limiting cooperation because he intended to address the debt question after he took office. On 22 December, tensions became public when Hoover authorized the release of his previously confidential correspondence with Roosevelt to the press: "Governor Roosevelt considers that it is undesirable for him to accede to any suggestions for cooperative action on the foreign proposals outlined in my recent message to Congress. I will respect his wishes."[99] Roosevelt responded by shifting the blame back onto his accuser, calling Hoover's statement "a pity not only for this country, but for the solution of world problems."[100]

The president-elect assured his team of advisers that he remained committed to the previously agreed approach to the war debts—

namely, avoiding an international "poker game," whereby war debts were traded for other concessions, and preventing foreign issues from affecting domestic recovery.[101] Roosevelt's preference for delay reflected a mix of optimism, self-interest, and ignorance. He may well have believed that he could realize a settlement, which would in turn provide valuable political and diplomatic capital, but he misunderstood the complexity of the issue.[102] A solution to these outstanding war debts remained deeply challenging. The U.S. press was keenly aware of the challenges. Newspapers ranging from the *New York Times* to the *Helena Independent* agreed that the United Kingdom's payment in December could be the last and expressed fears of widespread government defaults that might spread into the field of private debts.[103] Yet British calls for debt revision clashed with growing congressional and popular resistance to compromise.[104]

The Republican senator Hiram Johnson, a leading isolationist figure and a prominent supporter of Roosevelt, gained considerable support in Washington and across the United States when he argued that the Hoover moratorium had encouraged the fiscal irresponsibility of European governments and benefited only Wall Street.[105] In early January 1933, he challenged the claim that debt forgiveness would encourage prosperity: "That is, we put upon the overburdened American people more burden, and then Europe will buy more of our goods. . . . It is equally a fact that more burdens upon the people of America will make them less able to manufacture goods to sell. . . . We all know that they can pay these instalments. It may be hard for a period for Great Britain to meet them, but that they can be paid there is not any doubt."[106]

Johnson rejected all calls for compromise.[107] Writing to a close friend, he wrote, "I blew the lid off the debt situation in the senate . . . because I thought it high time something should be said from the American standpoint."[108] In early 1933, the issue of the debt revision remained politically toxic on both sides of the aisle. As the Democratic senator Tom Connally of Texas explained, "If it is immoral to scale down the debts of our own people, how does it become moral to scale down the debts of foreign governments?"[109] These speeches reflected growing economic concerns at home but also rested on lingering suspicions about the political motivations of Europe and especially Britain.[110] Demands for repayment would only be aided by Chamberlain's public statement later that month, when he stressed the difficulty of repayment but simultaneously expressed confidence in economic recovery.[111]

FIRST TOKEN PAYMENT

Hoover and Roosevelt met for a second meeting at the White House on 20 January 1933.[112] The president-elect's newfound willingness to meet with the president was less an important turnabout and more a gesture of goodwill, which reflected concerns about further bad press and confidence in controlling the outcome of the talks.[113] Hoover and Roosevelt had come together to draft an invitation to the British regarding preliminary talks on the war debts and the World Economic Conference that was to be held in London later that year. The Hoover administration was keen to link these subjects together. The president-elect, however, assumed what historians have varyingly described as a "masterful," "fuzzy," or "strange" position.[114] Roosevelt suggested that these two issues could be considered separately by different individuals, but resolution of one should be conditioned on resolution of the other. This position respected his advisers' guidance on the subject.[115] As Moley explained, the war debts required bilateral discussions because they were not a subject for international action. He rejected Hoover's quid pro quo about debt concessions for some vague trade advance because, he said, "we had the quid while nobody seemed to be clear about what the quo might be."[116] Downplaying the importance of such a deal complemented Roosevelt and his advisers' position that the issue of war debts was largely irrelevant to the progress of recovery at home or abroad.[117] Although Roosevelt and Hoover compromised on the final wording of a formal response to London, the president-elect retained freedom of political action on the issue. Roosevelt confirmed that he would be ready to receive the British delegation to discuss these issues in March.[118]

Lindsay met with Roosevelt on 29 January. The president-elect expressed his desire for a new agreement on the war debts and wished to begin negotiations soon after inauguration on 4 March. Lindsay later reported that Roosevelt was "willing to reduce them [the debts] as far as considerations of practical politics make it possible," by asking Congress to seek only payments for interest.[119] The size of such a potential haircut would therefore have been significant.[120] Roosevelt's proposal also encouraged hopes of securing a nonmarketability agreement—namely, a commitment that the U.S. government would continue to hold British debts rather than offering them to the markets and removing all hope of a settlement—which successive administrations had previously refused to contemplate. Roosevelt was also willing to keep France involved in negotiations, and he gave assurances that he would treat "their failure to pay as a deferment and not a default" if the French paid their December installment.[121] Indeed, earlier in the month, he had also rejected President Hoover's suggestion to bring direct pressure to bear on the French.[122] The president-elect's opening offer nevertheless remained a troubling compromise. Such a deal required the British government to pay £5.5 million a year and contradicted the Lausanne agreement, which the prime minister and chancellor had stressed should not be disturbed, by necessitating further debt collection from Europe. Roosevelt was unimpressed by arguments about imperiling the Lausanne agreement and was adamant on the sums required. As Lindsay recalled, the president explained that "if he were allied to Mr Hoover and the Archangel Gabriel he could not expect to induce his people to take less."[123]

On 30 January, members of the cabinet met to discuss U.S. attitudes to the British war debt. Chamberlain believed that Roosevelt was anxious to come to an understanding before he took office and sought to scale down the debt considerably. This confidence was no doubt aided by MacDonald's recent revelation of a secret channel of communication between himself and the president-elect via William C. Bullitt, who would soon become U.S. ambassador to the Soviet Union. Bullitt had ventured to London to hold "exploratory" meetings with MacDonald and Chamberlain in the previous week, which had raised hopes of an early and favorable settlement.[124] On the question of future payment in June, the chancellor was now clear to his colleagues: "Materially we could pay. We had collected a certain amount of gold, and might collect some more, and another shipment, therefore, would not be impossible. But this could not go on indefinitely, and the evil results would accumulate with every payment."[125] Although he favored repayment for the time being, he was clear: "if America was so foolish as to press us to pay we should default."[126] MacDonald supported Chamberlain but wanted to know the cabinet's attitude toward a June payment and, specifically, what the cabinet would be prepared to put before Roosevelt as a final settlement.[127]

The Cabinet Committee on British War Debts to the United States—or British Debts to America (BDA), which comprised MacDonald, Baldwin, Chamberlain, Simon, and Runciman—emerged as the forum in which to consider the government's war-debt strategy.[128] Through early February, the committee held six meetings. In the first meeting, held on 6 February, the cabinet committee reflected on Lindsay's summary of his recent exchanges with Roosevelt. The committee appreciated the difficulty of the president's situation given the "appalling economic conditions" in the U.S.[129] Yet the prime minister believed that Roosevelt's "ideas were still almost unknown," and Lindsay noted that he "had not even known the amount of the Debt!"[130] These difficulties and uncertainties encouraged the prime minister to suggest that the British government should make its case to the United States, even vaguely professing his readiness to use propaganda to assist such efforts.[131]

Five subsequent meetings, held between 7 and 11 February 1933, focused on converting U.S. public opinion on the debt question, preparations for sending a British minister to the United States, and the government's negotiation strategy. Chamberlain stated that if a deal did emerge, Britain would need to speak with France and other debtors, but he believed, "time was on our side."[132] The British, he suggested, had educated Europe on reparations before and would now do the same to the U.S. on the debt issue.[133] Questioned on the threat of default, Chamberlain was clear that the government made the last payment with reluctance and that the United Kingdom was not in the state of mind to go on paying indefinitely.[134] The cabinet committee accepted that there was little hope of obtaining an acceptable settlement of the war debts, and thus, as Chamberlain summarized, "we must hope to get a moratorium, in order to avoid default."[135] The gathered ministers agreed that the issue should be raised at the World Economic Conference scheduled for June of that year.[136] In the absence of progress, the United Kingdom would face a stark choice between either maintaining the terms of the Lausanne agreement and thereby suspending any further payments to the United States or making its repayments and resuming the collection of debts from European debtors. As both options were unpalatable, London recognized that Washington needed to support a moratorium on war-debt payments.

While the British cabinet sought to influence the Roosevelt administration, so too did Congress. Assumptions that Roosevelt favored debt reduction for the United Kingdom had provoked Senate debate on the president's role in foreign affairs and ultimately encouraged caution in the White House.[137] Roosevelt maintained close relationships with isolationists and remained mindful of their position within the Senate. As Self notes, "Roosevelt was far too shrewd as a player of the game of transactional politics to squander his personal capital and political leverage in hopeless and peripheral skirmishes when he had far more fundamental battles to fight over the New Deal at home."[138] Domestic politics dominated Roosevelt's attention in the depths of the Great Depression, not least as a growing banking crisis threatened complete collapse across the country before he had even assumed office.[139] As Robert Dallek put it, "Starvation, unemployment, business and financial collapse made foreign relations a secondary concern."[140]

By the next meeting between Roosevelt and Lindsay, which took place on 20 February, the president had come to understand that his previous proposals were unacceptable in London, but he also rejected the proposed moratorium by blaming Congress.[141] He acknowledged the United States' and United Kingdom's "irreconcilable opposition" over the debts issue but suggested that cooperation on broader economic questions could create "a favourable atmosphere" that would help Congress to accept some form of compromise.[142] By late March, Roosevelt was unimpressed to find that the British government had "not been sufficiently responsive" to his proposals.[143] The president, having now taken office, with William Woodin assuming the position of secretary of the Treasury, faced a series of economic crises, launching emergency initiatives to stabilize the banking system and provide relief to farmers.[144] Lindsay's exposition of the United Kingdom's difficult position created "an exceedingly bad impression" in the administration, which criticized the assumption that "in the long run [the United States] should be able to bear [the consequence] better than [the United Kingdom] could."[145] Nevertheless, fearing that a breakdown in international economic cooperation might exacerbate domestic economic challenges, Roosevelt gave a positive impression of the talks to the press.[146] Despite Lindsay's gloomy updates, the cabinet believed that personal contact with Roosevelt remained valuable, even in the absence of progress.[147]

On 31 March, the BDA committee met for its seventh meeting. There were doubts about U.S. views on the debt, which appeared "as stiff as ever," and whether the U.S. was simply "driving a hard bargain."[148] British ministers discussed the idea that MacDonald could overcome Roosevelt's resistance to a moratorium in a personal meeting, motivated in part by the renewed threat of Congress encouraging the administration to place British war bonds on the market. Transferring these debts from public ownership to private investors would remove all hope of a debt settlement and risked additional economic and legal consequences in the event of default. Chamberlain, who was concerned about the chances of success of a personal meeting and feared attacks from the government's enemies, grudgingly accepted this strategy as the best option available: "No debt settlement could be made now," he believed, "and all turned on getting moratorium."[149]

The gathered ministers were increasingly concerned about the danger of making another payment to the United States. The prime minister stressed "the great difficulty" of having to approach the French and Italians for their outstanding war debts to the United Kingdom to fund any further installments. In addition, and an inversion of the arguments advanced in the previous year, he was clear that "in spite of a large majority," if they paid in June, "the government would have to go out of office."[150] This argument was presumably driven by shifting public and press attitudes toward repayment in the light of ongoing economic challenges and defaults by other states, including debtors to the United Kingdom. Yet Chamberlain once again stressed the importance of continued repayment. "Assuming a default in June, even if the difference between this and other defaults was explained," he feared it would "involve a very serious risk that Australia and the Argentine might default. If so, other countries would default and the whole economic structure of the world would collapse."[151] He therefore hoped to delay a decision until the last possible moment. On 5 April 1933, the prime minister informed the cabinet that his colleagues on the BDA had agreed that he should journey to the United States accompanied by Leith-Ross to persuade Roosevelt of the need for a moratorium. The cabinet granted MacDonald its endorsement.[152]

On the same day, in an effort to pull the country out of depression, Roosevelt ordered Americans to sell all their gold holdings to the government. This would be followed in the coming weeks and months by his decision to formally suspend the gold standard and the eventual devaluation of the dollar. Roosevelt's willingness to abrogate the gold clauses in existing debt contracts to achieve these objectives can be viewed as an "excusable default" given its popular and legal support, evidenced by the eventual albeit narrow approval of the Supreme Court.[153] Leading economists such as Fisher, Rogers, and Warren had long supported and eventually lobbied for the idea of divorcing the dollar from gold.[154] Many believed that leaving gold and devaluing the dollar would help the U.S. economy, just as similar policies had aided the recovery of Sweden, Japan, and the United Kingdom.[155] Nevertheless, Roosevelt's own position was not always clear.[156] The British were initially shocked when the United States announced that it would soon leave the gold standard.[157] The decision undermined budding hopes of cooperation on the key issue of currency stabilization and jeopardized the success of the forthcoming World Economic Conference.[158]

The United States leaving the gold standard and the subsequent devaluation of the dollar in the following year proved in some ways positive for the United Kingdom. The dollar would lose value with respect to the gold-bloc currencies, and the value of sterling rose. British economists were soon keen to point out that this change could benefit the United Kingdom by lowering the relative sterling value of war-debt payments to the United States, helping to offset the costs associated with the earlier devaluation of the pound.[159] Furthermore, as elements of the U.S. press had foreseen, foreign debtors could now use the abolition of gold clauses to justify debt defaults.[160] Germany and the United Kingdom capitalized on the abrogation of gold clauses by canceling payment of nonwar debts in gold later that same year. Germany reneged on the gold clauses of the U.S. tranche of the Dawes Plan and all tranches of the Young Plan.[161] The British government held an additional wartime bond, placed with private U.S. investors, that included a gold clause. The House of Commons ultimately approved a provision that canceled payments of the additional loan in gold, which implied significant savings.[162] Chamberlain recognized a "moral obligation" attached to a loan raised in wartime, offering compensation to the affected bondholders via repayment in sterling, although his generosity also reflected the "inconvenient" challenge of repaying the principal of $137 million due in four years' time. As the chancellor put it, "there will be more money available in the course of the next few years in the Budget by reason of this proposal than there would have been otherwise."[163]

On 22 April, the day after the prime minister arrived in the United States, the president resumed discussions on the issue of war debts. Roosevelt, who privately criticized MacDonald's grasp of the issue and allegedly relished surprising him with the news of devaluation, eventually broached the idea of a "token payment" as a temporary solution to the deadlock, appeasing Congress and staving off default.[164] The British response was largely negative. MacDonald argued that this solution would still constitute a considerable burden and create "a bad House of Commons position."[165] Three days later, MacDonald and Roosevelt publicly announced that no deal emerged with regard to a moratorium or cancellation.[166] This joint statement allowed the president to allay any suspicion in Congress concerning a change in policy.[167] The details of private discussions, however, suggest some progress in negotiations. MacDonald's notes concerning the mission had recorded the president's "promise to seek . . . powers which would enable him to suspend the 15th June payment" and "to regard failure . . . to pay . . . as not a default but a deferment."[168]

There was also at least one other point of optimism. Leith-Ross and Moley continued technical talks into early May 1933. During this period, James Warburg, previously a Wall Street banker and now an adviser to the president, devised an ingenious but deceptive plan for significantly reducing the size of repayments required by all war debtors, while simultaneously using these potential funds to reform the gold standard and enable Roosevelt to issue more currency to support his domestic reforms.[169] This plan equipped Roosevelt with what Moley would describe as a "formula for the settlement of the debt question," albeit "tentative."[170] The president would remain interested in this plan over the course of the year, although growing concerns about it being seen as a fraudulent solution undermined progress.[171]

On 5 May, the prime minister provided a brief report to the cabinet concerning his recent "and satisfactory" visit to Washington, following a full account of his meeting presented to the BDA on the previous day. MacDonald recalled that he had not hesitated to say that repudiation was much nearer than he liked. Roosevelt said that he had absolutely no power to deal with the outstanding debts but could see his way to "an arrangement"—by which he meant a reduced payment—regarding the June and, if necessary, December installments.[172] Progress toward a moratorium nevertheless remained limited, and Roosevelt had distanced himself from such a solution by mid-May following stiff congressional resistance.[173] The president would subsequently challenge a *New York Times* story that claimed he was denying the existence of a definite plan for the war debts.[174] The U.S. also had, by now, good reason to believe that full payment would be forthcoming. Leith-Ross, who continued talks in Washington after MacDonald returned home, informed his hosts that if the British government had to make the payment, it would do so, although "it would be a terrific hardship."[175]

Two more BDA meetings took place later that month. On 16 May, the gathered ministers discussed a disturbing telegram from Lindsay that suggested the forthcoming World Economic Conference was likely to be a failure due to the United States' departure from gold and the impossibility of securing congressional approval for postponement. The chancellor feared that this decline in confidence undermined any hopes of a moratorium before the June deadline, and he suggested signaling to the president the government's worries "about the possibility of default."[176] The cabinet agreed to send another telegram to Roosevelt.[177] On the following day, in anticipation of a response, the chancellor stressed the serious ramifications of the president's position on whether a failure to pay would be treated as default. Once again, touching on Britain's status as an international creditor, he warned, "If we had to default it would provide a precedent for other countries."[178]

On 31 May, with another payment less than two weeks away, the chancellor informed the cabinet that the U.S. position remained obscure, but he considered the possibility of having either to pay the June installment in full or to default as very remote. Lindsay believed that the president might ask for a partial or "token" payment. The prime minister instead proposed to send to the president a letter arguing against any token payment, preferring instead to press for a complete moratorium.[179] There was by now growing support for default within the cabinet, ably evidenced by Runciman's memorandum on the war debts a week earlier: "Default and moratorium are ugly words. . . . But to make payment at the expense of our equilibrium and of our recuperative strength is still more dangerous. The ugly words we can survive, but the strain on our country's heart and strength may prove to be the beginning of a catastrophe."[180]

Runciman rejected arguments about a potential wave of defaults by states with debts to Britain: "The influence which restrains Australia, for instance, from default is not the good example of the Mother Country, so much as the fear that if she defaults she will not be able for many a long year to borrow again. Then I would suggest that we should not be frightened by a word."[181] Runciman's memorandum reflected lingering resentments about the special nature of these war debts, which arose as part of a cooperative wartime effort that had benefited the United States, but focused mainly on economic concerns. It stressed that the last payment was an "exceptional effort," which reflected the interregnum between two presidencies and the state of U.S. public opinion. Domestic pressure in the United Kingdom, he believed, now made any further payment impossible. In contrast to other ministers' fears about the political and social impact of default, he argued that the last payment was made "in spite of public opinion here."[182] The core of his argument rested on the public burden of continued payment.[183] The United Kingdom had struggled for years to meet its obligations, by increasing exports, reducing imports, and taxing itself more heavily than any other nation. "We have shown willing," he stated, but payment on 15 June would add one more strain to "the tottering structure of world trade and development." "The easiest course is to go on saying that, at whatever cost, we must honour our signature," he argued, but, "we cannot afford to break up Europe in order to placate America, and to ruin both in the process."[184]

By early June, Lindsay was confident that Roosevelt would present a moratorium to Congress and understood that the president had already prepared a first draft of such a message. On 4 June, the administration informed the ambassador that it had abandoned its support for any form of suspension in debt repayments due to a serious deterioration in the national and congressional situation.[185] The White House now proposed to Lindsay—and to MacDonald via private letter—that Britain plead poverty, make an interim part payment of $10 million, and make payment in silver. The president found inspiration for a token payment in the U.S. custom that an individual's credit should be maintained if they do their best to pay, however small the amount. He also took advantage of a recent congressional amendment that permitted payment in silver.[186] The president brushed aside Lindsay's objections that this figure exceeded Lausanne receipts and could establish a precedent for similar demands in December.

The British government's response was swift and unyielding. MacDonald reiterated earlier calls for a complete moratorium. Without a postponement, he warned, Britain would be forced into a policy of default. Roosevelt heard these threats but merely reiterated his position.[187] Chamberlain subsequently convinced MacDonald to make a counteroffer, whereby Britain would make a $5 million payment, as a down payment toward a final settlement rather than a plea of poverty, if the president guaranteed that such a payment would not be considered a default. Lindsay met Roosevelt on 8 June with the new offer. The president rejected the offer as too small given the political situation in which he now found himself.[188]

On 9 June 1933, the cabinet met to discuss the future of the war debts. All recognized that the previous payment in December had failed to effect change. The gathered ministers agreed that any payment would involve considerable difficulties at home but, disregarding Roosevelt's previous rejection, expressed their willingness to make a token payment of only $5 million if the president could provide assurances that this payment meant that the United Kingdom would not be regarded as being in default. Leith-Ross suggested that the government should make payment in ten million ounces of silver, at a value of 50c. to the ounce, which represented a "very favourable" rate given that it would only cost $4 million to purchase from India.[189] The prime minister initially rejected the chancellor's case of payment in silver, which was insufficiently dignified, and believed that the word "Judas" was likely to come into people's minds. The president of the Board of Trade thought that to a nation with such strong biblical knowledge, payment in silver would be regarded as a grim jest. Yet there was a consensus in the cabinet in favor of payment. In the meantime, the ministers agreed that the utmost secrecy should be observed concerning any agreement, due to concerns about the reaction of the press or the French government.

The content of the cabinet meeting reveals the ongoing difficulty of repayment. When the chancellor asked whether the cabinet agreed that, "if the worst came to the worst, we should not pay?" no dissent emerged.[190] The president's own advice—that the British government offer a part payment of $10 million—was problematic. Ministers feared that if they paid in June, there was no reason why they should not need to pay the same again next December. Two such payments would, despite the reduction, still "amount to a big figure in one year."[191] Such a large payment threatened to break up the Lausanne agreement, as Britain would have to ask more from its creditors than was provided for in the settlement. Three members of the cabinet now made a strong case for default. Runciman said that all the arguments were against payment and that he doubted whether any halfway house between full payment or no payment was possible; anything short of payment of the full installment would be termed repudiation by Congress and used as a precedent for other countries anyway. Secretary of State for War Hogg agreed and stressed that the cabinet "better make up [their] minds today instead of six or twelve months later when [the British government] should have paid out further money."[192] Finally, Secretary of State for the Colonies Philip Cunliffe-Lister thought that the public would take a token payment badly. Indeed, "probably most people did not wish to pay."[193]

A majority of the cabinet remained unwilling to default. Once again, a powerful reason for continued payments reflected ongoing concerns about the United Kingdom's own debtors. Thomas, as secretary of state for dominion affairs, wondered whether a repudiation by the United Kingdom could "stop at that point," encouraging other countries, from the Irish Free State to Australia, to do the same even if the context or reasons were "totally different." These factors, he stressed, pointed to "the danger of default" not only on governments but also on individuals. The chancellor conceded that many people would say that Britain was defaulting for the first time. If the British government could reply, "we did it with the assent of the Head of the American Government," however, those objections would be mitigated.[194] The prime minister then confirmed that the president had indicated that he would not regard nonpayment in such circumstances as a default. A majority of the cabinet and the governor of the Bank of England agreed. Nevertheless, there was uncertainty as to the amount. The president had asked for $10 million, but the prime minister thought that to offer more than $5 million would be a great mistake from the point of view of the House of Commons.[195]

On 9 June, Lindsay met with Roosevelt, Moley, and Secretary of State Cordell Hull. They accepted the use of the term "token payment" and remained adamant that $10 million was necessary to sway public opinion.[196] Roosevelt was keen to avoid the issue undermining the forthcoming World Economic Conference and welcomed the opportunity to postpone a major decision on the issue of war debts, especially as he focused his attention on more pressing domestic challenges.[197] A larger amount, however, would help to defend his actions.

On 12 June, the BDA committee met to consider the possibility of default if the president proved unwilling to accept a token payment, even going so far as to prepare a draft note to that effect. The committee agreed to summon the cabinet "in view of the gravity of the decision to be taken."[198] There followed an emergency meeting. The gathered ministers heard that the president was disappointed by the smaller offer and was not yet able to agree to the government's terms that the United States was not in the presence of a default. The cabinet was consequently unwilling to agree to any payment without specific and authoritative moral indemnity. It could increase the sum, however, if the president gave adequate support. The sum of $10 million would be difficult to justify to public opinion, especially the "considerable difference" in amount, and would necessitate a further meeting. Some ministers also now expressed concern that payment of the June installment would gravely imperil the success of the World Economic Conference and cause widespread political consequences of a most serious character.[199]

On the following morning, the cabinet met as a matter of urgency following receipt of a draft text from the president stating, "I have no personal hesitation in saying that I do not characterize the resultant situation as a default."[200] Nevertheless, the president remained adamant that public opinion in the United States would resent a payment of only $5 million, and he appealed for the larger figure of $10 million. The cabinet agreed with the prime minister and the chancellor that they should pay the larger figure, as the difference was not sufficiently great to warrant such a risk. Paying in silver also helped to reduce this amount, a financial sleight of hand that the U.S. was willing to support. As Moley recalled, "We arbitrarily fixed a price in silver that cost them seven million in American dollars."[201] The chancellor reminded the cabinet that if it proved possible to obtain a final settlement during the present financial year, the Lausanne agreement could be ratified, and possibly a final settlement with their own debtors might be achieved. In such an event, the British government might receive some payment to counterbalance these costs. The cabinet felt that it was essential to inform the French and Italian governments at once, largely in respect of the Lausanne agreement.[202]

The chancellor spoke to the House of Commons on 14 June. He remarked, "we felt the strongest objection to any course which would have placed us in the position of having repudiated our obligations."[203] Nevertheless, the chancellor was clear that it was impossible for the United Kingdom to continue payments the size of those that had gone before. This change was due to the provisional Lausanne agreement that had suspended the government's corresponding claims on its own debtors (see Figure 2.1). Resuming such payments would have necessitated putting an end to the Lausanne agreement, reopening all the vexed questions of reparations and war debts that had been provisionally settled. They also risked plunging the world once more into "the condition of uncertainty and despair" from which it was rescued the previous year. MacDonald and Chamberlain were pleased with the outcome, and the House met the decision with unanimous applause and congratulations.[204]

The British government had, by all contemporary standards, defaulted on its obligations. By choosing not to make a payment in full, it failed to honor the terms of its debts. Yet perceptions of what constituted default were evidently different at that time. Even the response from the opposition benches was supportive. Both Cripps and Herbert Samuel, of the Liberal Party, congratulated the government on a solution that satisfied the United Kingdom and the United States.[205] All parties appeared to be relieved that the government had safeguarded the country's position as a reputable international creditor. Samuel explained, "It would have been a most lamentable thing if we had been forced into a position of repudiation. . . . An Englishman's word is his bond has always been a most proud maxim in this country."[206] Robert Horne was also greatly relieved: "We cannot refuse to recognise that default is apt to be contagious. We are after all the greatest creditor nation in the world with a great number of debtors who would be delighted to take advantage of our example to fail in their obligations to us. Accordingly, from a point of view which is purely selfish, I am sure it is a good thing that we have been enabled to evade that trouble."[207]

The available data from the first half of 1933 therefore add further weight to the argument that British thinking was motivated by a complex mix of factors, including hopes for a debt settlement with the

United States, diplomatic anxieties, and domestic-political and normative concerns. Of particular importance, evidenced both in private cabinet discussions and in public speeches by senior members of the government and opposition, was also the fear of opportunistic default by Britain's own debtors. The available data therefore generate confidence in a mix of factors driving repayment in this case but provide limited support for several competing explanations, such as future borrowing costs, the risk of punishments, or spillover effects within the state.

Keynes was pleased with the outcome. Having refused to accept the choice between full repayment or default, he too had supported a token payment. Keynes believed that such a compromise would not be considered a "genuine default" and therefore "could not possibly impair international confidence."[208] *The Times* reported on events in the Commons by highlighting the wide range of support for the decision, and *The Economist* explained that the token amount may be "well worth paying" as long as the World Economic Conference proved successful and the debt issue was finally resolved thereafter.[209] There were nevertheless growing hints of frustration in the press by now. *The Scotsman* suggested that "the spirit to continue these payments is admittedly lacking," and in the week preceding the decision, the *Daily Herald* had sarcastically noted that "this most amazing of Governments has still not made up its mind what it will do," a situation that *The Economist* had admitted was "farcical."[210]

The United Kingdom's token-payment solution to the United States was also adopted by Italy.[211] These efforts contrasted favorably with the debt policies of the other major European powers. Although the Lausanne agreement had effectively canceled reparations payments, Germany continued to service its large and costly Reich loans—including the Dawes and Young loans, which enjoyed special privileges guaranteed by international treaty—until June 1933.[212] The new Nazi government's pursuit of an expansionist policy of public works and rearmament exacerbated an already precarious foreign exchange position. The Reichsbank subsequently sought opportunities to reduce the costs of servicing loans that consumed its scarce foreign exchange reserves.[213] On 8 June, the German cabinet gave approval for a unilateral moratorium on Germany's long-term foreign debts to begin 30 June 1933.[214] The Reichsbank subsequently announced that Germany's gold and foreign exchange reserves had reduced to the extent that it could not guarantee the service of external debts in full and subsequently suspended the transfer in foreign exchange of most German external liabilities.[215] As Adam Tooze concludes, "The decision in the summer of 1933 to initiate default marked a fundamental turning point."[216] It certainly represented a dangerous precedent for international investors. Within a year, Germany would reduce interest payments on both loans, paying partially in Reichsmarks instead of in foreign exchange, and accepting no amortization of bonds.[217]

Germany's partial default on external debts accompanied France's full and ongoing default on its war debts to the United States.[218] Prime Minister Édouard Daladier's decision not to pay the next installment of the war debt due on 15 June was accompanied by a warning from Paris to London that British payment would harm relations between the two countries.[219] By now, much of France criticized what it considered to be unfair press treatment abroad, and extreme-right opposition to the U.S. on the debt issue had come to the attention of French police.[220] Yet some French officials had begun to worry that trade relations might suffer given the negative mood in the administration and Congress regarding nonpayment.[221] The French default had certainly undermined Roosevelt's sympathy for France's economic demands on the United States.[222]

Although the United Kingdom had paid when Germany and France had defaulted, the mood in the United States was far from congratulatory. There was clear resentment at accepting as satisfactory a token payment.[223] Throughout June, there had been rising criticism of such a halfhearted installment. The Republican representative Hamilton Fish was puzzled why European nations such as the United Kingdom "would not have to pay more than 10 percent of the war debts to the United States, which means that the American people, already burdened with taxes, can pay the balance."[224] He continued, "What is the magic of London and the Thames that bewitches the intellects of our American statesmen? . . . Are the American taxpayers always to be shorn like lambs and pay for European armaments? Why should we loan a penny to any foreign nation until we can balance our Budget, put our own house in order, and pay our just debts to our own war veterans with service-connected disabilities?"[225] Such views existed on both sides of the aisle. The Democratic representative John Hoeppel expressed his doubts about the value of the forthcoming economic conference, where negotiations would soon begin with these "arch repudiators": "To me this is analogous to an honest man negotiating with confidence men. What value can we place upon their plighted word or any agreement which may be reached as long as they continue to default the just obligations they assumed, which we so freely gave in order to maintain their national and personal existence during the period of stress in the World War?"[226]

These comments were reflective of a growing resentment in Washington toward Europe's unpaid debts. As the *New York Times* described events, members of Congress had assailed the Roosevelt administration as having opened the way for cuts from all debtor countries.[227] The swift passage of the Johnson Act—which demanded full rather than token payments and effectively closed the New York securities and money markets to all governments behind on debt payments to the U.S. government—would ably express U.S. hostility toward Europe early in the following year. Roosevelt may have managed to avoid a default, but there was evidently little appetite in Congress or the United States at large for further concessions to the United Kingdom.

FINAL TOKEN PAYMENT

Representatives from sixty-six countries gathered in London's Geological Museum in mid-June 1933. The World Monetary and Economic Conference in London, organized by the League of Nations, sought to revive trade, stabilize prices, and restore the gold standard. British claims that a debt settlement was "absolutely essential" before the conference began had been countered by U.S. protests that its attendance required the exclusion of the subject from the agenda.[228] MacDonald's subsequent reference to war debts—and the need to complete the Lausanne agreement to improve world economic conditions—in his opening address on 12 June reflected an intentional effort to influence the United States rather than an act of senility.[229] Washington saw these diplomatic maneuvers as acts of bad faith that would sabotage the conference.[230] Nevertheless, war debts played only a small role in the failure of the World Monetary and Economic Conference to arrive at any agreement concerning exchange-rate stabilization or international economic cooperation more broadly.[231]

There were deep structural and political challenges to international cooperation, but a significant portion of the failure to reach a solution rests with the United States.[232] The president had increasingly distanced himself from the conference and was reluctant to make any agreements that would restrict his freedom to act boldly to revive the U.S. economy.[233] In addition, the president was keen to create space between himself and "Wall Street influences," especially given recent Senate investigations into stock exchange practices that had gained considerable momentum and revealed illicit ties between bankers and the current secretary of the Treasury.[234] On 3 July, Roosevelt telegraphed the conference accusing it of bad faith and self-interest, stating that "the old fetishes of so-called international bankers are being replaced by efforts to plan national currencies" around domestic needs. Roosevelt had fatally undermined progress, and talks collapsed in late July in a spectacular failure of economic diplomacy.[235] Hull, leader of the U.S. delegation in London and a committed free trader, noted that the message threw the conference into uproar.[236] He had long argued that the war debts could only be paid if U.S. tariff barriers were lowered so that debtor states could export more products, or otherwise policymakers "should have to forget about them."[237] Hull had wanted authority at the London Conference "to discuss war debt adjustment as a lever to induce the debtor countries to agree to more liberal trade throughout the world."[238] Any hopes that the United States could use the war debts to reverse or limit Britain's preferential trade agreements negotiated in the previous year had been dashed.

In the coming months, the British government grudgingly resumed diplomatic efforts to achieve a debt agreement with the United States. On 25 September 1933, the chancellor shared a note on the policy to be adopted in the forthcoming negotiations with the United States on war debts. He accepted that there was no prospect that Congress was yet ready to accept cancellation. A settlement was only possible by means of some compromise, but there was still good reason to try: "Default might have awkward repercussions on our own position as a creditor and should be avoided if possible. To avoid it, we must be prepared to pay a certain price."[239] Nevertheless, "we must not allow our anxiety in this respect to be exploited," he continued; the United States "must be prepared to scale down our existing obligations to an amount which will not be a serious burden to us."[240] The chancellor felt that if the United States was prepared to accept a settlement costing not more than $20 million a year, "it would be wise" for the cabinet to accept "rather than leave the much heavier burden of the existing agreement hanging over their heads."[241] In addition, the British government would show to its public and to the world its genuine anxiety to avoid default.[242]

The chancellor believed that a settlement could also preserve the Lausanne settlement and might not require payments to the United States larger than those the United Kingdom was likely to receive from its own debtors. He was confident that France and the relevant British dominions—which included Canada, Australia, New Zealand, the Irish Free State, Newfoundland, and South Africa—would consider further payment on a reduced scale. As such, the chancellor continued to approve the suspension of payments from the dominions and India to the United Kingdom at that time but remained unwilling to cancel these war debts formally.[243] Nevertheless, he thought it unwise to count on the possibility of collecting the full amount required. He warned that if the U.S. and Britain concluded a settlement, the cabinet should be prepared to make payment, in part or in whole, "out of its own pockets."[244] Chamberlain was also keen to guard against the possibility that other debtor countries might subsequently secure more favorable treatment, either as the result of an agreement with the United States or simply by withholding payments, and urged the inclusion of provisions for regular reviews and consistent terms.[245]

In October, the British government sent Leith-Ross to begin negotiations with the Roosevelt administration to reach a settlement that would appeal to Congress.[246] There was cause for optimism. By now, editorial opinion in the United States had widely come to accept the impossibility of full repayment and the danger of default.[247] The political commentator Walter Lippmann, for example, had recently suggested a settlement based on a lump sum payment of $1–1.5 billion.[248] Roosevelt had also become increasingly reliant on the advice of Warren and Rogers, both of whom favored a reduction or cancellation of the debt, and he remained attracted to elements of the Warburg plan.[249] Other economists in the administration, most notably Sprague, had long supported debt revision.[250] Furthermore, Undersecretary of the Treasury Dean Acheson, who was representing Roosevelt in these negotiations, was increasingly sympathetic to Britain's plight. As he recalled in his memoirs, he "urged FDR to relieve Britain of the intolerable and impossible burden of repaying the war debts."[251]

Yet Roosevelt remained wary of any such compromise. The ongoing domestic economic crisis, coupled with rising congressional tensions, did not bode well for transatlantic diplomacy. In addition, U.S. thinking on the terms of a possible solution remained underdeveloped since the new president had taken office. A variety of options existed, to be sure, but no agreed strategy had emerged, which undermined negotiations.[252] Opportunities to shape this policy in Britain's favor faded, however, following Acheson's and Sprague's resignations toward the end of the year, reflecting in large part persistent tensions with the president.[253]

By late October, after weeks of effort, neither Leith-Ross nor Lindsay believed a permanent settlement could be achieved.[254] Failure reflected a combination of factors. Roosevelt had chided the "ridiculous" British offer of $460 million in full settlement of more than a $4 billion debt.[255] In addition, British officials had aired concerns earlier in the year about Congress preferring failure to help spread blame for the ongoing depression.[256] Recent scholarship has also focused on the limitations of an overworked administration, which had concentrated its attention on other, more pressing issues.[257] These explanations can coexist. Roosevelt was certainly hoping for more than an offer of $460 million in exchange for full settlement, but placing blame on the British was helpful, especially given the mounting pressures on the fledgling administration as economic recovery stalled. It had become clear that the president's difficult political situation meant that he would have to avoid any controversial settlement. As *The Economist* later reported of the "palaver," there existed a clear "gulf that separates the two points of view," which would lead the *New York Times* eventually to describe negotiations as "futile."[258] Lindsay reported that Roosevelt was ultimately only willing to offer a reduction of the capital debt to $2.26 billion, based on fifty equal annuities of approximately $40 million, adding, "It was all nonsense to suppose that we could not pay. . . . The difficulty with us was political and not economic."[259] Leith-Ross conceded this point.[260] The chancellor also accepted that "it was both political and economic; that our people were becoming more and more reluctant to pay."[261] Nevertheless, as Britain had to take the action of payment, Chamberlain expected the U.S. to offer more acceptable terms.[262]

On 26 October 1933, the chancellor informed the cabinet that negotiations in the United States had been unsuccessful.[263] The details of this meeting reveal the government's steady progress toward default. The chancellor initially suggested that the cabinet should drop the idea of a permanent settlement and instruct Leith-Ross to pursue a temporary settlement. In the discussion that followed, the gathered ministers recognized that any kind of settlement was unlikely, which left the government to choose between default or continuing token efforts. The risks of the former were well known, but the latter risked the U.S. public growing accustomed to ongoing payments. By stopping all payments, many in the cabinet believed that they might get better terms when the United States was prepared to make a permanent settlement. Some believed that Paris would secure better terms than London, just as it had in the 1920s. Furthermore, British payments to the United States were becoming more and more unpopular, especially with "the rising generation," presumably referring to Britons born after the debts had been assumed.[264] Social attitudes toward debts were also evolving; the idea of imprisonment for debt had increasingly fallen out of favor, increasingly viewed as unfair and expensive.[265] Furthermore, the last interim payment had failed to pave the way to a final settlement as hoped. To make no payments until a permanent settlement had been achieved would show the president that "if he pushed [Britain] too hard he would get nothing."[266] Leith-Ross went on to suggest default if the president refused to accept a continuation of the token payments.[267]

Nevertheless, the cabinet understood that paying nothing risked "a violent attack on this country in the United States of America, where [Britain] should be described as a fraudulent bankrupt."[268] Equally pressing, however, were familiar arguments from proponents of repayment about significant domestic-political costs and a potential default domino effect around the world. The conclusions of the cabinet meeting are clear on these points: "In this country a number of people would be made extremely unhappy, and everywhere there would be serious loss of prestige. Ultimately other nations who owed us money might withhold payment and excuse themselves by alleging exactly the same reasons as we had given."[269] There was also a stubborn hope for a remission of the debt. Some in the cabinet accepted that this desirable result could not be obtained if the British government stopped payment. These views, however, were not advanced as an argument for payment to the United States of "the full pound of flesh" but rather to justify some reasonable form of payment to avoid potentially serious domestic and international consequences.[270]

According to the minutes of the cabinet meeting, "the general tenor of the discussion revealed some hardening of opinion on the subject of payments."[271] Chamberlain later noted that he faced considerable resistance from the "good many who wished to sit back & refuse further payments."[272] The chancellor remained convinced that a token payment was sensible and urged the cabinet to avoid being viewed as defaulters. Lord Irwin passed a note to Chamberlain during the debate that gave a valuable insight into the decision-making process: "Two or three of us who are ignorant & therefore silent, shall trust your judgement better than others; & you may as well know it."[273] The cabinet agreed that token payments of $10 million were worthwhile to avoid the odium of default. Some discussion then took place as to whether it might not be advisable to present to Roosevelt a document, partly financial and partly political in character, asking if the United States could find some way of helping and making quite clear that there were limits to what British public opinion would stand. The moment had not yet come for so decisive a step, however, which would remain a last resort.[274]

On 2 November, Chamberlain read to his colleagues extracts from telegrams from Leith-Ross containing an account of his interview with Roosevelt on the previous day.[275] The president had remained unwilling to support British proposals for renegotiation: "Probably he feels that while he could get a settlement through Congress he would lose a good number of tail feathers which he can ill afford to do," and, albeit less important in his decision-making, "there is no doubt that he thinks we can quite well afford to pay more than 20 million dollars and thus make things easier for him."[276]

The cabinet consequently faced another difficult decision about whether to default. Roosevelt's resistance toward any proposed settlement was accompanied by a request for a further token payment, which once again circumvented the difficulties posed by congressional approval. Roosevelt informed Leith-Ross that the political climate might have improved by May 1934 to allow "a more equitable settlement."[277] In these circumstances, the chancellor explained that there were now three new possible courses open to the British government: first, to accept Roosevelt's proposals, in the hope that a further delay would bring about a better atmosphere for arriving at a permanent settlement; second, to offer some smaller figure for a temporary payment, namely, $7 million instead of $10 million; third, to refuse Roosevelt's offer, making it clear that the government desired a permanent settlement and, as its offers had been rejected, could not undertake to make further temporary payments.[278]

The first course was felt by some members of the cabinet to be "extremely unsatisfactory," especially because improvement in congressional opinion was unlikely and because this situation might continue for years, but overall was preferred as the least objectionable choice.[279] The cabinet ministers rejected the second proposal as they felt it was hardly worthwhile to haggle over such a relatively small matter. The chancellor opposed the third course because it "would wreck all hope" of obtaining a cancellation of the debt.[280] As such, the gathered ministers agreed to make a payment of $10 million in December, which would virtually be a "token" payment, even if that term was not used. The prime minister again urged the utmost care to avoid any leaks prior to public announcement.[281]

Leith-Ross later successfully argued for a payment of $7.5 million largely because it was equivalent in value to the previous payment given the revised value of silver. The president privately accepted this revised amount on 4 November. The secretary of state for foreign affairs subsequently remarked, "in the circumstances the prevailing result is the best that could be attained and better than we at one time expected."[282] On 7 November 1933, the president issued a formal statement on the matter: "I have no personal hesitation in saying that I shall not regard the British Government as in default."[283]

On the same day, the chancellor addressed the House of Commons, defending the government's decision to pay and concluding with the president's statement.[284] He repeated familiar arguments about the dangers posed by default. Journalists in some newspapers had also taken the opportunity earlier in the month to stress the importance of repayment to stave off a wave of defaults by many of Britain's own debtors that "would not be slow to make the most of it."[285] The available evidence from the second half of 1933 further supports the claim that British motivation for repayment, even if only partial or token in form, and ongoing efforts to reach a debt settlement with the United States reflected a complex mix of variables, including diplomatic anxieties, domestic-political and normative concerns, and fears of default by Britain's own debtors. Yet the growing resistance in the cabinet toward even token installments suggests that the motivations for repayment were fading as the rewards of default were growing. In the absence of any significant changes, British default would soon become irresistible.

In contrast to the Parliamentary reaction in June, the British government's decision appears to have attracted little debate or celebration. National newspapers that had covered the previous installments in considerable detail, such as *The Times*, now offered only brief notices of a further token payment, while others, such as *The Economist*, provided no account of the government's decision.[286] Some policymakers familiar with events would subsequently forget that the United Kingdom ever made this final payment.[287] The United Kingdom's token payment was again imitated by Italy. These efforts contrasted favorably with further defaults by the other major European powers. Germany had unilaterally decided to extend its transfer moratorium and reduce interest payments by 30 percent, just as France chose to miss its next war-debt payment.[288] Despite these favorable international comparisons, the United Kingdom's token payments were increasingly unimpressive to U.S. onlookers. As the *New York Times* lamented, "It could have expected nothing more"; the idea of full repayment was now "dead in London."[289]

On 29 November, the prime minister welcomed Leith-Ross upon his return to London. The chief economic adviser conceded that a permanent settlement remained unlikely. Concerning the future, the president had spoken hopefully of getting authority from Congress to settle debts before next June, but it seemed improbable that he would succeed. Leith-Ross thought that the government might have to continue token payments for at least a year until U.S. opinion came to accept these smaller payments. Roosevelt seemed to have no settled convictions, Leith-Ross explained, but his principal and perhaps sole interest was domestic politics.[290]

In December, the British government made what would be its final token payment. The prime minister informed U.S. representatives that the decision had not been favored by the whole cabinet and "had aroused considerable resentment in many important quarters in England, and this resentment was greater than had been anticipated, particularly in view of the less generous attitude of other countries."[291] After fourteen months of difficult cabinet discussions, the British government was no nearer to solving the problems posed by its outstanding war debts to the United States. Despite growing resistance to compromise on both sides of the Atlantic, many policymakers in Washington and London still held out hope for a settlement.[292] Such expectations would prove unduly optimistic. The passage of the Johnson Act through Congress in the new year would undermine any chance of compromise.

3   British Default, 1934

THE UNITED KINGDOM suspended payment of its war debts to the United States in 1934. Failure to reach a settlement complements a growing body of research concerning the difficulty of resolving debt crises.[1] London's decision was informed by events in Washington, specifically the passage of the Foreign Securities Act through Congress earlier in the year. The Johnson Act, as it became known, demanded full rather than token payments and effectively closed the New York securities and money markets to any government behind on its debt payments to the U.S. government. The Johnson Act significantly raised the costs of repayment without offering any improvement in the chances of securing a favorable settlement. The British government now faced a choice between three unpalatable options. It could return to full payment every six months and meet the costs itself, which could imperil economic recovery and weaken chances of reelection. It could return to full payment and attempt to resume collection from its own European debtors, a difficult task given ongoing defaults by France and Germany, which risked reviving the destructive system of intergovernmental reparation and war-debt payments. Or it could cease payment entirely, which could well harm transatlantic relations and would probably prohibit future borrowing from the United States.

The British cabinet opted to suspend repayments. It was still anxious about the impact on the United Kingdom's position as a creditor but was motivated by the absence of a settlement, shrinking domestic-political support for repayment, and the limited repercussions that had followed French default.[2] The government justified its decision by stressing the need for domestic and international economic recovery rather than relying only on moral claims about the specialness of wartime debts or the difficulty of recovering its own foreign debts.[3] Default reflected the willingness rather than ability of the government to pay. The United Kingdom would have increasingly struggled to continue repaying its debts over the coming years, to be sure, but there was no urgent economic reason to suspend repayments in 1934. Eighteen months earlier, when economic conditions were far less favorable, Chancellor Neville Chamberlain had been clear on this point during cabinet discussion; the matter had always been one of willingness rather than ability to pay.[4] By the time of default, Britain had begun to enjoy a substantial fiscal surplus and larger gold reserves.[5] This historical case complements research showing that willingness to pay rather than ability to pay is the main determinant of sovereign default and also raises questions about the relationship between economic output in the borrowing country and default on loans from foreign creditors in some cases.[6]

Widespread support for the Johnson Act across the United States and its swift passage through Congress outlawed partial payments and halted further income from Europe's debtors, most of whom chose not to resume full payments thereafter.[7] This political stance cost the U.S. government tens of millions of dollars in 1934 and every year thereafter for decades to come. Chamberlain believed that the U.S. had "played a mug's game in depriving themselves of $40 million [from Britain] which they would have pouched if they hadn't given themselves the pleasure of passing the Johnson Act."[8] A small number of U.S. policymakers believed that hard-line tactics could encourage repayment. There was some logic to this approach; the United Kingdom could afford to pay more than British representatives claimed.[9] Yet most members of Congress were driven largely by short-term electoral concerns. The revision of European war debts was deeply unpopular across much of the United States. Overburdened American taxpayers remained indisposed to the reduction of foreign debts in the depths of the Depression. Even academic proponents of cancellation, such as Harold Moulton and Leo Pasvolsky, noted, "It is undeniable that from the fiscal point of view a remission of the war debts would mean that the American Treasury would have to collect larger sums from the American taxpayers than would otherwise be the case."[10] Few political leaders were willing to squander valuable political capital on such an unpopular issue. After the passage of the Johnson Act, and the wave of international defaults that followed, Washington could now blame European irresponsibility for U.S. woes.

More broadly, the Johnson Act complemented, and helped to represent, an increasingly popular noninterventionist mood in the United States, as evidenced by the Nye Committee and Neutrality Acts that soon followed. Historians such as Wayne Cole and Robert Self agreed that the act was "more of an angry nationalistic slap at Europeans than any real effort to win further payments."[11] Yet the act also represented a bolder strategic attempt to limit the United States' financial support of the European powers for the foreseeable future. Congress believed that this legislation meant that no president or financial elites, however clever or devious, could provide significant financial support to the Continent.[12] As such, European governments would not be able to sustain another lengthy war or draw the United States into a future conflict. Many members of the Senate and the House went on to celebrate the act in the following decade for its help in preserving the peace.[13] Political concerns evidently trumped economic interests, even when billions of dollars were at stake.

THE JOHNSON ACT

By early 1934, the British government's token payments had come to generate considerable resistance in Congress. Many members of the House and Senate already considered Britain in default and part of what the Republican representative Francis Culkin termed a European "concert of repudiation."[14] They decried nonpayment when the financial obligations were relatively small compared to national budgets, especially given rising defense expenditures on the Continent.[15] In addition, improving conditions in Europe contrasted with the woeful state of the U.S. economy, with official statistics suggesting that towns and districts were now defaulting at the rate of more than 150 a month.[16] Compromise or cancellation of Europe's outstanding obligations remained anathema to most Americans. The Democratic representative

Thomas Blanton spoke for many in both houses of Congress when he said that "Congress has uncompromisingly insisted that they should be paid."[17]

Congressional responses to these outstanding foreign debts varied from demands for their immediate marketization through to suggestions to leave them unsettled as a monument for the unaffordability of war.[18] London was keenly aware of these attitudes in Washington. Upon hearing of attempts to impose higher liquor duties on countries that had defaulted on their war debts, British ambassador Ronald Lindsay believed that the Senate had gone "off the deep end."[19] Speeches in Congress opposed to cancellation or revision were by now greeted with applause from both sides of the aisle.[20] The president had attempted to calm these passions by speaking directly to the House but nevertheless still played to his audience. Roosevelt encouraged cooperation with debtors but explained "in no uncertain language" that unless "the defaulting European nations who have agreed among themselves to pay [the U.S.] nothing . . . changed their dishonorable attitude he would bring about American reprisals which might cost them much more annually than their already greatly reduced obligations to [the U.S.]."[21]

By now it was too late to temper congressional ambitions to punish defaulters, which had become manifest in the form of the Johnson Act. The Republican senator Hiram Johnson, a senior figure on the Senate's Foreign Relations Committee, was the most vociferous critic of those states with unpaid war debts. He had criticized the Hoover moratorium as affording "exactly the excuse desired by [the United States'] debtors to demand reconsideration, revision, or cancellation" and had been critical of those that had subsequently defaulted or attached fresh conditions to repayment.[22] As Johnson informed the British embassy in February 1933, they "had been given a bond and must stick to it."[23] His proposed act would "prohibit financial transactions with any foreign government in default on its obligations to the United States."[24] Most pressingly for London, the terms of default would now include token repayments.[25]

This act, which had been introduced shortly after Roosevelt's inauguration a year earlier, was initially one of three laws Johnson had proposed to protect small U.S. investors in foreign bonds.[26] Johnson's proposals attracted considerable support given growing public sensitivity to banking and business malpractice in the depths of the Depression.[27]

The Senate's Special Committee Investigating the Munitions Industry, better known as the Nye Committee, would soon begin its investigation of the role of big business and banks in encouraging rearmament. The committee later alleged that U.S. loans to Britain and France in 1915–16 represented an illegal intervention in support of one side in the First World War.[28] As the historian Howard DeWitt explains, "Johnson's legislation and his rhetoric fitted nicely into the public mood."[29] Roosevelt's own attitude toward foreign investors was more complicated. He would support the creation of the Foreign Bondholders Protective Council, which was ostensibly designed to assist U.S. citizens and creditors in collecting on defaulted foreign government bonds. Yet the council principally served to protect his administration from the political pressure of bondholders in times of default.[30] Roosevelt would actively work against the interests of U.S. bondholders in some cases. His administration covertly conspired to overthrow the Cuban government in 1933 because it refused to default on its debts, which U.S. policymakers feared would result in political instability that threatened the security of U.S. direct investments.[31]

As the Senate debated the international debt problem in 1933, Johnson expanded his bill to include war debts. Some scholars have claimed that Johnson was unable to comprehend the complexity of the problem and consequently reduced it to a scheme by the Roosevelt administration, the British government, or big business to involve the United States in European controversies.[32] Johnson focused too much blame on the banking community, to be sure, but the *Congressional Record* and his private papers reveal a keener understanding of the debate.[33] Populist justifications obscured his political motivations—namely, winning favor domestically and advancing his noninterventionist ambitions. The Johnson Act was a rebuke to war debtors, but it was also a commitment to maintain strict neutrality at all costs. The act limited the president's flexibility in foreign affairs by forcing a clear and tough stand on unpaid war debts and served as a prelude to the Neutrality Acts of 1935–1937.[34]

In early 1934, Johnson reintroduced his bill during a heated debate surrounding a controversial arms-embargo law opposed by the Roosevelt administration.[35] In this political environment, senior figures in the State Department, Division of Western European Affairs, and Treasury—now headed by Henry Morgenthau Jr. who had replaced an ailing Woodin in January—encouraged the president not to oppose the proposed bill for fear of a serious confrontation with Senate isolationists. Some historians see the president's position as a grudging compromise, preferring that the arms embargo remain a dormant issue.[36] Roosevelt later said to Lindsay that he neither sponsored nor favored the proposed Johnson Act but would have paid a high price politically had he attempted to block it.[37] Lindsay believed that he had chosen to "lie low" to appease Congress.[38]

Yet suggestions of Roosevelt's grudging cooperation on the matter were contradicted by private exchanges within his administration that recognized the political value of the proposed act.[39] The State Department had explained to Johnson that "the President really favoured the bill" and "would like it as a weapon in dealing with these European welchers."[40] This position allowed Roosevelt to sidestep potentially serious charges of circumventing Congress by secretly authorizing token payments in the previous year.[41] Cooperation also provided greater influence over proceedings. Roosevelt pursued amendments to the act to exclude private debts to protect the administration's economic policies in Latin America and the Soviet Union, which were ultimately agreed, and also sought a clause to allow the president to decide if a default had occurred and the associated penalties, which Congress refused.[42]

Roosevelt and Johnson had also cooperated closely in the past. The senator had supported the candidacy of the president, who had in exchange promised not to reduce the debts at the London Economic Conference. Both men subsequently refrained from criticizing each other publicly. Johnson's continuing support for key New Deal legislation is therefore suggestive of a deal with the president to support the Johnson Act. As DeWitt concludes, "one can only deduce that a political compromise had been effected."[43] Roosevelt ultimately requested Assistant Secretary of State R. Walton Moore support the passage of the bill from February onward.[44] In the next two months, the bill journeyed from the Senate to the House and back to the Senate for final passage.

The British were initially calm concerning the smooth passage of the Johnson Act. Lindsay explained that he was "puzzled" by this "silliness," and Leith-Ross was not "worrying much"; they believed the law would not apply to war debts, an assumption for which Secretary of State Cordell Hull carried "some doubt."[45] Such optimism was repeatedly contradicted by the actions of Congress in February and March.[46] The Democratic senator Joseph Robinson provided an accurate account of the international tensions in this period: "Public sentiment in the debtor countries will not permit the governments to pay, even if they are able to pay, . . . and public opinion in the United States will not consent to or approve the cancellation or reduction of the debts. So I can see that we are approaching a time when the deadlock which has existed for some time may become permanent."[47] This impasse left the United States all the poorer. The Republican representative James Frear stressed that the $11 billion burden of Europe's unpaid war debts—of which the United Kingdom owed the largest share—would be shifted to American taxpayers and make the United States the highest taxed nation on Earth.[48]

On 14 March 1934, Lindsay informed Secretary of State for Foreign Affairs John Simon that the Johnson bill had passed the Senate and was now in committee in the House. This outcome, he explained, "indicate[d] an absence of opposition by the White House," and he noted that the president had "evaded the question" at several press conferences and had "been able so far to keep his intentions completely hidden."[49] Yet he believed that Roosevelt would allow "the Johnson Bill to die in the House Committee."[50] As the bill made its way through Congress, however, British concerns grew. By late March, it remained unclear whether the Johnson bill would affect countries that had made partial payments. The Foreign Office viewed this uncertainty as "all of a piece with the opportunistic bargaining policy of the Administration," which was "waiting deliberately to see which interpretation suits them best."[51]

In a message to Lindsay on 4 April 1934, London warned, "For the past few months War Debts have been very dormant here. . . . But they are only hibernating: the spring sunshine will revive them."[52] On the issue of repayment, the message said, "I think you can take it that the Government are certainly not prepared to pay in full. . . . On the other hand, the Chancellor would still be willing to make a permanent settlement on the basis of our proposal last November at a cost not exceeding 20 million dollars a year."[53] This offer of further token payments, however, required the president to say that the United Kingdom was not in default. As the Johnson Act appeared to rule out this concession, British policymakers saw few viable options left: "It looks therefore as if we should have no alternative to default and that the main question would be one of tactics."[54]

On 13 April 1934, the president signed the Johnson Act into law. Roosevelt had prioritized his own political interests above his country's ability to recoup some of its losses to foreign debtors. The British government now faced a choice between outright suspension or the resumption of full repayment and would need to make its decision within the next two months. Only four days later, Chamberlain's third budget, which enjoyed a £31 million surplus, made no commitment to any further payment, which some American observers interpreted as a sign of impending default.[55] This "sunshine budget," as the press termed the chancellor's decision to reverse heavy increases in taxation and cuts in allowances of all kinds, only intensified U.S. interest in the war-debts issue.[56] As The Economist explained events, the chancellor was "non-committal in the extreme," which had "aroused indignation of Congressmen."[57]

Chamberlain was simply following the same procedure as made in the preceding year; making no provision in the budget did not preclude the making of any payments. Yet there was by now "a considerable element" in the cabinet that opposed any further payments. Many ministers were convinced that public opinion in the United Kingdom had hardened so sharply after the Johnson Act that the "overwhelming majority" welcomed complete suspension.[58] The British government's dealings with its own debtors also provide further evidence of an intended default. Further exchanges with the governments of Australia and New Zealand reveal that Chamberlain had agreed that further payment to Britain should remain in abeyance, as all Commonwealth and colony payments had since 1931.[59]

The British government was also unclear as to whether it was already in default. On 24 April, despite the president's expressed opinion that the UK was "not in default," Lindsay informed his colleagues that it was "incontestable" that the UK had "failed to meet a legal obligation and that technically [it] must be regarded in default."[60] There was by now limited confidence in Roosevelt's words. As Lindsay warned, "I am inclined to think he would hardly dare to repeat it on a future occasion in any fashion, and indeed it seems to me quite possible that he may have encouraged passage of the Johnson Bill to relieve himself of [any] responsibility for carrying single-handed the whole burden of [the] debt situation as it has existed during the last year."[61]

Yet the ambassador, fearing rising tensions on the Continent, advised against default: "it seems to me at any moment His Majesty's government might be confronted with international situations in which it would be of capital importance to have as little bad blood as possible."[62] As such, he pressed for further talks with the president to consider "some further but final payment now, pending arrival of [the] moment when both governments will be able to consider debts in a realistic spirit."[63] Lindsay understood that his proposal might be unpopular, but he nevertheless considered it the correct course of action. As he explained to Leith-Ross, "I detest spending the hard earned millions of my Government and I am afraid that all of you over there will say that I only want to pitch good money after bad, . . . [but] the money would be well spent taking the long view of policy."[64]

In the Treasury, Leith-Ross responded by noting, "I shd lie low & say nuffin."[65] For London, the continuation of costly token payments with only the ignominy of default in exchange held limited appeal. The Foreign Office concluded that Lindsay's advice led to "the worst of both worlds": "for we should still be technically in default and should in addition be making a lump sum payment which would be embarrassing financially and prejudicial to world recovery."[66] As the Foreign Office put it, "We have no interest in continuing token payments unless we can thereby secure Presidential recognition of our own dislike for the word default. . . . It would be impossible to justify further payment to our public opinion. . . . Our present policy is to sit tight and to leave the solution to be decided in light of situation at beginning of June."[67]

Uncertainty about the terms of the Johnson Act persisted for several more weeks. On 6 May, Lindsay reported that in the opinion of the U.S. attorney general, the United Kingdom and other token-paying governments were not in default.[68] Three days later the ambassador reported that Johnson accepted the attorney general's ruling but believed that it dealt only with past payments. A different situation arose for the future payment due in June. Indeed, it was for him, a "perfect absurdity to accept a token payment from a country which boasted a surplus on its budget."[69] Lindsay noted that U.S. press reports now began to suggest that the president had decided that token payments would no longer be accepted, but he felt that Roosevelt had not yet come to a final decision and was still gauging reactions in Washington.[70]

The Roosevelt administration eventually made its position clear in May.[71] The United Kingdom was not in default, but the Johnson Act precluded the use of further token payments.[72] Initial reports suggested that the United Kingdom would also need to pay all its arrears to avoid being in default, but this assumption ultimately proved erroneous.[73] Lindsay declared that "the whole matter of war debts" had now become "ridiculous."[74] Correspondence between Lindsay and the Foreign Office was clear that the British government "must either pay the full instalments or be branded as defaulters," which left the government with "no choice now" but to suspend repayment.[75] In a final series of desperate talks between Lindsay and Roosevelt, the president stressed the need for transatlantic goodwill but accepted that without full payment, it was impossible to avoid default, although he was reluctant to use this "very ugly" word.[76] The ambassador subsequently informed the president that, in such circumstances, the United Kingdom would suspend payments.[77] On 21 May 1934, Lindsay sent a message to Leith-Ross in which he was resigned to British default: "One can hardly suffer disappointment at a decision if it does not also bring surprise, and of the latter there is none, though there may be regret, for I admit I do hate the prospect of these heaps of defaulted bonds poisoning relations between England and America in saecula saeculorum."[78]

SUSPENDED PAYMENTS

On 25 May 1934, the U.S. Treasury requested almost $262 million from the United Kingdom in respect of its debt arrears and the amounts due on 15 June 1934.[79] Four days later, the chancellor of the exchequer circulated the draft of a note that he intended to send to the United States on the subject of the war debt. The note ultimately favored default:

> His Majesty's Government are in fact faced with a choice between only two alternatives, viz: to pay in full the sum of $262,000,000 . . . or to suspend all interim payments pending the final revision of the settlement. Deeply as they regret the circumstances which have forced them to take such a decision, His Majesty's Government feel that they could not assume the responsibility of adopting a course which would revive

the whole system of inter-Governmental War Debt payments. . . . Such a procedure would throw a bombshell into the European arena which would have financial and economic repercussions over all the five continents and would postpone indefinitely the chances of world recovery. Accordingly His Majesty's Government are reluctantly compelled to take the only other course open to them.[80]

The chancellor's note was a skillful construction that advanced its case judiciously in five broad arguments.[81] First, it reiterated the difference between these war debts and normal credits for development purposes. Second, the note claimed the economic impossibility of making transfers on the scale required by these obligations and the disastrous effect that any further attempt to do so would have on trade and prices in the long run. Third, any resumption of payments on the past scale would intensify the world crisis and could provoke financial and economic chaos. Fourth, it emphasized the sacrifices that the United Kingdom had made and the injustice of the difference between its funding settlement and those accorded to other debtors. Fifth, the note explained that the recent improvement in the budgetary situation of the United Kingdom in no way invalidated the government's position. This improvement was due entirely to unprecedented sacrifices, and it would have been "a gross act of social injustice" to have denied this relief to the British people to pay war debts to the United States while suspending the war-debt payments of Europe due to the United Kingdom.[82]

The cabinet went on to express its full support for this "comprehensive and close-knit" series of arguments making the case for suspending repayments.[83] The note implicitly criticized the handling of the situation by the United States, which certainly held some responsibility for the war-debt controversy. At least one senior U.S. policymaker would come to accept that they could have adopted "a more mature approach" to interallied lending and that raising tariffs in the 1920s and 1930s had "worsened the situation."[84] Yet it is important not to ignore or downplay Britain's role in events.[85] Many of the arguments advanced in Chamberlain's note were open to criticism, especially among American audiences that may have viewed some of its claims as little more than casuistry.[86]

The first claim that stressed the differences between war loans and normal credits was almost as old as the debt itself. Yet Congress had already noted that a significant portion of British war debt came via post-armistice advances. In addition, critics claimed, much of the money borrowed had been used for commercial rather than war purposes. Examples included Britain meeting its preexisting commercial obligations maturing in the United States, furnishing India with silver, and maintaining its exchange position.[87] As Keynes would acknowledge, U.S. war loans "had not been limited to the purchase of munitions of war, even interpreted in the widest sense."[88] These claims aside, the United States continued to stress the sanctity of all loans, commercial or otherwise, noting the legal obligation into which the United Kingdom had entered during and immediately after the Great War and again in 1923, and expressed reluctance toward burdening American taxpayers with foreign debts of any kind that they could ill afford.[89]

The second claim regarding the economic impossibility of making transfers on the scale required by these obligations was also difficult to justify for U.S. observers. The Hoover and Roosevelt administrations, as well as successive sessions of Congress, appreciated the challenges but doubted that they were determinative.[90] Reserves could potentially have been replenished through further sacrifices or by mobilizing foreign holdings of U.S. assets, but British ministers evidently disregarded these alternatives. Expanding gold or dollar reserves may well have been challenging, but it was possible. During the financial crisis in the early stages of the Second World War, for instance, Britain adopted a variety of approaches to strengthen its exchange resources, including the sale of foreign investments and securities to the U.S.[91] Furthermore, the claim that transferring amounts of this magnitude would cause a sharp depreciation of sterling was not evidenced clearly or consistently by previous payments. Even if such challenges did emerge, however, the decision to default reflected a political choice—namely, the prioritization of sterling over outstanding obligations. The importance of this issue was also challenged by recent reports suggesting that Chamberlain's alleged refusal to stabilize the pound was a way in which to encourage the United States to accept a settlement of the British debt.[92] Furthermore, the chancellor's additional warning that such large transfers would harm the dollar, which would be inconsistent with U.S. monetary policy, surely remained a decision for the U.S. government.[93]

The third claim that the resumption of payments on the past scale would intensify the world crisis and might provoke financial and economic chaos appeared to be honestly felt by some policymakers. As MacDonald remarked, "Payments that would upset [the] financial order (such as it is) would be treason to the whole world."[94] War debts and reparations appeared to many observers as a major obstacle to recovery and had certainly generated considerable political ill will as well as serious tensions in the world economy.[95] Yet these serious problems were only part of the many structural and policy difficulties that beset the global economy.[96] Hoover had previously challenged such claims, noting the limited scale of European war debts in contrast to U.S. imports or exports.[97] Furthermore, the passage of the moratorium—which had removed this obstacle, albeit temporarily—had limited effect on the pace of recovery. The resumption of repayments by some states thereafter had also failed to provoke financial and economic chaos. Claims about the impossibility or recklessness of reopening the reparations and war-debt issue in Europe were further weakened, at least in part, by Chamberlain threatening to do just that on several occasions, both in the cabinet and in discussion with French representatives. For the chancellor, the failure to reach a settlement had invalidated the Lausanne agreement and consequently allowed the collection of existing claims should it prove necessary.[98]

Fourth, the sacrifices that the United Kingdom had made in honoring its debts thus far and the differences between its funding settlement and those accorded to other debtor states were undeniable. The British government had provided payments totaling $2.02 billion toward $4.28 billion advances, but despite these efforts, the nominal amount still outstanding amounted to $4.71 billion. In contrast, other European governments had only repaid $678.5 million in respect of war advances totaling $5.57 billion. Yet these were the terms to which the British government had agreed willingly in 1917 and 1923, a point that the Foreign Office would repeatedly stress in response to persistent claims of unfairness.[99] After lengthy negotiations, both sides had accepted a deal that reduced the size of future interest payments and effectively removed any possibility of marketization, concessions that clearly benefited the United Kingdom. It was true that the British government had made large advances to the Allied governments during the war but had suspended all claims to these loans and reparations from Germany following the Lausanne agreement (Table 3.1). The United States, however, had never demanded that the United Kingdom make

Table 3.1. Select unpaid war debts owed to the United States and the
United Kingdom, 1934

Country	Owed to US Debt outstanding in USD (w/arrears)	Owed to UK Debt outstanding in USD (w/arrears)	Total owed to US and UK Debt outstanding in USD (w/arrears)
United Kingdom	4,714,345,235	—	4,714,345,235
France	3,980,735,112	3,361,387,861	7,342,122,973
Italy	2,009,555,036	1,123,494,772	3,133,049,808
Belgium	413,430,000	64,631,010	478,061,010
Poland	226,248,308	17,107,860	243,356,168
Czechoslovakia	165,409,455	—	165,409,455
Yugoslavia	61,625,000	146,572,822	208,197,822
Romania	63,883,007	140,836,167	204,719,174
Greece	32,789,344	99,384,805	132,174,149
Austria	23,822,492	—	23,822,492
Estonia	18,079,383	1,432,045	19,511,428
Finland (fully repaid)	8,711,996	—	8,711,996
Latvia	7,435,784	6,222,619	13,658,403
Lithuania	6,650,080	—	6,650,080
Hungary	2,086,096	—	2,086,096
Australia	—	337,777,250	337,777,250
New Zealand	—	110,966,579	110,966,579
Portugal	—	99,459,373	99,459,373

Source: C. M. Reinhart and C. Trebesch, "A Distant Mirror of Debt, Default, and Relief," Munich Discussion Paper No. 2014-49 (2014), 20. Debt figures are given for 31 March 1934. These select examples
show that foreign debts owed to the United Kingdom exceed debts owed by the United Kingdom to the
United States. See table 4.2 for a fuller account in 1941.

these deals or accept such losses. Toward the end of the decade, some
members of the House of Lords openly conceded the weakness of such
arguments in defense of British default.[100]

The fifth claim, regarding the recent improvement in the budgetary
situation of the United Kingdom, seemingly reflected limited interest
concerning the economic conditions in the United States. To balance

its budget, the British government had for the past fifteen years, the chancellor's note claimed, relied on unparalleled levels of taxation. It made little reference to significant and rising national expenditures on arms, which outstripped any debt repayments.[101] The note suggested, erroneously, that the burden of taxation in Britain was twice that of the United States in 1929 and that these differences had only grown. For the United Kingdom, tax levels reached 26 percent. As an earlier HM Treasury report explained, however, the percentage of national income taken as federal, state, and local taxes amounted to 20.3 percent in 1932.[102] The accompanying argument that high levels of taxation in Britain had produced a prolonged period of industrial depression and an army of unemployed was also unpersuasive given the significantly worse situation facing the United States. If repayment was "a gross act of social injustice" to the British, surely the same logic applied to Americans who would absorb these costs.[103]

On 30 May 1934, the cabinet unanimously approved the chancellor's memorandum.[104] Chamberlain informed his colleagues that he was unwilling for the United Kingdom to carry the burden of full payment without receiving anything from its debtors. The British government would have been prepared to continue token payments, he argued, but there was little point as Congress would deem anything less than full repayment as a default.[105] Suspending payments therefore appeared to be the logical decision. The British government's willingness to continue paying the United States had now expired.[106]

It is interesting to observe that in this note and in official publications or speeches thereafter, the government typically shied away from references to "default," preferring instead to use the term "suspension."[107] Such wording may perhaps have represented a sincere willingness to resume payment at some point, but it certainly reflected a clear distaste for the term and a subtle effort to dissociate from the act of nonpayment. In many ways, the note served an important psychological function. Like many debtors, the British government had found ways of demonstrating that its decision was either inevitable and desirable or that it was all someone else's fault.[108] It is plausible that many of the claims advanced in the note were honestly felt by the chancellor and many of his colleagues, and it seems likely that the government would have been prepared to make another token payment. Leith-Ross recalls the final decision in his memoirs, stating, "The reluctance of HMG to take this step was perfectly genuine."[109] Nevertheless, there were several important arguments in favor of default that were entirely absent from the note but reveal a more self-interested series of motivations.

The British government had by now little to lose from a suspension of payments and much to gain. The limited costs of some unilateral defaults—in contrast to negotiated debt restructurings—has been downplayed or neglected in the extant literature.[110] Yet the major European debtors that failed to honor their financial obligations to the United States had suffered few consequences. As Leith-Ross explained, the British decision to default was "helped by France who had not lost anything by it."[111] Furthermore, fears about the possible effects of the decision on British credit and on its position as a creditor country, which had so exercised the chancellor and several of his colleagues, had faded.[112]

The risk of a wave of defaults or financial contagion driven by the British government's decision to suspend payments now assumed limited attention in the cabinet. This stance may have been aided by relatively stable income from many overseas investments throughout this period.[113] Maintaining a reputation for repayment may also have appeared insufficient to avert problems with some foreign debtors, evidenced most recently by Chile and Germany.[114] Furthermore, the British government saw no issue in attempting to recover its losses from both states despite its own default to the United States. In June, Johnson was "astonished to see" Britain considering reprisals against Germany following its own suspension of repayments, and he criticized what he saw as a double standard: "What a marvelous difference it makes whose ox is gored, Mr. President!"[115] Nor did the Johnson Act pose much direct harm to the British economy. There now existed an embargo against all foreign loans, to be sure, but there was already considerable difficulty in raising such loans.[116] In the United States, the flotation of long-term foreign government debt had been negligible since 1930.[117]

Chamberlain's note also made little mention of the domestic-political benefits of default.[118] The British government had just rewarded its people after many difficult years of sacrifice. The "sunshine budget" reduced taxation and cuts in allowances.[119] Such benefits would have been much more difficult to achieve had regular debt payments continued. The decision also had a significant effect on the debt profile of the United Kingdom. Dollar-dominated war debts had made up the lion's share of foreign debt, which at that time was 11.4 percent of total national debt.[120] Domestic-political considerations had certainly informed the British government's timing and management of the war-debt problem. As Chamberlain acknowledged, "I am sure that if we had done it last year the papers would have been full of protests, but the public have been led along so gradually, first with a full payment then a token payment & then a smaller token payment that they seem hardly to notice the final stoppage."[121]

Cabinet discussions support this interpretation. Ministers had increasingly come to argue that public opinion was more supportive of a suspension of payments, not least because of the burden of continued payment.[122] Default appears to have gradually become more rather than less acceptable in the United Kingdom. Support for a suspension of payments may have also been aided by a broader shift away from punishing debtors in society.[123] Britain's suspension of payments coincided with significant efforts toward domestic reform that would reduce levels of imprisonment in England and Wales following default on payment of fines.[124] Home Secretary John Gilmour appointed a departmental committee to review the position, and it proposed many sweeping reforms, including a reduction in prison numbers, shortly after British default took place.[125]

The logic underpinning the British government's decision to continue paying its war debts to the U.S. in 1932 and 1933 is consistent with its decision to suspend repayment in 1934. The avoidance of default and efforts toward achieving a debt settlement with the United States had been driven by a complex mix of interrelated factors, including domestic-political concerns, repayment norms, diplomatic anxieties, and the risk of consequent defaults by the United Kingdom's own debtors. As the rewards associated with repayment diminished and the risks associated with default faded, a change in policy appears entirely logical. As Michael Tomz explains, states may "prefer to default" when "the political and economic costs of debt service come to outweigh the benefits."[126] Shifting cost-benefit calculations as well as evolving attitudes about the fairness of repayment explain why the British government's focus now moved from restructuring to repudiating its war debts to the United States. The case for a unilateral default was by now more compelling than any other alternative. Washington remained unwilling to offer any viable concessions and had limited compromise by prohibiting token payments. Furthermore, other states had defaulted without major issue, the costs of opportunistic default by debtors appeared less serious, and there was growing political support for a suspension of payments. In such circumstances, default had become the rational and appropriate course of action for London.

ACCEPTING DEFAULT

The British government was wary of how the United States might react to what it had termed a suspension of payments. After the cabinet had reached its position, some discussion took place as to whether Lindsay should show the chancellor's note privately and confidentially to Roosevelt before its delivery, with the understanding that he should ask the president to reciprocate by showing the British ambassador the draft of his reply. The general view of the cabinet was that the chancellor's draft was so comprehensive and close-knit that it would not be possible to agree to any material omissions or amendments. In these circumstances, it was felt that it would be better not to run the risk of Roosevelt asking for changes or alterations of substance to which the cabinet "should find it difficult to assent."[127]

The British government nevertheless delayed official notice of default in the hope that Roosevelt's forthcoming message to Congress might provide a solution.[128] Such hopes were swiftly dashed. On 1 June, the president was clear that the war loans were made with the intention that they would be repaid: "The money loaned by the United States Government was in turn borrowed by the United States Government from the people of the United States, and our government in the absence of payment from foreign governments is compelled to raise the shortage by general taxation of its own people in order to pay off the original liberty bond and the later refunding bonds. . . . The American people would not be disposed to place an impossible burden upon their debtors, but are nevertheless in a just position to ask that substantial sacrifices be made to meet these debts."[129] Roosevelt concluded, "We are using every means to persuade each debtor nation as to the sacredness of the obligation and also to assure them of our willingness, if they should so request, to discuss frankly and fully the special circumstances relating to means and method of payment."[130]

Press comment in the United States proved mostly critical of the Johnson Act, not least for leading the United Kingdom into default, but was largely supportive of Roosevelt's message to Congress.[131] An overwhelming majority of Americans accepted the justice of the U.S. position even if they now believed that the war debts would never be paid.[132] The press response in the United Kingdom was less enthusiastic. *The Times* concluded that the speech "unfolds no new points of view" and "ignores the all[-]important question of transfers" and that Roosevelt had simply "passed the buck."[133]

In the absence of progress in Washington, Chamberlain decided to press ahead with his planned suspension of payments. The president was notified of the British government's position on 4 June and warned that the note would be released to the public the following day.[134] Chamberlain informed the Commons of the government's decision to default on 5 June. The chancellor had intended to publish his note simultaneously in London and Washington, but owing to a misunderstanding, it was published abroad first. His speech echoed the note and explained that it was not possible to arrive at a settlement because the government "could not assume the responsibility of adopting a course attended by such disastrous consequences"—namely, the breakdown of the global financial system. The chancellor concluded by saying that, while the government deeply regretted the circumstances imposed on the government that made a suspension necessary, it had "no intention of repudiating [its] obligations, and will be prepared to enter upon further discussion on the subject at any time when in the opinion of the President of the United States of America such discussion would be likely to produce results of value."[135]

The chancellor's statement brought much-needed clarity to the issue for the wider government, opposition, and press. *The Economist* said that his note had removed what "little uncertainty still remained" regarding future payment.[136] Throughout May, the government had repeatedly evaded questions relating to the war debts, leaving many onlookers baffled.[137] The immediate response to Chamberlain's speech in the House of Commons was muted. In the coming weeks, however, the issue reappeared in debate. The Labour MP Jack Lawson gave a scathing response: "As the Government have gone off the Gold Standard, and have defaulted, could the right hon. Gentleman give a guarantee that really the British Empire will be left intact before the next election?"[138] Labour Lord Strabolgi held "grave doubts and apprehensions about [the] policy of incurring a default": "We are a very great creditor nation and I think it will be a very serious matter indeed if we are adjudged defaulters on our American debt."[139] The Conservative MP Arthur Evans asked if the government had considered handing over Bermuda or other island territories adjacent to the United States, which he believed were no longer of defensive value to the British Empire to address U.S. demands for repayment. The prime minister was clear "that there could under no circumstances be any question of such an arrangement."[140]

The press reaction in the United Kingdom was largely supportive of a suspension of payments. The *Financial Times* had been appalled by the size of U.S. demands and believed Congress had had its way with Roosevelt: "Thus is the behest of Shylock fulfilled."[141] *The Telegraph* attributed Roosevelt's weakness on the issue to elections pending in Autumn.[142] A series of letters in *The Times* expressed a wide range of popular views on the subject prior to default. Some distinguished between war debt and commercial loans, while others criticized the United States' "illogical position."[143] Others still sought to prevent the "dreadful step of defaulting," warning that "this is a critical moment in the world's history—if the bond of Great Britain cannot be trusted in a matter of money, how can it be trusted in aught else?"[144] In the wake of the default, newspapers also took the opportunity to resurrect old memories of the United States' own unpaid debts, ranging from the Treaty of Peace with England in 1783 to the Southern states' debts from the Civil War.[145] These debts were of limited economic or political use to the British government, however, which helps to explain their limited role in cabinet discussions or transatlantic negotiations. Tracing the many private holders of these securities was unfeasible, and the success of diplomatic or legal action was doubtful given the relevant clauses of the 1853 Convention or the Pecuniary Claims Convention of 1910.[146]

The international response to the United Kingdom's suspension of payments to the United States was largely supportive. This decision meant that the British government would continue to honor its earlier decision to suspend any claims to its own war debts from the colonies and dominions as well as from many states across Europe. The size of the war debts and uncertainty regarding their status, for example, had been a serious concern for the antipodean powers.[147] The British government's decision was received with satisfaction in France, which was no longer the only major European power that had defaulted.[148]

The French government subsequently dropped the idea of token repayment and instead decided to remain in default.[149] Italy also chose to default.[150] Italian policymakers believed that repayment could create difficulties with London and undermine the Lausanne agreement; British default had been justified in part by its own debtors, such as Italy, ceasing payment to the United Kingdom. Moreover, Italian policymakers probably welcomed British default given their own challenging economic conditions and the difficulty of securing public support for further repayment.[151] Formally, all three states still expressed a commitment to settle these debts.[152]

In the United States, the reaction to the note was mixed. Georges Bonnet, a prominent French politician who had been involved in both the Lausanne and London conferences, asked the U.S. diplomat William Bullitt if the British default had "seriously injured the prestige of Great Britain" in the United States. Bullitt replied that he believed "it had relieved certain persons of the idea that Great Britain's sense of honor extended to matters in which her interests were involved."[153] Senators were swift to express their desire that the debtors honor their contracts.[154] The *Daily Telegraph* reported that, though Congress was evidently unhappy with this suspension of repayments, Roosevelt was "by no means displeased," as it moved the debt problem to a basis of reality and "allowed for a fresh start."[155]

U.S. press comment was mostly restrained in early June. Writing for the *New York Times*, Walter Lippmann said that the Johnson Act created a political deadlock that it was impossible to break except by paying nothing. Another editorial in the *New York Times* wrote that "Great Britain had a new experience today as she became signally and formally a defaulter on an international obligation."[156] In addition, the Hearst press papers published editorials questioning "British honor" and noting "how are the English fallen."[157] By 15 June, Lindsay informed Simon that U.S. press reaction was for the most part now friendly to the United Kingdom.[158] The British Library of Information subsequently informed the Foreign Office that reception to the note had "not been unsatisfactory" but warned, "we should be careful to realise that we are not yet out of the wood, and we must not relax our vigilance in regard to publicity."[159]

British officials had also recognized a growing trend in U.S. reporting of blaming Johnson for the loss to the American taxpayer of at least a token payment and possibly more from the United Kingdom.[160] A State Department summary of newspaper reports had indicated that only twenty-seven editorials favored the Johnson Act, with many "lukewarm in their praise," while 155 papers across forty states were "violently opposed" to its effect of encouraging the United Kingdom into default and encouraging other states to follow suit.[161] Senator Johnson denied that his bill affected the British government's decision: "The British have repudiated debts before, and have now done so again."[162]

Some scholars have suggested that Johnson and the United States had erred in pursuing this act. Rather than encourage debtor governments to resume payment, it led them into default.[163] Most of the press soon came to see the Johnson Act as a blunder and responsible for the present lack of payments.[164] The act was now regarded as "bad business."[165] Yet it was never pure folly. Johnson and many of his colleagues in Congress were correct that the British government could afford to pay more than it claimed.[166] Furthermore, though Johnson's tactics were ineffective in the current economic conditions, they had worked in the past. As Clavin explains, there was "little prospect of a revival in American international lending in the 1930s," but the "threat of withholding loans had been enough to persuade most debtor governments to pay up in the 1920s."[167]

Furthermore, critical assessments of the Johnson Act tend to assume that the goal was financial reward, at least in the main. As Johnson explained, however, "The one great desideratum of the measure was that something should be done, even in small degree, concerning the defaults that had occurred in the debts due by other governments to the Government of the United States."[168] Action was as much a matter of principle as politics. In addition to avoiding the odium of voting for a compromise, the passage of the act meant that Washington could now blame European fecklessness for some of the woes of overburdened American taxpayers. The Johnson Act also complemented a growing noninterventionist mood in the United States by successfully limiting U.S. financial support for the major European powers, thereby, its proponents argued, helping to preserve the peace.[169] In this sense, the Johnson Act was at once a political success and an economic failure.

The United States government's formal reply to the chancellor's note expressed disappointment in the British government's decision. Hull authored the U.S. note, but it expressed the personal views of the president: "I regret that the American government is unable to concur" with the basis of British arguments.[170] It clarified that the United Kingdom did not have to pay the previously published figure of $262 million to avoid default. The U.S. attorney general's ruling meant that the British government needed to pay the smaller figure of $85.67 million as it was not yet in default.[171] Despite the United Kingdom surrendering its own war loans to its allies, the U.S. note nevertheless continued to emphasize the independence of those debts and its loans to the United Kingdom. It also repeated that the debtor had a duty to approach the creditor to initiate any debt settlement. Hull went on to propose talks with regard to payment in kind as a potential solution to the current impasse.[172] Before sending the proposed note on 12 June, the president was asked if the tone was too severe. Roosevelt offered a straightforward response: "No—OK."[173]

Few observers expected a swift reply. Until the total was scaled down, The Telegraph reported, "this elaborate exchange of communications is no more than a barren exchange in Note writing."[174] On 21 June, the British government responded. After careful consideration, it reiterated its original position, stressing that the interdependence of intergovernmental loans was based on facts rather than laws. Saying that its war-debt payments were stopped because others would not pay was simply undebatable. The British government also took the opportunity to reject any suggestion of payment in kind, arguing that such a solution would not work as evidenced by its recent experience of the transfer difficulties surrounding German reparations.[175]

In the coming weeks and months, Washington generated more schemes for a settlement with London, including the rearrangement of annuities, reduction or elimination of interest, lump-sum settlements, deliveries in kind, and commercial credits. Some suggestions combined these ideas.[176] The British government rejected all these proposals and reiterated its position that war-debt payments were suspended because others would not pay. Chamberlain repeatedly denied rumors of a new formula for a settlement of war debts.[177] As the British understood it, there were no signs of coming down to a reasonable figure or a way out of paying in dollars.[178]

There remained little hope for effective negotiations given Congress's steadfast opposition to any revision of the debt. Toward the end of the year, Lindsay lamented the position of the United States:

"Such has been the recalcitrance of Congress that neither President has thought it worth while, or has had the courage, to talk common sense to it in public; while Senators and Representatives have been just as much afraid of their more ignorant voters as presidents have been of Congress, and have preferred to forgo all receipts . . . rather than face such odium as might be incurred by voting for a compromise. The deadlock is complete and seems likely to last a long time."[179] Lindsay had already informed Leith-Ross of his skepticism: "Americans fairly often talk of schemes for a settlement, . . . then they say . . . that the golden moment is at hand and must not be allowed to pass. . . . What is the good of talking one language to the American Administration when the American Legislature will only talk quite a different one?"[180] Furthermore, as he concluded, "From the purely financial point of view, it does not seem to me to be unfavourable to us that this deadlock should continue."[181] The chancellor agreed. As he informed Lindsay on 8 November, "the longer we postpone any payment, the more difficult it will be to resume."[182] By the end of the year, the British government had informed the United States that it was still not ready for negotiations: "it would be useless and, therefore, unwise to initiate negotiations at present."[183]

Some scholars have argued that the British government's decision to suspend repayments was an excusable default. The United Kingdom's suspension of payments had followed the forgiveness of German reparations at the Lausanne Conference in 1932, and this connection, they argue, had been implicitly accepted by the U.S. government, which could not forgive the interallied debt explicitly due to domestic-political concerns.[184] Yet such a reading of events downplays Hoover's and Roosevelt's unwillingness to accept such terms in public or private. It also overlooks the ongoing hostility toward British default within Congress and throughout the United States. The position was one of political stalemate rather than tacit agreement. Indeed, the U.S. Treasury would continue to record the United Kingdom's outstanding debts, as well as those of many other debtor states, which continued to grow each year as interest mounted (Table 3.2).

The British government went on to receive regular reminders of its unpaid debts. On 22 November 1934, in advance of the scheduled payment on 15 December, the United States issued its first semiannual reminder to the United Kingdom and every other indebted state concerning

Table 3.2 Indebtedness of foreign governments to the U.S. arising from World War I, 1934 (USD)

State	Total indebtedness (payments on principal deducted)	Total payments received	Funded indebtedness			
			Indebtedness		Payments on account	
			Principal (net)	Accrued interest	Principal	Interest
Armenia	20,813,124.89	0.00	0.00	0.00	0.00	0.00
Austria	23,757,934.13	862,668.00	23,752,217.00	5,717.13	862,668.00	0.00
Belgium	413,653,058.17	52,191,273.24	400,680,000.00	12,973,058.17	17,100,000.00	14,490,000.00
Cuba	0.00	12,286,751.58	0.00	0.00	0.00	0.00
Czechoslovakia	165,325,281.80[a]	20,134,092.26	165,241,108.90	84,172.90	19,829,914.17	0.00
Estonia	18,079,383.11[b]	1,248,432.07	16,466,012.87	1,613,370.24	0.00	1,246,990.19
Finland	8,711,996.26	3,685,673.77	8,478,840.04	233,156.22	521,159.96	2,855,198.54
France	3,980,735,111.59	486,075,891.00	3,863,650,000.00	117,085,111.59	161,350,000.00	38,650,000.00
Great Britain	4,714,345,235.02	2,024,848,817.09	4,368,000,000.00	346,345,235.02	232,000,000.00	1,232,770,518.42
Greece	32,789,343.56	3,429,712.01	31,516,000.00	1,273,343.56	981,000.00	1,286,636.00
Hungary	2,086,096.48[b]	468,466.32	1,908,560.00	177,536.48	73,995.00	393,717.78
Italy	2,009,555,035.78[b]	100,829,880.16	2,004,900,000.00	4,655,035.78	37,100,000.00	5,766,708.26
Latvia	7,435,783.76[b]	761,549.07	6,879,464.20	556,319.56	9,200.00	621,520.12

(continued)

Table 3.2 (*continued*)

State	Total indebtedness (payments on principal deducted)	Total payments received	Funded indebtedness			
			Indebtedness		Payments on account	
			Principal (net)	Accrued interest	Principal	Interest
Liberia	0.00	36,471.56	0.00	0.00	0.00	0.00
Lithuania	6,650,080.33	1,237,956.58	6,197,682.00	452,398.33	234,783.00	1,001,626.61
Nicaragua	425,295.38	168,575.84	0.00	0.00	0.00	0.00
Poland	226,248,307.86[b]	22,646,297.55	206,057,000.00	20,191,307.86	1,287,297.37	19,310,775.90
Rumania	63,883,006.54[a]	4,791,007.22	63,860,560.43	22,446.11	2,700,000.00	29,061.46
Russia	346,843,200.95	8,748,878.87[c]	0.00	0.00	0.00	0.00
Yugoslavia	61,625,000.00	2,588,771.69	61,625,000.00	0.00	1,225,000.00	0.00
Total	12,102,962,275.61	2,747,041,165.88	11,229,212,445.44	505,668,208.95[d]	475,275,017.50	1,318,422,753.28

Source: U.S. Treasury Department, *Annual Report* (1934), 391, table 42, "Principal of the Funded and Unfunded Indebtedness of Foreign Governments to the United States, the Accrued and Unpaid Interest Thereon, and Payments on Account of Principal and Interest, as of Nov. 15, 1934."

Note: Due to space limitations, the final four columns ("Principal [net]," "Accrued interest," "Principal," and "Interest") under the heading of "Unfunded indebtedness," have been removed. All figures in U.S. dollars.

[a] Difference between principal of funded debts and amounts here stated represents deferred payments provided for in the funding agreements, for which gold bonds of the respective debtor governments have been or will be delivered to the Treasury.

[b] Increase over amount funded due to exercise of options with respect to the payment of interest due on original issue of bonds of debtor governments.

[c] Represents proceeds of liquidation of financial affairs of Russian Government in this country. (Copies of letter dated May 23, 1922, from the Secretary of State and reply of the Secretary of the Treasury dated June 2, 1922, in regard to loans to the Russian Government and liquidation of affairs of the latter in this country, appear in the Annual Report of the Secretary of the Treasury for the fiscal year 1922, as exhibit 79, p. 283, and in the combined annual reports of the World War Foreign Debt Commission, exhibit 2, p. 84.)

[d] Includes balances of amounts postponed under provisions of joint resolution of Dec. 23, 1931. (For amounts postponed see p. 35 of report of Secretary of the Treasury for 1932.)

the outstanding amounts owed. The Roosevelt administration soon became accustomed to the evasive responses that followed and did not expect these messages to prompt a change of heart.[185] Nevertheless, these reminders helped to protect the president from popular and congressional criticism that he had allowed the United Kingdom, as well as many other states, to escape their war debts and burden the American taxpayer in especially challenging times. Unemployment remained a significant problem and levels of public and private debt remained historically high.[186] The United Kingdom's unpaid debts to the United States remained a source of tension between these two states. A December issue of the *Record*, a business newspaper, compared the United States to a grocery store with unpaid bills and Britain to an ungrateful customer.[187] Such simplistic comparisons are problematic, to be sure, but they highlight a sense of unfairness felt by many Americans.

In response to the U.S. reminder note, the British government repeated its position prior to the default. In sum, while it was prepared to discuss proposals for a settlement, such negotiations should wait because the considerations that governed the decision only six months earlier still applied "with equal force."[188] In explaining the response, Lindsay informed Secretary of State Cordell Hull that London still felt "that it would be useless and, therefore, unwise to initiate negotiations at present."[189] Many British citizens had expressed disappointment with their government's intention to default.[190] These regrets appear to have lingered in the absence of any attempt to resume negotiations. In 1935, Cecil Perkins, a British citizen residing in London, expressed his embarrassment concerning default and generously sent the State Department a check for £1 to cover his share of the outstanding debt.[191] Failure to resolve these unpaid debts went on to have a profound and deleterious effect on transatlantic relations in the coming decade.

4 Financial Isolation, 1934–1942

THE IMMEDIATE CONSEQUENCES of the British government's default on its war debts to the United States were surprisingly limited. "Well," Chancellor of the Exchequer Neville Chamberlain noted in a letter to his sisters in June 1934, "we have defaulted on the American Debt & not a dog has barked."[1] Such an outcome is unusual in most instances of sovereign default. The extant literature understandably tends to focus on the dire political costs to incumbent governments following a unilateral default as well as significant economic costs with regard to the domestic economy, international trade, and wider reputation.[2] Yet most of these consequences appear to have been relatively limited for the United Kingdom as well as for other European powers in the years immediately following default, with many governments benefiting from the unusual international economic conditions of the period.[3]

The British government subsequently reversed heavy increases in taxation as well as cuts in allowances of all kinds.[4] Prime Minister Stanley Baldwin went on to secure another large majority in the election of November 1935, in part benefiting from improving economic conditions and declining levels of unemployment.[5] Britain had limited interest in accessing foreign debt immediately after default but was able to borrow from the United States immediately after the Second World War.[6] The fears of the British government identified in the previous chapters—namely, a domino effect of defaults by Britain's international debtors or profound shock to a large section of public opinion that could harm the government—also failed to materialize.[7] Nor did default halt broader economic cooperation between the governments of the U.S. and the UK, as evidenced by the Tripartite Agreement of 1936 and the Anglo-American Trade Agreement of 1938.[8]

Yet this chapter reveals that there was one profoundly negative consequence to British default. As the United States struggled through the Great Depression, the memory of unpaid debts lingered. U.S. disappointment concerning Europe's unpaid debts and disillusionment with the Continent's drift to war produced powerful congressional and public barriers to international lending and diplomatic alliances, evidenced by the Johnson Act and successive Neutrality Acts. These responses complement suggestions that default can help to signal to creditor states that the indebted governments in question are unreliable, thereby limiting cooperation on other agreements or alliances.[9] In the buildup to the Second World War, the United Kingdom struggled to balance economic stability with military rearmament and increasingly hoped to regain access to U.S. debt markets.[10] Recent research has shown that governments that lack access to affordable credit face more constraints in conflict initiation, tend to become less self-reliant militarily, and are more likely to lose or avoid wars.[11] The United Kingdom evidences these claims, showing how default made allies harder to find just as they became more important.

Historians such as Robert Dallek and Paul Kennedy have rightly argued that the suspension of repayments was calamitous for the United Kingdom in the longer run because it weakened any anti-German coalition and denied easy access to the U.S. money markets.[12] British default had certainly strained transatlantic relations and helped to limit access to U.S. finances when they were most needed.[13] As Keynes understood events, "Our default on last time's war debts is presumably the real reason why the present law prohibits credits. The other ostensible grounds are not convincing."[14] Yet the experiences of Hungary and Finland suggest that resumed or continued payment may not have ensured adequate financial support given the climate of U.S. politics. Whether continued repayment would have been the most cost-effective use of British resources is also debatable. The British leadership certainly believed that repayment would have been unmanageable and disruptive. Some scholars are sympathetic to the British government's decision to suspend payments, stressing short-term economic rewards and the benefits of hindsight.[15] The distinction between short-term and long-term consequences is sensible, but the argument that these trade-offs only became clear in hindsight is less persuasive. Some observers on both sides of the Atlantic recognized the risks early on. The British government had ample opportunity to resume repayment but repeatedly chose not to do so, preferring not to resume the full payments necessary to appease Congress.

When the United Kingdom declared war on Germany on 3 September 1939, the British government became reliant on a U.S. policy of "Cash and Carry," which maintained the ban on loans but allowed the sale of material to belligerents if the buyer arranged transportation and paid immediately in dollars or gold. By late summer of 1940, following the collapse of France, fear of a German invasion across the English Channel led the British government to increase the procurement of essential materials from the United States regardless of economic concerns. Such efforts were unsustainable. By the end of the year, the United Kingdom expressed its urgent need for financial support from the United States. In response, the Roosevelt administration, which had become increasingly sympathetic to Britain's plight, proposed what eventually became the Lend-Lease Act.[16] In contrast to the loans of the First Word War, the United States allowed the direct transfer of supplies and material to the United Kingdom instead of requiring cash payments. This novel form of economic cooperation was an ingenious solution to the significant legal and congressional barriers to traditional forms of lending, keenly informed by the failures of international lending in the interwar period.[17]

The United Kingdom was in a perilous position as it awaited the ratification of Lend-Lease. The costs of the first eighteen months of conflict had ravaged the economy, and the British government found itself unable to pay the United States for existing orders.[18] Ongoing military struggles were the prime cause of this hardship, to be sure, but U.S. reluctance to lend money had exacerbated the costs of war. Much of the congressional resistance to Lend-Lease, which in turn informed the hard bargaining that followed during negotiations around the master Lend-Lease agreement in 1942, reflected bitter memories of unpaid war debts. The U.S. Treasury continued to maintain detailed records of these outstanding obligations, and the Roosevelt administration sent reminder notices every six months to all debtor countries during the early stages of the Second World War. After Allied forces had evacuated from Dunkirk and during the period in which bombs fell on London during the Blitz, Washington continued to send notices of payments owed.[19] Even when the United States entered the war, Roosevelt remained unwilling to settle or cancel the debts.[20]

DOWNPLAYING DEFAULT

The British government preferred to ignore rather than resolve the issue of its unpaid war debts throughout the 1930s. Nonpayment aided short-term economic objectives by removing the significant costs of servicing the debt and preventing the further erosion of gold and dollar reserves. Silence on the issue also avoided dredging up difficult conversations with Britain's own European debtors, especially France and Italy, that could destabilize the political and economic status quo. The same was true of outstanding war loans from the United Kingdom to the colonies and dominions, which had been suspended since 1931. Correspondence between the United Kingdom, Australia, and New Zealand, for example, highlights lingering concerns about significant outstanding debts held by the antipodean powers, which could potentially pose problems in the future.[21] Just as the United States refused to close the issue, however, so too did the United Kingdom. London repeatedly informed Canberra and Wellington that their war loans had not been canceled but remained in abeyance, pending further developments.[22]

Unpaid debts remained as a lingering source of tension on both sides of the Atlantic.[23] The Foreign Securities Act was a permanent reminder for policymakers of British default. As the British ambassador to the United States Ronald Lindsay had warned Chief Economic Adviser Frederick Leith-Ross, "The Johnson Act's penal clause is more serious than you make out. It would be a very formidable nuisance if we ever had the misfortune to be again at war."[24] Lindsay subsequently reiterated his apprehensions, noting that "politically the situation is full of peril, and if ever Great Britain found herself at war, the existence of this debt will be an extremely grave element in the situation."[25] Leith-Ross offered a curious response, which was at once remarkably pessimistic about U.S. motivations and unduly optimistic about securing future credit: "As the Americans would defend the war as a means of profiteering, they wd [*sic*] certainly sell to us & I don't believe the old govt war debt would affect the issuing of private credit."[26]

Despite Lindsay's well-judged concerns, London assiduously avoided the issue of war debts in subsequent discussions with Washington. There were many opportunities to reopen negotiations, especially in the months immediately after default, with the Roosevelt administration proposing ideas for repayment in exchange for goods that ranged from manganese to antiques.[27] By June 1935, proposals had expanded to include payments in kind in suitable commodities, such as tin, nickel, and chromium.[28] Other ideas in the coming years ranged from university and college scholarships, cotton and wheat exchanges, and territories such as British Guiana.[29] The British government doubted that the Roosevelt administration would be willing or able to overcome congressional resistance to achieve any viable compromise and consequently rejected all these proposals. Such doubts were reasonable. Roosevelt had by now started to avoid even considering questions from the press about the status of the war debts.[30] In the absence of a settlement, the British government preferred not to resume payment for its own benefit and welcomed the deadlock that made any resumption of payments more difficult.[31]

Ramsay MacDonald's worsening health led Stanley Baldwin to assume the premiership in June 1935. In October, the new prime minister called and won a general election that secured another majority for the National Government.[32] Baldwin was beset by foreign-policy challenges that would soon reintroduce the war-debts issue. The British government had for some time been concerned by Hitler's accession to power. Germany's withdrawal from the League of Nations and disarmament talks in 1933 was followed by growing evidence of German rearmament in 1934 and 1935. Although the British government erred by misunderstanding some of the strategic challenges it faced, successive cabinets understood that economic factors limited the pace of rearmament, which in turn influenced the course of British diplomacy.[33] Spending had to be restrained to protect the national economy and secure the country's long-term military potential. The British government would come to cautiously prepare to wage a long and costly war on multiple fronts.[34] Such efforts would eventually require considerable material and financial assistance from abroad. By early 1936, London became increasingly clear of the need to secure loans from Washington to fund rearmament. "We only just scraped through the last war with Germany with every assistance we could get from the USA," Permanent Under-Secretary at the Foreign Office Robert Vansittart noted in January 1936. "The deduction is plain. . . . In any crisis of life and death . . . this [the absence of U.S. support] might mean our 'death.'"[35]

The United States remained keen to distance itself from involvement. The passage of the second Neutrality Act in February 1936 had renewed the provisions of its predecessor from the previous year, which prohibited the export of arms to any belligerent in time of war, and now forbade all loans or credits to belligerents. Such noninterventionist or isolationist efforts compounded the challenges to the United Kingdom posed by the Johnson Act.[36] A commitment to neutrality and the memory of unpaid debts presented powerful and mutually reinforcing obstacles to U.S. support for British rearmament. The issue of British default certainly remained alive in Washington. On 14 March 1936, the *Washington Times* talked positively of a recent speech by Hiram Johnson, which stressed that the war debts still existed and that European nations were "welchers."[37] Twelve days later, the issue of repayment reemerged in Congress. Secretary of the Treasury Henry Morgenthau rejected the Republican senator Arthur Vandenberg's requests to invoke clauses in the war-debt funding agreement that would have made these outstanding obligations marketable. Vandenberg resentfully accepted this outcome: "Let them stand in default until paid. . . . Let them stand—as a warning against further American gullibility and as a further convincing justification of our new neutrality formula."[38]

The issue clearly remained important to the Republican Party. At its national convention held in the summer of 1936, the Grand Old Party adopted a platform that included demands for collection of the debts and criticized Roosevelt's inaction on the matter: "We shall use every effort to collect the war debt due us from foreign countries, amounting to $12,000,000,000; one third of our national debt. No effort has been made by the present administration even to reopen negotiations."[39] In the Senate, Republicans sought to revive and resolve the issue by creating a new debt commission for negotiating the payment of war debts with foreign governments. As one senator explained, "While nations arm to the teeth and spend billions in armament races, they have no right to repudiate the honorable debts of past wars. Of the billions owed us, as much as possible should—indeed, must—be collected, and I am convinced a determined effort on our part will be productive of results."[40]

British policymakers increasingly came to appreciate the importance of this issue in overcoming noninterventionism in the United States. In July, the head of the Home Civil Service, Warren Fisher, suggested to the chancellor that a final settlement "might well have an incalculable value in its influence on Middle West opinion as against a future when [the British] were in a European mess."[41] Prominent figures such as Lord Lothian, a respected member of the House of Lords, as well as Walter Runciman, president of the Board of Trade and previously one of the strongest proponents of default, also came to argue that a debt settlement could secure U.S. support for British rearmament, which could in turn serve as a powerful deterrent to any potential aggressor.[42] In late 1936, Lindsay took the opportunity to inform U.S. policymakers of an "ever-increasing desire" within the British government to consider further talks on the debt question, which reflected a "change in attitude demonstrated in high official circles."[43]

Such views were not representative of the British government more widely, however, especially at its highest levels. The prime minister and the chancellor remained opposed to reopening the issue of unpaid war debts. They were keen to secure U.S. financial support, to be sure, but years of bitter experience suggested that any progress on a settlement was unlikely given continuing congressional resistance. Moreover, they probably believed that the time and money necessary for progress in negotiations could be better spent on other areas. The British government sought only to avoid bringing any more attention to the issue, which explains why it retained the familiar language in its responses to the semiannual debt reminders it received from the United States.[44]

The United States, United Kingdom, and France were able to compartmentalize lingering tensions over war debts to pursue economic cooperation more broadly. Following further banking runs, France devalued the franc in September and left the gold bloc in October 1936.[45] The U.S., British, and French governments resisted a currency war and committed themselves to consult on daily exchange rates and to settle daily balances between national exchange equalization accounts.[46] The Tripartite Agreement brought a degree of stability to the international economy, but this "gentleman's agreement" was limited in its ambition.[47] As Stephen V. Clarke explains, the Roosevelt administration found unpalatable more substantial action, such as the remission of war debts or the initiation of discussions about longer-term exchange stabilization: "fear of being outwitted or snubbed by the British played a large part in the administration's attitude."[48] Speculative attacks continued and capital flight persisted. The U.S. Treasury provided indirect support for the franc but never provided much-needed credit. As France remained in default on war debts, the Johnson Act prohibited such loans.[49] The French government ultimately devalued the franc for a second time in June of the following year.[50]

In this period, France, in an effort to secure U.S. credit and to support currency stabilization, made renewed efforts to settle the war-debts issue with the United States. Despite such efforts, and the risk of unfavorable comparisons, the British government maintained a low profile. In November 1936, following rumors of French and also Italian schemes for settling war debts, Lindsay informed Leith-Ross that "there has been a certain stirring in the dry bones of the war debts" and that the subject was "rather more in the air than it was," but he warned, "we must wait a while longer."[51] The British Library of Information (BLI) reported news that "France and Italy both want to gain American good will and overcome [the] Johnson Act, so New York market will lend abroad."[52] These rumors proved correct.[53] By the end of the year, the U.S. government was convinced that France and Italy were "exceedingly anxious" to borrow money and sought a way to circumvent the Johnson Act's prohibition on lending.[54] On 16 December, the House of Commons organized a dinner in honor of U.S. ambassador Robert Bingham. Bingham took this opportunity to remind his hosts that Americans had not forgotten the war debts. Furthermore, as France now wanted to discuss the resumption of payments, Britain should follow this example or risk a "bad impression."[55] In a note to the president in the new year, Bingham explained, "Both in and out of the [British] Government, these people are becoming more and more anxious about the debt situation. . . . In the end, in my judgement, they will go to you with some form of proposal, especially if their outlook becomes darker, as it well may."[56]

International cooperation was increasingly important. U.S. neutrality legislation earlier in the year meant that the United Kingdom would have to rely more heavily on its own resources in any new conflict, requiring the running down of financial reserves in the absence of any public or private loans from the United States, which further helps to explain the cautious approach of British foreign policy in this period. Nevertheless, the British government remained unwilling to reopen the war-debt issue.[57] Leith-Ross informed Lindsay on 11 February 1937 that the government would not embark on any negotiations as "the less said about the war debts the better."[58] Such an approach proved sensible as France's and Italy's talks with the United States on war debts soon stalled. The Roosevelt administration had concluded that a settlement was not presently practical politics.[59] In the preceding months, the Americans had come to believe that they "should not accept anything less than a thoroughly reasonable offer," especially given suspicions that loans may once again not be repaid once a war began.[60] Roosevelt declared that there was "absolutely nothing doing on foreign debts": "[U.S.] policy for the last 3 yrs [was] for us to sit tight and let our debtors come to us and make proposals."[61] Despite the failure of French and Italian efforts, other states had persevered. By the end of the year, Hungary had decided to resume token repayments, albeit for uncertain rewards.[62]

On 10 March 1937, Secretary of State for Foreign Affairs Anthony Eden dispatched a coded telegram to Lindsay asking for a report on transatlantic relations: "The crucial importance of retaining the goodwill of the United States Government and public opinion in the event of a major crisis occurring in Europe is a matter which is keenly engaging my attention."[63] Eden resigned less than a year later and was replaced by Lord Halifax, but the report he requested still offers valuable insights into British interpretations of U.S. thinking at that time. Lindsay's dispatch suggested that "things have been going quite extraordinarily well" but warned, "war debts unfortunately still remain with us":

> They will always be exploited and will always be most capable of damage at the difficult moment when it is most desired to avoid friction. . . . Not only is Congress still unable to face the drastic reductions which alone would make a settlement possible, but the danger of war in Europe confirms them in their attitude. They almost welcome the defaults by which under the Johnson Act and under other legislation too, the potential belligerents are debarred from the New York market. They think that if Europe could borrow in America the chances of war would be increased. They therefore regard the existence of the debts as something of a bulwark against the possible danger of their

being involved themselves in a war. I think it better to leave this question alone rather than beat our heads against a brick wall. Meanwhile we shall have to suffer the in-conveniences of the situation. To the cheap orator the debts will always be a dripping roast—he can cut and come again as often as he likes.[64]

The Foreign Office supported the position outlined in Lindsay's dispatch. As it agreed, "The only dark spot on the horizon is the War Debt question which has presumably to be faced as insoluble for the present."[65]

The *Congressional Record* provides ample evidence for the insolubility of these outstanding war debts. In April, the Republican representative Charles Plumley expressed his frustration at the debtor states "welshing on their debts": "I take it, that our debtors have no intention of paying. One of the troubles with this war debt subject is exactly that which Mark Twain said was involved with respect to New England weather, namely, 'Everybody talks about it and nobody does anything about it.'"[66] He chastised the United Kingdom and France for having the audacity to attempt to induce the United States into joining another war and celebrated the Johnson Act as "accomplishing as much, if not more, to preserve the peace of the world than all the League of Nations has ever done" by starving Europe of U.S. supplies.[67] These strong and popular feelings in Congress help to explain why Roosevelt informed Lindsay on 27 May 1937 that now was not the moment to settle the war-debts question. The president nevertheless wanted the debts out of the way before 1940, which the ambassador considered "over sanguine."[68]

Delay would be welcomed on the other side of the Atlantic. On 28 May 1937, Neville Chamberlain replaced Baldwin as prime minister following the latter's retirement. A successful handling of a constitutional crisis concerning the abdication of Edward VIII provided a good opportunity to resign.[69] Chamberlain was wary of close cooperation with the United States and in no rush to resume payment.[70] On 15 June, Britain and the other European states' latest missed payments aroused considerable dissatisfaction in Congress. The Democratic senator Royal Copeland read approvingly from a short editorial in the *Washington Herald* relating to these unpaid debts. It suggested that the date be remembered as "Keep Out of War Day" and "seared into the national mind as a reminder that the debts of the last war still are unpaid and that the debts of future wars also never can be paid."[71] On the same day, the Republican senator Hamilton Fish also took the opportunity to ask the president directly what he was doing about the defaulted war debt. He proposed to "rise on every June 15 and every December 15 and ask the party in power what they are doing": "Why should we continue to be Santa Claus for the entire world?"[72] Fish was deeply unimpressed by Chamberlain's recent announcement that Britain had balanced its budget and enjoyed a surplus and that its financial house was the envy of the world. His conclusion that "they did not make any effort whatever to pay their debts" was greeted with applause from other members of Congress.[73]

In July 1937, Fisher informed the new chancellor of the exchequer, John Simon, that he thought the question of war-debt settlement might be reopened to gain influence on U.S. opinion. Second Secretary to the Treasury Richard Hopkins, however, advised the chancellor that it would be impossible to reconcile British public opinion to what would be acceptable to the Americans, namely, the reinstitution of large and regular payments to the United States. Simon, after consulting Chamberlain, accepted Hopkins's opinion.[74] The unsettled status of the war debts was therefore left to fester on both sides of the Atlantic.[75]

PAYING FOR REARMAMENT

By early 1938, the British government had become increasingly focused on improving the pace of preparations for war. The prime minister had heeded HM Treasury's warning that rapid rearmament could undermine and destroy "existing economic and social structures" and accepted that it must be carried out at a manageable pace.[76] After the Anschluss of Germany and Austria was formalized in March, however, Chamberlain told the cabinet that the appropriate response to Hitler's insatiable appetite was to accelerate rearmament, regardless of its broader economic cost.[77] Access to U.S. credit was now crucial, but unpaid debts continued to make cooperation challenging. "The impediment," as George Peden explains, "was American public opinion," reflecting in part the memory of unpaid debts, which explains why the Foreign Office consequently "kept a careful watch for signs that American resentment over default on war debts was easing."[78]

The U.S. press repeatedly claimed that there was a growing anxiety in London to settle the war-debts question, largely so that the British government would be "in a position to borrow again when the next war comes."[79] In May, the BLI reported that "war debts continue, like a grumbling appendix, to obtrude themselves on the attention."[80] The United Kingdom's continuing suspension of payments may have appeared increasingly conspicuous in light of the efforts of other debtors. Finland had continued to make its payments to the United States, but Hungary made a token payment in June 1938.[81] In the same month, the Czechoslovakian government, which sorely needed access to war materials, seriously considered making a settlement offer.[82] Moreover, there were some signs of change in U.S. foreign lending practices. Following pressure from major industrial companies and growing national-security concerns, the United States had decided to make new loans to states that were in default on their private foreign debts. By relaxing what constituted "satisfactory" settlements on unpaid debts, it was able to lend financial support to the Chilean state railways, Brazil's railway company, and even the Haitian government by 1938.[83] As more states resumed war-debt payments and the U.S. began to lend to debtors again, it may have appeared like a good opportunity for the British government to reconsider its own position on the matter.

Yet the prime minister rejected a proposal to establish a U.S.-UK committee on war debts, with a view to discovering areas of agreement, doubting that it would serve any useful purpose or be welcomed by the U.S. government.[84] Doing nothing not only saved considerable sums of money but also appeared to be working well. According to a sample poll carried out by the Institute of Public Opinion in March, there had been a significant change in public sentiment in the United States, with fewer than half of respondents seeking collection of debt in full and a rise in those seeking a reduction.[85] Furthermore, in that same month, there began long and difficult talks surrounding an Anglo-American Trade Agreement—which sought to craft a more liberal world economy by reducing U.S. tariffs by up to 50 percent on imports from states that would lower their tariffs against U.S. goods—that continued throughout the year, despite ongoing difficulties surrounding war debts.[86]

In late June, senior British Treasury officials concluded that despite claims that a clear statement on the war-debt question would secure the goodwill of American people, "the best thing in the interests of

Anglo-American relations is to keep the matter as quiet as possible."[87] As Lindsay informed Lord Halifax on 11 July 1938, lying low remained sensible. Even if Roosevelt won the next election, the ambassador remained skeptical about hopes for a settlement. Lindsay "could not help remembering a remark . . . just after the smashing Democratic victory of 1936, to the effect that the President's prestige was so high that he could have anything he wanted from Congress, except a settlement of the war debt."[88] The congressional elections later that year resulted in a remarkable political comeback for the Republican Party, meaning that any softening on the war-debts issue was unlikely.[89] Furthermore, much of the U.S. press remained suspicious of British intentions. Various papers had suggested that the United Kingdom was now so eager for U.S. cooperation in war that the alleged taboo on speaking about the debt had been lifted in the British press and in Parliament.[90]

There was some truth to these claims. The British government remained ill disposed to discussing the matter publicly but nevertheless accepted the need to occasionally defend its position to the United States. On 14 July, Lord Samuel decided to raise the question of war debts on the third reading of the Finance Bill in the House of Lords. Considering recent U.S. press and Hungary's latest offer, he sought to emphasize that the British government had not repudiated the debt and was willing to reopen discussions on the subject. The prime minister subsequently approved these efforts. He reasoned that "it may be well to contradict the suggestions sometimes made that H.M. Government fail to recognise the great importance of this question or that the Debt has been repudiated: such suggestions are entirely unfounded."[91] He was sure to emphasize, however, the importance of historical context. The United Kingdom was a net creditor in the Great War, and any resumption of payment had to be understood in relation to intergovernmental debts and the stability in international exchanges.[92]

On 21 July 1938, Samuel informed the Lords that any "additional burden" to the budget would not just be "unpropitious" but "impossible."[93] He raised the subject, however, to prevent the idea arising in the United Kingdom and in the United States that "this question of the British debt to America is a closed chapter of history" and stressed that states should honor their signatures.[94] Samuel conceded several familiar U.S. criticisms, including doubts about the relevance of Britain's own unpaid war debts to the debate on payment: "The Americans lent this money to us and not our Allies." As he explained, "Often a man will plead, when he is called upon to honour an obligation that he has undertaken on account of a friend, 'When I backed my friend's bill I never for a moment expected he would not pay.' But that is no answer. The money was lent to the friend for the very reason that he backed the bill, and we are in precisely that position vis-a-vis the obligations of the continent of Europe."[95] He also noted that it was "not nice" when Mexico—which had recently expropriated assets from foreign oil companies and subsequently faced demands for annuities to affected shareholders—had excused its own behavior by noting the United Kingdom's failure to honor its obligations.[96] There followed a lengthy discussion of the issue. Lord Snell also saw the debts as a problem and noted, "There is always a danger of clouds gathering on the horizon, and it may be dangerous to continue to encourage the belief in the mind of the average Briton that this is a closed chapter. . . . The time is overdue when this most difficult problem should be discussed with the American government."[97]

British interest in the war debts continued to grow following a serious deterioration in European security. The Munich Agreement of September, in which the British government agreed that Germany could have the Sudetenland region of Czechoslovakia in return for peace, was a clear sign of danger.[98] As a signal of Western cooperation after the Munich Agreement, the Anglo-American Trade Agreement was signed on 19 November 1938, even if it was soon contradicted by the British government's decision to introduce wartime controls and ration dollars, thereby discriminating against U.S. exporters.[99] As the threat of war loomed large, senior figures within the Bank of England believed that this new trade agreement created a "psychological opportunity" to make a war-debt settlement, thereby removing British nonpayment "as an excuse for other defaults" and generating goodwill in the U.S., which was "absolutely essential" as a source of credit in any future war.[100] Lothian also warned Simon on 29 December 1938 that the debt question remained a "sore thumb" in the United States.[101] He now suggested a resumption of the token payment when the next half-yearly note arrived: "£4,000,000 p.a. won't break us or the exchanges, and though the first reaction . . . will be that we are paying for something merely in order to entangle the U.S.A. in our wars, the effect . . . would . . . be immense."[102]

Early in the new year, Simon explained that such a solution was unlikely to succeed because the United Kingdom would need to at least equal the Hungarian offer of £15 million a year: "[That] is more than this country could pay without the risk of upsetting the stability of the exchanges, and comparable settlements between us and our debtors on this basis would not seem to stand any chance of being acceptable to the debtors."[103] Furthermore, the chancellor stressed that the Johnson Act was expressly designed to stop token repayments and that there was no reason to believe sentiment in Congress had changed sufficiently. As such, "the less said about the debt the better."[104] Simon's position was well attuned to public sentiment in the United States. The *New Yorker* had already offered an amusing response to such proposals: "British peers now feel that their government should make a token payment on the United States debt so they can get us for an ally in the next war. In that case, we would gladly send them a couple of fellows as a token army."[105]

With war on the horizon, France decided to approach the United States.[106] In February 1939, it offered the resumption of war-debt payments, alongside territorial transfers, in exchange for funds for its rearmament program. Roosevelt rejected these proposals as "inopportune."[107] Many in the British government would have been relieved that these efforts had failed. On 5 April 1939, Lindsay provided Halifax with a summary of the situation. The United Kingdom's unpaid war debt had grown to $5.4 billion, with an annuity of $243 million running for forty-five years. "The debt as it stands," he concluded, "is completely unmanageable. . . . It is obvious that the effort to transfer such vast amounts, year in year out, must infallibly disrupt all exchanges in a very short space of time."[108]

Yet the potential imminence of war kept the issue of unpaid debts alive. Nazi Germany's invasion and occupation of Czechoslovakia in contravention of the Munich Agreement in March and the subsequent decision by the British government to issue a statement guaranteeing Poland's independence encouraged renewed interest in the war debts in the United States. Some members of Congress had begun to more seriously consider the possibility of territorial concessions—most likely in Central America and the Caribbean—in exchange for a remission of the war debt.[109] Lindsay informed Halifax that the possibility of sharing islands and territories presently in British hands could become an important factor in addressing the war-debt issue if war occurred.[110]

The Foreign Office and the Admiralty considered ceding territory to the United States, especially West Indian territory of limited strategic importance, in exchange for significant reductions or complete cancellation. These ideas were not new and had occurred prior to default in March 1934—when MacDonald assured Parliament MPs that "there could under no circumstances be any question of such an arrangement" because colonial territories were "not property to be bartered or sold"—but thereafter assumed greater attention as the likelihood of war increased.[111] The British government, however, never changed its position. Although the Foreign Office remained supportive, the Colonial Office and Treasury remained deeply opposed.[112]

Much of the U.S. government and army were also opposed to the acquisition of additional territory, fearing accusations of "Yankee imperialism" and tensions with Roosevelt's "Good Neighbor" policies.[113] In private discussions, the president reportedly rejected the proposal, stating only that he did not want to limit British rearmament efforts.[114] Furthermore, much of Congress remained wary about agreements that could release states from the restrictions of the Johnson Act, thereby potentially drawing the United States into another war or allowing the creation of more debt to finance future conflicts. Congress thus refused all requests for settlement, including Hungary's recent proposal, for fear of establishing a dangerous or costly precedent. In April, a debate had taken place in the Senate in which the war debts came to the fore. The proposal to reopen the debate was rejected by forty-eight votes to eighteen.[115]

Later that month, the Republican senator William Borah drew attention to an editorial in the *Saturday Evening Post* that decried Britain's stance on the war debts and the "serpents-tooth rhetoric" of its politicians.[116] Similar views were expressed by Fish, who compared Hoover's and Roosevelt's efforts on the war debts and asked why only the former had managed to receive any payments.[117] The Republican senator Dewey Short also wondered why any American should even "contemplate forming an alliance with those people who have shown their gratitude and appreciation by pointing at us a finger of scorn and calling us Shylocks when we try to collect?" Both senators' questions were greeted with applause.[118]

On 19 June 1939, the new British ambassador to the United States, Lord Lothian, wrote to Simon to gain a better understanding of existing views of the war-debts problem before meeting with Roosevelt.[119] At the end of the month, in preparation for this meeting, there emerged a brief note explaining why Congress was unlikely to change its mind: "In fact many of the Isolationists in Congress at present are only too glad to keep the debts alive and in default because they provide an argument against American participation in any future war." Furthermore, as the note continued, "Token payments would not free us from the provisions of the Johnson Act. . . . They would, if we began making them, certainly be represented as an attempt to embroil the United States in the next European war and might well exacerbate isolationist feeling." In addition, there were significant costs involved: "Such payments would pro tonto increase our losses of gold and the inflow of gold into America, a result which would be unpopular with both parties. . . . It seems clear that it is better to do nothing whatever at the present stage."[120] The note concluded that it was "improbable" that Britain would "be able to borrow in the United States in war time": "Our only methods of financing our imports from the United States will be by the sale of gold and securities."[121] The expected duration of the war and the country's limited financial reserves were therefore problematic: "It will be seen that the situation is serious."[122]

The prospects of U.S. financial support for the United Kingdom looked bleak when examining events in Washington in June 1939. The *Congressional Record* was littered with critical references on both sides of the aisle to the unpaid debts of the United Kingdom and the other states of Europe; many of these statements were greeted with applause.[123] As the Democratic representative Edwin Schaffer explained, "If our foreign, welching debtor nations have the cash to buy arms, munitions, implements of war, and war supplies for future wars, let them use that cash to pay us what they owe."[124] The Democratic senator Robert Reynolds took the opportunity to remind his peers that another "semi-annual blackletter day" was coming and suggested that the Senate start "talk about collecting a few billion dollars in behalf of the American taxpayer": "If these war debts were to be collected, a lot of our economic ailments could be cured almost instantly."[125] Reynolds also took the opportunity to introduce a resolution creating a special envoy for the collection of these debts, which would receive widespread support, as a way to combat European efforts "to defraud Uncle Sam" and defend the United States' reputation against criticisms that it was "a gullible nation."[126] These excerpts from the *Congressional Record* capture the seriousness of Britain's unpaid war debts to many U.S. policymakers, some of whom appeared much more interested in outstanding loans than in current events in Europe.

On 30 June 1939, Roosevelt met with Lindsay to ask if the United States could lease base facilities in Bermuda, St. Lucia, and Trinidad to support its efforts to defend the western Atlantic. The British government eventually accepted this attractive request—it was a boon to transatlantic relations and allowed more warships for use in the Mediterranean or Pacific—and began arrangements for the use of facilities in July. Lindsay believed that this agreement might serve as a "half-way house" to eventual cession, which could itself help to return war-debt negotiations "into the field of practical politics."[127] Yet the leaders of both governments still disliked the idea of cession. Chamberlain argued that the political "storm" created by cession would have been so great that "no British Government could survive it."[128] Furthermore, as the prime minister rightly understood, the noninterventionist mood in the U.S. meant that many members of Congress preferred to keep European debts unpaid to prevent further loans.[129] The subject of cession was repeatedly raised in Congress, to be sure, but it went nowhere.[130] The U.S. government was far more interested in controlling rather than owning these European colonies and all their inhabitants. As Roosevelt later remarked, "If we can get our naval bases why, for example, should we buy with them two million headaches?"[131] Talks would continue until an agreement was reached two years later.[132]

CASH AND CARRY

By summer 1939, HM Treasury feared the "imminent collapse of the nation's economy."[133] A note for the cabinet on the financial situation summarized the situation as of July: "To-day under the Johnson Act we cannot borrow. . . . Unless, when the time comes the United States are prepared either to lend or to give us money as required, the prospects for a long war are becoming exceedingly grim."[134] HM Treasury believed that claims that gold reserves would barely last three years were optimistic and, moreover, feared that the limits of taxation appeared to have been reached with regard to the additional sums needed for rearmament.[135]

Access to external credit was by now critical. As Peden puts it, "Once more, as in the First World War, dependence upon American economic power would be necessary for victory."[136] Yet British default had done little to signal to many people in the United States that it was a reliable partner, consequently helping to limit transatlantic economic and military cooperation.[137] Just as Britain needed more external support, it had become increasingly difficult to secure. The United States' reluctance to involve itself in European affairs is well documented. Both houses of Congress were ardently opposed to U.S. intervention in 1939, but the stronghold of noninterventionism was the Senate, where a handful of members held the whip in foreign affairs, including Borah, Johnson, and Nye.[138] U.S. opposition to foreign lending remained immovable and largely unresponsive to international events. An important part of the reason for this resistance was the impact of European default only five years earlier. As Lynne Olson explains, adherents to isolationism pointed to unpaid war loans in debates across the U.S.[139]

In April 1939, Gallup polls revealed that only 21 percent of Americans believed that their government should amend the Johnson Act to lend money to the United Kingdom and France in case of war. Of particular interest were comments that "showed keen scepticism as to whether the money would ever be repaid if lent, a Yankee shrewdness that would not permit the U.S. to be duped a second time into throwing dollars toward a supposedly idealistic goal."[140] By the end of the year, and after four months of fighting, only 11 percent favored repeal of the Johnson Act. While an overwhelming majority of the U.S. public wanted the Allies to win the war, they were determined to remain neutral, especially to those who had not paid their debts.[141] Public resistance to financial cooperation helps to explain why Lothian's position as the British ambassador to the United States was to prove so challenging.[142]

On 4 September 1939, the day after the British government declared war on Germany, Secretary of the Treasury Henry Morgenthau asked the British and French ambassadors if they might be willing to dispose of the *Queen Mary* and the *Normandie* to the United States as payment toward the war debts. The administration swiftly disowned the idea before it could be rejected, but the British ambassador was clear that it would not create a favorable impression on U.S. public opinion. It would appear as an obvious maneuver to influence the neutrality debate, and British public opinion could not be bought to agree to abandon something of which it was extremely proud.[143] Self has argued that this suggestion was "a remarkable example of self-interested debt recovery" that "highlighted the threat posed by the Johnson Act."[144]

Such behavior appears to challenge claims that U.S. leaders did not exploit the potential leverage created by British dependence on the United States.[145] Yet it is worth noting that the United Kingdom could behave in a similarly rough manner in negotiations with its own debtors and do so without any such legal restrictions in place. In 1939, for instance, the British government extracted an onerous schedule of overseas debt repayments from New Zealand's Prime Minister Walter Nash to ensure that his government could roll over maturing debt and avoid default to external creditors. If war had not been on the horizon, thereby making relations with the dominions especially important, it is doubtful that the British government would have been willing to help at all.[146]

Cooperation between the United Kingdom and the United States had improved, even if financial support remained off the table. At a special session of Congress in September, Roosevelt sought the revision of the Neutrality Act of 1936 to allow the sale of war material to belligerents, if the recipients arranged for the transport using their own ships and paid immediately in cash, thereby transferring all risk in transportation. The Senate and the House had rejected the proposed bill earlier in the year due in large part to concerns about being drawn into European affairs. The bill passed in late October, following Germany's invasion of Poland in September and the sudden outbreak of war in Europe. Weeks of congressional debate revealed growing sympathy for the United Kingdom and the Allies. Criticisms had persisted, however, with many members of Congress expressing concerns that the proposal was a British scheme to place U.S. economic interests at the disposal of the Allied powers and ultimately draw the U.S. into war.[147] The president gave the "Cash and Carry" bill his signature on 5 November.[148] Bans on loans and U.S. transport of materials nevertheless remained in effect.[149] Morgenthau noted in his diaries that the Senate still resisted any effort to advance a loan or credit to a belligerent in late 1939.[150]

Europe's unpaid war debts were central to congressional resistance in this period, especially in the weeks preceding signature. Calls for a semiannual black-letter day and a special envoy for the collection of these debts resurfaced once again.[151] Senator Ernest Lundeen evoked Washington, Jefferson, and Jackson to support Borah's call for spirited public discussion of the unpaid war debts while the king and queen of Great Britain visited the United States.[152] Reynolds, with support from the Democrat Scott Lucas, went on to suggest that the United Kingdom had ample gold to make these payments, as evidenced by British loans to various other countries around the world and the government's decision to spend billions on armaments. Indeed, "the temerity of England" in advancing multimillion-dollar credits to Turkey in the preceding eighteen months, "less than 2 weeks before the semi-annual payment, . . . is beyond the bounds of adequate condemnation."[153] If the British government refused to pay its war debts, he argued, the U.S. could seize properties: "[if we] let the British governmental representatives know that we meant business, in the fix that they are now in they would not dare deny payment."[154]

Members of the House of Representatives were also resistant to cooperation. The Democratic representative James McGranery and the Republican representative Roy Woodruff recalled that the rewards for financial aid in the First World War had been "gross insults," "flagrant, and in some cases abusive, ingratitude," culminating in cries of "Uncle Shylock."[155] The progressive representative Merlin Hull warned of the risks of repealing the act and the possibility of "economic collapse which would seriously endanger our Government structure."[156] The Democratic representative Edwin Schaefer also opposed the repeal of the arms embargo: "It is about time that we move to collect the billions of dollars which foreign governments owe us instead of continuing to play Santa Claus to them. . . . If they do not [pay], we should . . . let the New Deal devote its foreclosure and collection energies and activities to collecting the many billions of dollars which foreign nations now owe."[157] The Republican representative Dewy Short warned, "The only thing we could get out of another conflict would be deeper debts, longer depressions, higher taxes, and more graveyards. We burned our hands once; should we be so silly as to rush back into the fire?"[158]

Much of Congress evidently still bristled at the thought of further lending when existing debts remained unpaid. These political and economic concerns help to explain why, even after the war began and the passage of Cash and Carry, the U.S. government was still sending half-yearly reminders to the United Kingdom about its war debts. The British response to these notes remained the same—namely, that it was "willing to reopen discussions . . . whenever circumstances are such as to warrant the hope that a satisfactory result might be achieved."[159] Britain's unpaid war debts evidently strained transatlantic relations and helped to limit financial support. Many Americans and much of Congress supported the United Kingdom and respected its crucial opposition to German expansion. Yet advocates of closer cooperation would struggle to defend fresh loans in the wake of billions of dollars of outstanding debt, especially in the context of widespread noninterventionist sentiment. It remains an intriguing counterfactual as to how far resuming payment—or having never defaulted in the first place—would have improved access to more credit on better terms.

Default certainly harmed relations between the states, but the rewards of a resumption of payments may still have been limited.[160] The U.S. government gave little credit to the Hungarian government for its resumption of token payments, which suggests that British efforts short of full repayment may not have been especially helpful at that time.[161] Even full and continued payment may not have been enough, as evidenced by the experience of the Finnish government, which had continued to honor its debt obligations. Roosevelt denounced the Soviet invasion of Finland on 30 November 1939 and placed its annual debt installment in a separate account, extended the Finns $10 million in credit to buy agricultural supplies, and applied a moral embargo against the Soviet Union. Finland's continuing repayment of its war debts had generated great approval in the United States, and a special ceremony celebrating these efforts was held and filmed in Washington in December.[162] Yet Roosevelt refused to antagonize Congress by asking for an unrestricted loan that Finland could use to buy urgently needed arms in Sweden or additional credits that would have been necessary to cover Finland's financial requirements. The president remained cautious of involvement in European wars and feared that Congress might suspect that he intended to make a similar effort toward France and the United Kingdom. As Senator Johnson put it, "I would go [to] any length to show my appreciation of what they do and what they have done, but I want to be very certain before I do it that this is not to be taken as a precedent."[163] Roosevelt thus left full responsibility in this case to Congress, which was indisposed to help.[164] When the Democratic senator Prentiss Brown filed a bill that would authorize a $60 million loan to the Finnish government to buy arms, Congress amended the measure to the extent that it no longer mentioned Finland and provided only another $20 million credit for nonmilitary supplies. As other historians have noted wryly, the Finns, by capturing Russian arms on the battlefield, received more military aid from the Soviet Union than from the United States.[165]

To be sure, the British government had borrowed—and defaulted on—much larger amounts to the United States than had any other state. The two countries also enjoyed a much closer political, strategic, and cultural relationship than Finland or Hungary did with the United States. Steady repayment could therefore have had a more significant impact on their relationship, generating more support in Congress and improving the terms of borrowing, even despite strong support for neutrality.[166] Keynes certainly believed that it was Britain's unpaid debts rather than U.S. neutrality that obstructed financial assistance.[167] Yet, as evidenced in the case of Finland, the provision of financial assistance by the United States to the United Kingdom may still have been disappointing, at least initially, given the wider political climate. Whether it was therefore an appropriate strategy to suspend payments remains difficult to determine. Such an assessment would depend on whether British policymakers believed that the actual costs of repayment outweighed the potential rewards. As the preceding years had shown, successive prime ministers and chancellors had been understandably wary of resuming such costly payments in exchange for what they felt to be largely uncertain rewards.

In the absence of more generous lending, the United Kingdom was now reliant on a U.S. policy of "Cash and Carry" limiting British purchases to a cash basis. There followed a rise in dollar expenditures. A financial crisis swiftly developed, which was not resolved until the Lend-Lease Act. The idea of the U.S. government or U.S. firms accepting sterling in lieu of dollars, an arrangement that the Canadians had made in the form of a "sterling overdraft," was never seriously discussed within the Roosevelt administration.[168] This decision reflected enduring assumptions about British opulence and lingering distrust. As Roosevelt had previously admitted to Morgenthau, "The trouble is that when you sit around the table with a Britisher he usually gets

80 percent of the deal and you get what is left."[169] Furthermore, such terms presented an opportunity to drive a hard bargain elsewhere. With an Anglo-American Trade Agreement under negotiation, the U.S. was keen to open the prize of Britain's empire to healthy competition.[170]

The terms of the Cash and Carry scheme also avoided the dangers of war loans to Europe that the United States so well remembered. A Gallup poll published in November 1939 had found that on this subject, the public "bear Europe an unforgettable grudge, more emotional than intelligent, but clear cut enough to be influential."[171] A British survey of U.S. press and radio two months later concluded that the subject of war debts was "still capable of arousing a mass emotion," with many papers expressing a preference for the Cash and Carry scheme over "the old method which led to such unfortunate economic aftermath."[172]

The idea of payment by territory remained popular in both syndicated editorials and in national polls: 66 percent of the U.S. public would have liked to see debts exchanged for islands.[173] Reflective of the mood at that time, Senator Lundeen—later revealed as a National Socialist agent and imprisoned following a violation of the Foreign Agents Registration Act—ostensibly formed a "Make Europe Pay War Debts" committee in early December 1939.[174] The true creator of the committee was George Viereck, Nazi Germany's chief publicist in the United States, who used German money to fund this anti-British group. Viereck cultivated isolationist members in Congress, including Fish and Lundeen, and helped the German war effort by buying reprints of their speeches and mailing them to hundreds of thousands of Americans.[175]

In January 1940, the British pushed their own propaganda. Lord Beaverbrook, publisher of the largest-circulation newspaper in the world, produced an article for his *Daily Express* titled, "We Hired the Money—They Hired the Soldiers."[176] The article sought to convince the United States of the unfairness of these outstanding war debts but only generated widespread criticism after being reprinted in the *New York Times*.[177] Paul Mallon, a widely syndicated Washington columnist, suspected the piece to be "the beginning of a campaign to circumvent the Johnson Act; but no one around here seems to be leaning that way."[178] Halifax had warned Beaverbrook against publishing such a story, stressing Americans' resistance to propaganda given an "intense fear of being inveigled into war."[179] HM Treasury officials also described it as "most ill-advised."[180] The British government was keen to dissociate itself from the article, renewing its commitment to a low prolife on the matter, recognizing that "the war debt question persists as an irritation to the U.S.A."[181] The Foreign Office was deeply unimpressed, criticizing a "lack of understanding" by those who were raising the issue and noting that "it seems to have been forgotten . . . that not merely in 1917, but again in 1923, Great Britain firmly pledged its word to repay the debt in full."[182] It was "no good" to argue about war debts at this stage, and the government was keen to stop debate on the subject.[183]

In April 1940, HM Treasury responded to fresh calls to start negotiations for a settlement on war debts by means of a token payment. It conceded that the government "clearly have not dollars available to make a token payment" and that public discussion of the matter was now embarrassing for both states.[184] Senior officials believed that the president remained reluctant to bring up the issue and that congressional resistance was still likely to be strong. The Foreign Office was in full agreement, believing that a token payment would "almost certainly do more harm than good."[185] Halifax also accepted the importance of maintaining a low profile. In a note on 6 July, he argued instead that U.S. views "depend not so much on the attitude of Americans to war debts but their view that [Britain's] ability to defeat the Nazi regime is conditional upon their granting [Britain] the necessary facilities . . . to win the war." As such, it would do Britain "much more harm than good" to raise the issue of war debts now.[186]

Such views appear largely accurate. Although the Roosevelt administration expressed its eagerness to provide financial support to the United Kingdom, it faced stiff opposition from both congressional and public attitudes that remained unreceptive to cooperation.[187] Senior figures in both houses of Congress continued to express anger toward these unpaid war debts throughout the first half of 1940, evidenced by growing support for the "Make Europe Pay War Debts Committee" and members' introduction of a resolution seeking the acquisition of certain British islands in the Caribbean and British Honduras to liquidate some of the outstanding war debt.[188] Over the summer, Johnson took the opportunity in Congress to reiterate his staunch opposition to forgiving European states for the "contemptuous disregard of their plighted obligations."[189]

For the United States, the fall of France on 25 June 1940 came as a shock.[190] The issue of its outstanding war debts was left unsettled. As Marvin Zahniser rightly notes, "France never developed the political will to resolve the debt problems to US satisfaction until she was facing the cocked gun of the German. By then it was too late."[191] Following the rout of British land forces at Dunkirk, followed by Nazi gains in northern and western Europe, the United Kingdom now faced a daunting German threat without the aid of another major power. In July, HM Treasury representative Frederick Phillips traveled from London to Washington to explain that the United Kingdom would require "massive assistance" from the United States within a year. According to Self, Phillips was under pressure to discuss a settlement on the war debts from those who were seeking to borrow from the U.S. market.[192] When discussing Britain's financial needs, Phillips projected a net balance of payments deficit of £400 million ($1.6 billion) by June 1941, contrasting with British reserves of only £375 million ($1.5 billion).[193] Roosevelt was sympathetic but offered no firm commitment to help. The president still believed that the British held considerable wealth, despite mounting evidence to the contrary, not least from the Commerce Department and the Federal Reserve Bank. The approaching presidential election and the unpopularity of the subject helped to slow any progress to address the looming financial crisis.[194]

Fear of a German invasion across the English Channel over the summer of 1940 led the British government to purchase more war materials in the United States at a quicker rate. As the United Kingdom's exporting capacity deteriorated, it had to cover imports from the United States by selling U.S. securities and transferring gold, which was unsustainable. HM Treasury believed that it lacked dollar reserves to sustain Cash and Carry purchasing. By the end of the year, British reserves would be "virtually exhausted," and new liabilities were accumulating "at a frightening rate."[195] These burdens were exacerbated by the liquidation of over $1.5 billion of overseas assets and the deterioration of Britain's international trade position brought about by the war. Lothian consequently predicted that the looming crisis would revive debate surrounding the Johnson Act, which would raise "many fierce memories, [including] war debts."[196]

Despite such desperate circumstances, the British government chose not to tackle this challenge head-on. Reopening the issue of unpaid war debts could have offered a way in which to improve the United Kingdom's standing in the United States, especially when few alternatives were available. Yet a note by the Foreign Office titled, "British War Debts to the United States," produced on 2 August 1940, helps to explain the British government's position: "we cannot pay our debt substantially in full even if we would."[197] Payment in gold, dollar securities, or excess of exports to the United States over imports was simply too difficult in the present situation. As Keynes later put it, Britain was already "scraping the bottom of the box."[198] Although the British government could have theoretically surrendered some colonial possessions, the Roosevelt administration and much of the U.S. government had little interest in taking them. Indeed, both sides reached agreement on the Destroyers for Bases Agreement on 2 September without the protracted and difficult nature of a takeover of British Caribbean possessions.[199] The idea of cession rumbled on, to be sure, generating further discussion in Congress and remaining popular in U.S. opinion polls, but neither government seriously attempted to progress the issue.[200]

According to a note produced by the Foreign Office, the only solution left was cancellation, which remained unlikely given that these debts had "become a part of the American national tradition."[201] The note conceded, "Very possibly the debt will never be settled, it will just lose its importance; as in the case of the unsettled debts still owing to us by the Southern confederation. . . . [Nevertheless] the war debt remains for an indefinite period as a source of irritation between the two countries."[202] As such, "by far our wisest course, it would appear, is to initiate no action or discussion of any kind on the subject of war debts."[203]

In October 1940, HM Treasury, including Keynes and Thomas Catto, who had recently become a director of the Bank of England and would become governor four years later, had begun to produce papers about approaching the United States for financial aid, all of which recognized the problem and popularity of the Johnson Act.[204] Yet few viable options existed for regaining access to U.S. credit. The British government therefore continued to avoid any talk of a settlement as it received its semiannual reminder about war debts from the United States on 7 December 1940.[205] As normal, it acknowledged receipt of the note and provided the standard response.[206]

LEND-LEASE

On 9 October 1940, Winston Churchill assumed the premiership following Neville Chamberlain's resignation. The new prime minister held out hope for closer financial links between the United Kingdom and the United States.[207] On 5 November, Roosevelt won a third term. The U.S. embassy in London reported that the London financial district now assumed that financial credits for the United Kingdom would naturally follow.[208] Roosevelt was certainly sympathetic to Britain's plight, especially given the untimely end of the Anglo-French front, but expectations of immediate and unqualified financial assistance were unfounded.

On 23 November, Lothian allegedly informed reporters in New York, "Well boys, Britain's broke; it's your money we want."[209] Although it is questionable that he ever used these words or that he did so with the permission of the government, his announcement established Britain's immediate financial needs and prepared the way for a letter from Churchill to Roosevelt.[210] The president and his key advisers had already begun to consider the dilemma of how to relieve Britain's dollar problem.[211] Yet Lothian's "calculated indiscretion" annoyed more than it surprised; Morgenthau and Roosevelt feared that it would antagonize Congress.[212] Any suggestion of a loan was unlikely to pass through Congress given lingering resentment over war debts, suspicion of Britain, and worries about foreign entanglements.[213]

Lothian's words challenged some of Roosevelt's doubts, especially about the seriousness of Britain's financial and dollar situation, and helped the White House into action.[214] This turnabout is evidenced in early December, both in Roosevelt's sudden encouragement to the British government to place orders exceeding $2 billion for which it could not pay and in Morgenthau's admission to key officials that the president required a solution to Britain's financial difficulties.[215] Roosevelt nevertheless faced a strong and vocal body of noninterventionism in the U.S. coupled with legal obstacles in the form of the Johnson and Neutrality Acts. Between 1939 and 1941, economic nationalists in the State Department had led efforts to repeal the Johnson Act, to be sure, but they had failed.[216] As such, direct aid to the United Kingdom, paid for by the United States, remained impossible.

Lingering memories of unpaid debts haunted policymaking in both states. On 6 December, London received its semiannual reminder note about outstanding war debts from Washington.[217] As government officials noted, "The situation has become rather farcical, but I think the least ridiculous thing is to send the usual reply."[218] Only two months earlier, Keynes had warned Phillips of the need to secure U.S. financing of British military purchases in the United States via grants rather than loans. As Keynes explained, Britain could not once again bear "the dishonour and the reproaches of default."[219]

On 8 December, following weeks of preparation, Churchill produced a letter for Roosevelt detailing the United Kingdom's financial difficulties. The prime minister had been reluctant initially, but Lothian convinced him; and over the course of several weeks, a draft was aided by feedback from the Treasury, the Admiralty, the Foreign Office, the Chiefs of Staff, and the War Cabinet.[220] It was an open and detailed letter that compelled action: "The moment approaches when we shall no longer be able to pay cash for shipping and other supplies. While we will do our utmost . . . I believe you will agree that it would be wrong in principle and mutually disadvantageous in effect, if at the height of this struggle, Great Britain were to be divested of all saleable assets."[221]

Upon returning from vacation, Roosevelt met with Morgenthau on 17 December. The president was keen to address Britain's imminent dollar crisis and suggested that he wanted to avoid loans and "get away from the dollar sign."[222] He instead proposed providing the United Kingdom with the required material, which it would return after the war.[223] This decision was motivated by many concerns but was clearly informed by the United Kingdom's unpaid debts. As Hull explained, "A loan to Britain was not the best method. We were still sending Britain the semi-annual demands for payment of instalments on the war debt for the previous war. More loans would probably produce eventually the same ill feeling that resulted from Britain's non-payment of the remainder of her First World War debt."[224]

Later that day, Roosevelt talked to the press. The president argued that democracies needed to find nontraditional methods of support as the Axis was waging war without money. There was no need to repeal the Neutrality Act or the Johnson Act; nor was there the need for an outright gift to the British.[225] Roosevelt's solution was the U.S. wartime aid program known as "Lend-Lease," and he gave a speech to persuade the American people of the merits of his solution, based on "a selfish point of view": "the best immediate defense of the United States is the success of Great Britain in defending itself."[226] He went on to justify his method by drawing an analogy of a neighbor fighting a fire. It was in the interest of the home owner to lend his neighbor a garden hose and think about repayment later.[227]

Robert Skidelsky calls this decision "the most adventurous political coup of Roosevelt's presidency, . . . breaking with the whole American tradition of making loans on business terms."[228] The president insisted that he was not seeking to repeal the Neutrality Act but wanted to circumvent its anti-loan provisions and to avoid the war debts that had poisoned Anglo-American relations in the 1920s and 1930s.[229] Lend-Lease certainly was a remarkable innovation. As Self explains, "Roosevelt had effectively created a new mechanism capable of avoiding the disastrous repetition of the network of inter-governmental indebtedness which had bedevilled international relations."[230] The U.S. ambassador to Britain Joseph Kennedy informed Hull two days later that Roosevelt's speech was "universally praised" in the United Kingdom. He noted that *The Times'* long editorial on the subject "points out that America realises that loans on the scale needed would simply create difficulties after this war similar to those which helped to wreck the world after the last war."[231] It continued that "there will be relief that at the end of the war the 'world may be spared the nightmare of unpayable war debts.'" The day's cartoons, he noted, "present the President as Santa Claus."[232]

The passage of the Lend-Lease bill, HR 1776, was often challenging, requiring considerable debate, backroom dealings, and amendment. There were also tensions within the administration. Hull and the State Department demanded that the United Kingdom repay Lend-Lease aid and post collateral. Roosevelt rejected such proposals before the passage of the act.[233] Congressional hearings on Lend-Lease took place in mid-January 1941. Opponents hoped to stymie the measure. For more than two weeks, senators rose to deliver diatribes against Lend-Lease. Historians typically ascribe these difficulties to U.S. fears about being dragged into war or doubts about the value of such financial assistance to national interests. Unpaid debts and lingering resentment toward them also played an important role.[234] The CBS correspondent Eric Sevareid described the debate in Congress in mostly negative terms and noted the use of "the old, evil shibboleths," which included "the war debts, Uncle Sap, and decadent France."[235]

Many members of Congress raised the unhappy memory of the war debts to oppose HR 1776. The Democratic representative Martin

Sweeney explained, "What an ironic gesture to identify the lend-lease, give-away bill with 1776. . . . Our money, our blood saved Britain in the last World War and made possible her security as a world power. For that we received from the same officials, who are now begging us to once more save imperial Britain, the contemptible designation 'Uncle Shylock,' because we dared to remind our former ally of the huge war debt due this country."[236] The Republican representative John Robsion warned that the bill's wording would "repeal the neutrality law that Congress was urged to pass to keep this country out of war . . . [and] repeal the Johnson Act, that protects the United States Treasury from future raids by defaulting nations."[237]

The Republican representative Paul Shafer expressed sympathy for Britain but was greeted with applause when he warned of becoming "Uncle Sap": "It seems to me that England's attitude regarding her debts should be a sufficient lesson to us. We would be fools to be burned in the same place the second time. Almost a quarter of a century has passed since the World War and during those years England has persisted in her refusal to pay her debt to us. . . . Let us spend our money in preparing our own armed forces so that there can be no question in the future as to who is protecting who, and why."[238] The Democratic representative Knute Hill asked his colleagues, "[Have you] forgotten how the leaders of the British Empire pleaded on bended knees with us to come to their rescue in 1917 and how they repaid us by calling us 'Shylock'?"[239] Hill went on to conclude, "She [Britain] has untold assets here. Let her pay for whatever supplies we give her. Her leading statesman has denounced us as a Shylock in view of her failure to pay her World War debt, let us 'have the game as well as the name.'"[240]

Congressional debate also drew on the November issue of *Commentator* magazine, referencing an interview from the *New York Inquirer* in 1936, in which Churchill had discussed British war debts, allegedly stating, "Legally we owe the debt to United States but logically we don't because America should have minded [its] own business and outstayed World War."[241] Members of Congress had raised attention to this interview over the preceding two years, but it gained renewed interest during the Lend-Lease debate. Churchill denied the statement, a stance that led to a suit against him for slander in the courts of New York.[242] Churchill subsequently called it a "malicious lie," and the matter passed.[243] The Roosevelt administration felt it to be untrue. In response, following exchanges within the administration in February 1941, doubts grew about its accuracy: "In all probability, Mr Churchill never made any such remark."[244]

Lend-Lease passed in the House with a majority of 260 to 165. After the White House agreed to yet more amendments, a weary Senate approved legislation by a vote of 60 to 31 on 8 March 1941.[245] The bill came into law three days later. The difficult legislative process, which reflected in part unhappy memories of unpaid war debts, helps to explain why the outcome was what scholars have described as "deeply warped" from the original fire-hose analogy.[246] The final bill differed markedly from Roosevelt's initial proposal and ultimately required some form of "payment or repayment in kind or property."[247] For Kathleen Burk, "Lend-Lease aid was always to be paid for in some sort of coin."[248] As Benn Steil explains, U.S. representatives—including Morgenthau, Hull, and Treasury official Harry Dexter White—went on to use Lend-Lease "to press the British relentlessly for financial and trade concessions that would eliminate Britain as an economic and political rival in the postwar landscape."[249]

The very creation of Lend-Lease reflected the learning of economic lessons of the interwar period. Roosevelt had after all initiated this unusual approach to wartime assistance in part to avoid what he considered "the wretched business of war debts."[250] In contrast to the loans of the First World War, the United States would now allow the direct transfer of supplies and material to the United Kingdom without direct compensation. This novel form of economic cooperation was an ingenious solution to the significant legal and congressional barriers to traditional forms of lending, most notably the Johnson Act, which continued to prohibit loans to states such as the United Kingdom.[251] As Peter Clarke puts it, Roosevelt "jumped over the hurdles of ancient war debts by refusing to do the sums in the old fashioned way."[252]

Roosevelt and the U.S. Treasury Department officials who wrote the Lend-Lease Act left repayment clauses purposely vague to help avoid a repetition of the debt problems that had followed World War I.[253] As the future secretary of state Dean Acheson recalled in his memoirs, "Twenty years of painful experience with the war debts of 1914–18 had dictated an admirable opening provision."[254] Such views were widely held by the staff members who worked on the bill. According to John M. Leddy of the State Department, "the reason for Lend-Lease" was to avoid a system of onerous and divisive repayments from Britain to America, "as [the U.S.] did after World War I with the World War I debts—and everybody was conscious that that was a stupid thing."[255] The success of Lend-Lease and Mutual Aid, alongside the technique of foreign exchange accumulation in the form of sterling balances, explains why the United Kingdom borrowed much less money from the U.S. in the 1940s when compared to the Great War.[256]

Churchill later praised Lend-Lease as "the most unsordid act in the whole of recorded history."[257] In an unsent memo, the prime minister revealed his relief that these credits would be granted "without any real prospect of the debt being repaid or the debt from the last war being repaid."[258] Although Lend-Lease was greeted initially with joy and relief, the British government and its people would suffer a series of humiliations in the process of ratification. As Steil explains, they had to endure "the U.S. Treasury Secretary testifying on the depths of British penury and speculating on what little might remain to be picked off the empire's carcass in return for American support."[259] In response to congressional arguments that the British government was trying to fleece the United States, the White House demanded that the United Kingdom liquidate its most valuable industrial holdings in the U.S.—including, most notoriously, a textile company called American Viscose—to prove that it had exhausted all financial options. Viscose was then sold to a group of American bankers who promptly resold it for a higher price. Churchill was infuriated, describing himself as a helpless debtor.[260]

Although Lend-Lease solved Britain's longer-term financial problems during the war, its generosity was limited to orders that the United Kingdom would place after the act became law. The British government struggled to pay for preexisting orders and faced outright default or the stripping of more resources.[261] The U.S. led by Morgenthau pushed for significant sales of British securities and thus the further reduction of national reserves, which Keynes felt would place Britain in "an intolerable position": "without any reserves he [Morgenthau] can blackmail us at every turn."[262] This interim financial crisis between December 1940 and March 1941 ultimately necessitated additional sales of South African gold, the purchases of sterling by Canada, and a loan of $300 million in gold from Belgium.[263] It also required Keynes to secure a $425 million loan from the Reconstruction Finance Corporation (RFC), one of Roosevelt's New Deal agencies, which appeared to flout the Johnson Act but did secure congressional approval and bolstered British reserves.[264] Morgenthau and the U.S. Treasury eventually convinced Roosevelt to accept a solution to the interim finance problem in early 1941.[265]

On 28 June 1941, the British government received no half-yearly reminder about debts.[266] This milestone in the history of the war-debts saga had only become possible a month earlier when Hull had written to Morgenthau and advised, "under existing circumstances . . . it [was] undesirable to send notices to debtor governments now defending themselves against aggression, to some of which we are at present extending aid under the Lend[-]Lease Act."[267] This subtle shift in U.S. policy helps to explain why the British government now chose to stop recording what its wartime allies still owed to the United Kingdom, a figure that still exceeded its debts to the United States (Tables 4.1 and 4.2).[268] Retiring these reminder notices, however, was a far cry from the cancellation of the war debt itself. By the end of the year, Morgenthau had sent to Roosevelt a draft of a bill to cancel the indebtedness of the governments of Britain and Russia to the U.S. government that arose out of the First World War. On 2 January 1942, the president responded, "I am very much of two minds on it."[269]

The formal entry of the United States into the Second World War and the Lend-Lease agreement overshadowed but never resolved the issue of the United Kingdom's unpaid First World War debts. Only weeks earlier, on 8 December 1941, following the surprise attack on Pearl Harbor by Japanese forces, the United States had joined the Second World War and begun to mobilize its full economic and military power.[270] The military crisis in Asia resulted in a temporary suspension of negotiations on the master Lend-Lease document.[271] The British government hoped that talk of costs concerning Lend-Lease would be replaced by the rhetoric of mutual sacrifice for a common cause and the pooling of resources.[272] In February 1942, Churchill argued that three-fourths of the cabinet opposed making the elimination of imperial preference part of the Lend-Lease settlement. In response, the president denied that he had ever considered such a condition but nevertheless wanted "a bold, forthright, and comprehensive discussion" on the subject, leaving the British with little option but to accept in principle "the elimination of all forms of discriminatory treatment in international commerce."[273] Lend-Lease nevertheless remained a preferable alternative to wartime

Table 4.1. Indebtedness of foreign governments to the U.S. arising from World War I, 1941 (USD)

State	Total indebtedness (payments on principal deducted)	Total payments received	Funded indebtedness			
			Indebtedness		Payments on account	
			Principal (net)	Accrued interest	Principal	Interest
Armenia	24,999,095.85	0.00	0.00	0.00	0.00	0.00
Belgium	470,204,713.74	52,191,273.24	400,680,000.00	69,524,713.74	17,100,000.00	14,490,000.00
Cuba	0.00	12,286,751.58	0.00	0.00	0.00	0.00
Czechoslovakia	165,855,717.87[a]	20,134,092.26	165,241,108.90	614,608.97	19,829,914.17	0.00
Estonia	22,193,246.28[b]	1,248,432.07	16,466,012.87	5,727,233.41	0.00	1,246,990.19
Finland	8,413,044.53	6,050,689.77	8,039,601.83	373,442.70	960,398.17	4,780,976.33
France	4,297,758,632.70	486,075,891.00	3,863,650,000.00	434,108,632.70	161,350,000.00	38,650,000.00
Germany[c]	26,020,579.44[d]	862,668.00	25,980,480.66	40,098.78	862,668.00	0.00
Great Britain	5,805,850,288.81	2,024,848,817.09	4,368,000,000.00	1,437,850,288.81	232,000,000.00	1,232,770,518.42
Greece	35,337,865.42	4,127,056.01	31,516,000.00	3,821,865.42	981,000.00	1,983,980.00
Hungary	2,494,151.10[b]	537,263.44	1,908,560.00	585,591.10	73,995.50	462,514.90
Italy	2,032,082,255.48	100,829,880.16	2,004,900,000.00	27,182,255.48	37,100,000.00	5,766,708.26
Latvia	9,154,628.45[b]	761,549.07	6,879,464.20	2,275,164.25	9,200.00	621,520.12
Liberia	0.00	36,471.56	0.00	0.00	0.00	0.00

Lithuania	8,198,754.04[b]	1,237,956.58	6,197,682.00	2,001,072.04	234,783.00	1,001,626.61
Nicaragua[e]	0.00	168,575.84	0.00	0.00	0.00	0.00
Poland	277,731,410.31[b]	22,646,297.55	206,057,000.00	71,674,410.31	1,287,297.37	19,310,775.90
Rumania	67,654,695.39[a]	4,791,007.22[f]	63,860,560.43	3,794,134.96	2,700,000.00	29,061.46
Russia	414,252,222.20	8,750,311.88[g]	0.00	0.00	0.00	0.00
Yugoslavia	62,164,218.78	2,588,771.69	61,625,000.00	539,218.78	1,225,000.00	0.00
Total	13,730,365,520.39	2,750,173,756.01	11,231,001,470.89	2,060,112,731.45[b]	475,714,256.21	1,321,114,672.19

Source: U.S. Treasury Department, *Annual Report* (1941), 611, table 49, "Principal of the Funded and Unfunded Indebtedness of Foreign Governments to the United States, the Accrued and Unpaid Interest Thereon, and Payments on Account of Principal and Interest, as of Nov. 15, 1941."

Note: Due to space limitations, the final four columns ("Principal [net]," "Accrued interest," "Principal," and "Interest") under the heading of "Unfunded indebtedness" have been removed.

[a] Differences between principal of funded indebtedness and amounts here stated represent deferred payments provided for in the funding agreements, for which "bonds" of the respective debtor governments have been or will be delivered to the Treasury.

[b] Increase over amount funded due to exercise of options with respect to the payment of interest due on original issue of bonds of debtor governments.

[c] The German Government has been notified that the Government of the United States will look to the German Government for the discharge of this indebtedness of the Government of Austria to the Government of the United States.

[d] Includes additional bonds aggregating $3,489,482.75 received July 23, 1937, in exchange for bonds aggregating $1,207,742 and annuities aggregating $69,634.46, payable on Jan. 1, 1933, 1934, and 1935, but postponed as provided by agreements of May 8, 1930, and Sept. 14, 1932.

[e] The United States held obligations in the principal amount of $289,898.78, which together with accrued interest thereon, were canceled on Oct. 6, 1939, pursuant to agreement of Apr. 14, 1938, between the United States and the Republic of Nicaragua, ratified by the United States Senate on June 13, 1938.

[f] Does not include payment of $100,000 by Rumanian Government on June 15, 1940, which was made as "a token of its good faith and of its real desire to reach a new agreement covering" Rumania's indebtedness to the United States.

[g] Represents proceeds of liquidation of financial affairs of the Russian Government in this country. (Copies of letter dated May 23, 1922, from the Secretary of State and of reply of the Secretary of the Treasury dated June 2, 1922, in regard to loans to the Russian Government and liquidation of affairs of the latter in this country appear in the Annual Report of the Secretary of the Treasury for 1922, as exhibit 79, p. 283, and in the combined annual reports of the World War Foreign Debt Commission, as exhibit 2, p. 84.)

[h] Includes balances of amounts postponed under provisions of joint resolution of Dec. 23, 1931. (For amounts postponed, see p. 35 of Annual Report of the Secretary of the Treasury for 1932.)

Table 4.2. World War I debt: the balance, 1941

Country	GBP (millions)
France	756
Italy	253
Portugal	22
Belgium (inc. Belgian Congo)	13
Austria	9
Greece	22
	1,075
Romania	32
Yugoslavia	34
Poland	4
Estonia	1
Latvia	1
Czechoslovakia	—
Lithuania	—
Russia	1,691
Armenia	1
	1,766
Australia	80
New Zealand	26
Newfoundland	0
	106
Grand Total	£2,948/$11,800 (rounded)

Source: T 385/204, Binns to Morris, "World War I Debt: 'The Balance,'" 8 February 1974. This grand total conversion is based on the pegged value of the pound to the dollar, which stood at $4.03 in 1941.
Note: Figures in the second grouping total 1,764 but round to 1,766.

loans despite such concessions. As Roosevelt reminded Churchill at the end of his response, he had tried to approach the matter "in a manner that will not lead [the two countries] into the terrible pitfalls of the last war."[274]

The formal entry of the United States into the Second World War and the Lend-Lease agreement overshadowed but never resolved the issue of the United Kingdom's unpaid First World War debts. Many Americans retained a deep-seated resentment toward the debtor that had once again become a wartime ally. Congress was quick to point out the rising national debt and concerns about the costs of the war in Europe, which were significantly larger than for the one that had preceded it.[275] As a British embassy report for the Foreign Office noted in July 1942, many Americans believed that "Lend-Lease is stripping America to supply the British who have not even paid their [First World] war debts."[276] At the same time, Catto noted that the war-debts issue was "an open sore that continues to fester": "For the moment it may seem a thing of the past," he noted, "but someday, somehow it has to be got out of the way."[277] Part of the ongoing problem was identified by Keynes three months later. Anti-British feeling, he noted, "springs in part" from the feeling that "America is always the sucker."[278]

An important element of subsequent negotiations concerning the Lend-Lease master agreement was British concessions to the United States.[279] As Steil points out, U.S. demands reflected public and congressional resistance to foreign aid, premised on lingering beliefs about rearming "economic rivals" and resentment at those who had "shamefully walked away from their Great War debts."[280] Roosevelt only played a limited role in subsequent negotiations on specific terms, leaving others to fill in the gaps.[281] Hull and the State Department never accepted that the United Kingdom could be short of dollars while still maintaining vast colonial and economic interests and consequently drove a hard bargain. The use of Lend-Lease as a lever to commit Britain to eventually eliminate the imperial preference system was not openly discussed in the State Department prior to the passage of the Lend-Lease Act. Yet Hull's State Department quickly made up for lost time thereafter, especially when it replaced Morgenthau and the U.S. Treasury in handling the negotiations, ensuring that "Great Britain had to stand and deliver."[282] Keynes, like many of his British peers, had long been wary of allowing U.S. influence in British markets, thereby undermining the United Kingdom's means of repayment and "picking the eyes out of the British Empire."[283] He was nevertheless careful not to claim that the United States had exploited the United Kingdom's crisis, even if he believed it had.[284] The British government had little choice but to accept the terms offered by the United States.

5 New Loans and Old Debts, 1943–1951

MANY SCHOLARS AND policymakers assume that the Second World War settled the United Kingdom's unpaid war debts to the United States. Historians have tended to claim that the matter was "laid to rest" well before the end of the conflict.[1] Such views complement the work of economists and political scientists that largely downplayed the postwar consequences for states that defaulted in the 1930s.[2] Some Treasury officials on both sides of the Atlantic believed until recently that the economic agreements reached in this period effectively overcame the issue.[3]

Yet neither government proved able to resolve the problems surrounding these outstanding obligations, whether by payment or cancellation, despite the end of the Second World War and the onset of the Cold War. Throughout the 1940s, the United States persisted in recording the United Kingdom's First World War debts, which continued to grow as unpaid interest mounted.[4] Postwar presidents and prime ministers seldom dealt with the issue directly, but the politics of these war debts still gained the attention of their closest advisers and senior officials. Neglected archival materials, congressional records, and oral histories reveal that these outstanding obligations went on to play a significant role in two major postwar events in transatlantic economic and political history—namely, the rapid termination of Lend-Lease in 1945 and the creation of the Anglo-American Economic and Financial Agreement ratified in 1946.

The Second World War had, among many other challenges, generated a remarkable series of economic problems and a formidable debt burden for the British government.[5] The United Kingdom was not bankrupt, to be sure, but did face significant financial pressure.[6] A key challenge concerned the U.S. decision to end its wartime aid program, better known as Lend-Lease, on 21 August 1945.[7] The British government was confronted by what John Maynard Keynes termed a "financial Dunkirk."[8] President Harry Truman later referred to this decision as the greatest mistake of his presidency.[9] The United Kingdom's precarious economic situation necessitated urgent support that only the United States could provide.[10] There eventually followed an Anglo-American loan, which was a key element of the larger Anglo-American Financial and Commercial Agreement, that provided an interest-bearing loan to the United Kingdom of $3.75 billion and arranged a generous final settlement of outstanding Lend-Lease claims.

Negotiations surrounding the loan were challenging. The United States ultimately managed to secure several major political and economic concessions from a weakened United Kingdom. For G. John Ikenberry, "negotiations over the British loan provided the most coercive use of American power" in the postwar period, but such an approach was "largely self-defeating."[11] The British government proved unable to adhere, in any meaningful sense, to many of the obligations of the agreement.[12] Nevertheless, the Anglo-American Financial and Commercial Agreement clearly stipulated major reforms to British trading practices that ruled out imperial preference as a substantial policy for the future.[13] A further condition required the free conversion of sterling to dollars, which encouraged the convertibility crisis of 1947.[14] These concessions, which London grudgingly made to Washington, have led the historian Peter Clarke to conclude that the agreement marked the humiliation of the British Empire.[15] In addition, the United Kingdom agreed to become a member of the Bretton Woods institutions, allowing the International Monetary Fund (IMF) and World Bank to begin operations, expediting U.S. plans for multilateral trade.[16] Membership of these institutions did provide some benefits for the United Kingdom, however, including a convenient solution to the lending restrictions imposed by the still-active Johnson Act.[17]

This chapter reveals the important but contradictory ways in which the United Kingdom's unpaid First World War debts informed U.S.

decision-making concerning financial aid in this period. On the one hand, the Truman administration was keen to avoid a repetition of the economic failures of the interwar period and crafted international agreements with these outstanding debts in mind. It sought to provide affordable financial assistance to the United Kingdom to support economic reconstruction, promote multilateralism, and eventually help in the defense of Europe against communist expansion.[18] On the other hand, the spirit of cooperation was hampered by the memory of the United Kingdom's unpaid debts. The Johnson Act continued to present a significant legal obstacle to further financial support.[19] More important was the political and popular resistance to economic cooperation, driven by anger at outstanding debts and fear of another British default. Democratic Party whips and the British embassy recognized that one of Congress's main arguments against the proposed loan was that it would not be repaid.[20] Throughout the difficult process of ratification, Congress made frequent reference to outstanding debts and the risks of future default passed onto American taxpayers.[21] These concerns were empowered by the United States' own difficult reversion back to a peacetime economy.[22] They were also amplified by doubts about the credibility of the socialist government recently elected to power in the United Kingdom, which Truman understood as a "revolution."[23] As Randall Bennett Woods explains, these powerful political pressures encouraged the Truman administration to "extract a pound of flesh for every pound of aid extended."[24]

Recognition of the war debts' importance to postwar decision-making complements rather than corrects the historiography. Scholars have traditionally suggested that the Truman administration was constrained by congressional and public resistance to foreign aid, reflecting latent isolationism, anxiety about the national economy, indifference or ignorance of international affairs, apprehension concerning the cost of further loans for other countries, the inherent contradictions of multilateralism, anti-imperialism, or concerns regarding the socialist Labour government.[25] This important collection of factors is nevertheless incomplete. Britain's unpaid war debts to the U.S. represent a crucial addition in their own right, and they also exacerbated the existing suspicions, resentments, and prejudices between the two states on which many existing explanations rest.[26] This addition certainly helps to explain the curious timidity of U.S. economic diplomacy in this period.[27]

The course of events also helps to temper popular criticisms of congressional and public ignorance on economic affairs. U.S. apprehensions had some merit. The United Kingdom defaulted on the terms of the agreement within a year of ratification and deferred several payments thereafter.[28] Concerns about establishing a precedent for further lending were also vindicated by subsequent U.S. support to France in the form of a $650 million loan, even if it was a much smaller amount than initially requested and officially came via the Export-Import Bank.[29]

The continuing relevance of these war debts also casts light on the content and conduct of British economic diplomacy before, during, and after the loan negotiations. The British government's approach to securing a grant-in-aid was not a wholly naïve appeal to U.S. largesse. London had a keen appreciation of Washington's ambitions and concerns and tailored its negotiating approach accordingly. The British government repeatedly stressed its belief that generous financial support was the best way to avoid the economic failures of the interwar period, not least the risk of default.[30] It also threatened to withhold support for a new global monetary and financial system in exchange for better terms.[31] Without British cooperation, the Bretton Woods system, designed to overcome the economic problems of the interwar period, could collapse.[32] Once the terms of the agreement were approved, the British government went on to play an important role in convincing Congress to support its ratification, including advising the Democratic Party on how to present the war-debt situation in a more favorable light.[33]

The termination of Lend-Lease and the creation of the Anglo-American Economic and Financial Agreement took place in a brief window of opportunity between the final stages of the Second World War and the dawn of the Cold War. The temporary absence of a major external threat, coupled with concerns about the costs of the war and the transition to a peacetime economy, helps to explain why concerns about unpaid debts from the First World War resurfaced so significantly but also so fleetingly in the United States. Indeed, the subject was far less relevant before and after this brief period in transatlantic history. Indeed, war debts had enjoyed a relatively limited influence on earlier wartime economic negotiations, including the Bretton Woods financial system that included the establishment of the IMF and the International Bank for Reconstruction and Development (IBRD) or the failed International Clearing Union.[34] Nor did unpaid war debts appear to exert a significant effect on subsequent discussions concerning the unsuccessful International Trade Organization, the emergence of the General Agreement on Tariffs and Trade (GATT), or the European Recovery Program thereafter.[35]

The lingering memory of these unpaid war debts, which now extended well beyond a decade after repayment had ceased, complements research by a small number of economists that suggests investors retain a long memory of sovereign default.[36] This chapter reveals that, in this instance at least, governments were also unwilling to forget large debts quickly. Politicians in creditor states can vary in their responses to these unpleasant memories, however, from advocating policies that restrict debtors' ability to borrow through to offering new loans on more favorable terms that improve the chances of repayment. Such variation reflects the wide range of political and economic influences that inform economic decision-making at the highest levels of government.

THE TERMINATION OF LEND-LEASE

The Lend-Lease agreement never overcame many Americans' deep-seated resentments toward their European debtors. In April 1943, Keynes reiterated his long-standing concerns on this matter, stressing that the U.S. remained deeply suspicious about supporting the British: "Our American friends cannot run the risk of being branded and pilloried in their own country as having been 'had for mugs.'"[37] Congress was adamant throughout the war that the United Kingdom would have to pay its way and reacted angrily following the publication of a government report in September that stated the United States wanted no debts following victory. Roosevelt later denied the report and apologized to Congress.[38]

The British government nevertheless expected, or at least hoped, to wipe the slate clean. Chancellor Kingsley Wood's budget of 1943 warned that the national debt had doubled in size and was a growing concern for Britain's postwar creditor-debtor position.[39] In addition, the "sterling balances," which were major debts in sterling to other countries—most notably India, Egypt and Sudan, Eire, Australia, Palestine, and Transjordan—accumulated during the war in exchange for vital goods, had become a major source of concern.[40] These liabili-

ties exceeded £3.2 billion and represented a serious burden, even if re-
deemed gradually, and a political complication within the Empire and
Commonwealth.[41] As David Edgerton explains, the sterling balances
and Lend-Lease were of comparable size and importance in supporting
the war effort, but there would be a big difference: "Lend-Lease would
not have to be paid back."[42] The United Kingdom's export trade position, which declined by over 50 percent during the war, could no longer
solve these mounting difficulties. The prospective postwar balance of
payments problem consequently became an obsession for the British
government.[43] U.S. Department of State officials commented privately
that a recent memorandum titled "Post-War Position of British Balance
of International Payments" should have been subtitled "The Decline
and Possible Fall of the British Empire."[44] They concluded dramatically that the British economy, relative to its prewar position, "has now
taken such a fall as being impossible to recover."[45]

The chancellor used his budget speech to express undue confidence
that U.S. support for the United Kingdom would be both forthcoming
and unquestioning after the war. "The American people have never put
the dollar sign in the help that they have given us," he explained, "and
we are not putting the pound sign in the help we give back to them or
give to others."[46] For this reason, Wood explained, the government was
not "keeping tables" on reciprocal aid.[47] Labour MPs expressed astonishment at this admission, especially given the well-known existence
of U.S. records on British debt.[48] U.S. onlookers were also surprised
by what they considered recurring efforts by the British government to
evade its obligations. As the head of the Division of European Affairs
noted, "[Wood's] statement is in a sense an echo of the ill-starred Balfour note of August 1, 1922. . . . Lend-Lease has, of course, practically
eliminated any question of interallied debts in this war but Sir Kingsley's statement is clearly a further step to building up the British case
that Lend-Lease aid from the United States to Great Britain involves
not only no debt but no obligation."[49]

The chancellor's speech reflected in part the British government's
long-standing desire to avoid any form of financial dependence on the
United States that could produce a humiliating repetition of the war-
debts imbroglio.[50] U.S. suggestions of a transitional loan to follow the
potential cancellation of Lend-Lease were cause for concern rather
than celebration in April 1944. Chancellor John Anderson, who had

assumed the role following the sudden death of his predecessor, warned Churchill of the risks of accepting such a loan, not least the specter of default that could erode rather than cement relations.[51] The prime minister agreed. Senior members of the government were determined to defend the country's reputation as a creditworthy state. In June 1944, preparing for a preliminary conference in advance of the Bretton Woods conference, Keynes produced a ten-thousand-word memo for ministers that highlighted the challenges of such an objective. He noted that the United Kingdom had "shuffled out of its First World War debts": "The fact that we owe money all over the place . . . means that the effort required to emerge without loss of honour, dignity and credit will be immensely greater."[52]

The approaching U.S. election of 1944, coupled with expectations of a swift end to the war, were, according to senior figures in HM Treasury, "unfavourable factors" that resulted in closer congressional scrutiny of British government expenditure, especially Lend-Lease, that threatened to place considerable strain on the economic relationship.[53] The Quebec Conference of September offered a glimmer of hope. On the side lines of this meeting, Roosevelt offered Churchill $6 billion in Lend-Lease aid for Phase II Lend-Lease negotiations, which referred to the period between the defeat of Germany and the defeat of Japan, to assist the reconstruction of the British economy.[54] Roosevelt's death meant that he was unable to fulfill his promise, but there had already been serious doubts in the White House and State Department about selling even this modest postwar program to the American people and Congress, given the "very grave danger that the settlement of Lend-Lease" would entangle the U.S. "in another international war debts mess."[55]

The already existing war-debts mess also continued to pose problems for U.S. policymakers. Roosevelt had repeatedly ignored suggestions from within the government to settle these outstanding obligations or to repeal the Johnson Act, which meant that any form of lending to Europe remained difficult and prone to "political opposition."[56] Throughout the first half of 1945, Congress repeatedly raised the issue of unpaid war debts in discussions concerning Lend-Lease. There were occasional suggestions in the Senate and in the press that the United States should cancel the First World War debts, if only because they were impossible to collect.[57] Yet references to these outstanding obligations were typically used to make the case for rapid termination of Lend-Lease when it came up for renewal in February 1945. Concerned members of Congress eventually compelled the administration to accept a highly restrictive interpretation of the act whereby any supplies shipped after hostilities ceased would require cash payment.[58]

The *Congressional Record* reveals widespread dismay regarding these still-unpaid debts and considerable doubts about the prospect of future repayment. As the Republican representative Noah Mason explained to his peers. "Mr. Speaker, after World War No. 1, Uncle Sam permitted himself to become the financial scapegoat of the world. Is history about to repeat itself? . . . We do not know today how many billions of dollars we have given and loaned to our allies during this war, but we do know that the money we have loaned will not be repaid, that it will all be cancelled or defaulted, just as the First World War debts were. Europe's method of meeting her debt, both internal and external, was a resort to further credit."[59] The Republican representative Roy Woodruff provides a similarly striking example of the war debts informing the debate: "Before voting upon [Lend-Lease], every one of us should ponder our fantastic national debt. . . . We loaned our allies billions 'on the cuff' [in World War I]. . . . It was not long before the French named us 'Uncle Shylock' and the British led all other debtor nations, except Finland, in their repudiation of the debts."[60] Such arguments appeared frequently in Congress throughout February and March. Lingering memories of perceived European ingratitude, and the risk of further defaults in the future, encouraged stiff political resistance to further generosity. As the *Congressional Record* also reveals, these political tensions existed alongside and complemented a renewed focus on the country's own economic interests.[61]

Few presidents could have ignored such congressional pressure. This was especially true of Roosevelt's successor. Harry Truman took office following Roosevelt's sudden death on 12 April and assumed the presidency with limited experience of international politics. His position on Lend-Lease largely reflected congressional views, not least because he believed that there would be a "lot of trouble" if he ignored its wishes.[62] It is also possible that Truman held some personal sympathy for Congress's position on the matter given his own painful struggles with debt repayment following the failure of his business in 1922. He and his partners had found it immoral to leave creditors with losses.[63] In addition, Truman lacked detailed knowledge of the precarious state of the British economy. Most of the reports received by the White House in the first months of the new administration misunderstood the United Kingdom's difficulties and thus downplayed the need for ongoing financial support. Presidential adviser Bernard Baruch, for example, informed Truman that he should not "rob Britons of their native self-reliance."[64]

The subsequent path toward the termination of Lend-Lease is well documented.[65] British efforts to secure financial support, and representations concerning the Quebec agreement, met with little success. On 28 May, Churchill appealed to Truman for continuing economic assistance but was rebuffed, reflecting pressure from Congress to resist seemingly unjustified British demands.[66] On 31 May, the president had received a stern warning from House Republicans that any attempts to use Lend-Lease for reconstruction might have "disastrous consequences."[67] When Truman and Churchill met at Potsdam in July, the president said that the United States owed the United Kingdom much for "having held the fort" at the beginning of the war but stressed that he must "abide strictly by the law" with respect to Lend-Lease.[68]

The shifting political situation in the United Kingdom did little to strengthen support in the United States for more financial aid. The Labour Party achieved a decisive victory in the general election of July 1945 and enjoyed a popular mandate for political reform.[69] Clement Attlee's government now called for greater levels of state intervention and social protection. A strong commitment to social welfare generated intense suspicion in many parts of the United States. Fears of socialism and policies of nationalization alienated many members of the U.S. business community and exacerbated popular resentments about offering foreign aid, especially to those countries that provided comparatively generous welfare for their own citizens.[70] More broadly, Attlee's policies were also opposed to the Bretton Woods program of rigid and convertible currencies that favored U.S. interests.[71]

The new Labour government was keenly aware of the significant risks—and strong likelihood—of U.S. financial support ceasing in the immediate postwar period.[72] London had nevertheless expected the war to last for another year. The use of the atomic bomb on Hiroshima and Nagasaki in early August proved devastatingly effective, and, in conjunction with the Soviet Union's entry into the Pacific war, Japan surrendered shortly thereafter.[73] On 17 August, without consulting the British government, Truman followed the advice of most of his advisers that Lend-Lease was inappropriate outside of wartime and ordered its immediate termination, recalling some shipments in midtransit. He explained his decision "in order that the best faith may be observed toward Congress and the administration protect itself against any charge of misuse of Congressional authorization."[74]

Truman later conceded that this decision was mistaken, but he still considered it to be unavoidable.[75] In his memoirs, he stressed that since Lend-Lease Act was exclusively an instrument of war, the outcome was inevitable.[76] Under Secretary of State Dean Acheson later claimed that the president's interpretation of the act was "unnecessarily rigid" and reflected "thoroughly bad advice" from his advisers.[77] Nevertheless, popular and congressional opinion gave the president limited room for maneuver. The Roosevelt administration's failure to prepare for postwar assistance or to address the problem directly in Washington made this challenge seemingly insurmountable.[78] Historians such as George C. Herring Jr. have suggested that the American people and their political representatives were largely uneducated about Britain's needs.[79] Ignorance surely existed alongside skepticism, however, as European defaulters now retuned to ask American taxpayers for further support. The British government was increasingly aware of a changing mood in the U.S., shifting away from wartime cooperation toward peacetime negotiation. As John Balfour, a senior British official based at the Washington embassy, warned later in the year, "The dollar sign is back in the Anglo-American equation."[80]

Postwar relations between former allies certainly appeared to be suffering. The termination of Lend-Lease was accompanied by divisions over the sharing of nuclear technology and serious rows over the future of Palestine.[81] One major obstacle to financial cooperation, however, had been removed. Congressional approval of the Bretton Woods proposals, following the successful conclusion of the U.S.-led conference a year earlier, provided a legal route by which the United Kingdom could secure a loan from the United States.[82] House and Senate backing not only ensured support for a new postwar financial and monetary system but also encouraged international cooperation by exempting all states that became members of the bank and fund from the provisions of the Johnson Act.[83] The Bretton Woods Act secured a majority of 345 votes to 18 in the House on 7 June and 61 votes to 16 in the Senate on 19 July.

Debate had been colorful despite the lopsided result. The Republican Jesse Sumner described the bill as "the worst swindle in American history. . . . Why the amateur diplomats who represented the United States at the conference last summer were babes lost in the Bretton Woods."[84] Resistance to the bill in the House had repeatedly referred to unpaid war debts. As Howard S. Ellis of the Federal Reserve Board warned the House, "We all remember the defaulted loans of our Allies of 25 years ago that was extremely distasteful. . . . So here we have a brand new sugarcoated plan which is trying to be made painless to continue giving away our resources."[85] Even those who supported the proposal expressed regret and concern at these unpaid debts. As the Republican David Brumbaugh explained, "Many of the debtor nations defaulted and even failed to pay the annual interest on their loans. . . . Surely we should have learned a bitter lesson from our experiences in World War I? . . . [But] if the Bretton Woods proposal will promote international friendship and world peace, such a goal cannot be measured in monetary terms."[86] In the Senate, the Republican Robert Taft had warned of more defaults such as those that occurred in the 1930s, leaving the United States to catch the buck.[87] Appeals to long-term security and international cooperation ultimately ensured congressional approval for the Bretton Woods system, but there remained a general unease regarding some of the lending provisions within these agreements.[88] The president signed Bretton Woods into law on 31 July and, in so doing, established a legal path to resume lending to the United Kingdom and the other states of Europe.

The political legacy of outstanding war debts nevertheless continued to limit the administration's room for maneuver, especially with regard to future lending should it ever be required. Truman's official files contain letters from members of the public who strongly objected to any revision of outstanding Lend-Lease debts: "Who do you think you are recommending we Americans write off forty-two billion dollars period as you well know they owe us from world war number one."[89] The State Department had warned that a loan or direct subsidy would face congressional opposition and, in view of the troubled history of war debts, that the British government might actually regard a government loan as the least desirable alternative.[90] The U.S. embassy in London had claimed in early 1945 that British public opinion opposed the incurring of any future dollar indebtedness given fears of nonrepayment. The embassy suggested that Britons might prefer U.S. capital on an equity rather than fixed interest basis, as these instruments do not carry with them "the stigma of 'default,' an epithet for which the British have little liking."[91]

A U.S. LOAN

The abrupt termination of Lend-Lease threatened a financial crisis for the British government. The United Kingdom now had the largest external debt in its history and few easy solutions given its depressed export industry, significant government expenditure, and painful transition to a peacetime economy.[92] This economic situation necessitated urgent external support, which the United States was best placed to provide.[93] British thinking on the looming crisis is detailed in a note produced by Keynes in April, which set out three solutions to the financial predicament: "Starvation Corner," "Temptation," and "Justice."[94]

"Starvation Corner," referred to as "Austerity" in an earlier draft, denoted a policy of economic isolation, risking serious political and social disruption at home and the state's withdrawal from the position of a first-class power in the outside world. Keynes noted that this policy necessitated a dramatic decline in the standard of living for the British people.[95] "Temptation" would involve a line of credit from the United States, between $5 and $8 billion, in exchange for accepting an array of troublesome conditions including sterling convertibility and commitments to free trade. "Justice" involved the United States reimbursing the United Kingdom and the dominions $5 to $6 billion for pre–Lend-Lease expenditure in the United States as well as debt cancellation and retrospective war-cost contributions. This solution was, as it is possible to infer from the name, Keynes's preferred option.[96]

Keynes defended the pursuit of "Justice" by stressing that the United States would recognize that the United Kingdom's postwar financial burden was "entirely disproportionate to what is fair": "It is precisely that expenditure which we incurred in the United States itself whilst we were holding the fort alone for which retrospective repayment would be made."[97] The British government also held one valuable negotiating chip. Keynes and the chancellor had delayed Parliamentary discussion concerning the ratification of the Bretton Woods agreements until after the Americans had passed their own legislation.[98] The United Kingdom and the British Empire—comprising sovereign territories, protectorates, and dominions—remained one of the most important economic and commercial forces around the globe. Without the cooperation of the British government, U.S. ambitions of a new monetary and financial system would probably collapse.[99] Time also appeared to be against the Americans: 31 December 1945 was the last day that Britain could ratify and still become an original member of the World Bank and IMF.[100] As Keynes explained, the United States required the United Kingdom "to be their partners and coadjutors in setting up a post-war international economy of the character on which they have set their hearts," but this would be impossible in the absence of a loan or grant.[101]

For Keynes, the chances of securing a grant were good given that the United States was now so wealthy: "The help asked from them is on relatively so small a scale that it costs them almost literally nothing."[102] In some ways, he was correct; the U.S. had benefited from the war, and its economy stood in stark contrast to the depressed conditions of the 1930s. British confidence in U.S. generosity was nevertheless misplaced. U.S. government spending reduced markedly as the economy shifted to peacetime, resulting in a significant decline in gross domestic product and a technical recession. The cost of the war had been immense, with the U.S. debt-to-GDP ratio reaching its then-all-time record of 113 percent by 1945. The U.S. national debt soared to $241.86 billion in the following year.[103] Furthermore, hopes of generosity based on wartime prosperity neglected a renewed wariness of European affairs and lingering memories of unpaid debts. In sum, the U.S. was not ideally placed to lend abroad, and there was limited support for such efforts.[104] There were also persistent doubts about the severity of the economic challenges facing the United Kingdom. Truman believed, largely mistakenly, that the British government had overstated the seriousness of its financial predicament, with regard to both its balance of payments deficits and its dollar holdings.[105]

There were evidently strong reasons for the United States to reject a loan or a grant to the United Kingdom in the immediate postwar period. Scholars have traditionally explained the Truman administration's eventual support for economic cooperation with the British government with regard to a U.S. commitment to multilateralism and eventually as a component of Cold War strategy.[106] Outstanding war debts also played a role. Postwar planners recognized the inadequate handling of economic problems following the First World War and were keen to avoid their return. Indeed, during the war, officials in the United States and the United Kingdom had undertaken an extensive study of loans and reparations to "learn the lessons" of history.[107] As Truman explained in August 1945, "We have declared our intention to avoid the political and economic mistakes of our debt policy after World War I."[108] In exchanges with Congress, the president rejected concerns about being cheated by foreign governments: "there is no intention on my part to allow the British Empire, the Russians, or anybody else to fleece the people of the United States."[109] Yet he was clear that financial aid should be forthcoming given the high price the British had paid in the Second World War: "I know it is a difficult situation to remember your fighting Allies after the fight is over, especially if you come out practically whole and unscathed, while they are practically prostrate and destroyed."[110]

In the summer, Churchill had asked Truman for permission to send a mission to Washington to discuss financial and trade problems in the postwar period. Truman instead suggested that Assistant Secretary of State for Economic Affairs William L. Clayton should venture to London in early August to begin exploratory talks.[111] Churchill agreed, and these talks came to lay the groundwork for the financial and economic negotiations in Washington scheduled for the following month.[112] Clayton and his team met with Keynes and British officials on 3 August. Keynes suggested that the United States offer a gift of around $5 billion, in return for which the United Kingdom would ratify Bretton Woods, liberalize the sterling area, and move toward the convertibility of sterling. If the U.S. failed to accede to this request, the British government would be forced to insulate itself in the sterling trading bloc, with "all the repercussions that implied" for both states.[113]

As one of the U.S. delegation noted, "[thc] British are obviously holding up action on Bretton Woods to force our hand."[114] This "threat" was treated by the Americans as merely a tactic "to cover a basically very weak financial position."[115] Clayton was clear that the British should not expect to secure a free grant.[116] Yet he was also keenly aware of the need for economic cooperation. Clayton had stressed during the war his desire to avoid making "a mess of [the United States'] international

economic and financial relationships as [it] did in the last peace conference and during the interwar period."[117] It remained unclear to both
sides how the incoming Labour government would react to these preliminary negotiating positions, and further discussions were postponed
until later in the year.[118]

On 23 August, senior ministers—including Attlee, Chancellor Hugh
Dalton, Foreign Secretary Ernest Bevin, President of the Board of Trade
Stafford Cripps, and Deputy Prime Minister Herbert Morrison—
alongside the British ambassador to the United States Lord Halifax,
head of the Treasury delegation to the United States Robert Brand, and
Keynes gathered to discuss the government's approach to transatlantic
economic negotiations.[119] At the meeting, Keynes repeated the comments made in his earlier note about the fairness of financial aid but
also reiterated veiled threats about the possibility of renewed economic
competition between the two states and the potential failure of Bretton
Woods. He concluded that ministers should not accept anything except
a grant and was only willing to advise them to support the proposal if
"they were not coupled with any dangerous concessions."[120] Halifax
and Brand urged caution and warned that the U.S. would not provide
a grant. Nevertheless, the gathered ministers concluded that the matter
should be "handled by Lord Keynes and his colleagues on the basis that
he had outlined that evening," with reports relayed to ministers as and
when necessary.[121]

Keynes's expectations of a generous grant-in-aid encouraged unwarranted optimism in Whitehall, which had embraced "Justice" with
enthusiasm but some trepidation.[122] "When I listen to Keynes," Bevin
said, "I can hear the money jingling in my pocket," while acknowl-
edging, "I'm not sure it's really there."[123] There was good reason for
doubt. For Congress and much of the United States, suggestions of a
moral debt to the United Kingdom and further grants to a state still in
default of existing debts were galling. A Gallup poll found that most
of the U.S. opposed even an interest-bearing loan to the United Kingdom.[124] As Attlee later recognized, U.S. public opinion was preoccupied
with its own postwar problems, remained suspicious of entanglement
in European affairs, and was convinced that the situation in the United
Kingdom was much exaggerated.[125]

The prime minister may have been optimistic about negotiations
initially, but he was always willing to engage in rough diplomacy. Af-

ter informing the House of Commons that the British government intended to reach a financial agreement with the United States, Attlee
contacted Truman. Attlee was clear that if negotiations were unsuccessful, his government would be forced to buy all its goods outside the
dollar area, launch an all-out export drive, and reject Bretton Woods.
To survive in this difficult environment, the United Kingdom would
have to close its markets to the United States via the imposition of tariffs and controls.[126] Truman appears to have appreciated Attlee's stark
warnings. From the start, the president stressed the need for the United
States to furnish substantial aid to the United Kingdom to encourage a
foreign economic policy on a multilateral basis rather than a sterling-
bloc arrangement.[127] None of this is to suggest that Truman was cowed
by such threats, only that he understood that international cooperation
was not a foregone conclusion and that the financial situation "was
obviously serious."[128]

The Washington negotiations commenced with a meeting of the top
committee on 11 September 1945.[129] The U.S. was represented by Secretary of the Treasury Frederick Vinson, Clayton, and a wide collection of experts and officials. The smaller British delegation was led
by Keynes, even if it was commanded officially by Halifax. The talks
divided into four groups, each of which would deal with a different
topic—namely, financial problems, Lend-Lease, commercial policy, and
disposal of surplus war property—before reporting to the top committee.[130] At the first meeting, Halifax expressed his hopes for "sanity
and cooperation" in the face of "the difficulties of the post war era."[131]
Recognition of Britain's unpaid war debts, and the lingering memory
of default from over a decade earlier, helps to provide a fuller and more
nuanced account of the negotiations that followed. The available evidence shows clearly that these outstanding obligations were relevant
to negotiations and helped to influence international diplomacy at a
pivotal moment in postwar history.

The opening press conference on 12 September provided the British delegation with an opportunity to present its case to the United
States. Keynes warned that the "easy course" would be to offer a commercial loan, but he advised against such an outcome: "We are not in
the mood, and we believe and hope that you are not in the mood, to
repeat the experiences of last time's war debts."[132] Vinson and Clayton had also previously expressed their desire to avoid the mistakes

of intergovernmental debt in the interwar period.[133] Vinson spoke from firsthand experience, having been involved in such debates in the House of Representatives a decade earlier.[134] Clayton was also clear that these "extremely important discussions" were "the most important economic problem" that would face the U.S. in its relations "with foreign countries in the post war period," and he could not "over-stress the importance of reaching a satisfactory conclusion."[135] Yet while the American negotiators recognized the importance of financial cooperation, they remained keenly aware of stiff congressional and popular resistance to further lending.[136] Critical newspapers such as the *Chicago Tribune* reacted poorly to British requests for a grant, recalling unpaid war debts in articles titled "The Dining Room Is Closed" and "Santa Claus Dies Hard."[137]

The initial meetings, which took place between 13 and 17 September, allowed the British to outline their predicament and the need for around $5 billion as well as an unspecified amount necessary to "clean up" what remained of Lend-Lease.[138] The proposed size of financial support did not appear to cause much concern, but Vinson and Clayton "repeated in unison that neither a Grant in aid nor an interest free loan was practical politics."[139] As Clayton would tell Vinson until the end of talks, the agreement had two goals: getting the world trade back on a multilateral basis for the future peace and prosperity of the world and being acceptable to Congress.[140] These issues were connected; trade liberalization was key if any deal was to pass Congress.[141] As Clayton explained privately, "The reason given for the loan, 'to help the British people get back to peacetime business' is only a fraction of the real story. If we make the loan one of the principal purposes will be to enable the British people to open up their commerce to the United States and to all other countries instead of confining it to the British Empire."[142] Popular and congressional opinion was certainly an imposing influence on negotiations. As Keynes recalled, "during the time I was in Washington there was not a single Administration measure of the first importance that Congress did not either reject, remodel, or put on one side."[143] Halifax noted, "it is quite plain that the Americans would like to help us, but are quite genuinely doubtful about what they can get through Congress."[144]

The general contours of debate soon emerged. Both sides agreed that it would be wise to avoid unduly burdening the United Kingdom again, but the U.S. delegation insisted that interest charges at least equal to the cost of borrowing by the U.S. Treasury remained essential to appease congressional and popular opinion.[145] Two other major issues remained: the timing of free convertibility for sterling and British negotiations with its sterling creditors. Both sides agreed on the need for a commitment to convert foreign holdings of sterling, but the Americans were impatient for change and demanded a fixed timetable of one year, against a British preference for delay to allow time for recovery.[146] On sterling balances, the U.S. expected the major holders of this debt to make a substantial contribution to any solution. Keynes initially agreed despite the potential consequences for the government's domestic and international monetary policies, presumably in the expectation of a grant.[147] The negotiations also came to include discussion of waivers, which were without precedent in previous U.S. loan agreements and signaled lingering doubts about the political dangers of default.[148] London greatly disliked waivers and escape clauses because they legitimatized defaults that could eventually create conflict and risk the loss of goodwill with Washington.[149]

In the coming days, Halifax was encouraged by a positive meeting with the president and, alongside Keynes, a successful dinner with senior senators.[150] At the end of September, Clayton informed Truman that Keynes was willing to provide a commitment to convertibility by 1 January 1947 and had accepted U.S. demands concerning sterling balances—effectively conceding many of the British government's key negotiating points with little in return, probably in the hope of still securing a generous settlement.[151] Yet the U.S. refused to budge on the need for an interest-bearing loan. By early October, "Temptation" rather than "Justice" had become the only viable alternative to "Starvation Corner." The British delegation came to accept a loan that included a modest level of interest that could be waived or deferred in difficult times.[152] Keynes subsequently requested permission from London to seek just such a loan and made the case that "substantial assistance" would be forthcoming if the government accepted liberalizing arrangements in the sterling area, supported Bretton Woods, and ensured that the sterling area made a contribution to any settlement.[153]

Ministers gathered to discuss these proposals on 5 October. The chancellor was stunned by the request from the British delegation. He struggled to understand how Keynes had misread Washington and misled London. Dalton's surprise reflected misplaced confidence in Keynes, to be sure, but also his failure to keep apace of the delegation's numerous telegrams.[154] Senior members of the government now seriously considered rejecting U.S. offers of financial assistance and thus the Bretton Woods system.[155] Dalton cabled Washington setting out ministers' views: "If best American offer is large loan at 2 percent interest we would not accept it. We remain firm that we will not accept obligations which we do not see reasonable certainty of discharging."[156] From now on, the inner cabinet—comprising Attlee, Morrison, Bevin, Dalton, and Cripps—met most weekday evenings to review telegrams from Washington.[157]

Halifax and Keynes consequently returned the cabinet's revised demands to Vinson and Clayton on 9 October; the demands were swiftly rejected. The U.S. would consider an interest-bearing loan of $5 billion over fifty years with repayments beginning in five years and with flexibility on interest and capital payments in difficult periods. The rate of interest would be somewhere between 1 percent and 2 percent. The mission cabled London with this informal proposal. On 13 October, Dalton responded to Keynes using his words against him: "we do not find a loan on these terms acceptable" as it lacked "the sweet breath of justice."[158]

By 15 October, as Keynes explained to Dalton, there had been "no progress whatever."[159] After a further meeting on the following day, he informed the chancellor that both sides still sought compromise: "When we remark as we are constantly forced to do, that nothing will induce us to repeat the experience of last time's war debts and sign an obligation we have no confidence we can meet, [Clayton] accepts our position and offers us any escape clause in reason to provide against this risk."[160] The memory of British default little more than a decade earlier therefore helped to drive both sides away from harsher or more inflexible terms. Nevertheless, Vinson and Clayton remained deeply concerned about the reaction of Congress to any deal, as evidenced by their correspondence during the period.[161] Such resistance was itself based on popular sentiment. In a Gallup poll of Americans on the prospect of a loan "to help England get back on its feet," only 27 percent approved.[162]

On 18 October, Keynes, with the support of Halifax, sent a telegram to London imploring ministers to consider a compromise position of a loan of $5 billion at 2 percent: "we cannot demand what they tell us does not lie within their power to give."[163] Shortly thereafter, the opportunity to secure $5 billion was lost. Scholars have variously suggested that Harry Dexter White, director of Monetary Research at the U.S. Treasury, reworked the numbers or that Keynes's subsequent attempts to secure a better deal and his willingness to dilute waiver conditions resulted in Vinson believing that Britain must be exaggerating its needs.[164] In either case, the original offer was rescinded. Later the same day, the U.S. offered a revised figure of $3.5 billion at 2 percent repayable over fifty years, with the Lend-Lease portion at 2.375 percent repayable over thirty years.

Despite the revised offer, the governor of the Bank of England, Thomas Catto, believed that Keynes could revive a deal based on justice with a sufficiently strong offer. With the chancellor's agreement, Catto telegrammed Keynes and suggested that he request an interest-free credit for $5 billion repayable over fifty years. In return, the United Kingdom would accept a nominal figure for the settlement of Lend-Lease, liberalize the sterling area, and begin negotiations on its sterling balances and commercial policy. Crucially, he also suggested repaying to the United States "at once" its First World War debt liabilities, albeit free of interest and scaled down to $1 billion.[165]

Keynes responded six days later, suggesting that he had received no pressure to repay "the old war debts" by members of the administration, the press, or the many Congress members to whom he had spoken thus far and therefore counseled silence on the subject of repayment: "I feel that this deeply sleeping dog one would let lie."[166] This response is curious, especially given the importance the subject had already generated and would receive in Congress and across the United States in the coming months. It is just as likely that Keynes was keen to avoid being side-tracked once again, with all the risks such tactics generated, or was simply reluctant to act on unsolicited advice. No Bank of England officials had accompanied the British negotiating party, in large part because they had clashed with Keynes's plans.[167]

Keynes nevertheless accepted the importance of using these unpaid debts to frame negotiations: "Of all the various lines of argument the Ambassador and I have tried, the one to which I find them always readily responsive is that we must not repeat the experience of last time's war debts and they must not press us to sign a bond we are not confident we can meet."[168] These concerns reflected the difficulties that large debts could create but also the risk of outright nonpayment: "There is nothing that they are more anxious to avoid than any sort of appearance of default. They agree with us that that would be fraught with all sorts of evil consequences and could lead to nothing but bad."[169] Keynes's regular exchanges with Dalton and Vinson repeatedly stress the importance of avoiding the lending failures of the past.[170] The U.S. certainly sought to ensure repayment of any loan. During the latter stages of talks, the governor of the Federal Reserve Board, Marriner Eccles, requested assurances that the United States would be repaid, much to Keynes's displeasure at assumptions about future bankruptcy.[171]

By 22 October, Keynes had conceded that obtaining a grant-in-aid was "simply off the map."[172] Congress would never accept a loan without interest, though the rate of interest would be kept as low as possible, and significant commercial reform in the sterling area. Keynes had cabled Dalton earlier in the month with news of the $3.5 billion proposal. Delayed by preparations for the first budget, the chancellor sent his instructions the day after a discussion of ministers held on 26 October. The cabinet was troubled by the inadequate size of the loan, worried about the difficulty of servicing it, and suspicious of any attempt to undermine the government's domestic policies. As such, it now advanced new proposals to the delegation in Washington, which Keynes and his colleagues feared would cause an irreversible breakdown in negotiations.[173] The Americans sensed these difficulties between the mission and London. As Clayton informed Vinson in early November, final negotiations were in a "serious" position and the British cabinet was "greatly worried."[174]

Following further exchanges, a revised set of proposals emerged on 6 November. The British government now informed the delegation in Washington, "our limit is an open credit for $4 billion at 2% on the amount of the credit in use, with an option on a further $1 billion at 2%."[175] This shift toward a larger loan with interest probably reflects a growing appreciation of what was now possible for both sides. Ministers in London were increasingly mindful of the "complete contrast between the Administration, anxious to be helpful to [Britain], and the public and Congress, who were losing interest rapidly in the outside world."[176] Dalton also feared that failure to secure a loan would lead to "sure defeat" in the next election.[177] The chancellor subscribed to

Keynes's belief about the dangers of a "Starvation Corner," which he had previously compared to "less than an Irish peasant's standard of living for the British people."[178] The prime minister shared these concerns and deferred to Keynes's expertise.[179] As Attlee later recalled, "We had to have the loan. Without it, it would have been impossible to exist, certainly without hardships on a scale no one had a right to ask of the British people at the end of a long war. . . . The critics could shout. We had to run things."[180]

In addition to accepting a large interest-bearing loan, London was now prepared to consider some form of waiver clause from Washington, albeit with certain conditions attached. This change represented another noteworthy compromise. Keynes had initially stated that if the repayment terms carried any danger of default, the British government would have to refuse.[181] Brand had helped to overcome London's doubts about such a clause by offering some historical context in late October: "Having been closely in touch with American opinion throughout the last war debt controversy and seen the serious consequences in the relations between the two countries . . . I cannot believe any trouble arising out of a waiver could possibly equal that which would be caused by another default."[182]

Despite these efforts, the U.S. rejected the British government's new proposal and eventually provided a counteroffer on 15 November. This preliminary draft contained new requirements, including the condition that any waiver would be dependent on a proportionate reduction in the release of sterling balances, which would prove unacceptable to London. Keynes bewailed the offer, conceding, "we had better pack up and go home."[183] Halifax consequently "warned that if the draft embodies the final and considered view of the US Administration the United Kingdom Government would be forced to the conclusion that the present negotiations had failed."[184]

Halifax explained that in such circumstances, the British government would suspend the approval of Bretton Woods and the proposals for future commercial policy, a threat that shocked the Americans.[185] So too did Keynes's presentation of an update from the chancellor on the British position on the following day. Vinson suggested that this update introduced a "disturbing note into the discussions," which he interpreted to mean that if talks broke down, Bretton Woods would not be ratified or, even if talks did proceed, the scale and terms might result in a delay in acceptance: "I am disappointed and somewhat astonished by the position the Chancellor has taken."[186] In response to British warnings, the U.S. withdrew the draft. Nevertheless, the terms of an agreement remained uncertain, and the delegation in Washington warned London of "further troubles ahead."[187]

After a meeting of ministers on 23 November, Attlee informed the mission in Washington that the British government would accept a credit of at least $4 billion, including Lend-Lease, at 2 percent, to be paid over fifty years alongside the commercial policies that had been agreed. The meeting had been difficult, eliciting a variety of strongly held views, including suggestions from some ministers that now was the time "to take the risk of a break."[188] The gathered ministers agreed that the British government would not complete negotiations with its creditor countries by the end of 1946, which represented a clear refusal to commit to convertibility by the agreed deadline, and nor would it rank U.S. debt ahead of all other obligations.[189]

The British mission in Washington reacted poorly to these conditions and pushed back. When the cabinet met again on 29 November, however, its position remained unchanged; these conditions were the final terms that ministers were prepared to accept. The mission responded by describing this position as "disastrous," but Attlee and Dalton offered a clear and immediate response: "It is now our firm opinion that you should put that text to the Americans as soon as possible."[190] As Dalton would write in his diary, "those who represent us out there and we here at home have drifted into a condition of mutual incomprehension."[191] To overcome such resistance and avert a potential mutiny, Dalton sent the Treasury permanent secretary Edward Bridges to assume leadership of the negotiations. Bridges arrived on 1 December and put forth the cabinet's proposal, which he swiftly realized was untenable. The outcome of efforts to achieve something better was, as reported by an unnamed member of the British delegation, "exactly as expected, humiliation."[192]

The final terms were agreed shortly thereafter. The British government would have a year from the date of ratification to prepare for convertibility. The loan was set at $3.75 billion at 2 percent interest, and the bill for Lend-Lease was significantly reduced to $650 million. Keynes believed that the amount offered would satisfy British needs and was less interested in securing a larger sum, given the troublesome inclusion

of interest payments. Furthermore, payment would consist of fifty annual installments, beginning on 31 December 1951. This five-year grace
period meant an effective interest rate of only 1.6 percent. On the final
major issue, the U.S. delegation continued to push for dramatic scaling
down of sterling balances. Keynes eventually agreed but avoided spe-
cifics. There followed several more days of tense cabling before both
sides reached agreement.[193] The British government finally capitulated,
fearing the consequences of securing far-less-favorable terms or possibly no loan at all.[194] It attempted to secure further concessions in early
December, including a five-year transitional arrangement outside the
sterling area, but was swiftly rebuffed. As Vinson explained, "we kept
firm to our position."[195] Both parties signed the Anglo-American Economic and Financial Agreement on 6 December.[196]

Dalton subsequently thanked Keynes: "you have got us the dollars,
without which—though I have more than once thought that a break
might have to come—the near future would have been black as the
pit!"[197] Yet, when the chancellor described the negotiations in his memoirs, he was less favorable: "we retreated, slowly and with bad grace
and with increasing irritation, from a free gift to an interest-free loan,
and from this again to a loan bearing interest; from a larger to a smaller
total of aid; and from the prospect of loose strings, some of which
would only be general declarations of intention, to the most unwilling
acceptance of strings so tight that they might strangle our trade and
indeed our whole economic life."[198] Such an account rightly highlights
Britain's misunderstanding of U.S. intentions and its own capabilities.
Attlee nevertheless went too far when he ruefully acknowledged, "We
weren't in a position to bargain."[199] Given the prime minister's reluctance to adopt austerity measures, especially considering his commitment to the welfare state, it would be accurate to suggest that he was
negotiating from a position of weakness. Yet it remains an intriguing
counterfactual as to whether a more robust stance utilizing Britain's
ratification of Bretton Woods would have helped the U.S. to come to
better terms.

In London, much of the reaction to the deal was critical. It was
true that the United Kingdom was the first state to secure a loan from
the United States and secured better terms than most postwar borrowers.[200] Yet, for the Bank of England, the loan epitomized what it
did not want and had advised against.[201] Elements of the press and

Parliament described the offer as "cruelly hard" and concluded, "we have been forced into a disastrous bargain."[202] An intense debate in the House of Commons began and ended on 13 December. The necessity of agreement ultimately drove Parliament toward acceptance.[203] Attlee and Dalton forced an early vote to stop any opposition gathering momentum. Leading the opposition, Churchill urged his fellow Conservatives to abstain against an agreement put before the House with "indecent haste."[204]

The memory of the First World War debts resurfaced during the debates. Churchill raised the issue directly, albeit confusing the date of suspension, stressing the risks to British creditworthiness and honor: "We shall have to do our very best, our very utmost, in future years to bear the heavy load. . . . Although in 1931 we had to default upon our American debt incurred in the First World War, nevertheless the character and conduct of our people, and the whole conduct of our State, is such that our name and honour still stand high in the world."[205] The bill passed by a vote of 345 to 98.[206] An hour later, the Bretton Woods agreement bill passed by 314 to 50. This latter debate was entirely perfunctory, reflected in the greater number of abstentions and absences. The House had to approve the Bretton Woods agreement to receive the loan on which it had just voted.[207] British membership of the IMF and IBRD provided the only solution to the lending restrictions imposed by the still-active Johnson Act.[208] The United Kingdom joined both institutions on 27 December 1945.

The House of Lords could have opposed both decisions but ultimately acquiesced. Debate began on 17 December. Keynes, having only just returned to England, made his case on the following day. He accepted that the deal was imperfect, lamenting, "I shall never so long as I live cease to regret that this is not an interest-free loan."[209] Yet he explained that U.S. negotiators deemed it necessary to charge interest if Congress and the U.S. public were to accept the agreement. The interest charges were also considerably below those charged via the Export-Import Bank to other states.[210] He invoked the memory of default in a bold peroration, stressing that "the case of last time's war debts has not been repeated."[211] The resolution to approve the financial agreement was carried by a margin of ninety to eight.[212] Keynes believed that his speech "made the difference" to convincing his initially reluctant audience, although it is difficult to see what viable alternatives were ever truly available.[213]

British press reaction was largely muted, typically offering only a dry report of events, but letters to the editor in papers ranging from *The Times* to the *Birmingham Daily Post* recorded considerable doubts about the fairness and feasibility of the terms attached to the loan and the Bretton Woods agreement.[214] *The Economist* said that it was the only possible decision in the circumstances but expressed doubts about the government's ability to pay its way without the expansion of British exports.[215] These concerns about repayment and criticisms of the terms, alongside what some American observers would come to perceive as ingratitude toward the loan, did not bode well for the course of U.S. ratification. Vinson, who congratulated Keynes on his hard-won efforts, warned his friend of more political difficulties to come: "The fireworks here will extend over a longer period of time than over on your side."[216]

RATIFYING THE AGREEMENT

The future of the Anglo-American Economic and Financial Agreement now lay in the hands of a Congress largely opposed to foreign aid. U.S. policymakers, in keeping with their British counterparts, were also unhappy with the proposed agreement but largely for the opposite reason—namely, that it was too generous. As the president later explained in his memoirs, "There was criticism that the loan was unsufficient [*sic*] and that it was extravagant, and Uncle Sam was cartooned both as Santa Claus and as Shylock."[217] Debate in London had done little to generate support in Washington. Much of the press was favorable to the idea of a loan, but journalists writing for the *Christian Science Monitor*, *Journal of Commerce*, *Washington Post*, and *Washington Star* all raised concerns about perceptions of British ingratitude.[218] Such views were also common in smaller papers around the country. Critical editorials in the *Canton Ohio Repository* and *Wichita Beacon*, for example, both raised the memory of the outstanding debts as a reason to reject the loan.[219] As Senator Vandenberg remarked, "Our prospective debtors are already beginning to 'shylock us' before the papers are signed. We are notified in advance that we will get no good will out of this largesse. If we are not going to get good will what are we going to get?"[220]

The president was in no position to answer such questions. Polls showed that Truman's job-approval ratings were suffering, which left him in a weak position from which to build political support for a loan, especially given the forthcoming midterm elections in November 1946.[221] Nor was the proposed loan especially well liked. The administration kept a close eye on Congress's attitude to the loan, tracking levels of support from December until the closing of the debate in May. The available figures made difficult reading for proponents of economic cooperation. Even after almost six months of campaigning, the administration remained unsure about the intentions of a clear majority of Congress but understood that most representatives and senators who had expressed an opinion were opposed to the loan.[222] Lingering memories of British default, which have been largely neglected in the existing literature, help to explain the persistence and strength of resistance to financial assistance in Washington and across the U.S. Analysis of the available evidence—including opinion polls, radio interviews, and congressional debates—strengthens claims about the relevance of war debts to the unpopularity of the proposed loan.

The administration recognized that Americans were generally unsupportive of a loan.[223] Polling by the Truman administration in November had revealed that 70 percent of the country were opposed.[224] A major Gallup poll in the new year revealed most respondents against any lending. The poll cited concerns about improving domestic economic conditions before spending money abroad, but it also included references to outstanding debts. As one respondent explained, "The British can't be trusted so far as loan matters are concerned. We have yet to see the first dollar in payment of the loan we made them previously."[225] The administration was keenly aware that a consistent element of opposition in Congress stemmed from outstanding war debts. As early as December, the Republican representative Dewey Short questioned the prudence of another loan to a country in default of its First World War debt.[226] In the following month, the Republican senator C. Wayland Brooks gave a speech in which he explained, "The British couldn't pay a $4,000,000,000 debt after the last war. They themselves tell us they can't pay it now. And still our negotiators insisted on calling it a loan."[227]

On 30 January 1946, Truman sent the proposed Financial Agreement to Congress. Work on securing approval, however, had started much earlier. The administration had been "getting busy with the business community, with organised labour, and with the farm groups and hoped to influence Congress indirectly rather than directly."[228] It had also run private polls and encouraged support via radio, press, and off-the-record talks as early as November. News of these efforts and the negative poll results leaked to the *Wall Street Journal*, which the administration's team described sarcastically as "a fine way to get an effective campaign launched."[229] The administration's strategy to promote the agreement was also increasingly circumscribed by domestic and international politics. Congressional and public resistance to seeing a loan as a generous gift, which made the U.S. a "sucker," or as an investment against Soviet imperialism, which encouraged charges of antagonism, limited the ways in which the administration could defend the proposal. The administration instead promoted it as a key element of progress toward multilateral trade, world prosperity, and peace. Few viable alternatives existed, yet, in approaching the loan in this way, Truman claimed too much for the Financial Agreement and exaggerated the extent of agreement, risking future tensions between both states. As Richard Gardner puts it, the administration was "sowing dragon's teeth for an eventual harvest."[230]

Vinson and Acheson campaigned to secure approval for the proposed agreement early in the new year. They were keen to stress that it would be "not an expenditure but an investment."[231] On 12 January 1946, both men were interviewed by Sterling Fisher, who directed a popular radio series for the National Broadcasting Company in the United States. Fisher had prepared a lengthy series of questions concerning the proposed loan. The first asked both men to consider if "we are being taken for a ride by the wily British."[232] Their response was clear; it was in U.S. interests to restore the British economy. As such, it would be wrong to think of the loan as a business arrangement or to try to make money out of the United Kingdom. As Acheson explained, reiterating the criticism of the war loans that he had made during the first Roosevelt administration, "we don't intend to repeat the history of the World War I loans."[233] Fisher then asked, "Can we be sure that the British won't default on this loan?"[234] Acheson responded clearly: "There's always some risks involved in making loans. But the total context of the agreement makes it possible for them to pay this time."[235] Vinson also stressed that this credit was an investment rather than an expenditure: "We will get it back with interest. . . . And in view of what's at stake—a healthy Britain and a healthy world trade—I don't think we can afford *not* to make the loan."[236] As Vinson stressed, "this time" would be different: "we are making the loan on terms we believe will make repayment possible."[237]

The preparation for this interview, which took place nine days earlier, sheds more light on how the Truman administration would handle the issue of unpaid debts from the First World War. When asked if the agreement meant writing off the First World War loan, Acheson responded clearly: "No. They have not dealt with that at all. They are still left for future discussion."[238] These debts remained inexcusable, but, for the first time, the U.S. government was willing to share publicly some of the blame for British default. In an attached but undated thirty-three-page document titled "Answers to Arguments against the British Loan," there is a strong rebuttal to criticisms of British default. Britain did not "welch" but found it impossible to pay after the economic depression of the 1930s destroyed world trade and Britain became unable to earn dollars. Until 1931, such payments were made in full. The note also conceded that the U.S. worsened the situation by raising tariffs in 1922 and 1930 to the highest levels in history.[239]

On 19 March, Acheson presented the mutual advantages of the British loan in an address before the Economic Club of Detroit. Asked whether the United Kingdom's repudiation of its First World War debts would be dealt with as a term or condition of the proposed loan, Acheson downplayed any connection between the two: "Forgiving World War I debt does not give the British any purchasing power now. . . . Because the British have not paid World War I debt, does this mean that they will not pay these debts? To my mind there is no relation between these two things."[240] He continued, "World War I loans were a first in world history—take transactions between allies in war and translate them into commercial transactions, and burden future commerce with the repayment of that amount."[241]

The Truman administration's bold claims about the rewards of multilateralism evoked limited enthusiasm in Congress or across the United States. Despite official and unofficial efforts by the State Department and the British government to win public support, Congress remained unconvinced of the value of a $3.75 billion loan and failed to approve the agreement by early spring as expected.[242] As early as 1946, the British government had started to doubt the outcome and begun preparations for the eventuality of the loan not being approved. Keynes nevertheless encouraged patience: "I should do nothing at this juncture. If indeed we have any ammunition, it should surely be reserved for use later on."[243]

Nevertheless, the British government understood that the failure to secure financial aid from the United States would have had profound effects on the international economic order. Keynes was clear that "if the worst does befall, some much more drastic change will be called for" and went on to elaborate his remarkable plan: "We should at once set about a reinvigorated and re-formed Sterling Area, which would . . . invite a considerable part of the rest of the word, including all North-West Europe either to join it or become linked to it by suitable payment agreements. At the same time, we should, of course, also be cutting off all dollar imports that we could and generally providing an ocular demonstration of what the Congress decision means to American interests.[244] Other senior British officials were confident that the United Kingdom could "develop a perfectly workable multilateral system based on sterling, excluding USA," which would involve leaving Bretton Woods and gathering support from the dominions. As one official put it, "On the whole our policy would have to be based upon the fact that in a world of bankrupts the half solvent is king."[245]

Yet the period surrounding the ratification debate brought two significant interventions. The first intervention reflected a significant deterioration in relations between the United States and the Soviet Union, which greatly aided the political advance of the proposed loan.[246] The Soviet threat to Iran and its boycott of the United Nations cast a shadow over Washington, even if the administration remained reluctant to present the proposed loan as an investment in the strength of the non-Soviet world.[247] Attlee had also avoided linking the two issues together in public, probably to avoid upsetting foreign audiences or unnecessarily complicating the path of ratification, even if he and much of the cabinet were keenly aware of the Soviet threat.[248] While political leaders on both sides of the Atlantic treated the issue cautiously, key figures such as Acheson and Churchill proved more than willing to defend the proposed loan in the context of an emerging Cold War.[249]

The second intervention was Churchill's trip to the United States, where he met senior U.S. politicians, including key Republican and Democrat members of the Senate and House in March. Churchill managed to convince many of them, including Senator Arthur Vandenberg, of the merits of a loan, not least as a valuable response to the Soviet threat. Vandenberg was an important figure in Republican circles who, as a member of the Senate Committee on Foreign Relations, could obstruct the progress of any measure.[250] Vandenberg's eventual speech in favor of the loan on April 22 therefore helped to turn the tide of debate.[251] Keynes judged the loan to be quite safe by April.[252]

The British government supported such efforts. Attlee, Dalton, and Bevin all repeatedly bit their tongues as members of Congress depicted them as "sponging socialists crawling to Uncle Sam so they could feather-bed their people."[253] Dalton also agreed to help Churchill and sent material to him to help with his talks.[254] Furthermore, following advice from sympathetic Americans and British diplomats, the chancellor carefully raised the subject in his second budget as an appeal to his potential creditors: "The proposed Anglo-American loan is now before the American Congress; and it would not be proper for me to intervene in that debate. But it is right for me to emphasise now how greatly we need and how greatly shall appreciate the proposed measure of assistance."[255] As the Conservative MP Joseph Gurney Braithwaite noted, "I could not escape the impression that he was addressing himself to the American Congress rather than to the British House of Commons, so ostentatiously did he soft pedal Socialist policy."[256]

Truman also continued to support the proposal in subtle ways. The president's recommendation to Congress had been, according to Halifax, "framed in such a way as to ensure that the agreement is referred, in the first instance, to the banking and currency committee . . . which is judged by the administration to be the friendliest."[257] This approach proved successful. The Banking and Currency Committee of the Senate began open hearings on 5 March. On 10 April, the committee voted by fourteen to five in favor of the proposed agreement, and debate in the Senate began a week later.[258] The Senate approved the loan by a vote of forty-six to thirty-four on 10 May. This final vote should not obscure the significant amount of opposition the vote generated, especially in the form of proposed amendments. The Democrat Ernest McFarland said that he would oppose approval unless Britain handed the U.S. permanent possession of the bases now held on a ninety-nine-year lease in exchange for fifty old destroyers, arguing that the United Kingdom should settle its First World War debts first.[259] The British government was unlikely to have accepted this amendment, and the Anglo-American

Financial Agreement would therefore have been wrecked. The Senate narrowly defeated this motion with a vote of forty-five to forty.[260] Ardent isolationists who had never previously shown support for multilateral arguments had helped to defeat these problematic amendments. They were probably converted in opinion by the growing Soviet threat and the need for stability in the Western world rather than by any efforts by the administration.[261]

Popular discontent persisted, however, as evidenced by letters to the president and Congress members criticizing the "welching British" and their outstanding debts from the First World War.[262] The bill was scheduled to come before the House in July. The president took this opportunity to stress publicly that the British financial agreement was "an integral part of the international economic policy of the United States" and warned of the economic and security risks of a "conflict in economic policy" between the two states if they failed to support the proposal.[263] Truman wrote to Brent Spence, chairman of the House Banking and Currency Committee, urging support for the agreement.[264] After three weeks of hearings, the committee reported favorably to the House, making special effort to engage with, and rebuff, arguments that the United Kingdom would not honor its obligations given its failure to repay First World War debts.[265] The House eventually approved funding with a vote of 219 to 155 on 13 July. Although this looked like a comfortable majority, there were dozens of attempted amendments, many of which were hostile and only narrowly defeated.[266]

An important but neglected element of the ongoing hostility to the Anglo-American Financial Agreement was the memory of British default.[267] In the week leading up to ratification in the House, criticism on both sides of the aisle focused on the United Kingdom's enduring wealth, the risks of a socialist government, and its unpaid war debts.[268] Democratic whips believed that the two main arguments against approval were the danger of inflation and the assertion that the loan would not be repaid, like the First World War loans. As the British embassy reported to the British government, "charges that we 'welshed' on the last war debt" were "almost inevitable."[269]

The Democrat Dudley Roe explained what voting in favor of the loan would mean: "We would be making the most serious blunder in the whole history of our Nation. . . . Are we going to squeeze the last drop of blood out of the American taxpayers and subsidize our industries and natural resources and be a 'sucker' all over again as in World War I?"[270] The Republican William Lemke continued this line of argument by stressing, "The time has come for Congress to decide whether we are more interested in the British Empire than the United States. . . . Great Britain never kept a promise to America or to any other nation," referring to "the so-called loan we made to Great Britain after World War I that is still unpaid."[271] The Republican Leon Gavin stressed "the fact that the British record is not the best record as to payment of World War I debts."[272]

The Republican Jessie Sumner took the trade argument head-on: "Several people have used the expression that England was our best customer. Does the gentleman believe it would be to his advantage if a customer bought a lot of goods in his store but never paid for it?"[273] The Republican Raymond Springer was clear that when considering the history of the United States' "past transactions with Great Britain," the assessment was poor: "The huge loans we extended to her, both before and after World War I, are largely unpaid. Our people have worked, and they have paid, for the benefit of Great Britain."[274] The Democrat Luther Johnson suggested that the British government should give its bases in the Pacific Ocean as collateral, because if it had done so, "after World War I, the first British loan would have been paid," and he explained that the United Kingdom should "not object now if they did not consider Uncle Sam sort of a sucker and figure that he would make this loan anyhow, which they would forget to pay."[275]

Such views were aided by press reports in both countries suggesting that the British government would not repay these debts. *The Economist* stated, "The odds are billions to one that this new credit will be paid."[276] The Republican John Robsion cited this source in an impassioned challenge to the proposed loan: "With these disclosures, how can American farmers, businessmen, and workers, who must make good in the end, the defaults of Britain on her other loan and this, hope to profit by this improvident deal? . . . She still owes her debt of World War I. . . . Of course, no one is so naive as to think that any part of the principal or interest will be paid."[277] Such statements highlight the powerful and enduring memory of British default in the minds of many U.S. policymakers despite the passage of more than a decade. As the British embassy noted, in "cloak-room discussions" among Republican representatives, attempts by those who were sympathetic to the United

Kingdom to set the record straight on the subject of war debts "had been met with howls of derision and disbelief."[278]

The Truman administration was well prepared for such criticisms, benefiting from the support of the British government and its embassy in the United States. The diplomat and congressional liaison officer Alan Judson closely monitored passage of the bill through Congress and worked with ministers and officials to help guide the Democratic whip's office.[279] Judson was keenly aware of the popularity and power of arguments based on Britain's unpaid debts from the First World War. He, together with Brand, prepared a list of facts relating to the debt for use by the Democratic whip, of which Judson was assured they would "make excellent use."[280] Furthermore, Judson managed "to get into the Congressional record" what he considered "a really satisfactory account of the World War I debt situation," detailing British efforts at repayment and justifying default on the basis of uncontrollable economic conditions.[281] He also placed a statement regarding Britain's handling of its war debt "quietly" into the hand of "thirty or forty carefully selected members of the House."[282] There followed a series of impassioned defenses concerning these unpaid debts in congressional debate.[283] Given such a close-run race, these efforts were surely important. In early July, it had been "touch and go," and the British embassy had begun to prepare for failure given the "decidedly gloomy picture."[284]

Following approval in the House, the Anglo-American Financial Agreement was enacted by the signature of the president. The U.S. then authorized a loan of $3.75 billion to the United Kingdom on 15 July 1946. Britain would ultimately have to repay $5.96 billion, making a payment every year of $119,336,000.[285] The United States had agreed to waive interest payments in time of emergency, so as to "not to force a default which might have serious consequences to the world economy."[286] The British government had by now also received a further loan of $1.25 billion from Canada, after it too had ceased wartime economic assistance.[287] This smaller loan, repayable over twenty years at 2 percent interest, was motivated by Canada's political ties to the dominion, dependence on British markets, and a commitment to free trade, especially given that it was not a member of the Sterling Area.[288]

Significant financial aid from the United States and Canada nevertheless proved insufficient. The U.S. loan was intended to last for three years, but difficult economic conditions—including inflation and a fuel crisis, alongside rising payments to support West Germany, the costs of the welfare state, and international obligations—meant that the British government had drawn $1.45 billion of the U.S. loan and $963 million of the Canadian loan by the first half of 1947.[289] As uncertainty about the British economy mounted, countries with sterling balances took advantage of the newly agreed convertibility option, choosing to solve their own financial problems by converting their holdings to dollars or gold rather than risk the devaluation of sterling. The conditions of the loan consequently helped to worsen the UK financial position as ever-larger sums were required to fill the gap that sterling convertibility created.[290] The British government ultimately announced the suspension of sterling convertibility on 18 August.[291]

Truman later recorded in his memoirs that he had been disturbed by this failure.[292] Popular opinion—with regard to both Congress and the American people more broadly—had been proved right in its doubts about the creditworthiness of the United Kingdom.[293] U.S. Treasury Secretary John Snyder regarded the suspension of sterling convertibility without consultation as a clear violation of the terms of agreement.[294] Transatlantic negotiations followed thereafter, which involved both sides seeking "legal loop-holes in the Agreement" to avoid a technical default and "a stigma upon [Britain's] reputation."[295] Representatives from each country issued a joint statement declaring that the suspension was an emergency and only temporary, but there was no agreement on when convertibility would be reestablished.[296] In a subsequent meeting with Snyder on 1 October 1948, the new chancellor of the exchequer, Stafford Cripps, noted that another effort at convertibility might risk "a second default."[297]

Powerful trade swings, limited reserves, and high levels of short-term indebtedness meant that sterling remained vulnerable to speculative pressure. As dollars continued to flow out of British coffers, reserves were drained, and a new balance of payments crisis emerged.[298] These events highlighted what would become a recurrent challenge to the Bretton Woods system.[299] Attlee and Cripps agreed to devalue the pound to stem the drain on reserves in an effort to conclude what Cairncross and Eichengreen have called "a slow motion train wreck."[300] On 18 September 1949, the government cut the value of sterling from $4.03 to $2.80.[301] Despite sterling's value falling by 30.5 percent, the relative amount was closer to 9 percent, as other European and sterling-bloc countries devalued simultaneously.[302] These devaluations, in conjunction with support from the European Recovery Program, would help to improve the competitive balance between Europe and the United States, shifting the former's current account deficit to a surplus.[303] Moreover, despite emerging from the war with an unprecedented level of sovereign debt, nearly 250 percent of GDP, devaluation did not force the government to default. Liabilities were largely denominated in domestic currency, and sterling retained its status as an international currency.[304]

British devaluation would help to introduce significant governance problems for the IMF. The IMF approved the devaluation but had only received twenty-four hours' notice for a reduction larger than suggested initially. This event revealed the IMF's limited ability to prevent powerful states from pursuing their own national interests. The British devaluation also generated political tensions within the IMF. Some states feared an adverse effect on their own interests, not least because the devaluing countries accounted for almost half the world's exports. The precedents established in this case led the IMF to become increasingly tolerant of member states' refusals to play by the newly established rules.[305]

For the United States, the devaluation of the pound revealed the United Kingdom as a weakened ally that required support.[306] London had at least been spared the difficulty and embarrassment of immediately seeking help to avoid defaulting on its new debts to Washington. Payments on the Anglo-American loan would only begin on 31 December 1951. The United Kingdom now carried a new and significant debt to the United States that would take decades to repay. Winston Churchill later lamented "why Britain should be the only debtor country in the world while those she had rescued and those she had conquered went into the future without having to drag a terrible chain of war debt behind them."[307] This chain of debt was especially long given that the U.S. Treasury also continued to record the United Kingdom's outstanding debts from the First World War. These debts continued to grow at the size of more than $150 million a year in interest, which compares to payments of only $119 million for the Anglo-American loan. In contrast to U.S. bookkeeping, the British government ceased to carry any reference to either its debts or credits concerning war loans in its books from 1945.[308] HM Treasury would always acknowledge that the matter was unresolved, however, and remained aware of U.S. record keeping on the subject (Table 5.1).[309]

These lingering war debts still mattered to policymakers on both sides of the Atlantic. The U.S. provided billions of dollars to the United

Table 5.1. Indebtedness of foreign governments to the U.S. arising from World War I, 1946 (USD)

| Country | Total indebtedness (payments on principal deducted) | Total payments received | Funded indebtedness | | | |
| | | | Indebtedness | | Payments on account | |
			Principal (net)	Accrued interest	Principal	Interest
Armenia	27,989,075.20	0.00	0.00	0.00	0.00	0.00
Belgium	511,895,077.60	52,191,273.24	400,680,000.00	111,215,077.60	17,100,000.00	14,490,000.00
Cuba	0	12,286,751.58	0.00	0	0.00	0.00
Czechoslovakia	179,659,821.93	20,134,092.26	165,241,108.90	14,418,713.03	19,829,914.17	0.00
Estonia	25,064,230.81[a]	1,248,432.07	16,466,012.87	8,598,217.94	0.00	1,246,990.19
Finland	8,418,516.01	7,430,029.73	7,734,932.45	683,583.56	1,265,067.55	5,855,646.91
France	4,683,681,394.40	486,075,891.00	3,863,650,000.00	820,031,394.40	161,350,000.00	38,650,000.00
Germany[b]	26,024,539.59[c]	862,668.00	25,980,480.66	44,058.93	862,668.00	0.00
Great Britain	6,567,564,782.58	2,024,848,817.09	4,368,000,000.00	2,199,564,782.58	232,000,000.00	1,232,770,518.42
Greece	37,527,295.10	4,127,056.01	31,516,000.00	6,011,295.10	981,000.00	1,983,980.00
Hungary	2,807,308.21[a]	556,919.76	1,908,560.00	898,748.21	73,995.50	482,171.22
Italy	2,057,195,159.34	100,829,880.16	2,004,900,000.00	52,295,159.34	37,100,000.00	5,766,708.26
Latvia	10,354,198.04[a]	761,549.07	6,879,464.20	3,474,733.84	9,200.00	621,520.12

Country						
Liberia	0	36,471.56	0.00	0.00	0.00	0.00
Lithuania	9,279,708.11[a]	1,237,956.58	6,197,682.00	3,082,026.11	234,783.00	1,001,626.61
Nicaragua[d]	0	168,575.84	0.00	0	0.00	0.00
Poland	313,663,444.20[a]	22,646,297.55	206,057,000.00	107,606,444.20	1,287,297.37	19,310,775.90
Rumania	76,741,399.37	4,791,007.22[e]	63,860,560.43	12,880,838.94	2,700,000.00	29,061.46
Russia	462,402,546.57	8,750,311.88[f]	0.00	0	0.00	0.00
Yugoslavia	63,704,843.78	2,588,771.69	61,625,000.00	2,079,843.78	1,225,000.00	0.00
Total	15,063,973,340.84	2,751,572,752.29	11,230,696,801.51	3,342,884,917.56[g]	476,018,925.59	1,322,208,999.09

Source: U.S. Treasury Department, *Annual Report* (1946), 561, table 66, "Principal of the Funded and Unfunded Indebtedness of Foreign Governments to the United States, the Accrued and Unpaid Interest Thereon, and Payments on Account of Principal and Interest, as of Nov. 15, 1946."

Note: Due to space limitations, the final four columns ("Principal [net]," "Accrued interest," "Principal," and "Interest") under the heading of "Unfunded indebtedness" have been removed.

[a] Increase over amount funded due to exercise of options with respect to the payment of interest due on original issue of bonds of debtor governments.

[b] The German Government has been notified that the Government of the United States will look to the German Government for the discharge of this indebtedness of the Government of Austria to the Government of the United States.

[c] Includes additional bonds aggregating $3,489,482.76 received July 23, 1937, in exchange for bonds aggregating $1,207,742 and annuities aggregating $69,534.46, payable on Jan. 1, 1933, 1934, and 1935; but postponed as provided by agreements of May 8, 1930, and Sept. 14, 1932.

[d] The United States held obligations in the principal amount of $289,898.78, which, together with accrued interest thereon, were canceled on Oct. 6, 1939, pursuant to agreement of Apr. 14, 1938, between the United States and the Republic of Nicaragua, ratified by the United States Senate on June 13, 1938.

[e] Does not include payment of $100,000 by Rumanian Government on June 15, 1940, which was made as "a token of its good faith and of its real desire to reach a new agreement covering" Rumania's indebtedness to the United States.

[f] Represents proceeds of liquidation of financial affairs of the Russian Government in this country. (Copies of letter dated May 23, 1922, from the Secretary of State and of reply of the Secretary of the Treasury dated June 2, 1922, in regard to loans to the Russian Government and liquidation of affairs of the latter in this country appear in the Annual Report of the Secretary of the Treasury for 1922, as exhibit 79, p. 283, and in the combined annual reports of the World War Foreign Debt Commission as exhibit 2, p. 84.)

[g] Includes balances of amounts postponed under provisions of joint resolution of Dec. 23, 1931. (For amounts postponed see p. 35 of Annual Report of the Secretary of the Treasury for 1932.)

Kingdom as well as other war-debt defaulters via the European Recovery Program, also known as the Marshall Plan, to promote economic redevelopment and halt the spread of communism on the European continent.[310] Yet policymakers and Congress did occasionally raise the issue of unpaid war debts to variously criticize or support the European Recovery Program, even if debate was overshadowed by broader Cold War concerns.[311] The Johnson Act was no longer an obstacle to further borrowing, to be sure, and the United Kingdom went on to secure further financial support from the United States in the coming years. As Figure 5.1 reveals, by 1971, the United Kingdom had five separate loans

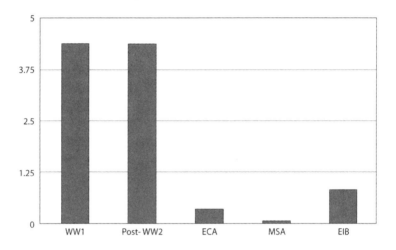

Figure 5.1. UK long-term debts to the U.S., 1971 ($ billion). This graph shows original debt totals and therefore excludes repaid amounts. Column 1 refers to debts owed to the United States following and immediately after the First World War. HM Treasury gave an outstanding figure of $4,368 million at the time of default. Column 2 refers to debts accrued during and soon after the Second World War, which comprises a U.S. line of credit totaling $3.75 billion and Lend-Lease aid, which was reduced to $622 million. Column 3 refers to support via the Economic Cooperation Administration totaling $337 million, which began in 1948. Column 4 refers to loans from the Mutual Security Agency, which began in 1952 and totaled $47.9 million. Column 5 refers to Export-Import Bank loans, comprising five lines of credit since 1966, of which $800 million had been drawn but $915 million was available. Figures exclude smaller "internal debt" whereby Kenya and Tanzania were the effective borrowers of a loan of up to £2.39 million via the Mutual Security Agency for the development of Mombasa and Tanga ports. (Source: T 385/204, Pierson note, 16 December 1971)

totaling $4.05 billion of long-term debt to the United States, which included the Anglo-American loan.[312] Nevertheless, the outstanding balance of First World War debts remained an emotive subject. As a note from HM Treasury explained in 1948, "allied indebtedness is one of the subjects to which U.S. public opinion is particularly sensitive."[313]

In the immediate postwar period, HM Treasury felt it "important for the record that Britain's effort [toward repayment] should not be minimized in the least."[314] The government's sensitivity to the issue is clearly evidenced by its reaction to the publication of Churchill's memoirs in 1947, which erroneously downplayed the scale and effort of Britain's repayments prior to default in 1934.[315] HM Treasury believed it worthwhile trying to secure a correction before the book was printed and shared in the United States, especially with excerpts due in *Life* and the *New York Times*, and sent a formal letter to Churchill requesting corrections.[316] The letter explained that extracts were "misleading," which was significant given ongoing "sensitivity" on this issue.[317] Churchill responded by saying that the Americans had complained that his draft overstated the matter, but "these new facts of yours" show "our case is even stronger."[318] Churchill asked for a corrected paragraph in order to prepare an errata slip, which HM Treasury duly provided, and the corrections were actioned.[319]

London ultimately expected a reckoning with Washington. As a British Treasury official warned in 1948, "Some day the United States must take action with regard to the war debts of World War I in order to clear the Treasury's books."[320] These concerns explain why the British government never formally forgave its own debtors, even if it never expected repayment. On successive occasions in the immediate postwar period, it clarified that it had still not canceled its own First World War loans to its European and Commonwealth allies. Furthermore, the Lausanne Agreement had never been ratified, which meant that French and German debts had never been written off. Similar situations existed around the world. The United Kingdom had provided a £400,000 loan to Newfoundland in 1917, for instance, but had suspended interest on this debt in September 1935. In 1947, correspondence initially suggested that the "debt can be considered cancelled."[321] A subsequent letter swiftly corrected this error, clarifying that cancellation was an "overstatement" that could only be approved by Parliament, even if there was "no intention of seeking repayment."[322]

The same was true of British loans made to Australia and New Zealand during the First World War. Antipodean debt to the United Kingdom still stood at just £105 million, which continued to arouse popular interest in the Southern Hemisphere.[323] The British government never attempted to collect these debts, evidently preferring to avoid the issue despite its own difficult negotiations with Australia and New Zealand on their sterling balances.[324] Avoidance helped to maintain strong relations between Commonwealth countries, especially as they would go on to make generous postwar donations to the United Kingdom and assume a greater burden of providing for Commonwealth security than they had in the past.[325] The British government evidently remained sensitive to the war-debts controversy and wary about a potential resurgence of the issue in the United States. Such concerns proved entirely reasonable. Congress would eventually come calling for the prompt repayment of these outstanding war debts.

6 A Long Shadow, 1952–2020

THE UNITED KINGDOM has sometimes forgotten its First World War debts, but the United States has never forgiven them. This chapter builds on one of the core arguments advanced in chapter 5 by showing that governments can retain a long memory of sovereign default. It refutes popular assumptions and potential counterarguments that Britain's war debts have been excused by the U.S., revealing instead how these outstanding obligations informed policymaking in governments on both sides of the Atlantic in the following seven decades. Unpaid war debts may no longer have assumed a central role in political debate, but they continued to linger and occasionally emerged as a significant concern for policymakers in Washington and London. British default has cast a far longer shadow over the course of international relations than scholars and policymakers have appreciated.

The claim that these debts still exist should not be controversial. The U.S. Treasury has maintained records of these outstanding loans well into the twenty-first century (see Table I.1). In 1952, Britain's unpaid debts stood at just under $7.5 billion. In the more recently published U.S. Treasury report in 2009, this figure had grown to more than $16 billion.[1] The comparative value of these outstanding obligations has been eroded by decades of inflation, and many policymakers may well have forgotten about their existence; but the U.S. Treasury has repeatedly defended its right to recover these debts in the future, actively pursuing various legal options in the 1990s.[2] Senior policymakers on both sides of the Atlantic accept the ongoing existence and delinquent status of these outstanding obligations.[3]

Recognizing the lingering memory of British and other European defaults on U.S. loans in the 1930s provides a fuller and more nuanced understanding of transatlantic relations in the postwar period. The United Kingdom's First World War debts—as well as those of other major European states—became an increasingly important and viable political tool with which to exert control over mounting economic challenges in the United States from the late 1950s to the mid-1970s. Throughout this period, Congress repeatedly raised the subject of Europe's outstanding obligations in connection with U.S. balance of payments problems, whether as a way in which to influence Cold War allies to make financial concessions or to excuse unpopular domestic policies by blaming the fiscal irresponsibility of foreign governments. Tensions peaked in 1973 when more than one hundred members of the House of Representatives sponsored a resolution that asked the U.S. Treasury to pursue the prompt repayment of these long-standing war debts. The United Kingdom, as well as France and the Federal Republic of Germany (FRG), remained largely silent throughout this period. Behind the scenes, officials in HM Treasury were preparing to deal with the issue of payment should diplomatic pressure intensify. The Watergate scandal and U.S. economic revival in the following years eventually turned Congress's attention elsewhere and helped the issue to fade from the political landscape.

Policymakers in Congress and the Houses of Parliament continued to raise the issue on occasion, and there were also infrequent periods of press interest in the many decades that followed. The most important discussions concerning these outstanding loans, however, took place behind closed doors. Treasury officials in London and Washington faced serious legal challenges to the status quo throughout the 1980s and 1990s. Much of the controversy reflected a private citizen's will, which bequeathed a multimillion-dollar donation to the United Kingdom to pay down some of its outstanding war debt to the United States. A series of protracted legal rulings followed, which ultimately led to a deposit of $2.1 million to the United States on behalf of the British government in 2002.[4] Throughout this period, the U.S. Treasury remained keen to avoid any policy or concession that might "undercut prospective efforts to collect the debt" in the future.[5]

In 2006, Britain finally paid off the Anglo-American loan of 1946. Celebrations were short-lived as media attention briefly returned to the First World War debts. The British government subsequently informed the British Broadcasting Corporation (BBC) that these outstanding obligations had not been serviced since they were suspended, but nor had they been written off.[6] Two years later came the global financial crisis of 2008. This international crisis failed to revive the issue of unpaid war debts. Part of the reason why may reflect the swift and coordinated nature of the international response but also the nature of the credit crunch itself, which more greatly concerned issues of private finance rather than states' trading surpluses or national debts.[7] The resultant austerity policies that emerged in many states around the globe, however, did encourage a brief renewal of popular interest in past debt transgressions. Yet interest in the British government's large and outstanding obligations to the United States remained largely subdued, and attention continued to fade in the years that followed, even despite major economic events ranging from the United Kingdom's departure from the European Union to the onset of the coronavirus pandemic. The etiolated condition of the debate has left the war debts fixed in a state of political limbo. Neither government has provided a formal statement on the subject in the past decade, and there is little evidence of any progress toward a resolution on either side of the Atlantic.

BALANCE OF PAYMENT CRISES

On 4 November 1952, President Dwight Eisenhower secured a dominant electoral victory. Shortly after he took office in the following year, British and U.S. representatives signed the London Debt Agreement whereby the Federal Republic of Germany assumed responsibility for all external obligations of the extinct German Reich. These debts included reparations obligations after the First World War as well as postwar loans such as the Marshall Plan. Burdened by high levels of debt, the FRG sought relief via international debt restructuring. The ensuing Conference on German External Debts involved representatives of thirty-one states meeting between February and August 1952.[8] The gathered representatives agreed to relieve the FRG of external debts totaling nearly fifteen billion Deutsche marks, which equated to 50 percent of total external debt, comprising both pre- and postwar obligations.[9] The agreement reached at the conference was signed in London on 27 February 1953 and ratified on 16 September later that year.[10] This charitable solution made a significant contribution to the West German postwar "economic miracle" of the 1950s and 1960s.[11] It was also the first example of a bankruptcy under international law.[12]

The generous approach toward the FRG's debts reflected doubts about the viability of repayment as well as West Germany's importance as a "bulwark against communism" in the early Cold War.[13] Nevertheless, White House staff warned the president that his support for the German debt settlement could feature negatively in the approaching congressional elections, on the basis of "the specious reasoning that the American taxpayers . . . were in reality paying for the external debt."[14] Such concerns help to explain why the London agreement on German external debts, to which both the United States and United Kingdom were signatories, avoided rather than addressed the European-wide issue of unpaid First World War debts.[15] As a later HM Treasury note explained, the 1953 London agreement "had put the WWI debts question into cold storage but neither the US nor the UK . . . had completely renounced their claims for repayment."[16]

The U.S. Treasury has always been clear that the "resolution of this issue [World War I debts] was deferred by 1953 agreement" but stressed that the "London Debt Agreement would not prevent the US from raising, on a bilateral basis, the question of payment of any debtor (except for Germany)." Yet it conceded that any effort to do so would "undoubtedly raise the problem of German World War I reparations. From the practical viewpoint, therefore, there does not seem to be any possibility of reaching an agreement on repayment in the absence of an overall settlement."[17] As European debtors would only be willing to resume payments following the settlement of World War I reparations, which in turn rested on the reunification of Germany, the United States had tacitly deferred the issue of war debts for decades to come.[18]

On first inspection, this decision to ignore these outstanding war debts seems like a missed opportunity for the new administration. Eisenhower had launched a successful campaign for fiscal discipline and committed himself to enhancing the economic strength of the United States.[19] Reopening the issue with the United Kingdom or any other major European power could have provided a way to recover some lost income or at least blame Eisenhower's difficult decisions on the failure of foreign borrowers to cooperate. Furthermore, the United Kingdom had also begun to enjoy a period of economic recovery by the early 1950s. Successive Conservative governments from 1951 oversaw steady growth in invisible exports, and the dollar shortage began to ease. The balance of payments improved as terms of trade became more favorable and reserves began to increase.[20] The Eisenhower administration nevertheless avoided using or invoking the issue of war debts to advance its own interests. The major challenge, as administration officials recognized, was that "most foreign countries consider World War I debts as completely dead."[21] Furthermore, any attempt to recover the debts via bilateral negotiations "would raise problems regarding the status of all World War I debts" and therefore require a broader and more complex international solution.[22] Such an outcome risked reopening a difficult subject that had bedeviled European relations in an already fraught Cold War setting.

The Eisenhower administration's failure to resolve the issue left it prone to further reappearances, especially as the United States continued to send billions of dollars overseas. The specter of these unpaid war debts haunted congressional debates concerning foreign aid programs.[23] The United Kingdom and the rest of Europe's unpaid war debts would also emerge from time to time in the popular press.[24] The first instance of the United Kingdom missing a repayment on the Anglo-American loan following the Suez Crisis generated considerable hostility in certain quarters of the U.S. media, which swiftly recalled the memory of Britain's default on its war debts.[25] The *Chicago Daily Tribune*, for instance, advanced a scathing argument in an article published in 1957: "No one familiar with the record in these matters had the slightest belief that Britain's government would pay its debts to us. It never had. . . . [After World War I and initial repayment] they quit paying and repudiated the debt . . . at the expense of the American taxpayers. . . . It is no surprise to us that another British debt is in the process of turning sour."[26]

The British government did little to challenge such criticism and simply preferred to avoid rather than address the matter. The war debts do not appear to have had much relevance to the major British currency debates of the 1950s, with regard to either the Robot plan of 1952 to adopt convertibility via a flexible exchange-rate regime, for example, or the Radcliffe Committee report of 1959 on the working of the monetary system.[27] As an internal memorandum within HM Treasury noted in August 1960, "The British government in no way denied or repudiated the debt . . . [but] the matter has not been reopened since."[28] This political limbo extended to the United Kingdom's own war loans. The British government did not attempt to pursue the collection of its own outstanding war debts with European or Commonwealth states. Australia and New Zealand, for instance, remained in more than £100 million of war debt to the United Kingdom. Yet all these debts remained dormant rather than forgiven.[29]

The war-debts issue would return to prominence in Washington in the 1960s as balance of payments problems become increasingly important, moving from what Barry Eichengreen describes as "benign neglect" to "malignant preoccupation."[30] The Bretton Woods agreement of 1944 meant that the dollar now operated as the pivot of the global exchange system, sustained by the promise of conversion into gold at US$35 per ounce. All signatories pegged their currencies to the dollar.[31] The major economies of western Europe, most notably France and the FRG, recovered their strength and became increasingly competitive. As a result, payments deficits vis-à-vis the United States transformed into surpluses in the 1950s. By the end of the decade, the dollar gap had grown considerably. Eisenhower attempted to meet this challenge by restraining government expenditures overseas, particularly military commitments, but was nevertheless thwarted in large part by bureaucratic resistance within Washington.[32]

The John F. Kennedy administration inherited these difficulties after coming to office in January 1961. By 1963, a cabinet committee report noted that the U.S. balance of payments deficit was "a serious threat to national power and security and to international economic order."[33] The document considered a wide range of ways in which to reduce the deficit, ranging from restraining defense and aid spending through to a drawing from the IMF.[34] Kennedy adopted an "offset arrangement," whereby the West German government would purchase U.S. or British military equipment to offset the exchange costs associated with stationing forces in Europe.[35] The United States continued to lose substantial amounts of gold, however, which underlined the importance of pursuing further reductions to defense expenditure and the elimination of the deficit.[36] Monetary stability would require the support of the European countries maintaining surpluses.[37] Yet international cooperation proved challenging. In addition to competing national interests, the growth of gold holdings was also driven by institutional memory and the persistent habits of European central bankers, which presented an unexpected and intractable problem for the Bretton Woods system.[38]

Balance of payments difficulties continued throughout the 1960s. The Lyndon Johnson administration's obligations to the Vietnam War and the Great Society, alongside its commitment to full employment, exacerbated the deterioration of the U.S. balance of trade position.[39] It was in such circumstances that the payment of war debts regained wider congressional and public attention as a way to address this challenge. Interest in such solutions may also have been stoked by the Greek government's decision to resume payment of its First World War debts in 1964.[40] On 5 November 1965, the U.S. Treasury noted that one possible action to deal with balance of payments surpluses abroad was to pursue the collection of outstanding First World War debts, focusing initially on France and West Germany given their increasingly large gold reserves. Yet, even at this early stage, U.S. Treasury officials recognized that it would be "difficult" and that the possibility of raising a "significant sum" within two to three years was "small," an attitude reflecting considerable doubts about the likelihood of European cooperation.[41]

By May 1966, Deputy National Security Adviser Francis Bator informed the president that the balance of payments was still a serious issue. The first-quarter results painted a "dismal picture" of an overall deficit running at $2.4 billion per year: "Unless we take drastic action, the rest of 1966 is not likely to improve much."[42] Bator blamed the rise in spending in Vietnam and the rapid expansion of the domestic economy, but France's resistance to U.S. economic policy and the further stockpiling of gold were also creating problems.[43] Only weeks earlier, in a memorandum to the secretary, administration officials had clarified the position of outstanding First World War debts, noting that France was still "legally obligated to the United States" to repay its loans, of which approximately $4.7 billion was due and unpaid.[44] Further exchanges within the administration underlined ongoing press, public, and congressional interest in the status of the war debts.[45]

Memories of the war debts had generated less political attention in the United Kingdom but would arise occasionally in Parliamentary questions. Lord Barnby had asked the government about the size of these unpaid debts in May 1965. Lord Shepard provided a detailed response, albeit erroneously suggesting that payments had stopped in July 1932, thereby overlooking one further full payment in 1932 and two token payments in 1933.[46] Perhaps reflecting growing interest in the United States, the issue generated further attention in 1966. Chancellor of the Exchequer James Callaghan was asked for an update concerning the present state of these debts. Callaghan confirmed only that payments on these loans were suspended and had not since been resumed.[47] The British press was also by now increasingly aware of rising political interest in the United States concerning unpaid war debts and the potential risks for the United Kingdom. *The Times* went on to cover the subject in some detail.[48]

By October 1966, the U.S. Treasury, frustrated by still-growing European gold reserves, proposed that France should be requested to repay its First World War debts. The State Department resisted the proposal. Officials warned that this strategy risked reviving the complex and problematic issue of reparations. In addition, such a claim would make a similar demand of the United Kingdom, whose war debts were larger and which would be ruined financially by such a demand, resulting in not much being left of NATO.[49] The State Department's analysis appears somewhat extreme and ignored a wide variety of repayment strategies, but it appreciated the serious challenges facing the United Kingdom. The Labour government had already sought U.S. support to avoid the devaluation of the pound, which required acceptance of a deflationary package that would "put in order" the British economy. Even then, the pound required further and urgent external support.[50] As Prime Minister Harold Wilson recalled in his memoirs, the governor of the Bank of England had "felt that the financial end of the world was near," with the dollar falling soon after the pound.[51] Furthermore, the British government was struggling to maintain its significant international military commitments. It would eventually succumb to longer-term trends and agree to withdraw completely from East of Suez in the following decade.[52] Economic weakness and an overstretched military therefore helped to protect the United Kingdom and thus, indirectly, France and West Germany from U.S. demands for repayment.

Under Secretary of State George Ball had detailed his concerns about renewed interest in unpaid war debts on 15 August 1966, two months earlier than the U.S. Treasury proposal. In a lengthy note, he opposed recent proposals for a change in the form of the government's response to public and congressional inquiries regarding First World War debts.[53] Ball argued that the sensible course of action was to downplay or ignore the issue given that the "possibilities of practical financial results are negligible and the political costs enormous":

> What kind of chain reaction might we be starting by creating a new ambiguity as to our position on this issue? Undoubtedly it would create a public row. . . . The slightest whisper that we might be thinking of pressing Britain for payment could further rock the sterling boat which is already taking water over the gunwales. If, on the other hand, it were thought that we might lay off Britain but proceed only against those nations in strong financial positions . . . we could expect cries of anguish and outrage. All governments that felt threatened by possible pressure for payment would automatically assert the linkage of debt to reparations, making it clear that if we moved to collect war debts they would demand reparation payments from Germany. This would almost certainly trigger a violent reaction from the Germans. . . . Worst of all, it might revive old resentments not only against us but between Germany and her neighbours. . . . I can think of nothing more dangerous than a Germany feeling disaffected and isolated. It could make our troubles in Vietnam seem small by comparison.[54]

Ball believed that returning to the issue of unpaid war debts would be a costly mistake. He was right to be concerned about rocking "the sterling boat." A little more than a year later, the British government would once again devalue sterling against the dollar, dropping from $2.80 to $2.40, and would waive interest payments on the Anglo-American loan in the following year.[55] Ball's concerns about reviving "old resentments" were especially acute given the Johnson administration's recent decision to reject two of the FRG's major international objectives—namely, access to nuclear weapons and reductions to the current offset agreement. The U.S. was instead attempting to stem the proliferation of nuclear weapons in Europe to secure a nonproliferation agreement with the Soviet Union and remained reliant on West German military purchases to reduce worsening balance of payments deficits.[56]

Ball continued his response by concluding that "too much water has gone over the dam to risk revising old angers and anxieties by stirring up an old argument."[57] He also followed in Dean Acheson's footsteps by conceding that the United States held some of the responsibility for the war-debts imbroglio, suggesting that the credit extended was toward a "common effort" and that only in the last war did the U.S. develop "a more mature approach to the basic philosophy of an alliance": "I think it the part of wisdom, therefore, that we regard our fifty-year indebtedness from the First World War as very much like our assistance during the second. It was a form of lend-lease for which we have received substantial repayment—partial payment in cash and a more important payment in victory that reinforced our own security. This is, I think, the way in which the world has come to understand it. Under these circumstances, I can see no real benefit and considerable harm in risking the renewal of old passions and resentments."[58] This position paper ably explains why successive administrations had chosen—and would continue to choose—not to pursue the issue, even if publicly they appeared willing to keep their options open.

Outside of the administration, congressional and press interest in a resumption of payments nevertheless continued to grow as the balance of payments deficit worsened and relations between the United States and France deteriorated in the latter half of the decade.[59] In 1967, senators read approvingly from the *Nashville Banner*, noting that not only were these war debts outstanding despite U.S. support for France and Britain but inflation had reduced their worth in terms of buying power: "Surely, after 45 years of loaning good money after bad it's time to serve notice on these delinquent debtors that payday is here."[60] In the following year, senators proposed an amendment to a proposed bill that would forbid sale of gold to countries that had not paid their First World War debts.[61] Such efforts were aimed at the French government, which continued to stockpile gold, but would inevitably affect all war debtors, especially larger debtors such as the United Kingdom. The State Department then began to recognize the possibility of being "confronted with the necessity of some legislation on this subject."[62]

Despite mounting pressure from Congress, a workable solution appeared no more likely. A U.S. Treasury report from 1968 celebrated recent success recovering war debts arising from the Second World War, observing the collection of advance repayments totaling nearly $3 billion and noting that Germany, Italy, and Sweden had prepaid all or nearly all of war and postwar debt obligations to the U.S. It accepted, however, that "the situation is different with respect to World War I debts" and conceded the difficulty of collection: "Any effort to do so would undoubtedly raise the problem of German World War I reparations. From the practical viewpoint, therefore, there does not seem to be any possibility of reaching an agreement on repayment in the absence of an overall settlement."[63]

THE END OF THE BRETTON WOODS SYSTEM

President Richard Nixon took office in 1969.[64] Nixon encouraged his administration to adopt a harder line in managing the reform of the international monetary system. He believed that persistent balance of payments deficits reflected an excessive international defense burden and protectionist policies abroad. After beginning troop withdrawals from Vietnam, his attention turned to the surplus countries.[65] Yet the new Republican president displayed limited enthusiasm for the economic challenges that had confronted his predecessors. Early on, he informed his White House advisers, "I do not want to be bothered with international monetary matters."[66] Nixon would not let dollar and gold problems interfere with his administration's pursuit of more important goals, specifically reelection, domestic economic recovery, managing the war in Vietnam, and détente with the Soviet Union.[67] None of this is to suggest that he favored inaction but rather that he would prefer to devolve responsibility when possible.

Throughout the 1960s, U.S. current account surpluses partially balanced large losses on capital outflow and government expenditures overseas. The challenges of inflation, declining U.S. productivity, an overvalued dollar, and worsening trade relations with Europe and Japan had led to the deterioration of these surpluses. By the end of the decade, foreign holdings of dollars had reached almost $50 billion, which contrasted with U.S. gold reserves of approximately $10 billion, highlighting the Triffin dilemma, whereby the operation of a global reserve currency produces tensions between national and global economic objectives.[68] In the absence of meaningful international monetary reform, which much of Europe continued to resist, the U.S. could no longer uphold its promise to convert dollars into gold at thirty-five dollars an ounce.[69]

In the summer of 1971, the U.S. government felt compelled to act. Nixon and his senior advisers discussed their options to address the adverse balance of payments position.[70] Treasury Secretary John Connally proposed a proactive approach, preempting a run on U.S. gold reserves by shifting the burden onto other states. As Connally explained, "foreigners are out to screw us, our job is to screw them first."[71] On 15 August, the president announced a series of policies designed to reduce inflation, increase employment, and stem the dollar glut. He authorized wage and price controls, closed the gold window—namely, the suspension of the convertibility between the dollar and gold—and imposed a surcharge on dutiable imports to encourage other countries to revalue their currencies.[72] The "Nixon shock," named for the surprise with which the decision greeted the international community, marked the end of the administration's willingness to engage in prolonged economic negotiations or to accept the pegged exchange-rate system as a constraint on economic policy.[73] In the aftermath of Nixon's announcement, the U.S. sought to develop a new system of international monetary management. In December 1971, the "Smithsonian Agreement" pegged the currencies of ten leading Western economies to the U.S. dollar and raised the price of gold from $35 to $38 per ounce.[74] Pressure on the dollar with regard to its value against gold persisted. In the following years, prices continued to rise, and further devaluations followed, leading eventually to a complete decoupling from gold. Problems with inflation and unemployment as well as wage price controls and the oil embargo only exacerbated the economic challenges of the first half of the decade.[75]

Many historians have argued convincingly that U.S.-European economic relations had turned into a "competitive relationship" by the early 1970s.[76] It is therefore unsurprising that in this period congressional interest in outstanding European debts peaked, especially large and unpaid First World War loans. In late 1971, HM Treasury officials initially reacted to the news that Congress had reopened the war-debt question with incredulity; they generally believed that these debts had expired.[77] Such an assumption perhaps reflected wishful thinking given the troubled state of the economy. The Conservative government under Prime Minister Edward Heath faced significant economic challenges, including costly international commitments, industrial unrest, and ongoing difficulties with inflation and unemployment.[78]

By February 1972, HM Treasury had become more concerned by events in the United States. The Nixon administration's work on collecting foreign debt arrears since the Second World War was faring well.[79] John Hennessy, deputy assistant secretary to the U.S. Treasury, noted that "important results have been achieved in arranging for the payment of problem debts that had been long in arrears," citing major debt settlements reached with Indonesia, Korea, and the United Arab Emirates.[80] U.S. success in managing recent international debts stood in stark contrast to Europe's older and unpaid obligations. Hennessy had recently testified before a House subcommittee that the National Advisory Council had established a working group on World War I debts. Hennessy's testimony revealed that the United States has stepped up its efforts to reduce long-standing debts.[81] Officials within HM Treasury "found this development a strange and puzzling one," as they considered the debts lapsed, and proposed to avoid rather than confront the issue, concluding, "we do not propose to try to discover what is afoot."[82]

By March, HM Treasury had become more interested: "The Americans seem to be threatening to claim what we owe them from WWI. I do not suppose it will get very far, but it could be embarrassing: I imagine the greatest use the Americans will make of the point is in the arguments over defence and aid burden-sharing, and possibly to a lesser extent in international monetary and trade negotiations."[83] U.S. Treasury officials had suggested using World War I debts in negotiations concerning NATO infrastructure several years earlier, to be sure, but these proposals had met immediate and significant resistance internally.[84] Nevertheless, HM Treasury had begun to consider how best to handle such potential challenges. Despite the United Kingdom's recent and successful attempt to join the European Community, there was a clear willingness to share the burden of any potential repayment across the Continent: "if the USA start claiming our debts perhaps we should start claiming our corresponding much larger post-WWI debts from our allies (unfortunately not including the USA), which we also allowed to lapse."[85]

Over the following weeks and months, HM Treasury came to understand or perhaps remember that, although British war debts were generally regarded as lapsed, no agreement was ever reached with the United States. As such, the political risks associated with these outstanding loans remained serious: "We are therefore a little afraid that the Americans will try to make use of the point in arguments over defence and burden sharing. . . . It could be embarrassing."[86] The principal outstanding stood at just over $10 billion, which gave considerable weight to any potential policy demands. These concerns rested on broader strains in the U.S.-UK partnership in this period, reflecting increasingly divergent economic and security interests.[87] Following insights from a senior but unnamed contact in the State Department, HM Treasury came to understand that these outstanding obligations "might be raised with the Europeans in the reasonably near future, perhaps as part of general negotiations on trade or monetary reform."[88] For British officials, the risk of a resumption of repayments was by now difficult to ignore.[89]

The impulse to respond in kind was strong. One note circulated in HM Treasury was clear: "If the Americans have dug up the files about our World War One debts to them, I suggest we should dig up the file about the defaulted debts of the Southern States of the USA to us. . . . We are still waiting for a reply to extremely cogent representations made by our embassy in Washington in 1906 or thereabouts."[90] Such a strategy would prove impossible, however, as officials rediscovered a Foreign Office memorandum from 1932, supported by a reference to a debate in the House of Lords in 1930, detailing the problems of bringing up the matter with the U.S. government.[91] Not only was it impossible to trace the many private holders of the securities in 1911 and 1912, but it was doubtful whether any diplomatic action was possible in view of the relevant clauses of the Convention of 1853 for the Settlement of Outstanding Claims by a Mixed Commission and the Pecuniary Claims Convention of 1910. Furthermore, research revealed that the amount of these debts was much smaller than the British war debts in question. As one internal exchange on the matter concluded, "we cannot use the southern states' debts as a weapon. . . . I think we can let the matter drop."[92]

Over the summer of 1972, U.S. policymakers continued their efforts to reclaim First World War debts. In July, a U.S. working group discussed the possibility of raising the issue with European governments in the reasonably near future.[93] HM Treasury now began to take threats concerning the resumption of payment much more seriously. Preparations focused on what might come next. HM Treasury officials began a process of stepping into the shoes of their creditors to better prepare themselves to handle such challenges.[94] One such position paper provides a valuable insight into this process:

> If I were in the US Treasury and asked to work up a constructive "position paper" on this subject at the present time, I am not sure that I would not try to work up an argument along the following lines:
>
> (a) the World War 1 loans were made at a time when the USA was economically prosperous and strong. . . .
> (b) the position has now changed fundamentally in that European countries have had many years of prosperity and intense economic growth, while the USA has been struggling with balance of payments problems;
> (c) moreover the European countries hold very large dollar balances: and indeed complain that the dollar balances in their hands are larger than they should be for the health of international monetary reform;
> (d) surely, then, the complaints of these countries would be met if they handed back the "excess" dollars about which they are complaining in settlement of the World War I debts?
> (e) it must be admitted that the wretched British probably do not have excess dollars, and at any rate do not talk about having any. But the complexity of these debts . . . is such that European countries owe the UK and the UK owes USA. Thus "excess" dollars can be extracted from continental Europe, passing through the UK as a conduit, without imposing burdens on the UK;
> (f) therefore the admitted need for a "consolidation" of excess balances should be combined with the settlement of the USA's justified claims in a single operation.[95]

The author of this note was nevertheless unsure if the U.S. would ever pursue such action: "Whether they will choose to take this line—which bristles with difficulty from their own point of view let alone that of international negotiability is another matter."[96] HM Treasury thus adopted a familiar position—namely, waiting patiently in the hope that the issue would once again fade from the political landscape.

Such hopes were swiftly disappointed. The House of Representatives had tabled a resolution on 7 July 1972, asking the U.S. Treasury to provide within ninety days a list and report on debts that were outstanding to the United States. In echoes of the World War Foreign Debt

Commission of the 1920s, the resolution also asked the U.S. Treasury to begin consultations "with foreign governments involved for the prompt repayment of these longstanding debts which are delinquent."[97] Some scholars might find it tempting to dismiss this as a small political protest, but the resolution was supported by 103 members of the House. Members included Wilbur Mills, the chairman of the influential House Ways and Means Committee, which held jurisdiction over all revenue-raising measures, and Thomas Morgan of the House Appropriations Committee.

The political repercussions of British default were evidently still being felt almost four decades later. HM Treasury was concerned by the pace of progress: "the fact that over 100 members have sponsored this resolution, including two very influential figures, . . . will probably jolt the Administration into completing the inter-departmental report on World War I debt more quickly than they might otherwise have done."[98] The Ways and Means Committee would next need to consider whether to recommend that the House of Representatives endorse the resolution, thereby sending it to the Senate.[99] By late August, the situation had grown even more serious. Moorhead Kennedy of the State Department informed British officials that "it was more likely than not that the US would raise the issue at some point during the negotiations on monetary reform in prospect but when, and in what form and with what degree of seriousness, it was impossible to predict," but he was clear that "outright refusal to discuss the debts would be taken badly in the US."[100] These fears were understandable given the potential costs involved. The U.S. Treasury now recorded a total outstanding debt of $10.67 billion for the British government (Table 6.1).

In February 1973, HM Treasury received further updates from Kennedy, who outlined the three main options before Congress following the conclusion of the report on First World War debts. The first option was to do nothing and regard the debts as valid but not to be repaid. This choice, he explained, was unlikely to satisfy Congress. The second option was to write off the debts. This option would require approval from Congress, which remained unlikely; U.S. policymakers still associated outflows of dollars to Europe now with past European indebtedness to the United States. The third option was to seek repayment of all or part of the debt. This option would create obvious problems for U.S. relations with Western countries and some eastern European countries.

Table 6.1. Indebtedness of foreign governments to the U.S. arising from World War I, 1972 (USD)

State	Original indebtedness	Interest accrued through June 20, 1972	Total	Cumulative payments			Total outstanding
				Principal	Interest		
Armenia	11,959,917.49	31,577,045.30	43,536,962.79	17.49	0.00		43,536,945.30
Austria[a]	26,843,148.66	44,058.93	26,887,207.59	862,688.00	0.00		26,024,539.59
Belgium	419,837,630.37	360,464,720.47	780,302,350.84	19,157,630.37	33,033,642.87		728,111,077.60
Cuba	10,000,000.00	2,286,751.58	12,286,751.58	10,000,000.00	2,286,751.58		0.00
Czechoslovakia	185,071,023.07	133,997,522.27	319,068,545.34	19,829,914.17	304,178.09		298,934,453.08
Estonia	16,466,012.87	24,732,430.01	41,198,442.88	1,248,432.07			39,950,010.81
Finland	8,999,999.97	12,212,615.96	21,212,615.93	5,322,999.97[b]	12,212,615.96[b]		3,677,000.00
France	4,089,689,588.18	3,911,498,274.64	8,001,187,862.82	226,039,588.18	260,036,302.82		7,515,111,971.82
Great Britain	4,802,181,641.56	7,739,631,958.11	12,541,813,599.67	434,181,641.56	1,590,672,656.18		10,516,959,301.93
Greece	34,319,843.67[c]	4,532,680.26	38,852,523.93[c]	1,326,242.35	4,445,303.76		33,080,977.82[i]
Hungary[d]	1,982,555.50	3,107,296.51	5,089,852.01	73,995.50	482,924.26		4,532,932.25
Italy	2,042,364,319.28	424,529,220.22	2,466,893,539.50	37,464,319.28	63,365,560.88		2,366,063,659.34
Latvia	6,888,664.20	10,446,750.91	17,335,415.11	9,200.00	752,349.07		16,573,866.04
Liberia	26,000.00	10,471.56	36,471.56	26,000.00	10,471.56		0.00
							(continued)

Table 6.1. (*continued*)

State	Original indebtedness	Interest accrued through June 20, 1972	Total	Cumulative payments		Total outstanding
				Principal	*Interest*	
Lithuania	6,432,465.00	9,689,950.86	16,122,415.86	234,783.00	1,003,173.58	14,884,459.28
Nicaragua[e]	141,950.36	26,625.48	168,575.84	141,950.36	26,625.48	0.00
Poland	207,344,297.37	315,271,564.38	522,615,861.75	1,287,297.37[f]	21,359,000.18	499,969,564.20
Rumania	68,359,192.45	60,337,262.80	128,696,455.25	4,498,632.02[g]	292,375.20[g]	123,905,448.03
Russia	192,601,297.37	524,240,003.81	716,841,301.18	0.00	8,750,311.88[h]	708,090,989.30
Yugoslavia	63,577,712.55	36,609,652.92	100,187,365.47	1,952,712.55	636,059.14	97,598,593.78
Total	12,195,087,259.92	13,605,246,856.98	25,800,334,116.90	762,409,612.17	2,000,918,734.56	23,037,005,790.17

Source: Statistical Appendix to U.S. Treasury Department, *Annual Report* (1972), 303, table 101, "Indebtedness of Foreign Governments to the United States Arising from World War I as of June 30, 1972."

Note: Due to space limitations, the final two columns ("Unmatured principal" and "Principal and interest due and unpaid") have been removed. In the published version of the U.S. Treasury report, Latvia's original indebtedness reads as $6,888,644.20, but this appears to be an error; when corrected to $6,888,664.20, it matches the total at the bottom of the column and the total debt figure in the third column. In addition, the total outstanding figure for Austria is presented as detailed in the original, but this figure is $20 more than the sum of the total minus cumulative payments.

[a] The Federal Republic of Germany has recognized the liability for securities falling due between March 12, 1938, and May 8, 1945.

[b] $8,480,090.28 has been made available for educational exchange programs with Finland pursuant to 22 U.S.C. 2455 (e).

[c] Includes $13,165,921 refunded by the agreement of May 28, 1984. The agreement was ratified by Congress November 5, 1966.

[d] Interest payment from Dec. 16, 1932, to June 15,1937, were paid in pengo equivalent.

[e] The indebtedness of Nicaragua was canceled pursuant to the agreement of Apr. 14, 1938.

[f] Excludes claim allowance of $1,813,428.69 dated Dec. 15, 1989.

[g] Excludes payment of $100,000 on June 14, 1940, as a token of good faith.

[h] Principally proceeds from liquidation of Russian assets in the United States.

[i] Includes $12,813,601.32 on agreement of May 28, 1964.

HM Treasury noted that "since all the options were politically sensitive, a decision would probably not be reached until the issue had been considered at the highest levels."[101] As such, it clung to a familiar hope that the president and his cabinet would overrule any effort to seek repayment. As one senior official in HM Treasury noted, "it is difficult to believe that the Administration would ever have much difficulty in firmly resisting Congressional pressure to take some action, if it were minded to do so."[102]

In the following month, Sidney Weintraub, deputy under-secretary for international finance and development, testified before the Subcommittee on Foreign Operations of the House Committee on Government Operations on 1 March: "[World War I debt present] immensely complex political and economic issues, involving the whole range of our relations with our Western allies."[103] For many members of Congress, however, these international challenges were less important than domestic-political concerns. On 11 April, the Democratic representative Lester L. Wolff spoke to the House arguing for the urgent need for the United States to collect its outstanding debts: "Neither the Treasury Department nor the State Department has initiated a workable method of recalling, or even naming, the delinquent debts owed to our government. Their method, or rather lack of method, is costing our country millions of dollars in losses, stemming from inflation, devaluation, write-offs, rescheduling, and concessional lending practices." As Wolff argued, these outstanding debts from World War I remained entirely relevant: "At a time when the United States is facing a budgetary and balance-of-payments problem of its own, when the American people are threatened with another tax increase, it is ludicrous not to insist that nations owing us longstanding debts begin to make regular payments and honor the terms of their contracts made in good faith."[104] In an interview with the author, Wolff recalled his position: "If we were having economic difficulties, the least we could do was to collect what was owed to us."[105] For HM Treasury, this speech served as "an example of how the issue of World War I debts have become enmeshed in the eyes of Congress, with current balance of payments problems. . . . They demonstrate again that this issue is not forgotten by Congress; Mr Wolff's resolutions have 224 co-sponsors, a clear majority of the House."[106] The data is clear in evidencing the enduring political relevance of the United Kingdom's unpaid debts to the United States.

By November 1973, senior elements of the U.S. government were looking at First World War debts. The archives provide limited detail on Nixon's attitude to these outstanding obligations, but senior officials were aware of the issue.[107] Deputies of the National Advisory Council, which included Paul Volcker of the Treasury and Willis Armstrong of the State Department, together with representatives from the Commerce Department and the Export-Import Bank, would shortly consider a report examining possible options for collecting the debt. HM Treasury was increasingly doubtful about the issue fading from the political landscape: "given continuing Congressional interest in these debts, it was unlikely that the matter would be allowed to rest even at that fairly exalted level and it would probably have to be considered at a later stage by cabinet level officials."[108] These insights complement a small body of research by economists arguing that debt markets retain a long memory of default.[109] The return of the First World War debts as a problem for the Nixon administration, almost forty years after the United Kingdom suspended payments, suggests that the same can also be true of governments. Both insights "contradict received wisdom" on the lingering effect of sovereign default.[110]

The U.S. committee on government operations produced a detailed study of delinquent foreign debts and claims owed to the United States in December 1973.[111] Yet congressional pressure for repayment, alongside the progress of sponsored resolutions, began to fade at this point. As a note from HM Treasury remarked several years later, "in the end nothing materialised."[112] British officials believed that the Nixon "administration stalled as long as it could, and the subject eventually died."[113] Wolff recalls that the Nixon administration, State Department, and U.S. Treasury all resisted efforts to recover these debts. He suggests that this outcome reflected, in part, a Republican administration resisting a Democratic Party proposal but also that Watergate and other international issues "crowded it out."[114] Improvements in the U.S. balance of payments from 1973 onward also help to explain why legislative efforts were derailed. HM Treasury favored this explanation, noting that with current improvements in the U.S. economy, calls for repayment "will die a natural death if it has not already done so."[115]

The eventual decline rather than sudden death of the war debts as a political problem may have been expected but was still a relief to HM

Treasury. The United Kingdom had at the very least been spared further diplomatic embarrassment. Whether economic advisers and policymakers in France, Germany, or Italy had been equally concerned about the political revival of this long-standing problem remains unclear. It seems reasonable to believe that they would also have been pleased with the outcome given the awkward challenges posed by any demand for payment. The war-debts issue nevertheless remained unresolved. British officials remained cautious, noting that the issue "could, presumably, flare up at any time."[116]

Whether sustained political pressure could have resulted in a change of policy in the 1970s remains an interesting counterfactual.[117] The available evidence suggests that even if the Nixon administration had eventually responded to congressional pressure for the resumption of repayment, real and significant progress—whether toward cancellation or collection—would still have been limited due to the political difficulty and uncertain rewards associated with any change to the status quo. Successive policymakers had reached the same conclusion. As Ball had warned six years earlier, there were few benefits and considerable risks for U.S. policymakers in returning to this difficult subject.[118] HM Treasury recognized that there had been many options for change—from introducing legislation to write off the debts through to seeking full repayment—but "none of them [held] any attraction" to U.S. policymakers.[119]

Nixon's sudden resignation in August 1974 resulted in Vice President Gerald Ford assuming the presidency. Ford would grapple with his own financial challenges, including rising national debt and New York City's default.[120] Although congressional demands for action on the war-debts issue had faded, interest in the issue itself lingered. A National Advisory Council working group had this complex matter under review but had been unable to find any feasible way to resolve the problem.[121] War debts also continued to play a role in international affairs. Ford met with President Urho Kekkonen of Finland in Helsinki on 29 July 1975. The two leaders celebrated Finland's final payment on its First World War debts, which was deposited in perpetuity so that the interest could be used to pay for exchange scholarships for Finnish and American students.[122] During a toast in honor of Kekkonen at a state dinner, Ford concluded his speech by saying, "Finland is respected as a nation that meets its obligations. Just a few weeks ago Finland wrote a new page in international relations by paying off, in full, its World War One debt to the United States—eight years ahead of schedule."[123] Finland is often purported to be the only state to have repaid its First World War debts to the U.S. Yet Hungary eventually repaid its war debts in the early 1980s, also using its final payment to finance cultural exchanges between itself and the U.S.[124] As the Finns cleared their slate, the ledger continued to grow for other debtors. By June 1976, the United Kingdom owed $11 billion after more than three decades of missed payments and accrued interest.[125] The war debts would return to inform policymaking on the other side of the Atlantic soon thereafter.

ENDURING DEBTS

By the late 1970s, the British government needed to manage the significant debts it had accrued during the tumultuous first half of the decade, which included a major bailout by the International Monetary Fund.[126] Scholars routinely describe this period with reference to "decline and fall," "crisis," "humiliation," and "collapse."[127] The economy nevertheless improved. In 1977, HM Treasury officials began to consider new avenues for borrowing to smooth out the demanding repayment schedule, with $20 billion falling due between 1979 and 1984 (Figure 6.1).[128] They came to focus on a return to the New York market and sought to secure a "triple-A" credit rating to improve the chances of a successful bond issue.[129]

A significant concern throughout the British government's attempts to secure favorable ratings from the two major U.S. credit rating agencies—Standard and Poor's and Moody's—was the country's default on its First World War debts, which posed "a tricky and potential formidable legal obstacle."[130] As early as May 1977, exchanges between senior officials revealed that there were concerns that this issue could constitute "a serious obstacle": "the sensitives here are plainly such that we should take no avoidable risks."[131] By October, HM Treasury was clear that these debts were still legally recognized by the U.S. Treasury as an open loan.[132] Although the French government had not mentioned its First World War debts when it applied for a credit rat-

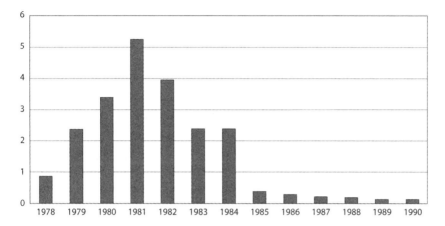

Figure 6.1. The British government's original debt repayment plan ($bn) (Source: BE 7A174/2, Couzens to PPS, 16 September 1977, attached note: "Debt Repayment and Bunching of Liabilities")

ing, that was not a good enough reason for the United Kingdom to avoid mentioning them: "we may be somewhat apprehensive that any references to this subject could just conceivably arouse some unwanted interest in it, not only in financial circles but possibly in anti-UK political circles in the United States also."[133] The issue remained salient. Only months earlier, Hungary had resumed its war-debt payments, paying the U.S. Treasury over $4.3 million to become current on its obligations.[134]

In an effort for the British government "to tell as good a story" as it could, it limited the relevant wording to a footnote, to "present as low a profile as possible" without risking legal action concerning the "suppression of material information."[135] HM Treasury and the Bank of England downplayed the issue and went on to control the flow of other information available to Standard and Poor's and Moody's throughout the review process, emphasizing the strengths of an improving national economy and downplaying the weaknesses.[136] The British government ultimately secured "triple-A" ratings from both rating agencies, in line with many other major economies (Table 6.2). It subsequently launched a bond issue in the New York market to high levels of investor demand.[137]

Table 6.2. Sovereign credit ratings, 1978

	S&P	Moody's
Australia	AAA	Aaa
Austria	AAA	Aaa
Canada	AAA	Aaa
Denmark	—	Aa
Finland	AAA	Aaa
France	AAA	—
Japan	AAA	Aaa
New Zealand	AAA	Aaa
Norway	AAA	Aaa
Panama	—	Aa
Sweden	AAA	Aaa
UK	AAA	Aaa
USA	AAA	Aaa
Venezuela	AAA	Aaa

Sources: moodys.com; standardandpoors.com.

Improving economic conditions were an important element of the United Kingdom's success in securing "triple-A" ratings and its successful return to the New York bond market. Approximately 90 percent of variance in sovereign credit ratings relates to six factors: GDP per capita, real GDP growth, the inflation rate, external debt relative to export earnings, level of economic development, and default history.[138] Nevertheless, as economists and political scientists accept, qualitative political considerations are also important determinants.[139] Senior officials in the Bank of England and HM Treasury went to considerable efforts to "persuade" and "convince" their assessors of the United Kingdom's creditworthiness, and a noteworthy element in this process was the successful handling of the state's unpaid war debts.[140]

At least one former member of Congress has suggested that there was a "psychological statute of limitations" in the United States on the issue of Europe's unpaid war debts by the end of the 1970s. This conclusion is only partially convincing. Although popular and political interest in the issue waned, British default lingered in the U.S. memory and in the

U.S. Treasury's records.[141] A resolution remained unlikely given that transatlantic relations during Jimmy Carter's presidency were riven with antagonism and disagreement.[142] In 1977, *The Economist* had included a humorous exchange of letters in which a British citizen asked for payment from the state of North Carolina for a bond on which it had defaulted in 1870. The American respondent kindly asked him to return the favor by recovering unpaid debts from the United Kingdom in the 1930s.[143] The U.S. Treasury certainly still considered it as "delinquent debt."[144] Its annual report put the precise figure at $11.16 billion in fiscal year 1980 but acknowledged that the "collection of this debt presents special problems."[145] The United States' own brief default a year earlier, in which congressional delays and operational problems meant that it failed to make its payments on maturing securities and was late redeeming T-bills, does not appear to have had any effect on its position.[146]

While governments on both sides of the Atlantic quietly accepted the political limbo in which these war debts existed, a private legal challenge based on the terms of a will made on 10 May 1927 threatened to upset the status quo. James Bertram, a wealthy native of Scotland who become a resident alien in the United States, had created a trust to pay the income to his wife for life and then to his daughter for life.[147] Upon the death of the daughter, the trust principal was to be paid to the daughter's children. If the daughter died without issue, then the trust was to be paid "absolutely to the Chancellor of the Exchequer of the United Kingdom of Great Britain to use and apply the same on account of the payment of the National Debt of Great Britain to the United States."[148] Bertram's daughter, Jean Ewing Bertram Underhill, was by now old and did not have children. Living in New York, she petitioned the Surrogates Court of Westchester County for a ruling on whether the bequest of trust principal to the United Kingdom was valid. Underhill thought that the trust, provisionally valued at $800,000, was invalid as the British government no longer recognized the debt.[149] She asked instead that the money should go to a foundation she had established to benefit animals and finance scholarships for veterinary students.[150] The case for honoring the payment to the U.S. Treasury was strong, however, given the legally outstanding nature of these debts. In addition, there was a precedent for such payment. In 1949, the estate of Mary Munday, a native of Great Britain, had successfully bequeathed funds to be applied to the interest on the First World War debt.[151]

HM Treasury was closely monitoring the situation, which it described as "an intriguing, and in some respects rather difficult, problem."[152] It was interested in securing this substantial sum for its own purposes but recognized that it would be difficult to get any of the money without the implication of repudiation. Indeed, it was "extremely dangerous" to admit to owing debts now after never repaying them.[153] Ultimately, HM Treasury recommended against taking any action; it chose not to contest the case and ignored the associated subpoena from New York. The Surrogate's Court eventually rejected Underhill's appeal. The court took the view that there had been no official settlement of the debt and no official repudiation of repayment obligations. As such, HM Treasury officials accepted that they would be "faced with a tricky problem when Mr Bertram's daughter dies."[154] Solicitors within HM Treasury conceded, "We could well be challenged if we sought to sign a statement that we are not in default on any loans. . . . We probably are, in law, in default even though the debt may not now be enforceable since the US may be stopped from pursuing their claim because of their inaction over the last forty years."[155] HM Treasury did go on to consider the possibility of repaying some of the war debt as a means of fulfilling the terms of Bertram's will, if only to "save an airing of [the] WW1 debt problem," or using the funds to help pay for the debts of the Second World War.[156] Yet it ultimately preferred to let sleeping dogs lie and patiently awaited the outcome.

The British government had originally agreed to repay its war debts to the United States by 1984.[157] In that same year, following a series of exchanges, the British and U.S. governments reached an agreement on the related matter of the Bertram estate. HM Treasury accepted that this payment should be made to the United States but, in a departure from its long-standing policy of claiming to have never written off the debts, did so only on the understanding that these debts were "otherwise irrecoverable" and would not prejudice the view that "with the passing of time and history any World War I debt should no longer be regarded as payable."[158] Chancellor Nigel Lawson approved this agreement.[159] The U.S. Treasury accepted that this payment did not alter the United Kingdom's position on the matter but, concluding ambiguously, noted that it "does not alter in any way the current status of the United Kingdom's World War I debts from the view point of the United States."[160] These exchanges represent the first time in the history of the war debts that the British government had suggested that it was no longer willing to negotiate on these outstanding obligations.[161] Publicly, however, the British government would continue to claim that these debts had not been written off.[162]

Underhill passed away in 1996. Two years later, when legal proceedings resumed, the British government reconfirmed its position that the U.S. should assume power over the trust. As such, the Chancellor of the Exchequer had limited interest in the case.[163] Although the British government had acquiesced to U.S. wishes on the matter, Underhill's executors continued to object to the use of her estate in this way. The U.S. Treasury resisted the tempting option of a settlement that could reduce litigation costs chiefly because of the risk of "large potential repercussions."[164] It was anxious that such a compromise could "potentially weaken" future attempts to pursue collection of these outstanding debts by "tacitly accept[ing] the argument that Britain's WWI debt is invalid."[165] The U.S. Treasury preferred to litigate because it believed the law was on its side: "We hold that Great Britain's debt to the USG from WWI, which continues to accrue interest, is legally due and payable, along with the outstanding WWI debt of other countries, unless and until Congress says otherwise."[166] Furthermore, "a court finding in the USG's favor would have provided a useful precedent for future debt collection negotiations."[167]

In 1998, the U.S. Treasury won its court case, underscoring the enduring political significance of Britain's unpaid debts. Following further testimonial in court, representatives from the U.S. Treasury were clear that British war debts were still a "legally enforceable" and "valid, outstanding debt, . . . evidenced by physical securities."[168] The judge presiding over the case agreed. He explained that it was irrelevant that the United States had made no effort to collect from the United Kingdom; there was no evidence that the United States had waived its right to be repaid. He also noted that Washington still listed the debt in a U.S. Treasury Department publication.[169] U.S. Treasury records would go on to indicate a donation of James Bertram's estate of more than $2.13 million in 2002 (Table 6.3).[170]

There was further evidence inside the U.S. Treasury that these debts remained unexcused and politically relevant. In 1998, Deputy Secretary

Table 6.3. Indebtedness of foreign governments to the U.S. arising from World War I, 2002 (USD)

State	Agreement obligation[a]	Interest accrued through 12/31/2002	Cumulative payments		Payments received		Total outstanding
			Principal	Interest	Principal	Interest	
Armenia	11,959,917	49,818,765	32	0	0	0	61,778,650
Austria[b]	26,843,149	20,518,950	862,668	0	0	0	46,499,431
Belgium	423,587,630	631,091,878	19,157,630	33,033,643	0	0	1,002,488,235
Cuba	10,000,000	2,286,752	10,000,000	2,286,752	0	0	0
Czechoslovakia	185,071,023	322,179,206	19,829,914	304,178	0	0	487,116,137
Estonia	16,958,373	43,267,365	11	1,248,432	0	0	58,977,295
Finland	9,000,000	12,661,578	9,000,000[c]	12,661,578	0	0	0
France	4,128,326,088	8,119,712,692	226,039,588	260,036,303	0	0	11,761,962,889
Great Britain	4,933,701,642	12,656,713,072	434,181,642	1,592,803,791	0	2,131,135[f]	15,561,298,146
Greece (I)	21,163,923	3,752,558	983,923	3,143,133	0	0	20,789,425
Greece (II)[d]	13,155,921	8,443,705	3,420,168	8,420,235	131,552	197,347	9,759,223
Hungary[e]	2,051,898	3,665,641	2,051,898	3,665,641	0	0	0
Italy	2,044,870,444	1,517,715,246	37,464,319	63,365,561	0	0	3,461,755,810
Latvia	7,094,654	18,190,081	9,200	752,349	0	0	24,523,186

Liberia	26,000	26,000	10,472	10,472	0	0	0
Lithuania	6,618,395	16,664,315	234,783	1,003,174	0	0	22,044,753
Nicaragua[f]	141,950	26,625	141,950	26,625	0	0	0
Poland	213,506,132[g]	547,180,167	1,287,297	21,359,000	0	0	738,040,002
Rumania	68,359,192	142,745,362	4,498,632[b]	292,375	0	0	206,313,547
Russia	192,601,297	818,003,154	0	8,750,312[i]	0	0	1,001,854,139
Yugoslavia	63,577,713	102,497,728	1,952,713	636,059	0	0	163,486,669
TOTAL	12,378,615,343	25,037,145,311	771,142,369	2,013,799,612	131,552	2,328,482	34,628,687,538

Source: U.S. Department of the Treasury and Office of Management and Budget, "U.S. Government Foreign Credit Exposure as of December 31, 2002," 30, table 7, "Indebtedness of Foreign Governments to the United States Arising from World War I as of 12/31/2002."

Note: Due to space limitations, the final three columns ("Unmatured principal," "Accrued interest not yet due," and "Principal and interest due and unpaid") have been removed. I present the totals as provided in the published version. Except for the two columns under "Payments Received 2002," the totals presented in the published version vary from the sum of their respective columns by $1–$2, which likely reflects the rounding of figures. Unless otherwise stated, all U.S. Treasury data in this book are presented in their published form.

a Includes capitalized interest.

b The Federal Republic of Germany has recognized liability for securities falling due between March 12, 1938, and May 8, 1945.

c $8,480,090 has been made available for educational exchange programs with Finland pursuant to 22 U.S.C. 2455(e).

d $13,155,921 refunded by the agreement of May 28, 1964, which was ratified by Congress November 5, 1966.

e Interest payment from December 15, 1932, to June 15, 1937, was paid in pengo equivalent.

f The indebtedness of Nicaragua was canceled pursuant to the agreement of April 14, 1938.

g After deduction of claim allowance of $1,813,429.

h Excludes payment of $100,000 on June 14, 1940, as a token of good faith.

i Includes proceeds from liquidation of Russian assets in the United States.

j Reduces WWI Great Britain's debt by the bequest of James Bertram's estate of $2,131,134.49.

of the Treasury Lawrence Summers received memos of an audit of the U.S. Treasury's financial statements on the status of World War I–era debt and policy options for collecting or forgiving the debt. Summers agreed that these memos should be circulated outside the U.S. Treasury with the intent of eliciting interagency deliberations on the available options.[171] The U.S. Office of the Inspector General had demanded that the U.S. Treasury resolve the accounting status of the loans, but senior officials worried that this approach would "undercut prospective efforts to collect the debt."[172] The accounting firm PriceWaterhouse (PW), which audited the U.S. Treasury's books in 1997, recommended a loss allowance be created for the loans, "which it considers delinquent."[173] Without the allowance, PW contended that "the Treasury will violate financial reporting laws."[174] Yet, as the U.S. Treasury warned, "a loss allowance, if sizeable and made public, would undermine prospective efforts to negotiate recovery of this debt."[175] The U.S. Treasury therefore sought an exemption to federal accounting standards to avert the potential loss allowance.[176] Senior officials in the U.S. government evidently remained unwilling to accept any approach that surrendered any control over these war debts.

Long-standing legal commitments to unpaid debts were not unique to the United States. The United Kingdom and France had only ended litigation over Russian bonds, which had been repudiated by the Soviet government in 1918, many decades later in 1986 and 1997, receiving merely 1.6 and 1 percent compensation of the bonds' updated value of the amounts claimed.[177] These outstanding financial obligations, which predated Britain's own unpaid war debts, had continued to cast a shadow over Russian finances. Alexander Zhukov, deputy chairman of the Duma's committee on finance, explained, "the debt was detrimental to our status as a reliable country and stopped us from obtaining new loans."[178] In 1995, a reunified Germany also took up the task of settling old debts, which it finished repaying fifteen years later.[179] The German government honored bonds issued between 1924 and 1930 and sold to foreign, mostly U.S., investors that it had yet to pay.[180] The settling of these outstanding obligations by a unified Germany raises interesting questions about the status of other unpaid debts from that period.[181]

Recently declassified materials in the British archives shed some light on this issue.[182] HM Treasury had been unimpressed by an article that appeared in the *Los Angeles Times* in January 1995, which stated that "Germany recently said it will pay interest on a World War I debt that most of the West had forgotten about. . . . Ironically, Germany is now repaying its entire debt—and France and Britain are not expected to pay theirs."[183] One official described the article as "a libellous slur on the British government" given that Germany was not paying any war debt or reparations but was instead honoring certain commercial debts from the 1920s.[184] The note goes on to reveal that the issue of British or French outstanding First World War debts to the United States had reappeared in diplomatic exchanges at the time: "The Americans surprised us in 1990 by suggesting that if the question of Germany's WWI reparations was raised in the context of German unification, the question of the UK's outstanding WWI debts to the US would be likely to come up too. Perhaps they said the same thing to the French. The American aim was seemingly to warn us off the subject."[185] Based on the available evidence, the United States appears to have been willing to use its knowledge of existing war debts as a tool with which to prevent the resurrection of German war debts and reparations despite the terms of the London Debt Agreement.

The value of these historical obligations as a diplomatic instrument helps to explain why the United States has remained unwilling to forgive these war debts. It remains unclear whether U.S. policymakers had acted preemptively or reacted to the behavior of other governments in this instance. There does appear to have been some attempt to collect outstanding debts by at least one state. News reports suggested that France had also sought reparations from the newly reunified Germany in December 1990. A foreign ministry spokesman in Bonn said that it was "normal procedure" that the question of war-reparation payments had come up after German unification. French sources confirmed that discussions "of [a] private character" with Germany started in early December.[186] In contrast, the available evidence from HM Treasury suggests that the British government had limited interest in resurrecting the issue of war debts at the end of the Cold War.

The subject of First World War debts reemerged publicly in exchanges in the House of Commons in the early twenty-first century. In February 2002, the Conservative member of Parliament Bob Spink asked the Labour chancellor of the exchequer Gordon Brown what plans he had to pay off or cancel the First World War debt owed by the United Kingdom to the United States.[187] Financial Secretary to the Treasury Ruth Kelly responded on behalf of the chancellor. She avoided his question and instead provided a brief factual account of the history of the debts up to 1934. Kelly then reiterated that Britain's wartime allies owed more to Britain than Britain owed to the United States.[188] On 17 and 30 July 2002, Lord Laird asked the government similarly worded questions about the status of the debts and received a similarly vague reply from Lord McIntosh of Haringey, who defended his response by explaining that more detailed answers could "be obtained only at a disproportionate cost . . . from the files (dating back more than 80 years) held at the Public Records Office."[189]

Lord Laird tried again on 23 October, asking whether the government considered that the debt owed to the United States by the United Kingdom from the First World War was still active. Lord McIntosh of Haringey offered a familiar response: "Neither the debt owed to the United States by the United Kingdom nor the larger debts owed by other countries to the United Kingdom have been serviced since 1934, nor have they been written off."[190] Lord Laird pursued his line of questioning concerning what arrangements were being made to clear the debt in January, July, and September 2003 and again in January 2005 but received no detailed answers.[191]

Press attention returned to these debts briefly at the end of the following year. On 29 December 2006, the British government paid the final installment of £43 million for the Anglo-American loan originally agreed in 1946.[192] The British government also made its final £12 million payment to Canada. That these debts had taken decades to repay reflected in large part their competitive terms. As HM Treasury had acknowledged in the 1990s, "the fact that they [debts to the United States] will remain outstanding into the next century is a result of a conscious decision to maintain these very low-cost loans, rather than repay them ahead of schedule."[193] Celebration was followed by difficult questions from the media concerning the status of the First World War debts.[194] The British government repeated its standard position.[195] The BBC went on to report that despite remaining "in limbo," these outstanding debts were "by no means trifling," equaling £40 billion when adjusted by inflation or £225 billion if adjusted by the growth of GDP.[196]

The global financial crisis of 2008 failed to revive the issue of unpaid war debts in transatlantic negotiations. Part of the reason why may concern the nature of the credit crunch itself, which reflected faltering flows of private finance rather than states' trading surpluses or national debts.[197] The swiftness and coordinated nature of the international response also helped to prevent the crisis from becoming a full-fledged depression, consequently providing little opportunity for such memories to resurface.[198] The resultant austerity policies that emerged around the globe, however, did encourage a brief renewal of popular interest in past debt transgressions, including the defaults of the European powers in the 1930s.[199] Germany had enjoyed considerable debt relief after the Second World War, but the struggling Eurozone economies—Portugal, Italy, Ireland, Greece, and Spain—now enjoyed little such help in reducing their own debts. The scholar Albrecht Ritschl highlights what he sees as the hypocrisy of Germany imposing austerity measures on European debtors, arguing that debt cancellation for the Eurozone would be equivalent to the debts that were canceled by the Allies after the war.[200]

The British government's postcrisis narrative, of fiscal rectitude and comparative credibility, underlined a commitment to reducing debts and deficits and signaling historical creditworthiness.[201] Such views were challenged by the United Kingdom loss of a "triple-A" sovereign credit rating from Moody's in 2013, which represented the United Kingdom's first downgrade since it had secured a rating thirty-five years earlier.[202] Chancellor George Osborne interpreted the news as a warning: "I think we've got a very clear message, a loud and clear message that Britain cannot let up in dealing with its debts, dealing with its problems, cannot let up in making sure that Britain can pay its way in the world."[203] Only a small number of commentators recalled that the United Kingdom had not always chosen to pay its way in difficult times. The columnist Peter Hitchens went on to recall the significance of these unpaid debts from the First World War: "the wretched fact, that this country is in fact one of history's greatest debt defaulters, rather contradicts our assumed reputation for probity and solidity."[204]

Scholars have noted many important similarities between the largest financial crisis of the twenty-first century and the Great Depression of the 1930s.[205] One neglected parallel is the unwillingness of the United States to alter its stance on the United Kingdom and the rest of Europe's unpaid debts from the First World War. U.S. policymakers continued to include these outstanding loans in their financial reporting for 2010. As the U.S. Treasury reported, "All the loans and credits [from the First World War] represent legally valid and outstanding obligations of foreign governments, and the USG has not waived or renounced its rights with respect to any of them. All such loans and credits remain due and payable."[206]

Conclusion

ALL SOVEREIGN LENDING carries risk. Even though most debtor governments meet their contractual obligations to foreign creditors every year, any state can default in the right circumstances. The United Kingdom is often presented as an exception to this claim. It is, for some observers, part of a small and exclusive club of states that has never defaulted on its sovereign debt despite centuries of financial challenges.[1] Yet the British government did just that when it unilaterally suspended repayment of its First World War debts to the United States. These obligations, worth $4.7 billion at the time of default, remain unpaid and outstanding to this day. The popular memory of these unpaid debts has faded over the course of almost nine decades. What the economist Sebastian Edwards has identified as a "collective amnesia" in financial history surrounding some instances of default has increasingly come to apply to the British government's suspension of payments to the United States.[2] This book has sought to recover and interrogate the legacy of these unpaid debts.

Many states defaulted on their war debts to the United States in the 1930s. There was nevertheless considerable variation with regard to timing. The United Kingdom was one of the last major powers to suspend repayment in 1934. In contrast, France, Belgium, and Austria were far quicker to default, having done so by 1932. This book has emphasized the importance of the United Kingdom's role as an international creditor in helping to explain the delay preceding the suspension of payments. Many factors certainly played a role, but there was considerable and widespread concern in the British government that the many states owing large sums to United Kingdom might use a default as an excuse to cease repayment on their own outstanding debts.

Some cabinet ministers believed initially that refusal to pay not only would weaken important traditions or norms of repayment but could also profoundly shock a large section of domestic public opinion. Continued repayment—in the form of one full payment in 1932 and two smaller or "token" installments in 1933—provided the British government with more time to manage such domestic-political risks and further opportunities to seek a settlement. The United States ultimately proved unwilling to compromise. The passage of the Johnson Act, which largely reflected the prioritization of political rather than economic interests in Congress, forced the British government to choose between returning to full payments or ceasing repayment entirely. In such circumstances, and as it became clear that the risks of default would be limited, the British government opted to suspend repayment indefinitely in 1934.

The United Kingdom's unilateral default—as well as those of other major European powers such as France—generated limited economic or political consequences in the short term.[3] This outcome contrasts with the extant literature's tendency to focus on the dire costs to incumbent governments and national economies following a unilateral default. To be sure, political scientists and economists have long recognized the existence of winners and losers from default by looking within a state.[4] Depending on the circumstances, some elements of society may secure a better deal from default than from repayment.[5] Certain sectors and industries can thrive in the conditions brought about by nonpayment or other contractual breaches. Political actors may gain popularity by promising not to repay foreign debts or simply benefit from the instability following default.

A small number of scholars have suggested that negotiated defaults can, in some cases, be relatively advantageous to debtor states as a whole, especially when coercing creditors into sizeable reductions or better terms.[6] The idea of unilateral default generating limited costs or even rewards remains much rarer in the literature. The United States in the 1930s represents an important example of such a phenomenon, however, albeit one focused largely on domestic rather than external debts. The abrogation of the gold clause and the subsequent devaluation of the dollar was largely positive, helping Roosevelt to pursue his broader economic recovery program without major cost to the country.[7] Key financial variables, including prices, gross national product, and investment, all evidence the relative success of this U.S. default.[8]

The United Kingdom's unliteral suspension of payments represents an even rarer case of a successful default on external debts. The British government used the sums allocated for repayment to reduce taxation and improve allowances.[9] Prime Minister Stanley Baldwin also went on to secure another large majority in the following election.[10] The United States even went on to provide considerable financial support to the United Kingdom, most notably via Lend-Lease during the Second World War and the Anglo-American loan afterward.[11] The unusual economic and political conditions generated by the Great Depression dampened the expected penalties, which suggests an aleatory element in the success of British default. This historical example may therefore be relatively rare, but it nevertheless generates an important qualification to much of the scholarship on sovereign debt: states can sometimes benefit economically or politically by defaulting, even in more extreme forms of unilateral repudiation.

None of this is to ignore the wider trade-offs involved in sovereign default. Scholars accept that credit may be more difficult to secure after nonpayment, which naturally poses significant risks for states, especially with regard to international security. The United Kingdom's unilateral suspension of its war-debt repayments to the United States in the 1930s evidences this point. The memory of these unpaid debts lingered in the United States, and access to U.S. finances remained closed in the wake of the Johnson Act, which shut the New York securities and money markets to any government behind on its debt payments. Default was therefore problematic for the United Kingdom because it harmed transatlantic relations, thereby weakening the possibility of any anti-German coalition, and denied easy access to the U.S. markets, which limited the British government's ability and willingness to wage war.[12]

Analysis of the British government's suspension of payments consequently complements sensible suggestions that default could signal to creditor states that the indebted government in question is unreliable, thereby limiting cooperation on other economic agreements, environmental pacts, and military alliances.[13] As political scientists have shown, states that lack access to affordable credit are less likely to win wars, tend to become less self-reliant militarily, face increased public opposition to war, endure more constraints in conflict initiation, and try to avoid paths to conflict.[14] As such, default makes allies harder to find just as they become more important. How states manage their defaults can therefore have profound consequences for their security in the international system.

This book has also attempted to analyze the longer-term consequences of sovereign default. Most research has analyzed only short-lived economic or political costs. A small selection of work suggests that the enduring cost of default has been underestimated.[15] Marc Flandreau and Frederic Zumer argued fifteen years ago that debt markets can retain a long memory of default, "which seems to contradict received wisdom."[16] Some governments also appear to have lengthy memories concerning unpaid debts, in this case concerning official or direct lending. A detailed examination of the longer-term, albeit often harder to assess, political consequences of default underscores the need to look beyond only short-term analyses. The political significance of the United Kingdom's unpaid war debts to the United States has ebbed and flowed over the past century but has never entirely disappeared, which highlights the risks of unpaid debts to the course of international politics. Memories of default help to explain U.S. resistance to lending to the United Kingdom after the Second World War, as evidenced most clearly in the congressional debates surrounding the rapid termination of Lend-Lease and the conditions of the Anglo-American loan.

Congress also went on to use these unpaid debts as a diplomatic tool with which to address the economic challenges facing the United States in the 1960s and 1970s, albeit unsuccessfully. Nevertheless, the fact that in 1973 over one hundred members of the House of Representatives sponsored a resolution that asked the U.S. Treasury to pursue the prompt repayment of these long-standing war debts highlights the enduring relevance of unpaid sovereign debts even among allies in the Cold War. Furthermore, ongoing legal and accounting issues concerning these outstanding financial obligations informed the British government's return to the New York bond market in 1978 and ultimately led to a further payment on behalf of the United Kingdom to the United States in 2002. Billions of dollars of taxpayers' money can evidently remain politically salient for decades, which largely explains why the

U.S. Treasury has long remained unwilling to support any policy that might undermine future efforts to collect British debts from the First World War.[17]

The United Kingdom's war debts to the United States remain unpaid and outstanding. Although the British government has never formally repudiated these obligations, nor has it ever resumed payment. Despite London's initial efforts to justify this decision and its studious avoidance of the subject in the many decades that followed, Washington has never forgiven these debts. Enduring bilateral difficulties have been compounded by the international context of reparations and war debts. Many other states dotted around the world remain indebted to the United States and the United Kingdom since the First World War. Whether these other outstanding war debts will ever be repaid or forgiven remains uncertain, which complicates progress toward a settlement between London and Washington. The challenge of reaching an equitable solution to such a long-standing problem helps to explain why interest in these financial obligations has largely faded from the political landscape. Governments may simply prefer to forget about these unpaid debts rather than deal with the difficulties posed by repayment or forgiveness.

Epilogue

THE FINANCIAL LEGACIES of the First World War extend well into the twenty-first century. During the autumn statement of 2014, Chancellor of the Exchequer George Osborne announced that he would "at last, pay off the debts Britain incurred to fight the First World War."[1] Although the British government subsequently repaid outstanding domestic war bonds worth £1.9 billion in the following year, it has made no similar effort to resume repayment of its international obligations. Treasury officials and policymakers on both sides of the Atlantic recognize that U.S. loans provided to the United Kingdom during the First World War remain unpaid and outstanding, but they appear mostly willing to accept this enduring political limbo.[2]

Despite the passage of more than a century since the end of the Great War, neither side has had the political will to resolve these outstanding obligations. Washington remains unable to forgive the debts, and London continues to ignore them. The question of responsibility has bedeviled war-debt negotiations on both sides of the Atlantic for more than a century. The United States and the United Kingdom recognize the enduring problem and its potential costs, but as Harold James warns of the psychology of debt, "each actor believes that . . . the burdens of adjusting to the unpleasant reality can and should be undertaken by the other."[3] Reaching a settlement today would probably resurrect many of the arguments advanced by both states over a century ago.

U.S. policymakers could stress the sanctity of commercial loans, noting the legal obligation into which the United Kingdom and the rest of Europe had entered, and go on to express their reluctance to burdening American taxpayers with the costs of unpaid foreign debts. Recently released memorandums from the late 1990s reveal that the U.S. Treasury still considered these outstanding debts as "legally due and payable" and resisted pressure from lawyers and accountants to change their status, stressing the possibility of "future debt collection negotiations" and "prospective efforts to negotiate recovery of this debt."[4]

British policymakers might respond by arguing that these war debts were special and different from commercial loans because they had arisen as part of a cooperative wartime effort, which garnered no advantage to the recipients and was of immeasurable value to the common cause. As the British government has always stressed, its wartime allies owed more to the United Kingdom than the United Kingdom owed to the United States.[5] If the British government was willing to sacrifice the collection of its own larger loans, it might contend that the United States should be willing to do the same, especially for a close wartime ally.

These unpaid debts remain in a state of political limbo and will probably remain there for some time. The British government's formal position on the matter, most recently provided to the BBC in 2006, reveals no great appetite for change: "Neither the debt owed to the United States by the United Kingdom nor the larger debts owed by other countries to the United Kingdom have been serviced since 1934, nor have they been written off."[6] There is no reason to believe that this policy has changed in the intervening years.[7] In the words of John Maynard Keynes, the British government would probably prefer to let lie this "deeply sleeping dog."[8] This approach, to which policymakers have largely but perhaps sometimes unknowingly adhered for almost nine decades, has served the United Kingdom well.[9] Much of the original value of the debt has been eroded by a century of inflation. In this sense, the British government has won what Irving Fisher long ago referred to as "the great gamble" of the war debts.[10] This quiet strategy appears to have been largely sensible in the long run, albeit with some significant trade-offs along the way, given the costs avoided and the persistence of close political relations.

The United States' management of the war debts represents a more difficult compromise. It has refused to cancel or reduce these war debts, encouraging expectations of repayment and occasionally antagonizing other governments in line with congressional demands, but has done little to recover its losses, quietly prioritizing cooperation with states in other areas despite popular calls for debt collection. This compromise leaves a thorny political problem unresolved. Demands for repayment have emerged in Congress from time to time, most notably in the 1930s and 1970s, and they could conceivably return in the future. In private, some policymakers accept that the issue could reappear on the political horizon. This presents both a risk and an opportunity for the British government. Calls for repayment could be embarrassing and generate unforeseen shocks, particularly if HM Treasury fails to consider these obligations as part of its fiscal risks register. Conversely, repaying this comparatively small sum, largely eroded by a century of inflation, could prove useful at some point in the future for venturesome policymakers.[11]

The United Kingdom's total outstanding war debts to the United States presently stand at approximately $18 billion. This relatively small sum, especially in light of the recent coronavirus pandemic that sent total British government debt surging to $2.4 trillion, could tempt some politicians or civil servants to return to the issue in the right circumstances.[12] London may one day be willing to pay such a price to clear this unusual mark on its financial reputation, for example, or win favor with Washington. Policymakers may well recognize that old debts can sometimes serve contemporary interests.[13] The United States could conceivably welcome the repayment of an outstanding foreign loan worth billions of dollars, especially if it encouraged other states to honor their unpaid war debts, but not if it risked the renewal of old passions and lingering resentments. Progress therefore remains possible but appears unlikely. There are no clear signs that the United Kingdom expects to repay these debts or that the United States plans to forgive them. This enduring political impasse leaves the issue unresolved. The shadow of British default looks set to extend well into the twenty-first century.

Notes

INTRODUCTION

1. Reinhart and Rogoff, *This Time Is Different*, 95–97, 99–100.

2. On investors using peer-group comparisons or "country categorizations," believing that "wealthy, established democracies are very unlikely to default on their sovereign obligations," see Brooks, Cunha, and Mosley, "Categories, Creditworthiness, and Contagion," 589, 599. Although the Eurozone debt crisis, and the specific example of Greece, has helped to highlight the possibility of default by advanced-economy democracies, many developed sovereign states with large external debts have previously been in "comparably precarious situations." See Barta, *In the Red*, 6.

3. Sebastian Edwards has ably revealed how the abrogation of the gold clause and the subsequent devaluation of the dollar by the United States government in 1934 represents another important case of collective amnesia in modern financial history. See Edwards, *American Default*.

4. Strachan, *Financing the First World War*, 155–158.

5. This figure ($4.714 billion) is based on total indebtedness (payments on principal deducted) as of June 1934. See U.S. Treasury Department, *Annual Report* (1935), 391, table 42. I am grateful to the Federal Reserve Archival System for Economic Research and to the Federal Reserve Bank of St. Louis for digitizing many of these U.S. Treasury reports. The United Kingdom had technically defaulted in 1933 by making only partial or "token" payments, but these were accepted by the United States. On the attorney general's ruling on this matter, see *Foreign Relations of the United States (FRUS)*, 1934, vol. 1, Memorandum by Hackworth, 15 May 1934. As President Franklin Roosevelt explained, "I have no personal hesitation in saying that I do not characterize the resultant situation at this time as a default." British Pathé, "Roosevelt's Decision on War Debts," YouTube, 13 April 2013, https://

www.youtube.com/watch?v=caMoxnIFL8c. For clarity and consistency, "billion" hereafter refers to one thousand million.

6. A comparison based on relative output of the economy would be closer to $1.5 trillion. This figure ($1.51 trillion), which compares relative output in 1934 and 2019, is for illustrative and general reference purposes given the challenges of historical comparisons. Nevertheless, as Liaquat Ahamed explains, "in order to grasp the true significance of sums of money that relate to the economic situation of whole countries, such as the size of war debts owed to the United States, it is most useful not simply to make allowances for changes in the cost of living, but instead to adjust for changes in the size of economies." In much the same way, Ahamed values British debts of $4 billion in the 1920s and at $800 billion in 2008: *Lords of Finance*, 505, 500. See also Rohrer, "What's a Little Debt between Friends?" On the logic of adjustments based on relative output of the economy or growth of GDP, see S. Williamson, "Seven Ways." Adjusted by inflation, this figure would be approximately $90 billion in 2019. The figure ($89.7 billion) compares dollar values in 1934 and 2019 and derives from the usinflationcalculator.com and officialdata.org websites, which use the U.S. Bureau of Labor Statistics inflation information provided in the Consumer Price Index. This figure is for illustrative and general reference purposes only. As the Bank of England rightly warns, comparisons of prices further back in time and over long periods are less accurate than comparisons over short periods in recent years. On this point, and for inflation data concerning the British pound, see the Bank of England's Inflation Calculator: www.bankofengland.co.uk/monetary-policy/inflation/inflation-calculator.

7. By way of contrast, Argentina had roughly $80 billion worth of debt that it did not repay in 2001, which is often cited as one of the largest defaults in history. In the same year, Britain's war debts would equate to approximately $57.7 billion in terms of inflation or $692 billion in terms of relative output. See Gilsinan, "65 Words Just Caused Argentina's $29-Billion Default." For more recent comparisons within Europe, the Greek government only briefly defaulted on $1.7 billion in 2015. See Jim Yardley, James Kanter, and Jack Ewing, "Greece, Missing I.M.F. Payment, Is Called Effectively in Default," *New York Times*, June 30, 2015, https://www.nytimes.com/2015/07/01/world/europe/greece-alex-tsipras-debt-emergency-bailout.html.

8. On a typology of sovereign default, see Roos, *Why Not Default?*, 45–48; and Gill, "Review Essay: Rethinking Sovereign Default." For valuable insights into other technical and contractual types of default, ranging from data misreporting to cross default, see Ams et al., "Sovereign Default."

9. For a recent example, see House of Commons Debates (HC Deb.), 28 February 2002, vol. 380, cc1439–441W, 1439W.

10. On lenders differentiating between excusable default, which is justifiably associated with implicitly understood contingencies, and debt repudiation, which would be unjustifiable and inexcusable, see Grossman and Van Huyck, "Sovereign Debt as a Contingent Claim," 1088–1097; and Edwards, "Sovereign Default, Debt Restructuring, and Recovery Rates," 1–29.

11. U.S. Department of the Treasury and Office of Management and Budget, "U.S. Government Foreign Credit Exposure as of December 31, 2009, Part I: Summary Analysis," 33, data as of year-end, 31 December 2009. The list contains some

curious errors, including outdated spellings, such as "Rumania," and states that have since broken up, such as Czechoslovakia. Nevertheless, this data provides a helpful guide to the status of these war debts.

12. The United Kingdom ceased to carry any reference to either its debts or credits concerning war loans in its books from 1945. On this point, see National Archives, London, HM Treasury file (T) 381/77, "First World War Debt," 11 May 1977, attachment entitled "History of WW1 Debt, 1931–77." More recently, see HC Deb., 28 February 2002, vol. 380, cc1439–441W; and House of Lords Debates (HL Deb.), 19 January 2005, vol. 668, cc110–111WA. The United Kingdom has never forgiven its own outstanding loans to wartime allies, comprising France, Italy, Portugal, Belgium (including Belgian Congo), Austria, Greece, Romania, Yugoslavia, Poland, Estonia, Latvia, Czechoslovakia, Lithuania, Russia, Armenia, Australia, New Zealand, and Newfoundland. In 1941, which was the last time that the British government compared wartime credit and debts, Treasury officials concluded that the United Kingdom owed the United States $4,368 million but was owed by its allies $11,880 (£2,948) million. This comparison is based on the pegged value of the pound to the dollar, which stood at $4.03 in 1941.

13. Irving Fisher recognized early on the power of inflation and deflation on the value of war debts. As he put it, "Governments lose and gain in the same great gamble" (I. Fisher, *The Money Illusion*, 99).

14. This figure would represent the total outstanding amount at year-end 2018. The debt will exceed $19 billion within the next decade. Most of the data is contained in U.S. Treasury Department, *Annual Report* and the Statistical Appendix (1932–1980). More recent data appears in the Office of the Assistant Secretary for Economic Policy, "Status of Active Foreign Credits of the United States Government," 1979–1991; and U.S. Department of the Treasury and Office of Management and Budget, "U.S. Government Foreign Credit Exposure as of December 31, 1999–2009, Part I: Summary Analysis" (1999–2009). Please note that annual figures of total outstanding debt are sometimes difficult to compare, as the U.S. Treasury has occasionally changed the month of publication. There are also two records in 1976: the three-month period—1 July through 30 September 1976—between fiscal year 1976 and fiscal year 1977. At that time, the fiscal year definition shifted from 1 July–30 June to 1 October–30 September.

15. For recent examples of work using historical research to study debt and default, see Edwards, *American Default*; Fleming, *City of Debtors*; and Lienau, *Rethinking Sovereign Debt*.

16. For policymakers or advisers addressing the subject directly, see Lloyd George, *The Truth about Reparations and War Debts*, 97; Keynes, "A British View of Mr Hoover's Note," in *The Collected Writings*, vol. 18, 382–386; Leith-Ross, *Money Talks*, 178–179; Churchill, *The Gathering Storm*, 23. On the U.S. side, see Moley, *After Seven Years*, 72; Hoover, *Memoirs*, vol. 3, 180–181; Blum, *Morgenthau Diaries*, vol. 1, 100; and Stimson and Bundy, *On Active Service in Peace and War*, 217.

17. To this list, we can technically add Joseph Schumpeter, who was Austrian finance minister in the postwar period, and Friedrich Hayek, who took a government job administering Austria's war debts in the 1920s. These experiences dealing with major debt crises—only a small part of which related to U.S. war loans—

influenced their own worldviews. See Dyson, *States, Debt, and Power*, 262; and Wapshott, *Keynes Hayek*, 29.

18. T 385/204, Thorp to Morris, 13 November 1973; Schuerch to Geithner, "World War I Debt: Treasury Audit," 21 October 1998, document provided to the author by U.S. Treasury in 2018 (hereafter cited as U.S. Treasury file).

19. Reinhart and Rogoff, *This Time Is Different*, 96. More recent work by Reinhart, however, has paid much closer attention to the war debts: Reinhart and Trebesch, "A Distant Mirror of Debt, Default, and Relief," 22–24. On the history of sovereign borrowing, see Eichengreen, "Historical Research on International Lending and Debt," 149–169; Tomz and Wright, "Empirical Research on Sovereign Debt and Default," 247–272; and Oosterlinck, "Sovereign Debt Defaults," 697–714.

20. See, for instance, Warner, "Britain Would Be Unwise"; and Leaviss, "What Happened the Last Time the UK Defaulted?" Warner and Leaviss rightly question some alleged examples of British default over the past century. Nevertheless, claims of "some debt forgiveness by the US in the interwar years" or of an "excusable default" whereby "Germany was the real defaulter" and the "Americans didn't seem to be especially cross about it" are problematic. The British government's unilateral suspension of repayments in 1934 raises serious questions about the conclusion that "Britain is part of a small and exclusive club of nations that has never defaulted on its sovereign debt" or that "there has never been a formal default."

21. For broader surveys of the field, see Floud, Humphries, and Johnson, *Cambridge Economic History of Modern Britain*; and DuBoff, *Accumulation and Power*. Scholars have also considered earlier credit events in English history. See, for example, Mortimer, *The Perfect King*; and Hunt, *The Medieval Super-companies*. On "the Great Stop of the Exchequer" of 1672, see also Ferguson, *The Ascent of Money*, 76; and Burnet, *History of His Own Time*, 111.

22. For book-length studies, see Moulton and Pasvolsky, *War Debts and World Prosperity*; Parrini, *Heir to Empire*; Schuker, *The End of French Predominance in Europe*; Leffler, *The Elusive Quest*; Trachtenberg, *Reparations in World Politics*; Costigliola, *Awkward Dominion*; Kent, *The Spoils of War*; and Cohrs, *The Unfinished Peace after World War I*. For smaller or indirect accounts in biographies, see, for example, Self, *Neville Chamberlain*; and Feiling, *The Life of Neville Chamberlain*, 218–221, 225.

23. Ahamed, *Lords of Finance*; Clavin, *Failure of Economic Diplomacy*; and Wormell, *Management of the National Debt*. The most detailed account appears in Self, *War Debt Controversy*. See also Self, "Perception and Posture in Anglo-American Relations," 282–312.

24. Differences with regard to data selection and research scope have also resulted in significant points of tension in the extant literature. Clavin and Self, for instance, diverge on the issue of whether an earlier default would have been a more rational course of action. Whereas Clavin focuses on the rewards of collaboration between European debtors in the short term, Self emphasizes the costs to Britain's relationship with the United States over the longer term. Both interpretations are plausible; differences of interpretation reflect emphasis rather than error. An earlier default may well have been the more rational course of action with the benefit of

hindsight, but it appeared unduly reckless at the time. See Clavin, *Failure of Economic Diplomacy*, 59, 180; and Self, *War Debt Controversy*, 132. On the dangers of the historian's fallacy, whereby one assumes that policymakers had access to the same information as those who are subsequently analyzing the decision, see D. Fisher, *Historian's Fallacies*.

25. Robert Self provides an excellent and detailed historical account in *War Debt Controversy* but only covers the period 1917–1941. In the last of the book's ten chapters, Self provides a valuable but relatively brief survey of events from British default to U.S. entry into the Second World War. Leading accounts of British and U.S. economic history that consider the onset of the Second World War and the decades thereafter largely overlook or downplay the issue of default or its connection to other events See, for instance, Sayers, *Financial Policy*; and Dobson, *Anglo-American Economic Special Relationship*.

26. A small number of scholars do touch on the issue in the late 1930s and 1940s, albeit fleetingly, in their accounts of the prewar rearmament program, Lend-Lease agreements, or the Anglo-American loan negotiations. These contributions remain brief and largely unconnected. No accounts examine the consequences of default for the United Kingdom or the United States in the many decades that follow. On these contributions, see Shay, *British Rearmament in the Thirties*, 279–280; Kimball, "Lend-Lease and the Open Door," 232–259; Steil, *The Battle of Bretton Woods*, 97–98, 105–106, 179–180; and G. Herring, "The United States and British Bankruptcy," 260–280.

27. See, for instance, Reynolds, *The Long Shadow*; Tooze, *The Deluge*; Gerwarth, *The Vanquished*; and Strachan, *The First World War*. On the Great War as the epicenter of a cycle of armed conflict that had a greater chronological dimension and wider territorial reach, see Gerwarth and Manela, *Empires at War*.

28. See, for instance, Keynes, *The Economic Consequences of the Peace*; Hirst, *The Consequences of the War*; Mantoux, *The Carthaginian Peace*; Milward, *The Economic Effects of the Two World Wars*; O'Brien, "The Economic Effects of the Great War"; Eichengreen, *Golden Fetters*; and Ferguson, *The Pity of War*, esp. ch. 14.

29. On the importance of historical contributions to the study of sovereign default, see Gill, "Review Essay: Rethinking Default." For key examples, see Tomz, *Reputation and International Cooperation*; Sturzenegger and Zettelmeyer, *Debt Defaults and Lessons*; Gilman, *No Precedent, No Plan*; and Roos, *Why Not Default?* More broadly, see also Drelichman and Voth, *Lending to the Borrower from Hell*; Álvarez-Nogal and Chamley, "Debt Policy under Constraints," 192–213; and Drelichman and Voth, "Duplication without Constraints," 999–1006.

30. Tomz, *Reputation and International Cooperation*, 3–4.

31. For an overview of this extensive literature, see Reinhart and Rogoff, *This Time Is Different*, 54–59; Panizza, Sturzenegger, and Zettelmeyer, "The Economics and Law of Sovereign Debt and Default," 651–698; and Roos, *Why Not Default?*, 23–39. On explanations focused on reputation in particular, see English, "Understanding the Costs of Sovereign Default," 259–275; and Tomz, *Reputation and International Cooperation*. A small number of scholars have also considered explanations based on the importance of institutions—specifically, an empowered

parliament, independent judiciary, strong rule of law, and central bank—acting as a constraint on governments seeking default. On this subject, see North and Weingast, "Constitutions and Commitment," 803–832; Stasavage, *Public Debt and the Birth of the Democratic State*, esp. 1–25; Stasavage, "Private Investment and Political Institutions," 41–63; Saiegh, "Coalition Governments and Sovereign Debt Crises," 232–254; and Kohlscheen, "Sovereign Risk," 62–85.

32. On scholars highlighting these limitations, see, for example, Reinhart and Rogoff, *This Time Is Different*, 57; and Tomz and Wright, "Do Countries Default in Bad Times?," 358.

33. For early work on domestic-political variables, see Frieden, "Winners and Losers in the Latin America Debt Crisis," 23–37; and Frieden, *Debt, Development, and Democracy*. On the role of economic and social variables in the transformation of many Latin American economies, see Edwards, *Crisis and Reform in Latin America*. More recently, see Alichi, "A Model of Sovereign Debt in Democracies"; Borensztein and Panizza, "The Costs of Sovereign Default," 683–741; Curtis, Jupille, and Leblang, "Iceland on the Rocks," 721–740; Ballard-Rosa, "Hungry for Change," 313–346; and Roos, *Why Not Default?* For work relating to state identity or public attitudes, see Lienau, *Rethinking Sovereign Debt*; and Nelson and Steinberg, "Default Positions," 520–533.

34. See, for instance, Clavin, *Failure of Economic Diplomacy*, 59; and Self, *War Debt Controversy*, 132.

35. On the logic of repayment for stalwart states, such as the United Kingdom, that are committed to defending their financial reputation to investors, in contrast to fair-weather or lemon-like governments, see Tomz, *Reputation and International Cooperation*, 18–20.

36. The minutes of the relevant meeting also refer to Austria, Chile, Ireland, Greece, and Russia. See the National Archives, London, Cabinet file (CAB), 23/73/3, 29 November 1932, attachment, 28 November 1932.

37. On the logic of ideas and norms functioning instrumentally, affecting cost-benefit calculations, but also substantively, making actions legitimate and appropriate, see Tannenwald, *The Nuclear Taboo*. See also Finnemore and Sikkink, "International Norm Dynamics and Political Change," 887–917.

38. For valuable exceptions, see, for instance, Lipson, "Bankers' Dilemmas," 200–225; Mosley, *Global Capital and National Governments*; and Tomz, *Reputation and International Cooperation*.

39. T 175/79/103–4, Leith-Ross to Fisher, 2 November 1933; and Cole, *Roosevelt and the Isolationists*, 92–93.

40. For an overview of these claims, see Borensztein and Panizza, "The Costs of Sovereign Default," 683–741; Sandleris, "The Costs of Sovereign Default," 1–27; and Fuentes and Saravia, "Are Sovereign Defaulters Punished?," 152. On defaulting being "clearly bad for political careers of heads of state" and that the chances of a prime minister or president being ousted from office within the following year double, see Malone, "Sovereign Debt Problems and Policy Gambles," 43.

41. In this way, the British government's suspension of payments joins a small universe of other cases in which default proved relatively advantageous to the debtor such as the United States in the 1930s. See, for example, Edwards, *Ameri-*

can Default, 186–200; and Edwards, Longstaff, and Garcia Marin, "The U.S. Debt Restructuring of 1933."

42. For a detailed account, see CAB 23/79/7, 30 May 1934.

43. Stannage, *Baldwin Thwarts the Opposition*.

44. Some foreign debtors certainly defaulted on their debts to the United Kingdom, but the available data shows that income derived from overseas investments— namely, dominion and colonial governments, dominion and colonial municipalities, foreign governments, and foreign municipalities—grew in 1934 and 1935. See Kindersley, "British Oversea Investments in 1935 and 1936," 644; Kindersley, "British Overseas Investments in 1934 and 1935," 647.

45. Hachey and Lindsay, "Winning Friends and Influencing Policy," 122–127; Peden, *The Treasury and British Public Policy*, 281–282; Schatz, "The Anglo-American Trade Agreement," 85–103; and H. James, *International Monetary Cooperation since Bretton Woods*, 24–25.

46. See Leith-Ross, *Money Talks*, 178–179. Other defaulting states also benefited economically. The rewards of default for Germany, for instance, exceeded what it paid in reparations. See Norbert, *Hitler's Magician*, 212–214.

47. Shea, "Financing Victory," 771–795; Allen and DiGiuseppe, "Tightening the Belt," 647–659; Flores-Macías and Kreps, "Borrowing Support for War," 997–1020; DiGiuseppe, "The Fiscal Autonomy of Deciders," 317–338; and Shea and Poast, "War and Default," 1876–1904.

48. This book therefore builds on earlier and briefer arguments advanced by P. Kennedy, *The Rise and Fall of the Great Powers*, 330; and Dallek, *Franklin D. Roosevelt and American Foreign Policy*, 74.

49. For the most recent example, see HL Deb., 11 July 2003, vol. 651, c66WA. In 2006, the British government confirmed that the debts it owed to the United States have not been serviced since 1934, but "nor have they been written off." See also Rohrer, "What's a Little Debt between Friends?"

50. None of this is to deny important differences between official lending by governments and public debt markets. On the latter, see Catão and Mano, "Default Premium," 91–110. For an example of economists who claim that markets retain a long memory of default, see Flandreau and Zumer, *The Making of Global Finance*, 57. On this topic, see also Özler, "Have Commercial Banks Ignored History?," 617. For a nuanced analysis of the consequences of sovereign debt restructurings, which stresses the importance of a longer-term perspective beyond initial default episodes and recognizes the significance of second-order ramifications, see Lienau, "The Longer-Term Consequences of Sovereign Debt Restructuring."

51. Other scholars have recognized the political persistence of unpaid debts. On the United States imposing a decade-long virtual embargo on the Soviet Union following default in 1918 and France and the United Kingdom ending litigation over these Russian bonds in 1986 and 1997, see Lienau, *Rethinking Sovereign Debt*, 99; and Toussaint, *The Debt System*, 204.

52. National Archives, London, Foreign Office file (FO), 371/52957, Judson to Balfour, "Notes on the Loan," 23 May 1946.

53. For a variety of sources that support this claim, see, for instance, FO 371/52957, Judson Minute, "World War I Debts and the Loan Debate," 25 June

1946; Our Own Correspondent, "Loan Debate Opens in Congress," *Financial Times*, 9 July 1946; and *Congressional Record*, House, 11 July 1946, 8697, 8701–8703, 8706, 8715, 8723. On the case for including war loans as a cost to the American people, see Rockoff, *America's Economic Way of War*, 144–145.

54. T 385/204, Thorp to Morris, 23 April 1973.

55. State of New York, Surrogate's Court, File No. P 1886/1934, 16 November 1998; and U.S. Department of the Treasury and Office of Management and Budget, "U.S. Government Foreign Credit Exposure as of December 31, 2002–2009, Part I: Summary Analysis" (2002–2009), data as of year-end, 31 December 1999–2009, n11.

56. Maurer, *The Empire Trap*, 20. There are many other good reasons to study economic history. As Richard N. Cooper explains, historians can "bring alive exciting or important events" and alert economists to "important but usually neglected characteristics of economies, namely that they are sometimes strongly influenced by non-economic factors," and "it is usually impossible to understand our institutions and attitudes without some appreciation of the events that shaped the legacy from our parents and grandparents." See R. Cooper, "Fettered to Gold?," 2120. Concerning the value of economic history more broadly, including narrative approaches, see Temin, "The Rise and Fall of Economic History"; Adelman and Levy, "The Fall and Rise of Economic History"; C.R., "Economic History Is Dead"; and Lipartito, "Reassembling the Economic," 101–139. More broadly, on the different methods within the study of history and their utility in other fields, see Fogel and Elton, *Which Road to the Past?*; Goldin, "Cliometrics and the Nobel," 191–208; and Gill, Gill, and Roulet, "Constructing Trustworthy Historical Narratives," 191–205.

57. For broader studies of international default episodes, see, for instance, Reinhart and Rogoff, *This Time Is Different*; and Sturzenegger and Zettelmeyer, *Debt Defaults and Lessons*. Scholars have studied the interwar debt crisis before, but many have neglected war debts. Barry Eichengreen and Richard Portes, for instance, have produced valuable research on sovereign debt and default in the 1930s, but they concede that their "treatment of war debts" represents an important aspect of their work that they have "left untouched" ("Debt and Default in the 1930s," 632). See also Eichengreen and Portes, "The Interwar Debt Crisis and Its Aftermath," 69–94.

58. Analysis of the available data, especially with regard to the strength of my own arguments against those of competing explanations, is informed by process-tracing techniques. See Collier, "Understanding Process Tracing," 823–830; George and Bennett, *Case Studies and Theory Development*. Process tracing has been used effectively by other social scientists studying economic decision-making, including Fairfield, "Going Where the Money Is," 42–57; Roos, *Why Not Default?*; and Barta, *In the Red*. For examples of social scientists using historical or detailed case studies as part of a mixed-method approach to the study of debt and default, see, for example, Ballard-Rosa, *Democracy, Dictatorship, and Default*; Bunte, *Raise the Debt*; Tomz, *Reputation and International Cooperation*; and Mosley, *Global Capital and National Governments*. Historical and case-study research can play a valuable role in the study of the international political economy. On the importance of

"problem-driven research" using "the method that shines the brightest light on the problem under investigation," see Oatley, "The Reductionist Gamble," 336.

59. Grossman and Van Huyck, "Sovereign Debt as a Contingent Claim," 1088.

CHAPTER 1. PRELUDE TO DEFAULT, 1917–1932

1. Of most relevance to this chapter is Self, *War Debt Controversy*, which provides an excellent and thorough account of events. See also important work by Wormell, *Management of the National Debt*; Clavin, *Failure of Economic Diplomacy*; and Ahamed, *Lords of Finance*. For an official history of events from 1914 to 1923, see CAB 104/28, P. J. Grigg, "History of the American War Debt, to the Conclusion of Settlement of 1923" (1934). For relevant book-length studies, see Moulton and Pasvolsky, *War Debts and World Prosperity*; Lloyd George, *The Truth about Reparations and War Debts*; Parrini, *Heir to Empire*; Schuker, *The End of French Predominance in Europe*; Hogan, *Informal Entente*; Leffler, *The Elusive Quest*; Schrecker, *The Hired Money*; Trachtenberg, *Reparations in World Politics*; Costigliola, *Awkward Dominion*; Kent, *The Spoils of War*; A. Turner, *The Cost of War*; Cohrs, *The Unfinished Peace after World War I*.

2. For an overview of the major differences in postwar viewpoints, see Moulton and Pasvolsky, *War Debts and World Prosperity*, 48–53.

3. On the viability of sovereign debt restructuring, see Barry Eichengreen, "Restructuring Sovereign Debt," 75–98; and Rieffel, *Restructuring Sovereign Debt*.

4. The "Great Depression" was a global phenomenon but was nevertheless experienced differently in many parts of the world. The U.S. economy suffered more greatly than the British economy did, for example. The term "slump" may therefore be a better description for the experience of the United Kingdom. On this comparison, see Weldon, *Two Hundred Years*, 109.

5. Concerning the importance of political and economic factors, or mixed-motive models, in explaining the timing of sovereign default, see Tomz and Wright, "Do Countries Default in Bad Times?," 352–360.

6. McVey, *The Financial History of Great Britain*. There is a variety of strategies states can use to pay for war. The United Kingdom's strategy in the First World War was different from that of France, Russia, and the United States. For a valuable study concerning how states finance wars—and why they sometimes do so differently—see Zielinski, *How States Pay for Wars*.

7. I base this valuation on an exchange rate of 4.93 ($:1) in 1914. In the absence of daily or monthly data, I determine the dollar-pound exchange rate via MeasuringWorth's "Dollar-Pound Exchange Rate from 1791," https://www.measuringworth.com/datasets/exchangepound/. This data set refers to annual averages of actual and large-scale transactions rather than advertised, posted, or otherwise hypothetical exchange rates. For further details, see Officer, *Between the Dollar-Sterling Gold Points*; and Officer, "Exchange Rates."

8. Goodman, "The Bank of England"; Anson et al., "Your Country Needs Funds." For a history of the Bank of England's activities during the war, see Bank of England Archive (BE), M7/159, John Osborne, *The Bank of England*, vols. 1–4 (unpublished, 1926).

9. Subsequent Labour proposals for a capital levy, however, risked a loss of confidence that could make it difficult to borrow in the United States. On these points, see Daunton, "How to Pay for the War," 890–891.

10. Grigg, "History of the American War Debt"; and CAB 104/28, Keynes to Playfair, 19 October 1933. Keynes recalled in 1933 that the U.S. Treasury asked why the British government gave loans and not subsidies to its allies. Keynes said that he "did not expect money to be repaid but was important in the interests of economy that allies look on them as loans, which would help them maintain a sufficient sense of responsibility in the spending of them." The American economist and first dean of the Harvard Business School offered a withering critique of the U.S. use of loans rather than grants, aided by historical comparisons to British lending during the Napoleonic Wars. As he explained of Britain, "while her allies shed blood in the common effort she furnished her share of the treasure." See Gay, "War Loans or Subsidies," 394–405 (quote on 396).

11. I use the term "HM Treasury" or "British Treasury" as shorthand for His or Her Majesty's Treasury.

12. Alstyne, "American Loans to the Allies," 180–193. The United Kingdom and France sought $1 billion in credit from the U.S. in 1916, but borrowers ultimately had to accept less than half that amount following a difficult and undersubscribed public offering.

13. Grigg, "History of the American War Debt," 4–5.

14. Burk, *Britain, America and the Sinews of War*; Burk, "A Merchant Bank at War," 155–172; Dayer, "Strange Bedfellows," 127–151; and Horn, "A Private Bank at War," 85–112.

15. By March 1922, the J. P. Morgan loan, dollar Treasury bills, Anglo-French loan, and notes and bonds held by U.S. industrialists, alongside most loans and advances from other countries, had disappeared. Domestic debts underwent conversion in the 1930s and were fully repaid in 2015. See Wormell, *The Management of the National Debt*, 450–452; and "UK Debt from First World War Finally Repaid," *Evening Standard*, 9 March 2015.

16. Moulton and Pasvolsky, *War Debts and World Prosperity*, 35; Burk, *Britain, America and the Sinews of War*, 95; and J. Cooper, "The Command of Gold Reversed," 211–214, 217.

17. J. Cooper, "The Command of Gold Reversed," 218.

18. Ibid., 227–229.

19. See, for instance, *Congressional Record*, Senate, 27 April 1917, 1362.

20. Lloyd George, "Address to the American Club." In his memoirs, Lloyd George lauded U.S. intervention but raised questions about the preparedness of U.S. forces. See Lloyd George, *War Memoirs of David Lloyd George: 1917*, 575; and Lloyd George, *Memoirs of David Lloyd George: 1918*, esp. 5, 80–81.

21. In the postwar period, the U.S. proposed effective rates of overall interest for the United Kingdom that varied from 5 percent to 3.31 percent. See Self, *War Debt Controversy*, 18–20, 24, 34, 218; Tooze, *Deluge*, 436.

22. Self, *War Debt Controversy*, 19; Grigg, "History of the American War Debt."

23. CAB 104/28, Note from Keynes to Chancellor, "Treatment of Inter-Ally Debt Arising Out of the War, March 1919." On the rate of 4.43 ($:1) in 1919, see "Dollar-Pound Exchange Rate from 1791."

24. Lloyd George, *Truth about Reparations and War Debts*, 97. As Martin Slater has written more recently, "one can see from the figures that Britain was still nominally a net creditor." Slater, *The National Debt*, loc. 2054.

25. The war officially ended on 2 July 1921. On these figures, see Self, *War Debt Controversy*, 18–19.

26. Grigg, "History of the American War Debt." Self provides a figure of $4.227 million, or £800 million, at par: *War Debt Controversy*, 19. For a detailed account of Britain's external borrowing from the U.S., as well as from Canada and the neutral powers, see Wormell, *The Management of the National Debt*, 242–315.

27. The United States remained on the gold standard, whereas the United Kingdom did not during World War I. When London borrowed from Washington, its sterling loans were now paper loans and not gold loans.

28. Most of this debt was owed to the U.S. Treasury and the U.S. private sector. See Wormell, *The Management of the National Debt*, 382, 731–733. On British national debt to gross domestic product, see Slater, *National Debt*, ch. 8, esp. fig. 6.

29. On the British government consistently reducing debt in peacetime, and the rationale for such policies in the interwar period, see Ritschl, "Sustainability of High Public Debt," 179–181.

30. Wormell, *The Management of the National Debt*, xiv–xv. See also, more broadly, Hargreaves, *The National Debt*.

31. This position had the unintended effect of France raising its demands to include not only full reparations but also war costs, which clashed with U.S. ideas of Germany paying a modest lump sum based on moral, legal, and practical grounds. On these points, see Stevenson, *1914–1918*; and Striner, *Woodrow Wilson and World War I*, 204.

32. Moulton and Pasvolsky, *War Debts and World Prosperity*, 49–50.

33. McAdoo, *Crowded Years*, 417; Costigliola, *Awkward Dominion*, 36. None of this is to suggest McAdoo's opposition to lending. He had supported efforts to widen the basis of Allied credit. He argued that the risks of not doing so outweighed the rewards as domestic prosperity rested on foreign trade. See Horn, *Britain, France, and the Financing of the First World War*, 104.

34. The first liberty loan was set to 3.5 percent, but the terms of all subsequent loans existed at U.S. discretion. As such, if the British government sought to protect the rate attached to the first loan, the U.S. could simply increase the rates elsewhere. HM Treasury nevertheless considered 5 percent reasonable at the time. On these points, see Grigg, "History of the American War Debt," 14, 16.

35. Trachtenberg, "Reparation at the Paris Peace Conference," 44–45, 47; and Marks, "The Myths of Reparations," 231 255.

36. Grigg, "History of the American War Debt," 23–25. On 18 September 1919, the British position stood as $4.27 billion ($4,267,000,000), payable on demand with interest at 5 percent.

37. Grigg, "History of the American War Debt," 16. On marketability also negatively affecting British market operations in the United States, see Wormell, *The Management of the National Debt*, 489–490.

38. John Keynes, "Personal Telegram by Keynes from Chancellor of Exchequer to Lord Reading, 20 April 1918," in *The Collected Writings*, vol. 16, 287.

39. On the economic costs of the war, see Ferguson, *The Pity of War*, 395–396. On the pandemic, see Johnson, *Britain and the 1918–19 Influenza Pandemic*, 174–175.

40. On the cross-party movement led by David Lloyd George and supported by his Conservative allies during and immediately after the war, see J. Turner, *British Politics and the Great War*.

41. Keynes to the chancellor, March 1919, in *The Collected Writings*, vol. 2, 178.

42. Cassel, *The Downfall of the Gold Standard*, esp. ch. 4, 99; and I. Fisher, "Cancelation of the War Debts," quoted in Pavanelli, "The Great Depression in Irving Fisher's Work," 153. The British economist Hubert D. Henderson referred to these debts as "a prodigious phenomenon without a parallel in the history of the world" (*The Inter-war Years and Other Papers*, 67).

43. Grigg, "History of the American War Debt," appendix F; Keynes, "Treatment of Inter-Ally Debt Arising out of the War, March 1919."

44. Austen Chamberlain to Robert Cecil, 22 April 1919, in Keynes, *The Collected Writings*, vol. 16, 437.

45. Concerning the influenza pandemic in the United States, see Crosby, *America's Forgotten Pandemic*.

46. On the reparation agreements and other war debts, see CAB 24/140/44, "Memorandum on the History of the Negotiations with Regard to the Payment of Reparation and of the Inter-Allied Debts (Excluding the American Debt)," printed 20 November 1922. See also MacMillan, *Peace Makers*, 194–195; and Skidelsky, *Keynes*, 354–357. For an important corrective to popular claims about French, as well as British and American, reparations policies during the peace conference and in the post-Versailles period, see Trachtenberg, "Reparation at the Paris Peace Conference," 24–55; and Trachtenberg, *Reparation in World Politics*, esp. 59–60.

47. Grigg, "History of the American War Debt," 20.

48. Ibid., appendix F; Keynes, "Treatment of Inter-Ally Debt Arising out of the War, March 1919." For a similar criticism of U.S. lending, see Gay, "War Loans or Subsidies," 394–405. On the war-debt problem allegedly playing a key role in explaining Keynes's decision to resign from the British delegation at the Paris Peace Conference, see Fuller and Whitten, "Keynes and the First World War," 1–39. On Keynes's private frustrations with the United States, see Schuker, "Keynes and the Personal Politics of Reparations," 463–464. See also Keynes, *The Economic Consequences of the Peace*; and Keynes, *A Revision of the Treaty*. To be sure, Keynes's own analyses of the Peace Treaty were not without flaws. As Jacob Viner explains, economists at the time had recognized that Keynes's analysis had been "technically defective at some crucial points, especially in its treatment of the alleged difficulties of 'transfer' of reparations." See Viner's review of Mantoux, *The Carthaginian Peace*, 69–70. These insights derive from Trachtenberg, "My Story."

49. Glass to de Billy, 29 January 1919, in U.S. Treasury Department, *Annual Report* (1926), 64–65.

50. Boyden, "Relation between Reparations and the Interallied Debts," 21. For a more detailed account of why the two issues are linked, see ibid., 24.

51. As Lloyd George pointed out, in such a scheme, a default by Germany "would have the same effect as a cancellation . . . of so much of the war-debts" (*The Truth about Reparations and War Debts*, 106).

52. R. Baker, *Woodrow Wilson and the World Settlement*, 289–290.

53. See, for example, Trachtenberg, *Reparations in World Politics*, 2–4, 15–16. On related arguments that "the German threat to the peace and stability of Europe would have been substantially lessened," see Jacobson, "Is There a New International History of the 1920s?," 633.

54. Kang and Rockoff, "Capitalizing Patriotism." McAdoo had hoped that patriotism would allow the bonds to be sold at lower interest rates but accepted the need for some exemptions to make the loan "more attractive" (*Crowded Years*, 378, 410).

55. Jacobson, "Is There a New International History of the 1920s?," 633; Artaud, *La reconstruction de l'Europe*.

56. Jacobson, "Is There a New International History of the 1920s?," 633; Artaud, *La reconstruction de l'Europe, passim*. See also, more broadly, Costigliola, "Anglo-American Financial Rivalry," 911–934.

57. Self, *War Debt Controversy*, 29.

58. Grigg, "History of the American War Debt," 25–29.

59. R. Baker, *Woodrow Wilson and the World Settlement*, vol. 3, 359–360. On the U.S. offer of deferment, and the British reaction, see Self, *War Debt Controversy*, 23–24.

60. Glass to Fordney, 18 December 1919, in U.S. Treasury Department, *Annual Report* (1920), 59–61. As Congress subsequently recognized, a large proportion of Britain's foreign investments had survived the war intact. See *Congressional Record*, Senate, 16 January 1923, 1786.

61. This concern also reflected the maturation of a large Anglo-Franco loan in October 1920, for which Britain owed half but might assume full liability. See Grigg, "History of the American War Debt," 25–29.

62. Ibid.

63. Ibid. For a detailed account of US and British negotiations, see Self, *War Debt Controversy*, 25–27.

64. Houston to Chamberlain, 1 March 1920, quoted in *Congressional Record*, Senate, 18 July 1921, 3950–3952.

65. Ibid.

66. Ibid.

67. *Congressional Record*, Senate, 26 April 1920, 6127.

68. Blackett memorandum, 11 May 1920, printed as CP 1259, CAB 24/105.

69. Grigg, "History of the American War Debt," 29.

70. CAB 24/105/59, "Inter-Allied and Anglo-American Debts," Note by the Chancellor of the Exchequer, 12 May 1920.

71. Wormell, *The Management of the National Debt*, 501–502.

72. Grigg, "History of the American War Debt," 30–31. See also Rathbone, "Making War Loans to the Allies."

73. Grigg, "History of the American War Debt," 30–31. As Jeremy Wormell notes, no minister mentioned the contractual nature of these obligations or the risks to future borrowing (*The Management of the National Debt*, 502–503).

74. Grigg, "History of the American War Debt," 32, letter printed in Annex L; ibid., 81–82.

75. *Congressional Record*, Senate, 18 July 1921, 3950–3952.

76. CAB 23/23/1, 3 November 1920. On the Harding administration and its approach to the war debts, see Murray, *The Harding Era*; and Grant, "Harding and the British War Debt Question," 479–487.

77. CAB 24/116/13, Memorandum by the Chancellor of the Exchequer, "Our American Debt," 30 November 1920.

78. Ibid.

79. Ibid. In addition to the problems of paying back interest, as detailed in Wilson's letter, London feared that Washington's issuance of marketable bonds could wreck any chance of eventual cancellation. There could also be no assurance of exchange stability for the United Kingdom if the United States held $4 billion of demand obligations. The chancellor therefore urged the government to send a representative to Washington to resume negotiations. On these points, see Grigg, "History of the American War Debt."

80. CAB 24/116/13, Memorandum by the Chancellor of the Exchequer, "Our American Debt." The interest due on 15 November amounted to $314,583,000 ($3.50 to the £ = £89,881,000).

81. CAB 24/116/14, Supplementary Note by the Chancellor, "Our American Debt," 3 December 1920.

82. Ibid.

83. Ibid.

84. Ibid.

85. CAB 23/23/17, Conclusions of a Meeting of the Cabinet, December 1920. On news from the United States, see Geddes, FO telegram no. 835, 15 December 1920. For an insight into congressional resistance to cancellation, see *Congressional Record*, Senate, 23 December 1920, 698–703.

86. CAB 23/23/17, Conclusions of a Meeting of the Cabinet, December 1920.

87. Self, *War Debt Controversy*, 32.

88. Grigg, "History of the American War Debt," 34–35.

89. Ibid., 82, Annex II.

90. Ibid.

91. Warren G. Harding, Inaugural Address, 4 March 1921, The American Presidency Project, http://www.presidency.ucsb.edu/ws/index.php?pid=25833.

92. Leffler, "American Policy Making and European Stability," 210–214.

93. Earlier histories have stressed the ignorance and provincialism of U.S. policymakers as well as deeply rooted belief in the sanctity of contracts. See, for instance, Moulton and Pasvolsky, *War Debts and World Prosperity*, 378; Rhodes, "Reassessing 'Uncle Shylock,'" 787–788. Since the late 1960s, however, a more nuanced view has emerged. See, for instance, Leffler, "The Origins of Republican War Debt Policy," 585–586; and J. Wilson, *American Business and Foreign Policy*, 123–156.

94. Leffler, "The Origins of Republican War Debt Policy," 588, 586, 589. Leffler explains, "The United States Treasury hoped to repay American bondholders with funds obtained from the Allied debtors. If the latter failed to pay, the government would have to obtain the necessary revenue from the American taxpayers" (589n19). Recent research has found that counties with higher rates of liberty-

bond ownership turned against the Democratic Party in the presidential elections of 1920 and 1924. This was a reaction to the depreciation of the bonds prior to the 1920 election and the appreciation of the bonds in the early 1920s under a Republican president. See Hilt and Rahn, "Financial Asset Ownership and Political Partisanship."

95. Leffler, "The Origins of Republican War Debt Policy," 589–590.

96. *Congressional Record*, House, 21 October 1921, 610–611; see also ibid., 6601–6628.

97. Self, *War Debt Controversy*, 34. See FO371/5662, A7885/247/45, "Inter-Allied Indebtedness and Attitude of the United States," April 1922; Moulton and Pasvolsky, *War Debts and World Prosperity*, 77–80.

98. Leffler, "The Origins of Republican War Debt Policy," 591–595.

99. Ibid., 595–596, 592–593.

100. Hughes would later preside over the U.S. Supreme Court when it took some of the most important cases related to the New Deal, including the gold cases at the heart of the United States' own default. See Edwards, *American Default*.

101. *Congressional Record*, Senate, 11 April 1922, 5281. On claims connecting the outcome of the Washington Naval Treaty of 1922 and subsequent negotiations on the war debts, see Dayer, "The British War Debts to the United States," 569–595.

102. Self, *War Debt Controversy*, 35; Grant, "Harding and the British War Debt Question," 479–480; *FRUS*, 1922, vol. 1, 391–399, 402.

103. See, for instance, CAB 23/25/21, Conclusions of a Meeting, 10 May 1921. The subrogated securities already posed increasing costs to the British government, but ministers continued to opt for delay with respect to the larger and more troublesome war debts. See Grigg, "History of the American War Debt." Elements within the Bank of England had argued that debt negotiations with the United States should be delayed "till conditions have cleared on both sides of the Atlantic": "To put it shortly; we should never pay in cash the principal or interest of our War Debt to America or make agreements when to do so: this debt was not incurred on our own behalf but on behalf of our allies. . . . We should discharge our War Debt to America by means of indemnity from Germany, an exchange which would be approved as right and equitable by the whole world." Osborne, *The Bank of England*, vol. 4, chap. 10, 9–10.

104. As Wormell explains, "The repayment was dramatic." By March 1922, net £223.6 million ($1,088,200,000 at par exchange) had been paid off in cash. The British government had repaid "the Morgan call loan, the dollar Treasury bills, the Anglo-French loan, the Notes and Bonds held by U.S. industrials, the loans from the Argentinian and Uruguayan governments, and the advances from European neutrals had disappeared, together with all but £3m of those taken from Japan. There remained small amounts to Canadian banks and government, Mauritius, the central Argentine railway, three public issues in New York but towering above all, the debts to the US Treasury" (Wormell, *The Management of the National Debt*, 450). On the Bank of England being "deeply interested in the liquidation of . . . short term indebtedness abroad" to "maintain the gold standard," see Osborne, *The Bank of England*, vol. 4, chap. 10, 8.

105. Wormell, *The Management of the National Debt*, 547. Wormell also recognizes the practical elements of the decision: "How could budgets be drawn up, fiscal policy planned, if a major item of expenditure was not known? How could a sustainable sterling rate be maintained with a huge demand liability hanging over the exchanges? . . . What would happen to the funding agreement already reached with the Empire if London refused to fund its own debt to the USA?" (547).

106. Grigg, "History of the American War Debt," 39.

107. A note to this effect was sent to France, Italy, Portugal, Romania, Greece, and Yugoslavia on 31 March 1921. Europe's reaction was muted, but the U.S. budget of 1922 subsequently provided for receipt of interest from the United Kingdom. See Grigg, "History of the American War Debt," 40.

108. HC Debs., 5s, 150 col. 1528; and HC Debs., 5s, 152 col. 240–241, 20 February and 21 March 1922. The U.S. was aware of this pending contribution. See *Congressional Record*, House, 23 March 1922, 4443.

109. For a useful overview of the troubled British economy in the 1920s, see Weldon, *Two Hundred Years*, 96–106. Concerning the serious political and social risks associated with increased taxation in the postwar period, see Daunton, "How to Pay for the War," 882–919.

110. CAB 23/24/6, Conclusions of a Meeting of the Cabinet, 7 February 1921.

111. The policies reflected the advice of the Geddes Committee on National Expenditure. On these decisions, see McDonald, "The Geddes Committee," 644–674.

112. International events also threatened to add to these burdens. During April and May 1922, Lloyd George attended a conference in Genoa attempting to revise the terms of the Treaty of Versailles. France had recently threatened to invade Germany, following Berlin's failure to pay Paris the required indemnities, and tensions remained high. Lloyd George believed that reparations were beyond Germany's means and proposed a reduction in its liabilities. France's relative share of payment should be increased, however, thereby ensuring that total receipts remained the same. Furthermore, he suggested that France's repayment of war debts to Britain should be suspended. Lloyd George's proposals lacked cabinet approval and generated resistance from backbenchers. See Hattersley, *David Lloyd George*, 552.

113. Grigg, "History of the American War Debt," 44.

114. Ibid.

115. Ibid., 45.

116. Ibid.

117. CAB 23/30/13, Conclusions, 16 June 1922.

118. Wormell, *The Management of the National Debt*, 547.

119. CAB 23/30/13, Conclusions, 16 June 1922.

120. Ibid.

121. On the occupation of the Ruhr and its relation to reparations and war debts, see Artaud, "Reparations and War Debts," 94–100.

122. CAB 23/30/20, Conclusions, 25 July 1922.

123. Ibid.

124. Ibid.

125. Ibid.

126. Ibid.

127. Ibid.

128. Ibid.

129. Ibid.

130. For the same conclusion, see Self, *War Debt Controversy*, 40. The Balfour Note was dispatched to diplomatic representatives in London of France, Italy, Yugoslavia, Romania, Portugal, and Greece. See Grigg, "History of the American War Debt," Annex P.

131. CAB 23/30/20, Conclusions, 25 July 1922.

132. Command Paper (Cmd.) 1737, 1922; *FRUS*, 1922, vol. 1, 406–409.

133. CAB 23/30/20, Conclusions, 25 July 1922.

134. Colby, "Should War Debts Be Cancelled?," 68.

135. Kent, *The Spoils of War*, 18–89.

136. *Congressional Record*, Senate, 14 September 1922, 12592, 12584.

137. *Congressional Record*, Senate, 16 January 1923, 1780–1786.

138. *Congressional Record*, Senate, 14 September 1922, 12600; Grigg, "History of the American War Debt."

139. Self, *War Debt Controversy*, 42–43; Trachtenberg, *Reparations in World Politics*, 257–258.

140. For an overview, see Jacobson, "Is There a New International History of the 1920s?," 633.

141. For an overview of the historiography, and a brief refutation, see A. Turner, *The Cost of War*, 265.

142. Orde, *British Policy and European Reconstruction*, 215–216.

143. CAB/23/30/20, Conclusions, 25 July 1922.

144. Self, *War Debt Controversy*, 40–41, citing Cmd. 1737, 1922; and *FRUS*, 1922, vol. 1, 406–409.

145. CAB 23/30/23, Conclusions, 12 August 1922.

146. Wormell, *The Management of the National Debt*, 547.

147. Quoted in Self, *War Debt Controversy*, 24.

148. On the significance of these strikes, with regard to both lost working days and the relationship between the government and organized labour, see Renshaw, "Black Friday, 1921."

149. For an overview of events, see Bogdanor, *The Coalition and the Constitution*, 78. Grigg, "History of the American War Debt."

150. Grigg, "History of the American War Debt."

151. HC Debs., 5s, 159 col. 3233, 14 December 1922; Self, *War Debt Controversy*, 44. I round the figures from the dollar-pound exchange rate, which at this time hovered around 4.8 ($:£). This figure resembles published exchange-rate data for 1923 that provides a figure of 4.58 ($:1): "Dollar-Pound Exchange Rate from 1791."

152. Schuker, "Keynes and the Personal Politics of Reparations," 581–582, citing Keynes to Baldwin, 16 December 1922, John Maynard Keynes Papers, King's College, Cambridge, FI/4/2; Cambridge University Library, Stanley Baldwin Papers (SBP), vol. 109, Keynes to J. C. C. Davidson, 30 January 1923, reiterating that American creditors stood "completely at [Britain's] mercy."

153. Quoted in the *Washington Post* and *The Times*, 5–6 January 1923.

154. U.S. Treasury Department, *Annual Report* (1923), 24.

155. Quoted in Self, *War Debt Controversy*, 46.

156. Ahamed, *Lords of Finance*, 140.

157. Grigg, "History of the American War Debt," 58–61.

158. CAB 24/158/16, Telegrams passed between the Chancellor of the Exchequer and the Prime Minister, 12–13 January 1923.

159. Ibid.

160. Self, *War Debt Controversy*, 47, citing SBP, vol. 109/96, Keynes to Davidson, 30 January 1923.

161. *FRUS*, 1922, vol. 2, 187–195; Kent, *The Spoils of War*, 203.

162. Quoted in Adams, *Bonar Law*, 348. Though the United States had paid in blood and not just treasure—more than fifty thousand Americans died in combat—such figures paled in comparison to at least seven hundred thousand British deaths.

163. Cannadine, *Mellon*, 320.

164. Grigg, "History of the American War Debt," 61–62.

165. CAB 24/158/18, Telegram from the Chancellor of the Exchequer to the Prime Minister, 15 January 1923.

166. Ibid.

167. Self, *War Debt Controversy*, 48–49.

168. Ibid., 49.

169. Grigg, "History of the American War Debt," 62.

170. *Congressional Record*, Senate, 16 January 1923, 1780–1786. For support of revision in Congress, see ibid., 1828.

171. Grigg, "History of the American War Debt," 64–65.

172. On 21 January 1923, Horne had telegraphed the prime minister and urged him to accept the deal. He feared the consequences of delay and doubted the chance of a better deal. In response, Bonar Law stressed the unjust nature of any agreement that placed "not less than a pound a head extra taxation for two generations." In addition, the prime minister believed it unlikely that the United Kingdom would get much back from its own debtors. On these exchanges, see ibid., 63–65. See also HC Debs., 5s, col. 402, 14 December 1932.

173. Grigg, "History of the American War Debt," 64–66.

174. Ibid., 66.

175. As James Harvey Rogers rightly noted in the 1930s, the United Kingdom had received some of the least favorable terms (*America Weighs Her Gold*). More recent analyses support these claims. States such as the United Kingdom and Finland that came to terms with the United States in 1923 typically received less generous settlements than those states that completed negotiations from late 1924 onward. On the terms of the various war-debt agreements, see Tooze, *Deluge*, 467, table 12. On improving conditions in the U.S., see Leffler, "The Origins of Republican War Debt Policy," 599–600. Cordell Hull notes in his memoirs that "great fights broke out in Congress over each settlement," and while he voted for some settlements, he opposed the Italian settlement "because it scaled down the debt too much" (*Memoirs*, 381).

176. The chancellor's deep-seated commitment to an agreement was further evidenced by a document he subsequently circulated to the cabinet on the international financial situation: CAB 24/97/100, Note for Cabinet, 31 January 1923.

177. Ibid.

178. *Congressional Record*, Senate, 1 February 1923, 2823. Others were more sympathetic. Cater Glass, former secretary of the Treasury and now a Democratic senator, criticized McKellar for "savagely assailing" Britain: "Britain is going to pay her indebtedness in dollars, just as she paid her obligation in blood for the cause which we assumed at one time to be our cause, but which now we seem to have forgotten" (ibid., 2826).

179. Self, *War Debt Controversy*, 50. The issue was divisive within the cabinet; Bonar Law wrote an anonymous article in *The Times* denouncing his government's handling of its war debts (H. James, *Europe Reborn*, 90).

180. Grigg, "History of the American War Debt," 65–66.

181. CAB 23/45/5, Conclusions of a Meeting of the Cabinet, 31 January 1923.

182. "Address of the President of the United States to the Congress, February 7, 1923, Submitting the Report of the World War Foreign Debt Commission," in U.S. Treasury Department, *Annual Report* (1923), 257–258.

183. *Congressional Record*, House, 9 February 1923, 3338–3363 (quote on 3344).

184. Ibid., 3344.

185. *Congressional Record*, Senate, 16 February 1923, 3786.

186. *Congressional Record*, Senate, 14 February 1923, 3607–3608, 3625–3627 (quote on 3625). See also *Congressional Record*, Senate, 15 February 1923, 3669–3786; *Congressional Record*, Senate, 16 February 1923, 3741–3764; and *Congressional Record*, Senate, 16 February 1923, 3741–3764.

187. *Congressional Record*, Senate, 16 February 1923, 3764.

188. Ibid., 3762.

189. Ibid., 3742.

190. Leffler, "The Origins of Republican War Debt Policy," 595–596; Leffler, "American Policy Making and European Stability," 217.

191. Wormell, *The Management of the National Debt*, 547.

192. Cannadine, *Mellon*, 320–321; Grigg, "History of the American War Debt," 6.

193. Jacobson, "Is There a New International History of the 1920s?," 635.

194. Leffler, "The Origins of Republican War Debt Policy," 599, citing Senate, Committee on Finance, Refunding of Obligations of Foreign Governments (Washington, DC, 1923), 11–19; House, Committee on Ways and Means, Refunding Foreign Obligations-British Debt (Washington, DC, 1923), 1–2.

195. Keiger, "Raymond Poincaré and the Ruhr Crisis," 56; Artaud, "Reparations and War Debts," 94–96. See also O'Riordan, *Britain and the Ruhr Crisis*.

196. On further disagreements about amortization, prepayment of principal, payment in U.S. bonds, exemption from British taxation, and other issues, see Grigg, "History of the American War Debt," 73–76.

197. Ibid., 75. Full texts of the proposal and acceptance appear in Annex R.

198. Cmd. 1912, The American Debt Settlement, 18 June 1923.

199. Lloyd George, *The Truth about Reparations and War Debts*, 121.

200. Quoted in Self, *War Debt Controversy*, 52.

201. Kent, *The Spoils of War*, 268.

202. For Baldwin's "exact statement" of his "settlement of the American debt," intended as a rejoinder to later criticism of the deal, see SBP, vol. 109, CR to Penny, 26 November 1930, attached documents; and "Mr Baldwin and the War Debt to America," *Daily Express*, 12 January 1931.

203. Costigliola, "Anglo-American Financial Rivalry," 928. The overvalued pound and London's tight money policy produced deflationary pressures and high unemployment without making British prices competitive in the world market. On these points, see Jacobson, "Is There a New International History of the 1920s?," 635.

204. Moggridge, *British Monetary Policy*, 93, 164.

205. Middlemas and Barnes, *Baldwin*, 148; Grigg, *Prejudice and Judgement*, 105; Grant, "Harding and the British War Debt Question," 484–485; Ellis, *Republican Foreign Policy*, 196–198; Hoover, *Memoirs*, vol. 2, 178–179.

206. The Dawes Committee proposed a complete reorganization of German finances under foreign supervision and attempted to raise revenues to fund reparations but never intended reparations to be financed primarily by U.S. loans. See Marks, "The Myths of Reparations," 246–247; Costigliola, "The United States and the Reconstruction of Germany," 485–494; and Schuker, *The End of French Predominance in Europe*, 180.

207. Each year there was a slight default, "but never enough to cause a stir" (Marks, "The Myths of Reparations," 249).

208. Temin and Vines, *The Leaderless Economy*, 33.

209. Sobel, *Coolidge*, 310. Some historians have claimed that Coolidge posed the rhetorical question, "They hired the money, didn't they?" There is no evidence of such a quote, but it was certainly in keeping with his attitude to the matter. See Boller and George, *They Never Said It*, 18–19.

210. Sobel, *Coolidge*, 310. In Coolidge's memoirs, he praises the "exemplary habits" of his childhood neighborhood, where, "If any debts were contracted, they were promptly repaid. Credit was good and there was money in the savings bank" (*The Autobiography*, 8).

211. Ferrell, *The Presidency of Calvin Coolidge*, 41, 145.

212. Daunton, *Wealth and Welfare*, 289.

213. Moggridge, *British Monetary Policy*, 27.

214. Eichengreen, *Golden Fetters*, 10. Some scholars attribute the world depression to financial chaos precipitated by the collapse of the gold standard. See, for instance, Kindleberger, *The World in Depression*. On British policymakers, including Keynes and Churchill, seriously considering paying a large portion of the war debt in gold rather than dollars to raise the value of the pound at the expense of the dollar, see Moggridge, *British Monetary Policy*, 27–28; and Costigliola, "Anglo-American Financial Rivalry," 920–921.

215. Howson, *Domestic Monetary Management*, 30–63; Moggridge, *British Monetary Policy*, 98–158; Sayers, *Bank of England*, 211–234. Scholars debate the extent to which devaluation would have reduced unemployment: Wolcott, "Keynes versus Churchill," 601–628.

216. On Keynes's criticisms of the return to the gold standard, see "The Economic Consequences of Mr. Churchill," which originally appeared as three articles in the *Evening Standard*, 22–24 July 1925.

217. On the price of indebtedness from 1924 onward, see Wormell, *The Management of the National Debt*, 554–588.

218. Self, *War Debt Controversy*, 53; Hayford and Pasurka, "The Political Economy of the Fordney-McCumber and Smoot-Hawley Tariff Acts," 30–50.

219. CAB 23/53/17, Conclusions, 21 July 1926.

220. Self, *War Debt Controversy*, 55; *FRUS*, 1927, vol. 2, 731–745.

221. FO 371/11197, Minute by Craigie, 7 August 1926. Chamberlain initialed his approval of this policy.

222. Costigliola, "Anglo-American Financial Rivalry," 928, citing *Literary Digest* 90 (31 July 1926): 507.

223. Moulton and Pasvolsky, *War Debts and World Prosperity*, 106–107. The U.S. agreed not to charge France any interest for the first five years after funding, and a rate of 3 percent was not to be reached until thirty-three years had elapsed. In the case of Italian debt, even the rate of 1 percent was not to be reached until forty-five years of funding. The British debt settlement was therefore equivalent to remission of 18 percent, whereas the French secured a remission of 50 percent and the Italians of 68 percent. On these points, see Grigg, "History of the American War Debt," 5.

224. Leffler, "The Origins of Republican War Debt Policy," 599–600.

225. For a full summary of the agreements, see Self, *War Debt Controversy*, 218. France moved toward and away from debt cooperation in the 1920s, reflecting changing economic and political circumstances, concerns against the dangers of German military and economic resurgence, and ultimately U.S. threats to halt the flotation of foreign loans in the United States from any country with outstanding and unfunded war debts. On these points, see Boyce, "Business as Usual," 107–108; Jacobson, "Is There a New International History of the 1920s?," 635; A. Turner, *The Cost of War*, 265; and Self, *War Debt Controversy*, 56.

226. SBP, vol. 109, "Mr Baldwin's Bargain," *Daily Express*, 12 January 1931. David Lloyd George would later accuse Baldwin of rushing to agreement on much worse terms. SBP, vol. 109, *The Times*, 15 January 1931.

227. SBP, vol. 109, Lloyd George, *The Times*, 16 January 1931.

228. For this reason, WWFDC member Herbert Hoover believed that the British settlement should have been more generous: "The concession to the British was about 30 percent, to the Italians about 70 percent, to the Belgians about 60 percent, and to the French about 40 percent. The British and Belgian debts should have been reduced still further" (Hoover, *Memoirs*, vol. 2, 178).

229. Self, *War Debt Controversy*, 56. The United States subsequently agreed to settlements with Greece and Austria in May 1929 and May 1930.

230. Moulton and Pasvolsky, *War Debts and World Prosperity*, ch. 5. These figures exclude Russia and Armenia as the United States did not recognize either government.

231. Cannadine, *Mellon*, 320. This optimism excluded the Soviet Union, which had repudiated its debts.

232. For a full schedule of war-debt repayments and postwar debt repayments to the United Kingdom from its debtors, including France, Italy, Portugal, Yugoslavia, Romania, and Greece between 1926 to 1989 and states ranging from Belgium to Lithuania from 1924 to 1956, see Moulton and Pasvolsky, *War Debts and World Prosperity*, 456–457. See also Self, *War Debt Controversy*, 219; and Moulton and Pasvolsky, *World War Debt Settlements*, chs. 3–5.

233. See Self, *War Debt Controversy*, 57.

234. Self, *War Debt Controversy*, 57; Leith-Ross, *Money Talks*, 95.

235. CAB 23/30/13, Conclusions, 16 June 1922; and CAB 23/30/23, Conclusions, 12 August 1922.

236. Moulton and Pasvolsky, *War Debts and World Prosperity*, 113–115.

237. Costigliola, *Awkward Dominion*, 210.

238. On British motivations, see Costigliola, "The Other Side of Isolationism," 606.

239. On the agreement, see Marks, "The Myths of Reparations," 250–252; Costigliola, "The United States and the Reconstruction of Germany," 499–500; and, more broadly, Schuker, *The End of French Predominance in Europe*.

240. The viability of Germany recovery is debatable. On the "strong but subtle link" between Germany's slump and reparations, see Ritschl, "The German Transfer Problem," 943–964; and Ritschl, "Dancing on a Volcano," 105–142.

241. Costigliola, "The Other Side of Isolationism," 606–610; Self, *War Debt Controversy*, 58–62.

242. On the Young Plan, see Marks, "The Myths of Reparations," 250–252; Costigliola, "The United States and the Reconstruction of Germany," 499–500; and Schuker, *The End of French Predominance in Europe*.

243. The Young Plan made the cancellation of war debts and reparations less likely. In the 1920s, some German policymakers had believed that high debts to the U.S. made it more probable that reparations and war debts would be canceled. In sum, if the Reich threatened to default on debts to private investors, wealthy U.S. creditors would apply pressure on the U.S. government to avoid this outcome. The Young Plan changed this calculation, however, by prioritizing official payments over the private payments. On these points, see Straumann, *1931*, 9–10; and H. James, "International Capital Movements and the Global Order," 279.

244. Rhodes, "Herbert Hoover and the War Debts," 130; Moley, *After Seven Years*, 72.

245. Hoover, *Memoirs*, vol. 2, 177–179; Self, *War Debt Controversy*, 62.

246. The president outlined four principles on which his debt policy rested, which respected the precedents established before him. First, these were business obligations rather than political debts. Second, debts should be dealt with on an individual basis on their own merits. Third, debts and reparations were not related. Fourth, a state's capacity to pay should inform policy. On these points, see Moley, *The First New Deal*, 30–31; and Self, *War Debt Controversy*, 103.

247. CAB 24/207/2, Memorandum Respecting the Conversations between Prime Minister MacDonald and President Hoover at Washington (4–10 October 1929), printed for the cabinet, November 1929.

248. Hoover, *Memoirs*, vol. 3, 345–346.

249. The causes of the Great Depression remain contested. For an overview, see Eichengreen, "The Origins and Nature of the Great Slump Revisited," 213–239; and Crafts and Fearon, "Lessons from the 1930s Great Depression," 285–317.

250. H. James, "1929," 129, 131; H. James, "The Great Depression and the Great Recession," 308–314; Schuker, "The Gold Exchange Standard," 77–94. See also H. James, *The Creation and Destruction of Value*, 36–38.

251. On doubts about the relationship between the Smoot-Hawley tariff and states defaulting on war debts, see Irwin, *Peddling Protectionism*, 141. Concerning the extent to which a rise in trade costs, rather than mainly a collapse in GDP, impacted trade flow during the Great Depression, see Irwin, "The Smoot-Hawley Tariff," 326–334; and Mitchener, Wandschneider, and O'Rourke, "The Smoot-Hawley Trade War."

252. On the degree of coordination of financial and banking crises as they spread across national frontiers, see H. James, "Financial Flows across Frontiers," 594–613. See also Bernanke and James, "The Gold Standard, Deflation and Financial Crisis," 33–68.

253. On the "twin crises" (banking and currency crises) facing Germany in 1931, see Schnabel, "The Twin German Crisis of 1931," 822–871; and Buch and Heinrich, "Twin Crises and the Intermediary Role of Banks," 313–323. For a similar explanation that predates these works, see H. James, "The Causes of the German Banking Crisis," 68–87.

254. Dayer, *Finance and Empire*, ch. 7.

255. H. James, "The Central European Banking Crisis Revisited," 121.

256. On the development of the moratorium, see Yale University Library, Microfilm Collection, Henry Lewis Stimson Diaries, esp. 6–22 June 1931. See also Stimson, *The Politics of Integrity*.

257. S. Clarke, "The Reconstruction of the International Monetary System," 25. On Hoover's shift to fighting the depression abroad, see also Rauchway, *Winter War*, 51.

258. Cannadine, *Mellon*, 442–445.

259. Hoover intended for the moratorium to ensure the safety of private investments, which were specifically exempted. On this point, see Marks, "The Myths of Reparations," 252.

260. Moulton and Pasvolsky, *War Debts and World Prosperity*, 403–422.

261. I. Fisher, "Cancelation of the War Debts."

262. Ibid.

263. Nasar, *Grand Pursuit*.

264. As Moulton and Pasvolsky conclude, "While the obliteration of the war debts would not solve all the manifold difficulties under which the world is laboring, economic analysis leads unmistakably to the conclusion that the restoration and maintenance of world prosperity will be rendered much easier if the disorganizing effects of the war debt payments are eliminated once and for all" (*War Debts and World Prosperity*, 422).

265. Clavin, *Failure of Economic Diplomacy*, 180.

266. Hoover, *Memoirs*, vol. 2, 179. Franklin Roosevelt had also believed that war debts were a "politically explosive but economically insignificant issue." Quoted in Self, *War Debt Controversy*, 100.

267. This point is conceded by Moulton and Pasvolsky in *War Debts and World Prosperity*, 403–404. Even this relatively modest counterfactual raises challenging questions about the relationship between political conditions and international trade in the 1930s as well as broader assumptions about debtor behavior in changed economic circumstances. Nevertheless, on the argument that "counterfactual reasoning plays an unavoidable implicit role in history," and the potential rewards of evaluating "minimal rewrites" or "idiographic counterfactuals" based on indirect evidence, see Bunzl, "Counterfactual History," 857; and Tetlock and Belkin, "Counterfactual Thought Experiments in World Politics," 7–8. See also Hawthorn, *Plausible Worlds*; Lebow, *Forbidden Fruit*; and Ferguson, *Virtual History*. Concerning the many challenges of counterfactual analysis, see Evans, *Altered Pasts*.

268. Self, *War Debt Controversy*, 64.

269. Herbert Hoover Presidential Library (HHL), Great Britain correspondence, 1931, Cable 196, Mellon to President, 18 June 1931. After speaking with MacDonald and Norman, Mellon says that the president "would be justified in initiating some proposal under [the] War Debt Agreements, toward a postponement of payments." See also Hoover, *Memoirs*, vol. 2, 67–68. The global situation was also worrying. Rumors had begun that Argentina, Uruguay, and Chile were approaching Brazil to try to arrange for a common default on all their foreign obligations. See Stimson Diaries, 16–17 June 1931.

270. Wapshott, *Keynes Hayek*, 84.

271. Hoover, *Memoirs*, vol. 3, 69; Stimson Diaries, 14 and 19 June 1931.

272. *Congressional Record*, House, 10 December 1931, 297; and *Congressional Record*, Senate, 15 December 1931, 523–524.

273. Stimson Diaries, 22 June 1931.

274. Leffler, "American Policy Making and European Stability," 226. On Hoover's unwillingness to change position, including the relationship between war debts and reparations, and his debate with Stimson on the insolvency of individuals versus the insolvency of states, see Stimson Diaries, 8 June 1931. See also Schwartz, *Interregnum of Despair*, 78–79.

275. DeWitt, "Johnson and American Foreign Policy," 233. DeWitt cites *San Francisco Examiner*, June 25, 1931, 1, 2; Bancroft Library, University of California, Berkeley, Hiram W. Johnson Papers (HJP), Johnson to Franklin Hichborn, 26 June 1931; and Johnson to Fogarty, 27 June 1931.

276. HHL, Great Britain correspondence, 1931, Atherton to Secretary of State, 22 June 1931; and Atherton to Secretary of State, 22 June 1931. Editorials in London papers—including the *Daily Telegraph*, *Times*, *Daily Herald*, *Daily Express*, *Daily Mail*, *Manchester Guardian*, and *Financial Times*—gave "enthusiastic praise." On MacDonald's positive reaction, see Stimson Diaries, 19 June 1931.

277. Self, *War Debt Controversy*, 66.

278. *Congressional Record*, House, 18 December 1931, 845–846.

279. CAB 23/67/10, Cabinet meeting, 24 June 1931.

280. The French ambassador described the news as "wonderful." Stimson Diaries, 8 June 1931.

281. Bennett, *Germany and the Diplomacy of the Financial Crisis*, 169. France enjoyed comparatively favorable economic conditions between 1926 and 1933,

especially as other European powers struggled with the Depression. See Boyce, "Business as Usual," 106–130.

282. Self, *War Debt Controversy*, 66, citing T 188/26, Leith-Ross, "Hoover Plan," 28 June 1931.

283. Self, *War Debt Controversy*, 67, citing HHL, 1015, "Moratorium Diary," 4–6 July 1931. It is worth noting that the Hoover library underwent a reboxing project whereby some folders shifted into different boxes as the archivists compressed box contents to save space and preserve the long-term health of the documents. Other scholars' references may therefore not reconcile with my own, which adopt the most recent version of the filing system.

284. Mouré, *Managing the Franc Poincaré*, 66.

285. On the National Government and the economic situation, see P. Williamson, *National Crisis and National Government*, 59; and Stevenson and Cook, *The Slump*, 10–12, 72–74. For further data, see Broadberry, *The British Economy between the Wars*. For the financial crisis of 1931 marking a turning point in British economic foreign policy, see Richardson, *British Economic Foreign Policy*.

286. Cairncross and Eichengreen, *Sterling in Decline*, 61. See also Eichengreen, *Sterling and the Tariff*, 27. There is limited primary evidence available on this matter beyond that already identified: CAB 58/169, "Minutes," EAC (H.) 147, 24 September 1931; and T/172/1768, "Capital Items in the International Balance of Payments," 15 December 1931. On press attitudes toward devaluation "making a present to the foreigner" more broadly, see "A Crisis of the £," *The Times*, 17 October 1931, 13.

287. CAB 24/225/15, Note, 11 December 1931.

288. The British government would stress these points in its justification of default in 1934. See CAB 24/249/33, 29 May 1934. See also Stevenson and Cook, *The Slump*, 2–3, 5. It is important to note, as Stevenson and Cook clarify in their revised version (2010), that despite these problems, "the 1930s were a period of rising living standards and new levels of consumption, upon which considerable industrial growth was based" (5).

289. Unemployment figures are contested, and international comparisons can be problematic, not least given different approaches. On British economywide unemployment rising from 8 percent in 1929 to 16.4 percent in 1931, see Boyer and Hatton, "New Estimates of British Unemployment," 667, table 6. For further context, see also Crafts, "Long-Term Unemployment in Britain," 418–432; and Denman and McDonald "Unemployment Statistics from 1881 to the Present Day," 6, table 1. The definitive source on U.S. unemployment data is provided by Cater et al., *Historical Statistics of the United States*, 282–283, which gives a figure of 15.65 percent. Scholars have debated unemployment figures, which have varied from 15.3 percent to 15.9 percent in 1931 and even more greatly thereafter, owing to different conceptual approaches regarding federal relief workers. For an overview, see Margo, "Employment and Unemployment in the 1930s," 43, table 1.

290. Trentmann, *Free Trade Nation*, 331.

291. As Albert Fishlow explains, "In the last analysis, the issue is not whether countries can service their debt but whether they choose to do" ("Lessons from the

Past," 438). For Robert Kolb, "default is always a choice and default by a government necessarily has a political element" ("Sovereign Debt," 4–7).

292. Stevenson and Cook, *The Slump*, 2–3.

293. Self, *War Debt Controversy*, 73, citing Documents on British Foreign Policy (DBFP), 2, vol. 2, MacDonald to Hoover, 16 December 1931, 379n2.

294. On differing responses to the flight of sterling, and evidence that the gold standard was an unintended but successful experiment to pursue a managed float, see Morrison, "Shocking Intellectual Austerity," 175–207.

295. CAB 24/225, Minutes, 11 December 1931.

296. Ibid.

297. *Congressional Record*, House, 10 December 1931, 297, 332–333, 341.

298. *Congressional Record*, House, 18 December 1931, 817–818, 857, 861.

299. Colby, "Should War Debts Be Cancelled?," 65.

300. Hoover, *Memoirs*, vol. 3, 171.

301. The result in the Senate was sixty-nine to twelve in favor of the resolution. For debate in the Senate, see *Congressional Record*, Senate, 15 December 1931, 523–524; *Congressional Record*, Senate, 17 December 1931, 724; and *Congressional Record*, Senate, 22 December 1931, 1081, 1116, 1126. For debate in the House, see *Congressional Record*, House, 10 December 1931, 341; *Congressional Record*, House, 14 December 1931, 470–471; and *Congressional Record*, House, 18 December 1931, 803–804, 841, 845–846, 862, 870.

302. Self, *War Debt Controversy*, 75.

303. CAB 23/69/16, 10 December 1931; and CAB 23/69/20, 15 December 1931.

304. Self, *War Debt Controversy*, 77, citing FO371/15905, C561/29/62, Tyrrell telegrams 9 and 15, 18 and 20 January 1932; and FO371/15906, C638/29/62, Sargent minute, 19 January 1932.

305. CAB 24/227, CP13(32), "Reparations and Debts: A Bird's-Eye View," 9 January 1932.

306. Ibid.

307. Self, *War Debt Controversy*, 79, citing Neville Chamberlain to Hilda Chamberlain, 17 January 1932, in *The Neville Chamberlain Diary Letters*, vol. 3, 302.

308. These ideas can be attributed to Chamberlain: see Chamberlain to Chamberlain, 17 January 1932, 302.

309. Self, *War Debt Controversy*, 77–81.

310. CAB 23/70/04, Meeting of Ministers, 20 January 1932.

311. Self, *War Debt Controversy*, 82.

312. Ibid., 83.

313. CAB 23/71/13, 8 June 1932.

314. Self, *War Debt Controversy*, 84.

315. CAB 29/139, 6th meeting, 2 July 1932 and Annex.

316. Self, *War Debt Controversy*, 84.

317. These events are more fully detailed in Self, *War Debt Controversy*, 84–85.

318. On the importance of this agreement to the course of war-debt negotiations, principally by depriving countries of reparation receipts and thereby affect-

ing their capacity to repay, see Moulton and Pasvolsky, *War Debts and World Prosperity*, 344–366, esp. 365.

319. Not only had Germany avoided honoring its postwar obligations, but it went on to repudiate most of its remaining debts in the coming decade. See Marks, "The Myths of Reparations," 233, 254–255. On later defaults, see Clement, "The Touchstone of German Credit," 33–50.

320. T 160/1411/11, Waley note, 1 July 1932; Bruce to Chamberlain, 22 September 1932; and Chamberlain to Bruce, 27 September 1932; Philips note, n.d.; Bruce to Chamberlain, 12 September 1933; Chamberlain to Bruce, 22 September 1933; Extract from minute, 8 November 1933; and Waley to Batterbee, 18 November 1933. For a useful summary, see also "Dominion War Debts to the U.K.," 13 June 1932, in the same folder.

321. Chamberlain seemingly encouraged the inference of U.S. approval but subsequently had to correct the misunderstanding that "the United States had approved, either tacitly or explicitly, what was done at Lausanne." See *FRUS*, 1932, General, vol. 1, Stimson to Lindsay, 7 December 1932. Other British policymakers assumed that the war-debts issue would soon be resolved. Writing before the conference, Winston Churchill, for example, believed the war debts "will be in one way or another cancelled or suspended anyhow." See SBP, vol. 119, Churchill to Baldwin, 3 June 1932.

322. Self, *War Debt Controversy*, 86.

323. CAB 23/72/4, 12 July 1932.

324. CAB 23/72/4, 12 July 1932, and Annex I and II. As the procès-verbal clarifies, "The Lausanne Agreement will not come into final effect until after ratification. . . . So far as the Credit Governments on whose behalf this Procès-Verbal is initialed are concerned, ratification will not be effected until a satisfactory settlement has been reached between them and their creditors."

325. Self, *War Debt Controversy*, 86, citing T 188/47/44–45, Chamberlain to Simon, 2 June 1932.

326. Self, *War Debt Controversy*, 87, citing T 188/47/44–45, Chamberlain to Simon, 2 June 1932.

327. T 172/1788, Leith-Ross note to Chamberlain, 27 May 1932.

328. Rhodes, *United States Foreign Policy in the Interwar Period*, 85.

329. CAB 23/72/4, 12 July 1932.

330. See, for instance, HC Deb., 11 July 1932, vol. 268, cc923–1047.

331. Costigliola, *Awkward Dominion*, 257; Self, *War Debt Controversy*, 87, citing HHL, 1012, Telegram 329, Davis to Stimson, 14 July 1932.

332. Self, *War Debt Controversy*, 88, citing Stimson Diaries, 13 October 1932.

333. Mills, "Our Foreign Policy," 565–566. See also Self, *War Debt Controversy*, 87.

334. Quoted in Self, *War Debt Controversy*, 89.

335. "Hoover at Washington," *The Times*, 12 August 1932; Self, *War Debt Controversy*, 91, citing; HHL, 1012, Bundy telegram to Joslin and Mellon, 2 November 1932, and HHL, 998, 1012, Mellon telegram to Stimson, 27 October and 2 November 1932, telephone conversation between Secretary Stimson, Mills, and Mellon, 31 October 1932.

336. Trentmann, *Free Trade Nation*, 331. On the British government's decision to move away from free trade, and its subsequent use of protection to bargain for trade advantages, see Roth, *British Protectionism and the International Economy*. Concerning India's voluntary and negotiated acceptance of preferential trade, beside the white self-governing dominions, see Stubbings, "Free Trade Empire to Commonwealth of Nations," 323–344.

337. Trentmann, *Free Trade Nation*, 333.

338. The fall in world income and output "can plausibly account for the majority of the 1929–33 trade collapse," but tariffs and quotas "were the major reason why the share of UK imports coming from the British Empire increased during the 1930s" (Bromhead et al., "When Britain Turned Inward," 327).

339. T 188/76/132, "Attitude of Democrat and Republican Parties." Roosevelt's claims are detailed more fully in his article "Our Foreign Policy."

340. Self, *War Debt Controversy*, 91. On the campaign trail, see Leuchtenburg, *Franklin D. Roosevelt and the New Deal*, 30–31.

341. Quoted in Self, *War Debt Controversy*, 92.

Chapter 2. Final Payments, 1932–1933

1. CAB 23/73/3, 29 November, attachment 28 November 1932.

2. For key meetings, see CAB 23/73/3, 29 November 1932, attachment, 28 November 1932; CAB 23/76/11, 9 June 1933; and CAB 23/77/9, 26 October 1933. For context concerning the final decision to default, see also CAB 23/79/7, 30 May 1934. In contrast to the available archival data, most biographies of and memoirs from key participants involved in the decision-making process offer few insights concerning the war debts. As Self puts it, "the subject of so much ministerial and Cabinet time barely figures at all" (*War Debt Controversy*, 13). See, for example, Dutton, *Simon*; Marquand, *MacDonald*; Macleod, *Chamberlain*; Middlemas and Barnes, *Baldwin*; Simon, *Retrospect*.

3. T 188/58/40, Leith-Ross minute to Fisher and Chamberlain, 20 December 1932.

4. See, for instance, Franklin D. Roosevelt Presidential Library (FDRL), President's Secretary's File (PSF), Roosevelt to MacDonald and reply, 22 and 24 May 1933; T 172/1805/101–102; and PSF, War Debts (WW1–1934), Subject File, Box 190, 7 November 1933.

5. FDRL, PSF, London Economic Conference, Roosevelt to MacDonald, 7 June 1933; and T 175/79/103–104, Leith-Ross to Fisher, 2 November 1933.

6. For full details, see U.S. Treasury Department, *Annual Report* (1933), 28. The United Kingdom was not the only major European power that delayed default. Italy would also go on to make two additional token payments, largely influenced by its position as a debtor to Britain. See Astore and Fratianni, "We Can't Pay," 208.

7. For an overview, see Reinhart and Rogoff, *This Time Is Different*, 55–58; Panizza, Sturzenegger, and Zettelmeyer, "The Economics and Law of Sovereign Debt and Default," 651–698; and Roos, *Why Not Default?*, 23–39.

8. See, for example, Roos, *Why Not Default?*; North and Weingast, "Constitutions and Commitment," 803–832; Lienau, *Rethinking Sovereign Debt*; and Nelson and Steinberg, "Default Positions," 520–533.

9. See, for instance, Clavin, *Failure of Economic Diplomacy*, 59; and Self, *War Debt Controversy*, 132.

10. At least one historian raises Britain's role as an international creditor as a deterrent to default in the 1930s but provides only passing detail, which downplays its ongoing importance throughout the decision-making process: Self, *War Debt Controversy*, 116, 132, 163. Wormell highlights the importance of being "a creditor of much of the rest of the world" in explaining why the United Kingdom did not default in the early 1920s (*The Management of the National Debt*, 513, 547).

11. Other states also mentioned by ministers were Austria, Chile, Ireland, Greece, and Russia. See CAB 23/73/3, 29 November 1932, attachment, 28 November 1932. The Irish Free State had already defaulted on debts to the United Kingdom by the summer of 1932. See Foley-Fisher and McLaughlin, "State Dissolution, Sovereign Debt and Default," 272–286.

12. Major British overseas investments comprised dominion and colonial governments, dominion and colonial municipalities, foreign governments, and foreign municipalities. Income from dominion and colonial governments was £44,997,000 ($152,989,800) and from foreign government securities was £11,984,000 ($40,745,600) in 1932. See Kindersley, "British Overseas Investments in 1932 and 1933," 367, table 2. On exchange rates of $3.40 in October 1932, see Howson, "The Management of Sterling," 53–60. Ministers' references to some states should not be treated as a definitive list of important debtors. The Interwar Debt database details borrowing from Canada, India, Japan, and South Africa. On the Interwar Debt database, see Sargent et al., *Debt and Entanglements between the Wars*, 283–290.

13. HC Deb., 14 June 1933, vol. 279, c290. Many of the states that the British government feared would default did so despite the United Kingdom honoring its debts to the United States. Nevertheless, the idea of contagion has some merit given the tendency for sovereign defaults to come in "clusters." See Reinhart and Rogoff, *This Time Is Different*, 94–96; and Sturzenegger and Zettelmeyer, *Debt Defaults and Lessons*, 4–10. There is an expansive literature concerning financial contagion, but the political rather than economic motivations for such behavior have generated limited attention.

14. Eichengreen and Portes, "Debt and Default in the 1930s," 601. On opposition support for such views, see HC Deb., 14 June 1933, vol. 279, cc289–290. "Financial contagion" was a reasonable concern given that it had also played a role in Britain's earlier decision to leave the gold standard. On this point, see H. James, "The Central European Banking Crisis Revisited," 121.

15. HHL, Personal File, 204, Hoover to Roosevelt, 12 November 1932; HHL, Financial, Monetary and Economic Conference (London), Correspondence, 1932, Nov.–Dec., Memorandum, 22 November 1932. U.S. concerns were not unique to the 1930s; fears of contagion would resurface following the Mexican default in 1982. In 1984, Argentina, Brazil, Columbia, and Mexico threatened a debtors' cartel. U.S. Secretary of State George Shultz feared the possibility of a "domino effect" of unilateral defaults. See H. James, "International Capital Movements and the Global Order," 287; and H. James, *International Monetary Cooperation since Bretton Woods*, 392–393.

16. Claims that domestic-political concerns eventually encouraged nonpayment are correct, but many policymakers nevertheless initially feared that default would harm the government. On the former argument, see Clavin, *Failure of Economic Diplomacy*, 175. Some social sentients have also begun to consider such claims. See Ballard-Rosa, "Hungry for Change," 313–346. On the latter, especially concerning the loss of trust between domestic constituents and the government, see Kolb, "Sovereign Debt," 4–7.

17. On the logic of ideas and norms functioning instrumentally and substantively, see Tannenwald, *The Nuclear Taboo*. See also Finnemore and Sikkink, "International Norm Dynamics and Political Change," 887–917.

18. On the Hoover campaign, see Carcasson, "Herbert Hoover and the Presidential Campaign," 349–365; Jeansonne, *The Life of Herbert Hoover*, 403–426; and Rappleye, *Herbert Hoover in the White House*, 387–408. On Roosevelt's rise to power, see Schlesinger, *The Age of Roosevelt*; and Leuchtenburg, *Roosevelt and the New Deal*, 1–18.

19. According to Cater et al., *Historical Statistics of the United States, Millennium Edition*, vol. 2, 282–283, unemployment had risen from 8.94 percent in 1930 to 22.89 percent in 1932. On the United States and the Great Depression, see, for instance, Bernstein, *The Great Depression*; and Eichengreen, *Hall of Mirrors*. For a revisionist account of economic growth in this period, see Field, *A Great Leap Forward*. More broadly, see Kindleberger, *The World in Depression*. On how war debts related to these challenges, see Moulton and Pasvolsky, *War Debts and World Prosperity*.

20. Stimson Diaries, 10 November 1932, quoted in Self, *War Debt Controversy*, 95. On the interdepartmental discussions within the British government that preceded this note, see Self, *War Debt Controversy*, 92–94.

21. CAB 24/234/38, Note, 10 November 1932.

22. Self, *War Debt Controversy*, 97–100, citing Stimson Diaries, 10–11, 13, 16, 19–21 November 1932; HHL, Personal File, 204, Hoover to Roosevelt, 12 November 1932. This proposed meeting is also consistent with the significant efforts taken by the Hoover administration in the preceding four years to salvage these debts. For an overview, see Ferrell, *American Diplomacy in the Great Depression*.

23. Dallek, *Roosevelt and American Foreign Policy*, 19, 23; Roosevelt, "Our Foreign Policy." Hoover had also swiftly reversed his opinion in the face of electoral considerations a decade earlier. On this point, see Hoover, *Memoirs*, vol. 2, 177–179; Rhodes, "Herbert Hoover and the War Debts," 133; HHL, 1006, Memorandum, 4 February 1923.

24. Dallek, *Roosevelt and American Foreign Policy*, 23–24; Leuchtenburg, *Roosevelt and the New Deal*, 31; and Moley, *The First New Deal*, 23–24.

25. S. Clarke, "The Reconstruction of the International Monetary System," 25.

26. Whereas Moley and Tugwell focused on domestic politics and stressed the importance of securing repayment, others such as Norman Davis and William Bullitt encouraged an international perspective and the forgiving of the debts. On this division, see Moley, *The First New Deal*, 22–23; and Tugwell, *In Search of Roosevelt*, 142.

27. FDRL, Rexford Tugwell Papers (Tugwell Diary), Box 30, 20 December 1932; Moley, *The First New Deal*, 25–26.

28. Tugwell Diary, Box 30, 20 December 1932. See also Moley, *The First New Deal*, 25–26.

29. Tugwell, *The Brains Trust*, 384.

30. HHL, Financial, Monetary and Economic Conference (London), Correspondence, 1932, Nov.–Dec., Memorandum, 22 November 1932. See also Jeansonne, *The Life of Herbert Hoover*, 427–430; and Dallek, *Roosevelt and American Foreign Policy*, 24–25.

31. Hoover, *Memoirs*, vol. 3, 179; Moley, *After Seven Years*, 72; Stimson Diaries, 22 November 1932. Moley later commented on Hoover's description, accepting both the compliment and his own ignorance (*The First New Deal*, 30).

32. Hoover, *Memoirs*, vol. 3, 180–181; HHL, 1012, Memorandum, 22 November 1933; Stimson Diaries, 22 November 1932; Moley, *The First New Deal*, 29, 30–32; Moley, *After Seven Years*, 72–77.

33. Moley, *The First New Deal*, 35.

34. According to Moley, "The course of events proved Roosevelt to be right. For while the debtors for the most part failed to pay . . . we and Europe had recovery" (ibid., 413).

35. Edwards, *American Default*, xxxi–xxxii, 99–100; J. Rogers, *America Weighs Her Gold*.

36. Fuller, *Phantom of Fear*, 165.

37. The Hoover administration had by now witnessed the Bolivian, Dominican, Panamanian, Peruvian, and Salvadorian defaults. The United States' other formal and informal economic protectorates, including Panama and Colombia, would also default in 1932, followed by Guatemala in 1933. As Noel Maurer reveals, "The US signed off on most of these defaults owing to fears of political instability" (*The Empire Trap*, 190, 203).

38. HHL, Presidential Papers, Foreign Affairs, Financial, British debt, Hoover Library, telephone conversation, Ambassador Mellon and President Hoover, 3 December 1932.

39. T 188/49/74, Fisher to Vansittart, 22 November 1932; FO 371/15914, Lindsay telegram, 461 and 463, 19 November 1932.

40. Self, *War Debt Controversy*, 115–116; Neville Chamberlain to Ida Chamberlain, 4 December 1932, in *The Neville Chamberlain Diary Letters*, vol. 3, 363; Self, *Neville Chamberlain*, 180–181. Mills had always sought a middle road on the debt, seeking a solution that "protects American interests and at the same time does not ignore [the United States'] moral obligation to help the world" ("Our Foreign Policy," 566). For evidence of a meeting, and subsequent discussions, see BE, ADM 24/31, Montagu Norman Diaries, 27–30 November 1932.

41. The chancellor refers to this consolation in CAB 23/73/3, 29 November 1932, appendix, 28 November 1932.

42. Ibid.

43. CAB 23/73/3, 29 November 1932.

44. On the National Government and the economic situation, see P. Williamson, *National Crisis and National Government*, 59; and Stevenson and Cook, *The Slump*, 10–12, 72–74.

45. U.S. Treasury Department, *Annual Report* (1932), 437.

46. On the war-debt burden in relation to the British economy, see CAB 23/79/7, 30 May 1934.

47. CAB 23/73/3, 29 November 1932, appendix, 28 November 1932. The chancellor had previously urged his cabinet colleagues to avoid "statements as to capacity to pay," presumably given the political sensitivities on this issue: CAB/23/73/1, 16 November 1932.

48. The Exchange Equalisation Account (EEA), established earlier in the year to provide a fund that could be used for "checking undue fluctuations in the exchange value of sterling," would never be able to address such significant and ongoing challenges. See Howson, *Sterling's Managed Float*.

49. Moley, *The First New Deal*, 26. Solutions might include export surpluses or inward investment. Congress understood that the United Kingdom would struggle to maintain these gold payments indefinitely, but some senators were confident that the British government would find a solution. As evidenced by British financial policy during the war, it was possible to mobilize substantial holdings of U.S. securities, tangible property, and bank balances, thereby obviating the transfer of large sums through the foreign exchange market. The British and French governments could then reimburse their own nationals in their own currency or internal bonds. These ideas were also advanced by the economist M. S. Rukeyser in 1939. On these points, see, *Congressional Record*, Senate, 1 June 1933, 4747–4752; and *Congressional Record*, Senate, 14 October 1939, 432.

50. CAB 23/73/3, 29 November 1932, attachment, 28 November 1932.

51. Shipping gold or buying dollars would naturally shrink British reserves, which some policymakers feared would result in deflation and a materially negative impact on business conditions. On the assumptions underpinning such thinking, see Middleton, "British Monetary and Fiscal Policy," 414–441; and Dimsdale, "British Monetary Policy and the Exchange Rate," 306–349.

52. CAB 23/73/3, 29 November 1932, attachment, 28 November 1932.

53. Ibid.

54. Ibid.

55. Ibid.

56. HL Deb., 6 December 1932, vol. 86, cc201–228.

57. Stevenson and Cook, *The Slump*, 2–3.

58. The 1932 war-loan redemption and conversion should not be considered a default because the existence of a call provision meant that it was achieved contractually. On the "great conversion" operation, see Wormell, *The Management of the National Debt*, 589–627. On the conversion operation's impact on long-term interest rates, see Capie, Mills, and Wood, "Debt Management and Interest Rates," 1111–1126. On the gold standard, see Barry Eichengreen and Jeffrey Sachs, "Exchange Rates and Economic Recovery," 925–946. On the conversion of UK and U.S. debts in the 1930s as "blows to the traditional status of public credit," see Macdonald, *A Free Nation Deep in Debt*.

59. Stevenson and Cook, *The Slump*, 6. The Conservatives had lost by elections to Labour and the Liberals in April and July 1932. On these losses, see Craig, *British Parliamentary Election Results*. On the earlier landslide election victory, see Thorpe, *The British General Election of 1931*.

60. CAB 23/73/3, 29 November 1932, appendix, 28 November 1932.

61. Self, *War Debt Controversy*, 109.

62. Ibid.

63. CAB 23/73/3, 29 November 1932, appendix, 28 November 1932.

64. CAB 23/73/3, 29 November 1932, attachment, 28 November 1932.

65. Ibid. Even though the risk of a British default leading to a wave of defaults and the end of capitalism proved to be unwarranted, such concerns still had some justification. In the 1930s, foreign defaults on British loans—alongside heavily curtailed overseas lending and larger payment for maturities and to sinking funds—moved the balance of payments from surplus to deficit. On this claim, see Sayers, *The Bank of England*, 32, 33.

66. On British overseas investments, see note 12.

67. On foreign defaults in part accounting for this decline, see Kindersley, "British Overseas Investments in 1932 and 1933," 367, 369. The relative importance of international lending in the British government's decision-making complements existing claims by Albrecht Ritschl that default was inhibited by a desire to maintain a "leading position in international financial markets." As Ritschl explains, "Credibility had to be maintained that investments in Britain and the assets emitted there were safe" ("Sustainability of High Public Debt," 181). On safe assets, and the claim that "the passing of the safe asset baton from the United Kingdom to the United States [occurred] in the 1930s," see Caballero, Farhi, and Gourinchas, "The Safe Assets Shortage Conundrum," 29–46.

68. See, for instance, HC Deb., 14 June 1933, vol. 279, cc289–290; and HC Deb., 14 June 1933, vol. 279, c290.

69. Quoted in "War Debt Payments in Gold," *The Times*, 2 December 1932, 7. The claim that "to default on the American debt would be to give a cue to many of [Britain's] own debtors, who would not be slow to make the most of it," would continue to appear in the press well into the following year: "War Debt," *Edinburgh Evening News*, 8 November 1933; and "War Debt," *Lancashire Evening Post*, 8 November 1933.

70. FDRL, Official File 212, Foreign Debts 1933, Eagle to Roosevelt, 24 April 1933; Moley, *The First New Deal*, 26. On the maldistribution of gold and how the cancellation or reduction of war debts would help alongside the easing of tariffs, see J. Rogers, *America Weighs Her Gold*. Kostolany quoted in Thomas and Morgan-Witts, *The Day the Bubble Burst*, 224. On French gold hoarding and its relevance to the Great Depression, see Mouré, *The Gold Standard Illusion*, esp. 181–182.

71. CAB 23/73/3, 29 November 1932, attachment 28 November 1932.

72. CAB 23/73/3, 29 November 1932.

73. Ibid. London subsequently communicated to Paris that the additional payment in December was merely a "transitional payment" and did "not reopen the question of French debt payment to Great Britain." *FRUS*, 1932, vol. 1, Mellon to Secretary of State, 7 December 1932.

74. For a detailed account of the British Note to the United States, Lindsay's additional "little separate paper," and "another Note from London," as well as the U.S. response, including the problematic marketable bond proposal, see Self, *War Debt Controversy*, 118–121.

75. Self, *War Debt Controversy*, 121–122, citing Stimson Diaries, 2, 3 December 1932; and FO 371/15915, Lindsay telegrams 513–515, 4 December 1932.

76. Stimson and Bundy, *On Active Service in Peace and War*, 217.

77. On this "astonishing breach of cabinet secrecy," see Self, *War Debt Controversy*, 123.

78. Stimson Diaries, 7 December 1932. Stimson rebuts claims that complete cancellation was essential to world recovery or that loans were for destructive purposes only. He also disputes that balance of payments or transfer difficulties justified default. For the letter and response in full, see *FRUS, 1932*, vol. 1, British Embassy to the Department of State, 1 December 1932; and Stimson to Lindsay, 7 December 1932.

79. CAB 23/73/5, 7 December 1932.

80. Stimson Diaries, 11 December 1932.

81. Self, *War Debt Controversy*, 126, citing Stimson Diaries, 12 and 13 December 1932.

82. The Bank of England was undertaking the cost of packing and shipping the gold, which might be as much as £70,000. The Bank of England and Treasury officials thought that an increase in the fiduciary issue was unnecessary and undesirable, especially as it might cause anxiety abroad.

83. CAB 23/73/6, 12 December 1932. See Appendices for HMG note to United States, the U.S. response, and a further British reply, 11–12 December 1932. On the politics of taxation in the 1930s, see Daunton, *Just Taxes*, 142–175.

84. HC Deb., 14 December 1932, vol. 273, cc367.

85. Ibid., cc363. On the morality of debt, see Dyson, "Morality of Debt."

86. For an overview, see Reinhart and Rogoff, *This Time Is Different*, 55–58; Panizza, Sturzenegger, and Zettelmeyer, "The Economics and Law of Sovereign Debt and Default," 651–698; and Roos, *Why Not Default?*, 23–39.

87. On the use of "doubly decisive" evidence to strengthen confidence in one explanation and simultaneously weaken other arguments, see Collier, "Understanding Process Tracing," 823–830; and George and Bennett, *Case Studies and Theory Development*.

88. HC Deb., 14 December 1932, vol. 273, cc369.

89. HC Deb., 14 June 1933, vol. 279, c289.

90. Keynes, "A British View of Mr Hoover's Note," in *The Collected Writings*, vol. 18, 382–386.

91. City Editor, "The War Debt Paid," *The Times*, 16 December 1932, Issue 46318, 1.

92. "War Debts—A Postscript," 1130; "The End of a Chapter," *The Times*, 16 December 1932, Issue 46318, 15. For examples of bolder headlines from smaller newspapers, see "We Cannot Default," *Western Gazette*, 2 December 1932; and "No Alternative," *Western Morning News*, 15 December 1932. Larger newspapers had already quoted the government's position approvingly and cited experts stressing the dangers of default. See, for instance, "War Debts" and "War Debts Payment in Gold," both in *The Times*, 2 December 1932, 7.

93. See, for instance, Benjamin Pollard's letter, in which he seeks to prevent the "dreadful step of defaulting." Quoted in "War Debts," *The Times*, 2 June 1934, 10.

94. On the course of French default, see Leffler, *The Elusive Quest*, 310; Clavin, *Failure of Economic Diplomacy*, 54–56; and Self, *War Debt Controversy*, 128–131. For Herriot's sentiments, see Herriot, *Jadis*, 355–357. For detailed reports on the debate in the Chamber, see National Archives II, College Park, MD (NAII), RG 59, 800.51W89, France/754, 760–763, Edge to Stimson, 10, 13, 14 December 1932.

95. Stimson Diaries, 15 December 1932, quoted in Stimson and Bundy, *On Active Service in Peace and War*, 217.

96. Following French default, Stimson had passed on a message from Hoover to MacDonald: "Tell MacDonald that I believe that the civilization which he speaks of can only be saved by the operation of Anglo-Saxons, we cannot count on the other races." Quoted in H. James, *The End of Globalization*, 130.

97. See, for instance, *Congressional Record*, Senate, 7 December 1932, esp. 112–113, 118–121.

98. Self, *War Debt Controversy*, 133; Moley, *The First New Deal*, 40; HHL, 1012, "Reconsideration of War Debts," 12 December 1932. For a detailed account of the debt issue during the presidential interregnum, see Self, *War Debt Controversy*, ch. 7; see also Jeansonne, *The Life of Herbert Hoover*, 427–450; Rappleye, *Herbert Hoover in the White House*, 409–428; and Rauchway, *Winter War*, 49–51, 55–56, 60, 62, 66–72.

99. HHL, Financial, Monetary and Economic Conference (London), Copresence, 1932, Nov.–Dec.), Hoover to Roosevelt, 20 December 1932; Roosevelt to Hoover, 21 December 1932; and note by Hoover, 22 December 1932.

100. Hoover and Roosevelt statements, *The Times*, 23–24 December 1932; Moley, *The First New Deal*, 40; Dallek, *Roosevelt and American Foreign Policy*, 24–25.

101. Tugwell Diary, 20, 27, 29 December 1932; Moley, *The First New Deal*, 39; Self, *War Debt Controversy*, 136.

102. On Roosevelt's mixed motivations, see Dallek, *Roosevelt and American Foreign Policy*, 24. U.S. and British officials were surprised by Roosevelt's apparent ignorance of the war-debt problem. See Self, *War Debt Controversy*, 139, 151. Charges of ignorance existed on both sides of the Atlantic. Roosevelt was also surprised by MacDonald's limited knowledge on the subject (Moley, *The First New Deal*, 415).

103. See, for instance, Arthur Krock, "Debt Revision View Gains in Congress," *New York Times*, 13 December 1932; and *Helena Independent*, 27 December 1932.

104. "U.S. Public's View," *The Times*, 5 December 1932, 12.

105. Such claims had some basis in fact. Subsequent investigations would conclude that J. P. Morgan had previously profited directly via the reduction of the Italian war debt. See DeWitt, "Johnson and Early New Deal Diplomacy," 378.

106. *Congressional Record*, Senate, 4 January, 1268–1283.

107. DeWitt, "Johnson and American Foreign Policy," 250–251, citing *Congressional Record*, 8 and 16 January 1933.

108. HJP, Johnson to C. K. McClatchy, 8 January 1933. This source appears in DeWitt, "Johnson and American Foreign Policy," 250–251.

109. *Congressional Record*, Senate, 24 January 1933, 2371. See also *Congressional Record*, Senate, 24 January 1933, 2477, 2502–2503. Arguments regarding

the scaling down of debts had also been used by the Soviet Union at the same time when negotiating with France, albeit in a different way. On this parallel, see Oosterlinck, *Hope Springs Eternal*, 87.

110. On the existence of much older suspicions, see Palen, *The "Conspiracy" of Free Trade*.

111. "British War Debts," *The Times*, 25 January 1933, 12.

112. On the preceding discussion between Rosewell and Stimson, see Self, *War Debt Controversy*, 137–139.

113. Dallek, *Roosevelt and American Foreign Policy*, 28. For more on the wider context surrounding this second meeting, see Rauchway, *Winter War*.

114. Dallek, *Roosevelt and American Foreign Policy*, 31; Leffler, *The Elusive Quest*, 322; Jeansonne, *The Life of Herbert Hoover*, 434.

115. Self, *War Debt Controversy*, 139, citing Stimson Diaries, 19–20 January 1933; and Tugwell Diary, 22 January 1933. See also Dallek, *Roosevelt and American Foreign Policy*, 28.

116. Moley, *The First New Deal*, 411.

117. Ibid., 413.

118. HHL, Financial, British Debt, British debt memorandum and White House statement, both 20 January 1933. On these talks, see Leffler, *The Elusive Quest*, 322–333; and Jeansonne, *The Life of Herbert Hoover*, 433–434. On the "battle royal" that followed between officials in both administrations over the phrasing for the aide memoire to be given to the British ambassador, see Self, *War Debt Controversy*, 140–141.

119. CAB 24/237/30, Telegram, Lindsay's interview with Roosevelt, 29 January 1933.

120. Such a haircut would nevertheless still have been within the wider range of historical and contemporary debt restructurings. See Oosterlinck, "Sovereign Debt Defaults," 700; Sturzenegger and Zettelmeyer, "Haircuts," 780–805.

121. CAB 24/237/30, Telegram, Lindsay's interview with Roosevelt, 29 January 1933. Lindsay's note reveals that, in contrast to Senate hostility toward defaulters, Roosevelt agreed in "bringing the French government along," describing their behavior as "deferment" not "default." He was prepared to talk to any debtor, in contrast to Hoover, who would only work with those in good standing.

122. Stimson Diaries, 3, 18–19 January 1933; HHL, 1015, Diary Memorandum, 13 January 1933.

123. Notes of the meeting appear in CAB 27/548, First meeting, 6 February 1933.

124. Talks between Bullitt and MacDonald had begun as early as November 1932, which helps to explain initial hopes of debt revision and moratorium. Roosevelt later denied his support for this secret mission when it later leaked to the press. On these points, see Self, *War Debt Controversy*, 148–150.

125. CAB 23/75/5, Meeting of the Cabinet, 30 January 1933.

126. Ibid.

127. Ibid.

128. All BDA committee minutes appear in CAB 27/548.

129. CAB 27/548, BDA, First meeting, 6 February 1933.

130. Ibid.

131. Ibid.

132. CAB 27/548, BDA, Second meeting, 7 February 1933.

133. Ibid.

134. CAB 27/548, BDA, Third meeting, 8 February 1933.

135. CAB 27/548, BDA, Fifth meeting, 10 February 1933.

136. Ibid.

137. DeWitt, "Johnson and American Foreign Policy," 251–252; Schlesinger, *The Coming of the New Deal*, 1–23.

138. Self, *War Debt Controversy*, 160.

139. S. Kennedy, *The Banking Crisis of 1933*.

140. Dallek, *Roosevelt and American Foreign Policy*, 23, see also 70–71.

141. Ibid., 32.

142. Self, *War Debt Controversy*, 159.

143. CAB 27/548, BDA, Seventh meeting, 31 March 1933.

144. Edwards, *American Default*, 30–49.

145. Self, *War Debt Controversy*, 159, citing Bullitt to MacDonald, in Roosevelt and Bullitt, *For the President*, 30.

146. Dallek, *Roosevelt and American Foreign Policy*, 31–33.

147. For the cabinet instruction for Lindsay's meeting, see CAB 24/237/29, 13 February 1933. See CAB 24/237/30, 10 February 1933, for a full account of Lindsay's interview with Roosevelt on 29 January 1933.

148. CAB 27/548, BDA, Seventh meeting, 31 March 1933.

149. Ibid.

150. Ibid.

151. Ibid.

152. CAB 23/75/23, Meeting of the cabinet, 5 April 1933.

153. Edwards, *American Default*, xxii–xxvii, 199. For the case that Roosevelt's decision to leave the gold standard helped to drive economic recovery, see Rauchway, *The Money Makers*; and Eggerston, "Great Expectations at the End of the Depression," 1476–1516.

154. On U.S. devaluation, see Edwards, *American Default*. Fisher had long been critical of the gold standard and proposed instead to allow the value of the dollar to change through time. See I. Fisher, *The Purchasing Power of Money*; and I. Fisher, "A Compensated Dollar," 385–397. Despite agreement on the issue of gold, Fisher and Warren diverged on many other issues. Moreover, Fisher's views contrasted with those of other economists working in the Brain Trust, including Rex Tugwell and Adolf Berle, who were wary of large devaluations. See Edwards, *American Default*, 208–213. On Keynes's flawed criticisms of the U.S. gold-buying program launched later that year, see Edwards, "Keynes and the Dollar in 1933," 209–238.

155. Edwards, *American Default*, xi; Nasar, *Grand Pursuit*.

156. Prior to Roosevelt's taking office, the available evidence suggests that neither he nor the Brain Trust had very strong views on gold or the dollar. See Edwards, "Gold, the Brains Trust and Roosevelt," 209–238.

157. On these points, see Leith-Ross, *Money Talks*, 160; and Edwards, *American Default*, 79–81.

158. Leith-Ross, *Money Talks*, 160–161; Self, *War Debt Controversy*, 64, citing PRO 30/69/1753/3, MacDonald Note book, 15, 19–21 April 1933; and Vansittart, *The Mist Procession*, 466.

159. Edwards, *American Default*, xxiii–xxiv, 74; Cairncross and Eichengreen, *Sterling in Decline*, 61.

160. Edwards, *American Default*, 75, citing "In Washington," *New York Times*, 30 May 1933, 14.

161. Clement, "The Touchstone of German Credit," 36–37.

162. Edwards, *American Default*, 98; HC Deb., 21 July 1933, vol. 280, cc2179–2197.

163. HC Deb., 21 July 1933, vol. 280, cc2181, 2194.

164. Feis, *1933*, 126; Moley, *The First New Deal*, 415; Leith-Ross, *Money Talks*, 171–172.

165. Self, *War Debt Controversy*, 164.

166. FDRL, Official File 212, Foreign Debts 1933, Note for Robinson, 28 April 1933.

167. Moley, *The First New Deal*, 415.

168. See Self, *War Debt Controversy*, 164.

169. Leith-Ross, *Money Talks*, 166. For a helpful summary of the plan, see Self, *War Debt Controversy*, 166.

170. Moley, *After Seven Years*, 202. This plan should not be confused with another idea developed by Warburg, which focused on a "modified gold standard" and held important similarities with a plan developed by Keynes. See Edwards, "Keynes and the Dollar in 1933," 209–238.

171. American and British policymakers shared these concerns. On the life of the Warburg plan, see Self, *War Debt Controversy*, 165–167, 179, 181–182, 184–185.

172. CAB 23/76/5, 5 May 1933; and CAB 27/548, Eighth BDA meeting, 4 May 1933. See attached appendix for full details of the meeting.

173. Dallek, *Roosevelt and American Foreign Policy*, 44.

174. Roosevelt noted that it was like a "story one day that the President had murdered his own grandmother and the next day saying that the President had refused to concede that he had murdered his own grandmother." Jimmy Carter Presidential Library, Collection: Office of Staff Secretary, Series: Presidential Files, Folder: 6/2/77[1], Container 23, "Franklin D. Roosevelt's first term press conferences: One method of influencing newsgathering," 17, referencing a press conference held on 31 May 1933.

175. Moley, *The First New Deal*, 416.

176. CAB 27/548, BDA, Ninth meeting, 16 May 1933.

177. Ibid. Appendices detail telegrams from Lindsay on 14 and 11 May 1933.

178. CAB 27/548, Tenth BDA meeting, 17 May 1933.

179. CAB 23/76/10, 31 May 1933.

180. CAB 24/241/14, War Debts: Memorandum by the President of the Board of Trade, 24 May 1933.

181. Ibid.

182. Ibid.

183. For evidence of such feeling at the time, however, see Reid, *Britain and the War Debts.*

184. CAB 24/241/14, War Debts: Memorandum by the President of the Board of Trade.

185. Self, *War Debt Controversy,* 168–169.

186. Moley, *The First New Deal,* 418.

187. CAB 23/76/11, 9 June 1933, appendices.

188. Ibid., appendix 1, telegrams from Lindsay, 8 June 1933.

189. On this latter point, see Leith-Ross, *Money Talks,* 171; Self, *War Debt Controversy,* 170, 172.

190. CAB 23/76/11, 9 June 1933.

191. Ibid.

192. Ibid.

193. Ibid.

194. Ibid.

195. Ibid.

196. Self, *War Debt Controversy,* 173, citing T 188/74/71–79, Lindsay telegrams 387–388, 395, 398–399, 9–11 June 1933; and CAB 27/548, BDA, Eleventh meeting, appendix.

197. Dallek, *Roosevelt and American Foreign Policy,* 48.

198. CAB 27/548, Eleventh BDA meeting, 12 June 1933. Appendices 1–4 contain various correspondence with Lindsay.

199. CAB 27/548, Notes of a conversation, 12 June 1933. Document also found in CAB 23/76/12, 12 June 1933.

200. CAB 23/76/13, 13 June 1933.

201. Moley, *The First New Deal,* 418.

202. CAB 23/76/13, 13 June 1933.

203. HC Deb., 14 June 1933, vol. 279, cc286–287.

204. Self, *War Debt Controversy,* 175.

205. HC Deb., 14 June 1933, vol. 279, cc288–89.

206. Ibid., cc289–290.

207. Ibid., c290.

208. Keynes, "An Economist's View of the Debt Payment Problem," in *The Collected Writings,* vol. 18, 387–390.

209. "The American Debt," *The Times,* 15 June 1933, Issue 46471, 7; "The Debt Finale," *The Economist* 116, no. 4686 (17 June 1933): 1287.

210. "The War Debts," *The Scotsman,* 15 June 1933; "War Debt," *Daily Herald,* 10 June 1933; "The Debt Finale," 1287.

211. Astore and Fratianni, "We Can't Pay," 197–222. For a chronology of events leading up to default by most debtors, see Reinhart and Trebesch, "A Distant Mirror of Debt, Default, and Relief," 22–24.

212. On these costs, see Tooze, *Wages of Destruction,* 50.

213. The Weimar government had also considered selective default to reduce foreign debt levels at the end of 1929. See H. James, *The German Slump,* 97. Nevertheless, it chose not to suspend repayment and went on to improve its reparations and debt problems before the Nazi government took power and chose to default.

On claims that a repudiation of foreign indebtedness formed part of Hitler's economic program, see Einzig, *Germany's Default*.

214. In April 1933, the German cabinet had given the president of the Reichsbank and future Reich minister of economics Hjalmar Schacht "carte blanche" to instigate a moratorium on Germany's international debt. When Germany eventually defaulted on international debt, Roosevelt allegedly "slapped his thigh" and said "it served the bankers right." Nevertheless, German hopes of an agreement were dashed by the State Department, which explained that the U.S. government expected ongoing payment. Schacht understood that since there was no chance of any new loans to Germany, the U.S. now had limited leverage. There was also little to fear from default with regard to U.S. trade sanctions. See H. James, *The German Slump*, 410; Tooze, *Wages of Destruction*, 28, 51, 86–87; and H. James, *The Creation and Destruction of Value*, 72.

215. Following discussions with creditors, the Reichsbank decided that foreign exchange transfers for interest payments falling due during the second half of 1933 would be reduced by half. Interest payments on the Dawes and Young loans would continue to be met in full, however, although the amortization of the Young loan was discontinued. See Clement, "The Touchstone of German Credit," 33–50.

216. Tooze, *Wages of Destruction*, 55.

217. Clement, "The Touchstone of German Credit," esp. 36–39, 47–49. Existing debt was now steadily decreased via partial and somewhat-hidden defaults: H. James, *The German Slump*, 97, 404, table 39. On the broader history of German debt and default in this period, see Schuker, *American "Reparations" to Germany*. Nazi Germany's ongoing defaults on loans had a strong influence on British economic policy. On this effect, see Forbes, *Doing Business with the Nazis*, 63–96.

218. On the claims that the French default encouraged the German default, see Tooze, *Wages of Destruction*, 51.

219. Self, *War Debt Controversy*, 171.

220. Armus, *French Anti-Americanism*, 96–97, 118, citing Archives Nationales, 7-13032.

221. Shamir, *Economic Crisis and French Foreign Policy*, 206.

222. Feis, *1933*, 182.

223. See, for instance, *Congressional Record*, Senate, 13 June 1933, 5877.

224. *Congressional Record*, House, 10 June 1933, 5646.

225. Ibid.

226. Ibid., 5675.

227. "Roosevelt Drafts Notes to Debtors," *New York Times*, 17 June 1933.

228. T 175/79/4–8, Hopkins and Waley note to Chamberlain, 27 March 1933; FDRL, PSF 38, Roosevelt to MacDonald, 22 May 1933.

229. Skidelsky, *Keynes*, 481; Rhodes, *United States Foreign Policy in the Interwar Period*, 98. See also Self, *War Debt Controversy*, 175.

230. Hull, *Memoirs*, vol. 2, 250, 256. On earlier U.S. skepticism about British intentions, in which "the Cabinet with the possible exception of MacDonald has now little real faith or interest in achieving [economic cooperation]" and has "only one real preoccupation" in its "economic and financial relations" with the U.S., "namely, the war debt issue," see *FRUS*, 1933, General, vol. 1, Atherton to Secretary of State, 9 May 1933.

231. Clavin, *Failure of Economic Diplomacy*, 159–160. For an analysis of the economic effects of the conference, see Edwards, "The London Monetary and Economic Conference of 1933," 431–459.

232. Large and small powers had an interest in "killing off" the negotiations, leaving it to resemble "an Agatha Christie novel in which there are too many suspects in a murder" (H. James, *The End of Globalization*, 131). On the narrowly focused and unrealistic ambitions of the World Economic Conference, as well as the politically trickier and unpleasant task of domestic adjustments, see H. James, "Deep Red," 338. See also Clavin, "Explaining the Failure of the World Economic Conference," 77–99. Long-standing difficulties also plagued cooperative central-bank efforts to revive the international economy, including the dilemmas facing central banks in their relations with their domestic governments. On this subject, see Clavin, "The Fetishes of So-Called International Bankers," 281–311. On links between war debts and the banking system, see Feldman, "Political Disputes about the Role of Banks," 18. In the same volume, see also Kunz, "American Bankers and Britain's Fall from Gold," 35–48; and H. James, introduction to *The Role of Banks*, 4. On war debts making international cooperation between leading central banks much more difficult, see Findlay and O'Rourke, *Power and Plenty*, 440.

233. Dallek, *Roosevelt and American Foreign Policy*, 47. On this approach being consistent with Roosevelt's earlier monetary policy or an effort to increase his freedom of maneuver for an as-yet-undetermined domestic policy, see, respectively, Clavin, *Failure of Economic Diplomacy*, 132–134; and Barber, *Designs within Disorder*. On political motivations more broadly, see also Eichengreen, *Golden Fetters*.

234. Horn, "J. P. Morgan & Co.," 522, 524, 526, 526n20. On the New Deal as an attempt to "devolatilize American capitalism" and Roosevelt "rolling back . . . the power of finance capitalists," see Levy, *Freaks of Fortune*, 313.

235. Clavin, *Failure of Economic Diplomacy*, 5, 196.

236. Hull, *Memoirs*, vol. 1, 62.

237. Ibid., 381.

238. Ibid., 381.

239. CAB 24/243/22, 25 September 1933.

240. Ibid.

241. Ibid.

242. Ibid.

243. T 160/1411/11, Bruce to Chamberlain, 12 September 1933; Chamberlain to Bruce, 22 September 1933; and T 160/1411/11, Extract from minute, 8 November 1933; Waley to Batterbee, 18 November 1933.

244. CAB 24/243/22, 25 September 1933.

245. Ibid. If a permanent settlement were to prove impracticable, the chancellor recognized two alternatives other than a complete suspension of payments. These were either a temporary five- or seven-year settlement, not exceeding $20 million a year, or a further token payment of $10 million on December 15 and at each installment date. Both alternatives risked the disadvantage of leaving the future uncertain, and so a permanent settlement remained preferable.

246. Leith-Ross, *Money Talks*, 172–176.

247. FDRL, Official File 212, Foreign Debts 1933, Memorandum for the Secretary, 9 October 1933.

248. FDRL, Official File 212, Foreign Debts 1933, Walter Lipmann to Phillips, 10 October 1933.

249. Edwards, *American Default*, xxxi–xxxii, 99–100; J. Rogers, *America Weighs Her Gold*; Self, *War Debt Controversy*, 181.

250. Fuller, *Phantom of Fear*, 165.

251. Acheson, *Present at the Creation*, 387.

252. Options ranged from the possibility of writing down of the debt in accordance with changes in the gold price since 1917 through to collecting part of the British debt through the transfer of cable and radio rights, fuel stations, and seadromes for transatlantic aviation. See Self, *War Debt Controversy*, 180; FDRL, Official File 48/1, Hull to Roosevelt, 12 September 1933; and Phillips to Hull, 25 September 1933. See also FDRL, PSF, 32/302, Office of Economic Adviser, "Skeleton Outline of Alternative Approaches to Possible Debt Agreement with Great Britain," 25 September 1933.

253. Watt, *Succeeding John Bull*, 67.

254. For further analysis of the Leith-Ross negotiations, see Self, *War Debt Controversy*, 180–189; and Clavin, *Failure of Economic Diplomacy*, 175–176.

255. FDRL, Official File 212, Roosevelt to Senator Frederic Walcott, 8 November 1932.

256. CAB 27/548, Second meeting, 7 February 1933.

257. See Self, *War Debt Controversy*, 188, citing "The Presidency: Tired Team," *Time*, 13 November 1933.

258. "War Debt Palaver," 857; "Cabinet Acts at London," *New York Times*, 7 November 1933.

259. Leith-Ross, *Money Talks*, 174.

260. Ibid.

261. CAB 23/77/9, 26 October 1933.

262. Ibid.

263. Ibid.

264. Ibid.

265. See, for instance, HC Deb., 30 June 1933, vol. 279 cc1836–1876.

266. CAB 23/77/9, 26 October 1933.

267. Self, *War Debt Controversy*, 187, citing Stimson Diaries, 27 October 1933.

268. CAB 23/77/9, 26 October 1933.

269. Ibid. The cabinet minutes suggest that the first domino to fall would have been the Irish Free State, which "would certainly use it as a precedent," and the argument "would be adopted by those extremists who favoured repudiation of the National Debt."

270. Ibid.

271. CAB 23/77/9, 26 October 1933.

272. Self, *War Debt Controversy*, 186.

273. Ibid.

274. CAB 23/77/9, 26 October 1933.

275. CAB 23/77/10, 2 November 1933.

276. Self, *War Debt Controversy*, 187.

277. T 188/74, Leith-Ross memorandum, 31 October 1933. See also Clavin, *Failure of Economic Diplomacy*, 175–176.

278. CAB 23/77/10, 2 November 1933.

279. Ibid.

280. Ibid.

281. Ibid. See also Self, *War Debt Controversy*, 188.

282. Self, *War Debt Controversy*, 188. On the British government's message to the United States, in which it admitted being "greatly disappointed" but also recognized "the difficulties in the way of reaching a final agreement at the present time," see *FRUS*, 1933, vol. 1, Lindsay to Secretary of State, 6 November 1933.

283. FO 371/16675, C9542, C9550, C9567, Leith-Ross to Fisher, telegrams 589–590, 596, 1–2 November 1933; T 188/74/450; Cmd. 4448, Simon telegram 481 to Lindsay, 6 November 1933.

284. FDRL, PSF, War Debts (WW1–1934), Subject File, Box 190, 7 November 1933; HC Deb., 7 November 1933, vol. 281 cc24–25.

285. "War Debts," *Edinburgh Evening News*, 8 November 1933; "War Debt," *Lancashire Evening Post*, 8 November 1933.

286. "News in Brief: British War Debt to America," *The Times*, 15 December 1933, Issue 46628, 14; "War Debt Payment by Britain," *The Times*, 16 December 1933, Issue 46629, 10. *The Economist* makes no reference to these final payments in its issues published on 16, 23, and 30 December 1933 (vol. 117, nos. 4712–4714).

287. Moley erroneously suggests that the earlier June payment was the last sum Britain ever made to the United States. He is correct, however, that these debts "stand on the Treasury's books today." On these points, see Moley, *The First New Deal*, 418. On mistakes regarding the scale and effort of Britain's repayments in the 1930s, see Churchill, *The Gathering Storm*, 23.

288. Clement, "The Touchstone of German Credit," 39; "France and Belgium Refuse to Pay Us; Decide to Default Again on the War Debt," *New York Times*, 13 December 1933.

289. "Tokens and Defaults," *New York Times*, 17 December 1933; "Issue Dead in London," *New York Times*, 15 December 1933.

290. CAB 23/77/17, 29 November 1933; Leith-Ross, *Money Talks*, 178, 176.

291. *FRUS*, 1933, vol. 1, Atherton to Acting Secretary of State, 18 December 1933.

292. Historians recognize that Chamberlain and Roosevelt had both expressed such hopes even at the end of the year. See, for instance, Clavin, *Failure of Economic Diplomacy*, 175–176; and Self, *War Debt Controversy*, 189.

CHAPTER 3. BRITISH DEFAULT, 1934

1. See, for instance, the collection of chapters in Guzman, Ocampo, and Stiglitz, *Too Little, Too Late*. For classic works on this subject, see H. James, "Deep Red," 331–341; and Fishlow, "Lessons from the Past," 383–439.

2. Leith-Ross, *Money Talks*, 178–179.

3. CAB 24/249/33, 29 May 1934; CAB 23/79/7, 30 May 1934.

4. CAB 23/73/3, 29 November 1932, attachment, 28 November 1932.

5. CAB 24/249/33, 29 May 1934; W.O.S., "Britain's Budget Surpluses and War Debt," *Foreign Affairs*, October 1935. On British gold holdings rising between 1931 and 1933, see Eichengreen and Temin, "Fetters of Gold and Paper," 373, figure 1. By 1938, Britain's reserves went on to reach new highs; gold became so plentiful that officials discussed using some of it to repay war debts to the United States. See M. Harris, *Monetary War and Peace*, 209.

6. Reinhart and Rogoff, *This Time Is Different*, 24, 54; Tomz and Wright, "Do Countries Default in Bad Times?," 352–360. On the limits of monocausal interpretations for the defaults of the 1930s, which tend to explain events with reference to "bad luck" or "political opportunism," see Papadia, "Sovereign Defaults during the Great Depression"; and Eichengreen and Portes, "Debt and Default in the 1930s," 599–604. More broadly, on the element of choice involved and the importance of political economy rather than "naked" economics, see Buiter and Rahbari, "Why Governments Default," 257–286.

7. Finland would go on to continue payments until completion. On the logic of Finnish repayment, as a tool to rebuilding the government's financial reputation, see Tomz, *Reputation and International Cooperation*, 112–113. Other smaller debtor states, such as Hungary and Greece, also eventually resumed payments. Furthermore, private donations within debtor countries also continued, as detailed in chapter 6.

8. Neville Chamberlain to Ida Chamberlain, 9 June 1934, in *The Neville Chamberlain Diary Letters*, vol. 4, 73.

9. T 175/79/103–104, Leith-Ross to Fisher, 2 November 1933; Cole, *Roosevelt and the Isolationists*, 92–93.

10. Moulton and Pasvolsky, *War Debts and World Prosperity*, 403–404. Nevertheless, as they stressed, "the losses to the Treasury from a remission of the debts would undoubtedly be greatly outweighed by the gains which would accrue to the Treasury with the recovery of business activity" (413).

11. Cole, *Roosevelt and the Isolationists*, 94; Self, *War Debt Controversy*, 194. See also DeWitt, "Johnson and Early New Deal Diplomacy," 383–384. On the neutrality legislation of the 1930s, see Divine, *The Illusion of Neutrality*, esp. 58–59.

12. Some scholars claim that the act precipitated a sharp decline in U.S. investment overseas. See DeWitt, "Johnson and American Foreign Policy," 2; and De-Conde, *A History of American Foreign Policy*, 563.

13. The Republican representative Charles Plumley, for example, suggested that the Johnson or Debt Default Act of 1934 did as much for world peace as, if not more than, the League of Nations ever did: "You know as well as I do, and nobody knows it any better than the European powers whose ace representatives and diplomats are now here in Washington, that none of them can carry on a major war, or over a considerable period of time, without American supplies; and what is more to the point just now, the purchase of such supplies would have to be financed by loans negotiated in these good old United States." *Congressional Record*, House, 1 April 1937, 3029.

14. *Congressional Record*, House, 29 January 1934, 1524; *Congressional Record*, Senate, 28 February 1934, 3372–3373.

15. *Congressional Record*, House, 30 January 1934, 1610–1611. Representative Wolverton noted that these debtors had already received generous reductions but now moaned that it "constitutes a burden that foreign nations are unable to carry." He explained that the amount to be paid by Italy to the U.S. each year represents only 1.41 percent of its entire budget; Belgium, 2.45 percent; France, 2.65 percent; and Great Britain, 3.75 percent. "The amount due us is so infinitely small as compared to the expense of maintaining these forces, that it is ridiculous to contend that prosperity can be brought to such nations by cancellation of the debts owing to us. . . . If we should cancel the debts, the burden of payment is thereby transferred from the foreign taxpayer and placed upon our own taxpayer. There is no justification for such a course. The remedy is for foreign nations to reduce their expensive armaments."

16. *Congressional Record*, House, 30 April 1934, 7641–7642.

17. *Congressional Record*, House, 2 February 1934, 1890.

18. *Congressional Record*, Senate, 22 January 1934, 1106, 1072; *Congressional Record*, Senate, 28 February 1934, 3375.

19. T 160/934, Lindsay to Moley, 11 January 1934.

20. *Congressional Record*, House, 29 January 1934, 1509–1510.

21. *Congressional Record*, House, 4 January 1934, 118.

22. HJP, "Moratorium–war debts" folder, typewritten statements and moratorium speech.

23. T 188/58/75, "Interviews in Washington with Senators and others, 6–9 February 1933." Also quoted in Self, *War Debt Controversy*, 189.

24. On this bill, see "The Johnson Act: Extension of Credit to a Government in Default," 102–104.

25. For more detailed analysis on the Johnson Act, see Vinson, "War Debts and Peace Legislation," 206–222.

26. DeWitt, "Johnson and Early New Deal Diplomacy," 378–379. Historians such as Allan Nevins have suggested that, "to strike at delinquent governments, Senator Johnson was willing to cause these citizens heavy loss" (*The New Deal and World Affairs*, 42–43). Yet, as DeWitt clarifies, the Johnson Act also prevented the sale of fraudulent securities to U.S. citizens and thereby protected small investors.

27. DeWitt, "Johnson and Early New Deal Diplomacy," 378–379. Recent investigations had concluded that the J. P. Morgan company had profited from the reduction of Italian war debt. Representative Gray, for example, claimed that the "industrial depression is a part of a worldwide crisis brought under an organized plan and deliberately carried out with the object, purpose, and intent to multiply and pile high the burden of war debts upon the people of the world." *Congressional Record*, House, 29 January 1934, 1508.

28. On the committee, see Wiltz, "The Nye Committee Revisited," 211–233.

29. DeWitt, "Johnson and American Foreign Policy," 259–260.

30. Adamson, "The Failure of the Foreign Bondholders Protective Council Experiment," 479–514.

31. Maurer, *The Empire Trap*, 250, 211.

32. For a detailed revaluation of Johnson, see DeWitt, "Johnson and American Foreign Policy," 38–39.

33. Scholarly research suggests that bankers tend to dread war, which helps to explain why governments oppose assertive foreign policies (Krishner, *Appeasing Bankers*, esp. 24–28). Indeed, the war had come as a "bolt from the blue" to most investors (Ferguson, "Political Risk and the International Bond Market," 72).

34. DeWitt, "Johnson and American Foreign Policy," 268–270, citing HJP, Johnson to Edwin M. Borchard, 16 April 1934; Johnson to C. K. McClatchy, 11 and 25 March and 16 April 1934; Johnson to Alex P. Moore, 9 April 1934; Johnson to John Francis Neylan, 25 March 1934. See also Divine, *The Illusion of Neutrality*, 58–59.

35. DeWitt, "Johnson and American Foreign Policy," 256, citing *Congressional Record*, 72nd Cong., 2nd sess., S. 682, Foreign Relations, I (1934).

36. DeWitt, "Johnson and American Foreign Policy," 268; Divine, *The Illusion of Neutrality*, 58–59.

37. Clavin, *Failure of Economic Diplomacy*, 177.

38. T 160/934, Lindsay to Simon, 14 March 1934.

39. Clavin, *Failure of Economic Diplomacy*, 177, citing Strauss to Roosevelt, 27 September 1933, in Roosevelt, *Roosevelt and Foreign Affairs*, vol. 1, 412–413.

40. Self, *War Debt Controversy*, 190, citing Hiram Johnson to his son, 4 February 1934; Blum, *Morgenthau Diaries*, 3 May 1934; Cole, *Roosevelt and the Isolationists*, 92–93.

41. *Congressional Record*, Senate, 28 February 1934, 3372–3373; *Congressional Record*, Senate, 15 February 1934, 2575–2576.

42. Self, *War Debt Controversy*, 190; Cole, *Roosevelt and the Isolationists*, 92–93.

43. DeWitt, "Johnson and American Foreign Policy," 263–264, citing HJP, Johnson to boys, 26 May 1933, 4 June 1933, 16 June 1933; and Schlesinger, *The Coming of the New Deal*, 208.

44. Self, *War Debt Controversy*, 190.

45. These quotes and a more detailed account appear in Self, *War Debt Controversy*, 190. Lindsay did warn Hull, however, that "should his government fall under the ban of the Johnson Bill just as France which had deliberately defaulted, it would be bitterly resented by his government." *FRUS*, 1934, General, the British Commonwealth, vol. 1, Memorandum by Hull, 5 February 1934.

46. *Congressional Record*, House, 2 February 1934, 1890. Hull argued to Lindsay that British inaction had encouraged the progress of the bill: "the Johnson Bill had been pending for many weeks and had once passed the Senate and was then reconsidered and held on the Calendar for two weeks without any complaint whatever from any representative of the debtor governments abroad, [which] naturally had led Congress to the conclusion that those governments were not seriously concerned about the passage of the proposed Johnson measure." Memorandum by Hull, 5 February 1934.

47. *Congressional Record*, Senate, 28 February 1934, 3372–3373.

48. *Congressional Record*, House, 27 March 1934, 5528, citing Crowther, *America Self-Contained*, 226.

49. T 160/934, Lindsay to Simon, 14 March 1934.

50. Ibid.

51. Self, *War Debt Controversy*, 191.

52. T 160/934, Message to Lindsay, 4 April 1934.

53. Ibid.

54. Ibid.

55. Self, *War Debt Controversy*, 191.

56. FDRL, Official File 212, Foreign Debts 1934, Department of State, "American Editorial Opinion, May 1 to June 11," 13 June 1934. On the budget, see CAB 23/79/7, 30 May 1934.

57. "The War Debts," 863.

58. T 188/75/96–97, Leith-Ross to Lindsay, 7 May 1934.

59. T 160/1411/11, Further exchanges between Bruce and Chamberlain concerning abeyance of payments for 31 March 1934; 18, 24, 30 September 1934; and 12, 15, 31 March 1935. On New Zealand, see Message to Britain, 14 June 1935 and response; Note to Dalton, 17 June 1935; and Note, 2 February 1937.

60. T 160/934, Note from Lindsay, 24 April 1934.

61. Ibid.

62. Ibid.

63. Ibid.

64. Self, *War Debt Controversy*, 192.

65. Ibid.

66. Ibid.

67. T 160/934, FO to Lindsay, 30 April 1934.

68. T 160/934, Note from Lindsay, 6 May 1934.

69. T 160/934, Note from Lindsay, 9 May 1934.

70. Ibid.

71. The president now "felt he was bound by the Johnson Act, . . . in other words, that partial payment after June 15th would not prevent a debtor country from being in default." *FRUS*, 1934, vol. 1, Memorandum by Phillips, 9 May 1934; and see also 8 May 1934.

72. The attorney general's ruling, which reflected both "the flexibility of the term 'default'" and "statements made" by the president and in the House of Representatives, explained that it "was not the intent of the Act that a government which had made a partial payment on an instalment when it became due should be considered in default." *FRUS*, 1934, vol. 1, Memorandum by Hackworth, 15 May 1934.

73. The attorney general rendered an opinion that "governments in the same category with Great Britain, namely, Czechoslovakia, Italy, Latvia, and Lithuania, would not fall within the prohibitions of the Act of April 13, 1934, should they pay the full amount of the instalment next due on their indebtedness." *FRUS*, 1934, vol. 1, Wright note, 12 June 1934.

74. FO 371/17585, A3755, Lindsay telegram, 11 May 1934.

75. T 160/934, Note from Lindsay, 11 May 1934; T 160/934, FO to Lindsay, 15 May 1934. On Lindsay giving "the impression that any payments on account were now exceedingly doubtful" four days earlier, see *FRUS*, 1934, vol. 1, Memorandum by Phillips, 11 May 1934.

76. For a more detailed account of these discussions, see Self, *War Debt Controversy*, 192–193. On Lindsay dwelling "on the iniquities of the word 'default'"

and the president's unwillingness to amend the wording, see *FRUS*, 1934, vol. 1, Memorandum by Phillips, 22 May 1934.

77. T 188/75/130–131, Lindsay telegram 156, 16 May 1934.

78. In the margins of the note, Leith-Ross says he "doesn't think it will." T 160/934, Lindsay to Leith-Ross, 21 May 1934.

79. Self, *War Debt Controversy*, 193, citing FO 371/17586, A4117/383/45, Lindsay telegram 168, 25 May 1933. A week later, Roosevelt's message to Congress was clear that it was "a just position to ask that substantial sacrifices be made to meet these debts" (FDRL, PSF 170, Presidential Message to Congress, 1 June 1934).

80. CAB 24/249/33, 29 May 1934.

81. In many ways, the note respects the advice Roosevelt gave to Lindsay earlier in the year: "The President said that if he were the British Government he would hand this Government a note setting forth at length the conditions of the British Treasury, referring to the favorable balance in their budget, but also to the extent of the taxation under which the British people were suffering; that, for social and other reasons, it was necessary to lighten this heavy taxation which would automatically unbalance their budget; however, that they recognize their responsibilities under their debt and desire to discuss the question of final disposition of the debt." *FRUS*, 1934, vol. 1, Memorandum by Phillips, 22 May 1934.

82. On the assumptions underpinning such thinking, see Middleton, "British Monetary and Fiscal Policy," 414–441; and Dimsdale, "British Monetary Policy and the Exchange Rate," 306–349. The British government did not discuss the issue of "sterilization," whereby central banks seek to limit the inflows and outflows of capital on the money supply. Both the United States and France, for instance, accumulated and sterilized gold reserves during the onset of the Great Depression. On this subject, see Irwin, "Did France Cause the Great Depression?"; Eichengreen, "The Bank of France and the Sterilization of Gold," 56–84; and Eichengreen, *Golden Fetters*.

83. CAB 23/79/7, 30 May 1934.

84. Document originally located via U.S. Declassified Documents Online, http://tinyurl.galegroup.com/tinyurl/4gyMW7 (accessed 19 April 2017). See also NAII, RG 59, Bureau of European Affairs, Memorandum from Acting Secretary of State George Ball regarding Congressional inquiries concerning WWI war debts and reparations to Germany, Department of State, 15 August 1966; and Harry S. Truman Presidential Library (HSTL), Acheson File, Box 27, British Loan, Interview, 3 January 1946.

85. Tariffs were not a one-sided issue. On the British government's decision to move away from free trade, and its subsequent use of protection to bargain for trade advantages, see Roth, *British Protectionism and the International Economy*; and Trentmann, *Free Trade Nation*. It is also important not to exaggerate the relationship between tariffs, and especially the Smoot-Hawley tariff, and the later series of defaults on war debts. See Irwin, *Peddling Protectionism*, 141.

86. Stimson had rebutted most of the claims now advanced by the British almost eighteen months earlier. See Stimson Diaries, 7 December 1932; *FRUS*, 1932, vol. 1, Stimson to Lindsay, 7 December 1932. At this juncture, British and U.S. approaches to the war debts ably support Harold James's claim that "the debate between debtors and creditors in the international economy swings dangerously

between two different ways of assessing legitimacy: power and morality" ("International Capital Movements and the Global Order," 296).

87. See, for instance, *Congressional Record*, House, 18 December 1931, 841, citing recent editorials in the *Washington Post*.

88. Keynes memorandum for the chancellor, 27 October 1940, in Keynes, *The Collected Writings*, vol. 23, 22. See also Keynes to Ronald, 11 March 1941, in Keynes, *The Collected Writings*, vol. 23, 47.

89. On taxpayers footing the bill if Allied debtors refused to pay, see Leffler, "The Origins of Republican War Debt Policy," 588, 586, 589; and Moulton and Pasvolsky, *War Debts and World Prosperity*, 403–404.

90. As policymakers in the Roosevelt administration believed, the transfer problem was "appreciable but not determinative." On this claim, see Moley, *The First New Deal*, 26. See also *Congressional Record*, Senate, 1 June 1933, 4747–4752; and *Congressional Record*, Senate, 14 October 1939, 432. The Hoover administration certainly recognized that the transfer problem could affect the British economy, but it was not swayed by such considerations. On Hoover's position, see Hoover, *Memoirs*, vol. 2, 179. See also Self, *War Debt Controversy*, 103.

91. Kimball, "Beggar My Neighbor," 771; on the infamous example of the sale of the Viscose Company, see HC Deb., 19 June 1941, vol. 372, cc820–821. See also *Congressional Record*, Senate, 16 January 1923, 1786.

92. FDRL, PSF, War Debts (WW1–1934), Subject File, Box 190, Report of Conversation, 14 July 1934.

93. For an amusing criticism of the British position, including how repayment could affect US monetary policy, see HJP, War debts, vol. 3, misc., Carlisle Bargeroon, "Along the Potomac," *Washington Post*, 6 June 1934.

94. Self, *War Debt Controversy*, 194.

95. H. James, "Deep Red," 337; H. James, introduction to *The Interwar Depression in an International Context*, ix–x; Schuker, "The Gold Exchange Standard," 77–94; Daunton, *Wealth and Welfare*, 290. The British government had argued that after the Lausanne Conference, "there was a marked tendency for prices to rise but that this tendency was reversed when the prospects of a final settlement of inter-governmental obligations receded, while the December payment was accompanied by a sharp fall in prices which was felt in America at least as much as in Europe. Experience, therefore, appears to show that the effect of these payments upon prices is very direct." *FRUS*, 1933, vol. 1, Lindsay to Acting Secretary of State, 13 June 1933.

96. Clavin, *Failure of Economic Diplomacy*, 180; H. James, "Deep Red," 337.

97. Hoover, *Memoirs*, vol. 2, 179.

98. FDRL, PSF, War Debts (WW1–1934), Subject File, Box 190, Report of Conversation, 14 July 1934.

99. See, for example, FO 371/24245, Darvall to Cowell, 22 January 1940.

100. HL Deb., 21 July 1938, col. 1050–1056.

101. Armaments spending in the United Kingdom had been a source of criticism in the United States that undermined calls for debt revision since the 1920s. See, for instance, Hoover, *Memoirs*, vol. 2, 179; *Congressional Record*, Senate, 16 January 1923, 1780–1786; and *Congressional Record*, House, 18 December 1931, 870.

102. T 160/934, Note, 14 May 1934. Since the war, Britain had been carrying a burden of indebtedness amounting to approximately £8 billion, or £170 per head of the national population, about one-fifth of which represented the war loans made to the Allied governments. It was true that war debts represented a smaller burden relative to gross domestic product for the U.S. than for the British economy. See Reinhart and Trebesch, "A Distant Mirror of Debt, Default, and Relief," 20.

103. CAB 24/249/33, 29 May 1934.

104. Leith-Ross, *Money Talks*, 178–179.

105. CAB 23/79/7, 30 May 1934.

106. The decision to suspend repayment was one of willingness rather than ability. The United Kingdom had the resources to fund the debt but prioritized other interests. As Citicorp chairman Walter Wriston has suggested, "countries don't go bankrupt" or "don't go out of business": "The infrastructure doesn't go away, the productivity of the people doesn't go away, the natural resources don't go away. And so their assets always exceed their liabilities which is the technical reason for bankruptcy. And that's very different from a company." As the British example reveals, and in contrast to the optimistic interpretations of international investors in the 1970s, this insight should not be interpreted to mean that states will always repay their debts. On these points, see H. James, *International Monetary Cooperation since Bretton Woods*, 352–353. See also Kolb, "Sovereign Debt," 4–7.

107. CAB 23/79/7, 30 May 1934.

108. H. James, "Deep Red," 333.

109. Leith-Ross, *Money Talks*, 178–179.

110. For a key exception, see Edwards, *American Default*, 186–200. On negotiated debt restructurings being, in some cases, relatively advantageous to the debtor, especially when coercing creditors into sizeable reductions or better terms, see Roos, *Why Not Default?*, 48.

111. Leith-Ross, *Money Talks*, 178–179. More broadly, the examples of Soviet repudiation of tsarist debt in 1918 and Great Britain's arbitration with Costa Rica in 1923 also suggest the feasibility of selective debt cancellation in the interwar period. See Lienau, *Rethinking Sovereign Debt*.

112. Leith-Ross, *Money Talks*, 178–179.

113. Some foreign debtors certainly defaulted on their debts to the United Kingdom, but the available data shows that income derived from overseas investments—namely, dominion and colonial governments, dominion and colonial municipalities, foreign governments, and foreign municipalities—suffered only a small decline in 1933 and then grew in 1934. See Kindersley, "British Overseas Investments in 1934 and 1935," 647; and Kindersley, "British Overseas Investments in 1932 and 1933," 367.

114. HL Deb., 6 June 1934, vol. 92, cc871–872; Clement, "The Touchstone of German Credit," 36–37; H. James, *The Reichsbank and Public Finance in Germany*, 342.

115. *Congressional Record*, Senate, 16 June 1934, 12067. Germany's default in the summer of 1934 resulted in the British government quickly approving legislation authorizing coercive action. Germany did eventually agree to a unilateral commercial agreement with Britain and also went on to resume repaying its Dawes

and Young loans. On these points, see Tooze, *Wages of Destruction*, 70, 87; and H. James, *The Reichsbank and Public Finance in Germany*, 342.

116. HL Deb., 6 June 1934, vol. 92, cc870.

117. Short-term loans, running from months to one year, had been granted to governments or their central banks, but these were infrequent and less significant. See "The Johnson Act: Extension of Credit to a Government in Default," 102, citing Trade Information Bulletin No. 814, Department of Commerce (1933), 77; and Trade Information Bulletin No. 819, Department of Commerce (1934), 40.

118. As Harold James explains, "The problem behind a high level of external debt is that the creditors are obviously not represented in any Parliament, and the political representatives of debtor classes (or those who have to pay taxes in order to service debt) may well have a powerful incentive to default" ("International Capital Movements and the Global Order," 274). For a detailed analysis of the domestic drivers of default, see Roos, *Why Not Default?*

119. CAB 23/79/7, 30 May 1934.

120. Wormell, *The Management of the National Debt*, 731–733.

121. Self, *War Debt Controversy*, 195.

122. See, for example, CAB 27/548, BDA, Seventh meeting, 31 March 1933; CAB 24/241/14, War Debts: Memorandum by the President of the Board of Trade, 24 May 1933; and CAB 23/77/9, 26 October 1933.

123. On the gradual shift from the punishment of debtors in society to control of creditors, see Strange, "Debt and Default in the International Political Economy," 9.

124. National Archives, London, Ministry of Pensions and National Insurance (PIN) 15/1010, *Hansard*, 29 November 1934.

125. PIN 15/1010, Cmd. 4649, Report by Departmental Committee, Imprisonment by Courts of summary jurisdiction in default of payment of fines and other sums of money (London: HM Stationery Office, 1934), esp. 2, 64. See also PIN 15/1010, Newspaper clipping, 24 July 1934. On the importance of good credit and punishment for default in prewar society, see Finn, *The Character of Credit*, 110, 259–261.

126. Tomz refers to "the benefits of future credit," but the rewards of repayment in this case extended beyond only the terms of potential borrowing. Policymakers repeatedly stressed the domestic-political, diplomatic, and debtor-based benefits that could be jeopardized by default. See Tomz, *Reputation and International Cooperation*, 225.

127. CAB 23/79/7, 30 May 1934.

128. Clavin, *Failure of Economic Diplomacy*, 179.

129. *Congressional Record*, Senate, 1 June 1934, 10192.

130. Ibid. See also T 160/934, Telegram from Lindsay, 1 June 1934.

131. Self, *War Debt Controversy*, 194.

132. FDRL, Official File 212, Foreign Debts 1934, Department of State, "American Editorial Opinion, 1 May to 11 June," 13 June 1934.

133. F. S. Tew, "War Debts," *Times*, 23 May 1934, 15.

134. FDRL, PSF, War Debts (WW1–1934), Subject File, Box 190, Under Secretary of State to President, 4 June 1934.

135. HC Deb., 5 June 1934 vol. 290, cc753–755. See also Cmd. 4609, "Papers Relating to the British War Debt," 1934.

136. *The Economist*, 9 June 1934.

137. HC Deb., 15 May 1934, vol. 289, c1621; HC Deb., 16 May 1934, vol. 289, cc1761; "M.P.s Baffled on War Debts," *Daily Mail*, 15 May 1934, 15.

138. HC Deb., 18 June 1934, vol. 291, cc15–16.

139. HL Deb., 6 June 1934, vol. 92, cc857.

140. HC Deb., 18 June 1934, vol. 291, cc15–16.

141. "The Latest War Debts Demand," *Financial Times*, 29 May 1934, 6.

142. "Debts and the War," *Daily Telegraph*, 12 May 1934, 12.

143. High Packard, "War Debts," *The Times*, 21 May 1934, 6; E. C. Dickinson, "War Debts," *The Times*, 31 May 1934, 10.

144. Benjamin Pollard, "War Debts," *The Times*, 2 June 1934, 10.

145. L. H. Elphinstone, "Eighteenth-Century War Debts," *The Times*, 11 June 1934, 13; "U.S. Experts and War Debts," *Daily Mail*, 27 November 1934, 3. For an earlier example of debts from the 1800s, discussed prior to British repayment in 1932, see HJP, War Debt Moratorium, vol. 5, Newspaper comment, "The Money America Owes Britain," *New York Times*, 28 October 1932.

146. Interest in using older U.S. debts as leverage in British war-debt negotiations is curiously rare up until the 1970s. On the difficulties of collecting these debts, see T 312/3360, Peirson to Lovall, Foggary, World War One debt, 7 July 1972; T 385/204, Peirson to Taylor, World War One Debt, 20 June 1972; T 312/3360, Memorandum respecting repudiated debts of the Southern States of the United States of America, 1932; and FO 371/24245, Note, "British War Debts to the United States," 2 August 1940.

147. See, for example, T 160/1411/11, Waley to Batterbee, 18 November 1933; Bruce and Chamberlain, 31 March 1934, 18, 24, and 30 September 1934.

148. "U.S. and British War Debts," *Daily Telegraph*, 6 June 1934, 11.

149. Clavin, *Failure of Economic Diplomacy*, 178.

150. Astore and Fratianni, "We Can't Pay," 208.

151. On the logic of Italian default and for a text of the letter by the Italian ambassador Augusto Rosso to the U.S. acting secretary of state, June 1934, see ibid., 208, 217.

152. FDRL, PSF, War Debts (WW1–1934), Subject File, Box 190, Report of Conversation, 14 July 1934.

153. Ibid.

154. T 160/934, Lindsay to Simon, 7 June 1934, attachment. See extract of *Congressional Record*, 5 June 1934.

155. "U.S. and British War Debts," 11.

156. HJP, War debts, vol. 3, misc., *New York Times*, 15 June 1934.

157. T 160/934, Telegram from Lindsay, 7 June 1934.

158. T 160/934, Lindsay to Simon, 15 June 1934.

159. T 160/934, Fletcher to Willert, 16 June 1934.

160. Ibid.

161. FDRL, Official File 212, Foreign Debts 1934, Department of State, American Editorial Opinion. For further analysis of the same data, see Self, *War Debt Controversy*, 194.

162. "U.S. and British War Debts," 11.

163. Clavin, *Failure of Economic Diplomacy*, 178–179.

164. T 160/934, Lindsay to Simon, 15 June 1934.

165. FDRL, Official File 212, Foreign Debts 1934, Department of State, American Editorial Opinion.

166. T 175/79/103–104, Leith-Ross to Fisher, 2 November 1933; Cole, *Roosevelt and the Isolationists*, 92–93.

167. Clavin, *Failure of Economic Diplomacy*, 176–177.

168. *Congressional Record*, Senate, 2 February 1934, 1823.

169. *Congressional Record*, House, 1 April 1937, 3029.

170. "America's Reply on War Debts," *Daily Telegraph*, 13 June 1934, 15.

171. Self, *War Debt Controversy*, 194.

172. T 160/934, Telegram from Lindsay, 12 June 1934.

173. FDRL, Official File 212, Foreign Debts 1934, Memorandum for Files, 12 June 1934.

174. "The Crux of War Debts," *Daily Telegraph*, 14 June 1934, 16. See also "No Immediate Reply to United States," *Daily Mail*, 14 June 1934, 15.

175. FDRL, PSF, Great Britain, 1933–36, Osborne to Hull, 27 June 1934; T 160/934, Note to Vansittart, 21 June 1934, attachment. Hull's letter and response published as Cmd. 4609.

176. FDRL, PSF, War Debts (WW1–1934), Subject File, Box 190, Undersecretary of State to President, 30 August 1934.

177. W. F. Sanderson, "Will Not Shirk the Issue," *Daily Mail*, 17 August 1934, 12.

178. T 160/934, Astor to Jones, ca. August 1934; FDRL, PSF, War Debts (WW1–1934), Subject File, Box 190, Undersecretary of State to President, 30 August 1934. On other suggestions concerning the war debt, see Secretary of State to President, 31 October 1934, attachment dated 27 October 1934; and Secretary of State to President, 8 November 1934, attachment dated 8 November 1934.

179. Quoted in Self, *War Debt Controversy*, 203.

180. T 160/934, Lindsay to Leith-Ross, 2 October 1934.

181. Ibid.

182. T 160/934, Note to Lindsay, 8 November 1934.

183. "War Debts to U.S.," *Daily Telegraph*, 12 December 1934, 11; FDRL, PSF, Great Britain, 1933–36, Lindsay to Hull, 10 December 1934.

184. Ritschl, "Sustainability of High Public Debt," 175–198. See also Schuker, *American "Reparations" to Germany*.

185. FDRL, Official File 212, Foreign Debts 1935–1938, Hull to President, 29 May 1935.

186. On employment levels, see Cater et al., *Historical Statistics of the United States*, 282–283. On rising debt levels in the 1930s, see Carmen M. Reinhart and Kenneth Rogoff, "Debt and Growth Revisited," *Vox*, 11 August 2010. https:// voxeu.org/article/debt-and-growth-revisited. As Paul Krugman notes, however, "Debt actually fell as the economy slumped, through a combination of deleveraging and default. The ratio to GDP spiked only because GDP collapsed." Krugman, "Debt in the 30s," *New York Times*, 11 August 2010.

187. FDRL, Official File 212, Foreign Debts 1934, The Record: A Business Newspaper, 13 December 1934.

188. FDRL, PSF32/302, Lindsay to Hull, 10 December 1934. See also Self, *War Debt Controversy*, 195.

189. FDRL, PSF, Great Britain, 1933–36, Lindsay to Hull, 10 December 1934.

190. See, for instance, Benjamin Pollard's letter, in which he seeks to prevent the "dreadful step of defaulting," "War Debts," *The Times*, 2 June 1934.

191. The check was duly returned to him in the following year. See FDRL, Official File 212, Foreign Debts 1935–1938, Note, 21 December 1935. See also Self, *War Debt Controversy*, 205.

Chapter 4. Financial Isolation, 1934–1942

1. Neville Chamberlain to Ida Chamberlain, 9 June 1934, in *The Neville Chamberlain Diary Letters*, vol. 4, 73. For similar arguments, and the same quote, see Self, *War Debt Controversy*, 195; and Clavin, *Failure of Economic Diplomacy*, 179.

2. For an overview of these claims in the extant literature, see Borensztein and Panizza, "The Costs of Sovereign Default," 683–741; Sandleris, "The Costs of Sovereign Default," 1–27; and Fuentes and Saravia, "Are Sovereign Defaulters Punished?," esp. 152. On defaulting being "clearly bad for political careers of heads of state" and doubling the chances of a prime minister or president being ousted from office within the following year, as evidenced by a sample of eighty-six countries over four years, see Malone, "Sovereign Debt Problems and Policy Gambles," 43.

3. On other major Europeans powers such as France and Germany suffering limited costs from suspending payments on their war debts or reparations prior to 1934, see Leith-Ross, *Money Talks*, 178–179; Norbert, *Hitler's Magician*, 212–214; and Tooze, *Wages of Destruction*, 50.

4. CAB 23/79/7, 30 May 1934. On British default as one of several important "steps" allowing "Britain to stabilize its precarious debt situation," see Weldon, *Two Hundred Years*, 115.

5. Existing accounts stress the importance of the improving state of the economy but make curiously little mention of the war-debts issue. See, for instance, Robertson, "The British General Election of 1935," 149–164; Stannage, *Baldwin Thwarts the Opposition*; and Fry, "A Reconsideration of the British General Election of 1935," 43–55. These outcomes emerged despite the government's limited program to promote economic recovery. On this point, see Shay, *British Rearmament in the Thirties*, 15–16. In the five years between ceasing repayment and entering the Second World War, there was strong and sustained growth in gross domestic product, and the pound remained historically strong against the dollar. On the decline in economy-wide unemployment after 1932, see Boyer and Hatton, "New Estimates of British Unemployment," 667, table 6.

6. Capital markets reacted to the defaults of the 1930s, to be sure, but scholars have questioned the relationship between the severity of default and the ability to borrow immediately after the Second World War. See Eichengreen and Portes, "The Interwar Debt Crisis and Its Aftermath," 69–94. Eichengreen and Portes do not record the United Kingdom as a defaulter in this period. In addition, although they include France as a "light defaulter," they specifically exclude war debts and reparations. On the broader relationship between default in the 1930s and borrow-

ing after 1945, see Eichengreen, "The U.S. Capital Market and Foreign Lending," esp. 243, 245. It is also worth noting that the United Kingdom also managed to retain a "triple-A" sovereign credit rating throughout the decade, according to the rating agency Fitch, although Moody's dropped its rating from "Aaa" to "Aa" in 1934. See Reinhart and Trebesch, "A Distant Mirror of Debt, Default, and Relief," 36; Gaillard, *A Century of Sovereign Ratings*, 41. See also Flandreau, Gaillard, and Packer, "To Err Is Human."

7. Income derived from overseas investments grew in 1934 and 1935 and was only slightly lower than in 1932. See Kindersley, "British Oversea Investments in 1935 and 1936," 644; Kindersley, "British Overseas Investments in 1934 and 1935," 647; and Kindersley, "British Overseas Investments in 1932 and 1933," 367.

8. Hachey and Lindsay, "Winning Friends and Influencing Policy," 122–127; Peden, *The Treasury and British Public Policy*, 281–282; Schatz, "The Anglo-American Trade Agreement," 85–103; and H. James, *International Monetary Cooperation since Bretton Woods*, 24–25.

9. Cole and Kehoe, "Self-Fulfilling Debt Crises," 91–116; Fuentes and Saravia, "Sovereign Defaulters," 336–347; Rose and Spiegel, "Noneconomic Engagement and International Exchange," 337–363; Tomz and Wright, "Sovereign Theft," 69–110.

10. CAB 24/287, Note for the cabinet on the financial situation, July 1939. Rearmament intensified rather than resumed. For an important corrective to claims about British disarmament and evidence that the government maintained a strong armaments industry and rearmed expensively during the interwar period, see Edgerton, *Warfare State*.

11. Allen and DiGiuseppe, "Tightening the Belt," 647–659; DiGiuseppe, "The Fiscal Autonomy of Deciders," 317–338; Shea, "Financing Victory," 771–795; Shea, "Borrowing Trouble," 401–428; Shea and Poast, "War and Default," 1876–1904. More broadly, on the pressures of war favoring states with the greatest public creditworthiness, see Macdonald, *A Free Nation Deep in Debt*.

12. Dallek, *Roosevelt and American Foreign Policy*, 74; P. Kennedy, *The Rise and Fall of the Great Powers*, 330.

13. Not all scholars accept the importance of the war debts to the course of relations between the U.S. and the United Kingdom. David Reynolds argues that the controversy "no longer seemed vitally important" by the late 1930s. He notes as "probably sound" some claims from within the British government that war debts would not, in a crisis, influence U.S. public opinion against the United Kingdom to more than a limited degree. On both points, see Reynolds, *Creation of the Anglo-American Alliance*, 53.

14. Keynes note, 2 November 1939, in Keynes, *The Collected Writings*, vol. 22, 26.

15. See, for instance, McKercher, *Transition of Power*, 176.

16. Kimball, "Beggar My Neighbor," 758–759. For a more detailed account of Britain's growing financial problems and the U.S. response, see Kimball, *The Most Unsordid Act*.

17. Dean Acheson, *Present at the Creation*, 28; Allen, "Mutual Aid between the U.S. and the British Empire," 272–273; HSTL, Oral History Interview with

John M. Leddy, 15 June 1973, 29–31. See also HSTL, Oral History Interview with Hubert F. Havlik, 20 June 1973.

18. On the costs of the Second World War, see Broadberry and Howlett, "The United Kingdom," esp. 68–69. Broadberry and Howlett cite Cmd. 6707, table 12, which provides an official balance-sheet evaluation of the effects of World War II on the United Kingdom's economy in 1945. The chancellor of the exchequer put the total deterioration in the national balance sheet at £7.3 billion, compared with a prewar national wealth estimate of £30 billion, which represents a loss of 25 percent. In contrast, Broadberry and Howlett reach a figure of 18.6 percent of prewar national wealth.

19. See FO 371/26209. By June 1941, Roosevelt had approved the cessation of notices of debtor government due dates. Even then, however, he was clear that "this constitutes, of course, no waiver on the part of the United States Government." See *FRUS*, 1941, General, The Soviet Union, vol. 1, Roosevelt to Welles, 16 June 1941.

20. FDRL, Official File 212, Foreign Debts 1939–1945, Note, 2 January 1942.

21. On these exchanges, see T 160/1411/11, Waley to Batterbee, 18 November 1933; Bruce and Chamberlain, 31 March 1934, 18, 24, and 30 September 1934, and 12, 15, and 31 March 1935; Dalton note and exchanges, 14 and 17 June 1935; and Note, 2 February 1937.

22. The British government's debt policies varied in some instances. Newfoundland's default on external debts resulted in the loss of its sovereignty, ultimately becoming a Canadian province. Egypt also became a British protectorate following default. See Reinhart and Rogoff, *This Time Is Different*, 81–83; and Hale, "The Newfoundland Lesson," 51–61.

23. In January 1935, for instance, Roosevelt asked the Senate to approve U.S. admission to the World Court. This request prompted an angry response in some quarters, which played effectively on lingering resentment toward Europe's unpaid debts. See Dallek, *Roosevelt and American Foreign Policy*, 95–96.

24. T 160/934, Lindsay to Leith-Ross, 21 May 1934.

25. T 160/934, Note to Lindsay, 8 November 1934.

26. Ibid.

27. T 160/934, Astor to Jones, ca. August 1934; T 160/572/3, Letter to Leith-Ross, 2 October 1934. On initial U.S. ideas for "handling the war debts," see *FRUS*, 1934, General, the British Commonwealth, vol. 1, Phillips to Roosevelt, 31 October 1934.

28. T 160/572/3, Note from Lindsay, 4 June 1935; FDRL, Official File 212, Foreign Debts 1935–1938, Hull to President, 29 May 1935.

29. FDRL, Official File 212, Foreign Debts 1935–1938, *passim*.

30. Jimmy Carter Presidential Library, Collection: Office of Staff Secretary, Series: Presidential Files, Folder: 6/2/77[1], Container 23, "Franklin D. Roosevelt's first term press conferences: One method of influencing newsgathering," 11, referencing a press conference held on 14 June 1935.

31. T 160/934, Note to Lindsay, 8 November 1934; "War Debts to U.S.," *Daily Telegraph*, 12 December 1934, 11; FDRL, PSF, Great Britain, 1933–36, Lindsay to Hull, 10 December 1934.

32. For a detailed account, see Stannage, *Baldwin Thwarts the Opposition*.

33. On the logic of "appeasement" and preparations for war, see Peden, "A Matter of Timing," 15–28. On the wider debate and claims of an early start to the rearmament period, see Ripsman and Levy, "Wishful Thinking or Buying Time?" 159–163. See also Ferris, *Men, Money, and Diplomacy*; and Parker, *Chamberlain and Appeasement*, 12–17.

34. P. Kennedy, *Strategy and Diplomacy*, 102; Ripsman and Levy, "Wishful Thinking or Buying Time?," 159–160.

35. FO 371/18761, Minute, 8 January 1936. See also Watt, *Succeeding John Bull*, 76; and Self, *War Debt Controversy*, 208. Over the course of the following year, as the demands of rearmament mounted, the British government became unable to meet defense expenditure from revenue alone. It therefore sought to raise a sum not exceeding £400 million in any manner acceptable under the War Loan Act of 1919, to pay for "the formidable nature of the task now facing HMG." The bond performed poorly: T 175/96, Cmd. 5374, Statement relating to defence expenditure, February 1937.

36. The term "isolationism" is problematic, but even its critics accept that these treaties were the strongest evidence of such sentiment. On this point, see Braumoeller, "The Myth of American Isolationism," 349–371.

37. HJP, "Moratorium-war debts" folder, "Cannot Afford to Lose Our Self-Respect," *Washington Times*, 14 March 1936.

38. CAB 104/28, Lindsay to Eden, 26 March 1936.

39. *Congressional Record*, Senate, 20 June 1936, 10384.

40. Ibid., 10815.

41. A proposal he repeated two years later. See Peden, *British Rearmament and the British Treasury*, 86; and Self, *War Debt Controversy*, 208.

42. Self, *War Debt Controversy*, 206–207.

43. Ibid.

44. T 160/934, Troutbeck to Walley, 19 November 1936; Walley to Troutbeck, 20 November.

45. On the French government's attitudes toward devolution, which moved from "absolute opposition" in 1933 to "grudging acceptance" in 1936, see Mouré, "Une Eventualité Absolument Exclue," 479–505.

46. Belgium, the Netherlands, and Switzerland signed on to the agreement in November. See Steil, *The Battle of Bretton Woods*, 33.

47. On the Tripartite Agreement as "the fundamental organising principle of the international monetary system until the outbreak of the Second World War," "the foundation of modern monetary cooperation," and a "force for democratic cooperation" but nevertheless "limited by design," see M. Harris, *Monetary War and Peace*, 4, 7–8. As Benn Steil explains, "Morgenthau characterized it as a 'gentlemen's agreement,' fearing anything that might smell like a formal treaty" (*The Battle of Bretton Woods*, 32). For Ian M. Drummond, "There was strictly speaking, no agreement at all" (*Floating Pound and the Sterling Area*, 217). Scholars continue to debate the motivations behind currency coordination. Harold James, for example, argues persuasively that the decision was "as much political as narrowly or purely financial," reflecting U.S. and British attempts to keep France economically and

politically stable to help resist the threat posed by Nazi Germany (*International Monetary Cooperation since Bretton Woods*, 24–25). For a similar explanation, see Oye, "The Sterling-Dollar-Franc Triangle," 193. Other scholars, however, suggest that security considerations were not important to the British during the consultations that led to cooperation. As Lars S. Skålnes argues, "Economic considerations, therefore, explain why Britain concluded the stabilization agreement. Political and strategic considerations probably better explain why the agreement survived than why it was concluded, but the importance of political considerations should not be exaggerated" ("Grand Strategy and Foreign Economic Policy," 606–607).

48. S. Clarke, *Exchange-Rate Stabilization in Mid-1930s*, 10–11.

49. Oye, *Cooperation under Anarchy*, 196.

50. H. James, *International Monetary Cooperation since Bretton Woods*, 24–25.

51. T 160/934, Lindsay to Leith-Ross, 23 November 1936.

52. T 160/934, Note from British Library of Information, 1 December 1936.

53. In June 1936, Italy had wanted to resume debt talks and reach a settlement, to which Roosevelt said, "OK." At the same time, France wanted personal debt talks and stabilization of currencies with the United States. Roosevelt said that the two issues were not linked but was glad to have assurance that these discussions were unofficial in nature. See FDRL, Official File 212, Foreign Debts 1935–1938, Notes, 3 and 5 June 1936.

54. FDRL, Official File 212, Foreign Debts 1935–1938, Note, 28 December 1936.

55. Self, *War Debt Controversy*, 206.

56. FDRL, PSF, Great Britain, 1937–38, Bingham to President, January 1937.

57. On the divisions in Whitehall, whereby the Foreign Office believed that Britain should open negotiations before either France or Italy and HM Treasury preferred a "wait and see" approach, see Self, *War Debt Controversy*, 206–207.

58. T 160/934, Leith-Ross to Lindsay, 11 February 1937.

59. See T 160/934 for a useful overview.

60. Self, *War Debt Controversy*, 205, citing FDRL, PSF, 29–30, Bullitt to Roosevelt, 24 and 28 October 1936; and FDRL, Henry Morgenthau Jr. Papers 1866–1960, 46/275/76, Bullitt telegram 1152 to Hull, 27 November 1936.

61. Quoted in Self, *War Debt Controversy*, 206, citing Morgenthau Papers, 48/114-17, Telephone conversation between Morgenthau and Moore, 11 December 1936; and 48/306, Morgenthau note, 18 December 1936.

62. Morgenthau Papers, Diaries, 4/27/1933–7/21/1945, File Unit: vol. 101, December 7–December 13, 1937, Morgenthau note, 12 December 1937.

63. Hachey and Lindsay, "Winning Friends and Influencing Policy," 120, citing FO 371/20651, Telegram No. 91, Eden to Lindsay, 10 March 1937.

64. Quoted ibid., 122–127.

65. Ibid., 120–121, citing FO 371, vol. 20651, Minute, 2 April 1937.

66. *Congressional Record*, House, 1 April 1937, 3025–3026, 3029.

67. Ibid.

68. T 160/934, Lindsay to Eden, 27 May 1937.

69. On Baldwin retiring "in dignity and silence," "loaded with honors and enshrined in public esteem," see Churchill, *The Gathering Storm*, 18.

70. Reynolds, *The Creation of the Anglo-American Alliance*, 52–53.

71. *Congressional Record*, Senate, 15 June 1937, 5967.

72. *Congressional Record*, House, 15 June 1937, 5769.

73. Ibid., 5770.

74. Peden, *British Rearmament and the Treasury*, 86, 193n95, citing T 175/94 (part 3), Hopkins to Simon, 2 September 1937; and Woods to Hopkins, 9 September 1937.

75. T 160/934, S.W. to Bewley, ca. September 1937; Morgenthau Papers, Diaries, 4/27/1933–7/21/1945, File Unit: Volume 101, December 7–December 13, 1937, Morgenthau to Hull, 9 December 1937.

76. Quoted in Shay, *British Rearmament in the Thirties*, 174.

77. Ripsman and Levy, "Wishful Thinking or Buying Time?," 167–169. Simon went on to warn the cabinet in April 1938 that rearmament spending risked turning the United Kingdom into "a different kind of nation" by abandoning, as Alan Allport explains, "the liberal-capitalist axioms of balanced budgets, low taxation, minimal inflation and non-state interference in wage and price levels" (*Britain at Bay*, 46). On the broader economic social context of this period and its relevance to rearmament policies, see Allport, *Britain at Bay*, ch. 3.

78. Peden, "A Matter of Timing," 18, citing T 160/19341/F13300/13, BLI, New York, to Foreign Office News Department, 22 June 1938; and Lindsay to Halifax, 11 July 1938.

79. T 160/934, Note from BLI, 22 June 1938; FO 371/21545, BLI to FO, 22 June 1938; Auld, "The British War Debt," 640–650.

80. FO 371/21545, BLI to FO, 26 May 1938.

81. FO 371/21545, *passim*.

82. T 160/934, Note to Waley, 30 June 1938.

83. Maurer, *The Empire Trap*, 292–293; Adamson, "Must We Overlook All Impairment of Our Interests?," 589–623.

84. FO 371/21545, British War Debt to the United States, 7 February 1938.

85. FO 371/21545, BLI to FO, 18 March 1938. Public sentiment, which favored collection of the debt in full by a majority of 54 percent in 1937, now favored reduction or cancellation by a majority of 53 percent. On these figures, see Auld, "The British War Debt," 640–650.

86. Schatz, "The Anglo-American Trade Agreement," 93. See also Whitham, "Seeing the Wood for the Trees," 29–51; Dobson, "The Export White Paper, 10 September 1941," 61; and McKercher, "Our Most Dangerous Enemy," 769.

87. T 160/934, S. G. Waley to Steward, 30 June 1938; T 160/934, Note from British Library of Information, 22 June 1938. In pen beneath this message, Steward responds to Waley on 7 July 1938, "I entirely agree with you."

88. T 160/934, Lindsay to Halifax, 11 July 1938.

89. Plesur, "The Republican Congressional Comeback," 562.

90. T 160/934, Note from BLI, 22 June 1938; FO 371/21545, BLI to FO, 22 June 1938.

91. FO 371/21545, Waley note, 18/7, attachment "Draft Statement on British War Debt."

92. Ibid.

93. HL Deb., 21 July 1938, col. 1048–1049.

94. Ibid.

95. Ibid.

96. Ibid. On this subject, see Meyer, "The Expropriation and Great Britain," 156. The U.S. press had certainly picked up on this point: T 160/934, Note from BLI, 22 June 1938; and FO 371/21545, BLI to FO, 22 June 1938.

97. HL Deb., 21 July 1938, col. 1062–1063.

98. On the economic and military background to British policy, see Peden, "A Matter of Timing," 15–28. See also Jervis, *Perception and Misperception in International Politics*, 78; Ripsman and Levy, "Wishful Thinking or Buying Time?," 175.

99. Whitham, "Seeing the Wood for the Trees," 29–51; and Dobson, "The Export White Paper," 61.

100. BE, OV179/1/66A, J. A. C. Osborne, "The American Debt," 9 December 1938; and BE, OV179/1/66A, J. A. C. Osborne, "Some Incidental Arguments," 9 December 1938.

101. Lothian's position on this matter was informed by his membership of the Council on Foreign Relations and the Royal Institute of International Affairs, which had created subgroups on war debts that exchanged confidential memoranda between Washington and London. Lothian argued that, in the interests of improving relations between the two states, the British government should resume partial payments on its war debts. On these points, see Saucier, "Mr. Kerry Goes to Washington," 122. See also Roberts, "Lord Lothian and the Atlantic World," 119–120.

102. T 160/934, Lothian to Simon, 29 December 1938.

103. FO 371/21545, Waley to Phillips, 14 July 1938.

104. T 160/934, Simon to Hopkins, 12 January 1939.

105. FO 371/21545, BLI to FO, 2 August 1938.

106. There is an extensive literature on French strategy and diplomacy prior to the Second World War, which provides important context for any understanding of Paris's handling of the war debts issue. For an overview of the historiography, see P. Jackson, "Post-war Politics," 870–905.

107. Self, *War Debt Controversy*, 208, citing Bullitt to Roosevelt, 22 February and 4 April 1939, and reply, 16 May 1939, in Roosevelt and Bullitt, *For the President*, 315–317, 334–336, 353.

108. T 160/934, Lindsay to Halifax, 5 April 1939.

109. Whitham, "Sore Thumbs and Beachcombers," 468–469.

110. T 160/934, Lindsay to Halifax, 5 April 1939.

111. The quotes appear in National Archives, London, Colonial Office (CO), 323/1750/10, Note, 12/6/1940. The broader subject is covered in detail in Whitham, "Sore Thumbs and Beachcombers," 466–488. Senator McAdoo had visited the prime minister in autumn 1934 and "laid before him a proposal that England surrender her West Indian possessions to the United States in return for debt cancellation." MacDonald had explained "that any time a Ministry presented such a scheme to Parliament it would fall over night." *FRUS*, 1933, vol. 1, Atherton to Acting Secretary of State, 18 December 1933.

112. Whitham, "Sore Thumbs and Beachcombers," 473–477. The Bank of England also favored a transfer of West Indies possessions. See Osborne, "The American Debt"; and Osborne, "Some Incidental Arguments."

113. Conn and Fairchild, *The Framework of Hemisphere Defense*, 11; and Conn, Engelman, Fairchild, *The Western Hemisphere*, 354.

114. Whitham, "Sore Thumbs and Beachcombers," 474, citing FO 371/22803 A4026/85/45, Perowne to Bewley, 16 June 1939.

115. T 160/934, Lindsay to Halifax, 5 April 1939.

116. *Congressional Record*, Senate, 25 April 1939, 4717–4718, referencing *Saturday Evening Post*, 22 April 1939.

117. *Congressional Record*, House, 25 April 1939, 4755.

118. Ibid., 4759.

119. T 160/884/16, Lothian to Simon, 19 June 1939.

120. T 160/884/16, W.S. note, 30 June 1939.

121. Ibid.

122. Ibid.

123. *Congressional Record*, House, 29 June 1939, 8308, 8328.

124. Ibid., 8318.

125. *Congressional Record*, Senate, 19 June 1939, 7445, 7454, 7455.

126. Ibid., 7448.

127. Whitham, "Sore Thumbs and Beachcombers," 475–476, citing FO 371/22831 A10742/9805/49, Lindsay to Halifax, telegram 319, 17 July 1939.

128. Ibid., 478, citing CO 323/1750/10, Chamberlain's letter, 28 January 1940.

129. Ibid., 479.

130. FO 371/24245 A957/290/45, "War Debts: Survey of American Press and Radio, November 1939–8 January 1940"; FO 371/24245 A958/290/45, "Lord Beaverbrook on War Debts," 7 January 1940: Survey of American Press and Radio."

131. L. Young, "Franklin D. Roosevelt and America's Islets," 211; and Whitham, "Sore Thumbs and Beachcombers," 482.

132. Whitham, "Sore Thumbs and Beachcombers," 475–476. See also Baptiste, "The British Grant of Air and Naval Facilities to the United States," 5–43.

133. Shay, *British Rearmament in the Thirties*, 274; see also 279–280.

134. CAB 24/287, Note for the cabinet on the financial situation, July 1939.

135. Daunton, *Just Taxes*, 173.

136. Peden, "A Matter of Timing," 27.

137. See, for example, Cole and T. Kehoe, "Self-Fulfilling Debt Crises," 91–116; and Tomz and Wright, "Sovereign Theft," 69–110.

138. Olson, *Those Angry Days*, 65.

139. Ibid., xvii.

140. Jacob, "Influences of World Events on U.S. 'Neutrality' Opinion," 62, citing data from Gallup, 18 January 1937, 19 April 1939, and 11 September 1939.

141. Ibid.

142. For a broader account of Lothian and relations between the United Kingdom and United States, albeit one that does not focus on the importance of war debts, see Reynolds, "Lord Lothian and Anglo-American Relations," 1–65.

143. T 160/934, Note to Lothian, 4 September 1939.

144. Self, *War Debt Controversy*, 209.

145. Kimball, "Lend-Lease and the Open Door," 232–259.

146. J. Baker, *The Official History of New Zealand in the Second World War*, 570, 573.

147. DeWitt, "Johnson and American Foreign Policy," 290, 304.

148. Divine, *Roosevelt and World War II*, 5–48.

149. Kimball, "Beggar My Neighbor," 759.

150. Blum, *The Morgenthau Diaries*, vol. 2, 100.

151. *Congressional Record*, Senate, 14 October 1939, 429.

152. Ibid., 8318, referencing the *Washington Times-Herald*, 11 June 1939.

153. *Congressional Record*, Senate, 14 October 1939, 432. Reynolds was also angered by news that earlier in June, the United Kingdom had extended substantial new credits to Turkey, after it joined the Anglo-French security front. The sum of $46,862,500 was mentioned, which followed an earlier loan of $74,980,000 in April 1938.

154. Ibid., 430; see also 432.

155. *Congressional Record*, House, 1 November 1939, 1215, 1233, 1236. See also comments from Representative Landis (ibid., 1226).

156. Ibid., 1246, 1248.

157. Ibid., 1275, 1276.

158. Ibid., 1166–1167.

159. T 160/838, Philips to Perowne, 9 December 1939, and attachment detailing UK debt between 1933 and 1939.

160. Even this "minimal rewrite" counterfactual raises complex questions about the relative importance of war debts to transatlantic relations and the value of comparative analysis in this instance. On the use of indirect evidence and the need to recognize complexity, see Bunzl, "Counterfactual History," 845–858; and Tetlock and Belkin, "Counterfactual Thought Experiments in World Politics," 1–38.

161. T 160/838, Lothian to Halifax, 28 December 1939.

162. T 160/838, Lothian to Halifax, 28 December 1939.

163. *Congressional Record*, Senate, 14 June 1940, 8228.

164. FDRL, Official File 212, Foreign Debts 1935–1938, Note, Secretary of State, 29 December 1939; and Roosevelt to Garner, 16 [ca. January] 1940; Blum, *The Morgenthau Diaries*, vol. 2, 129–132.

165. Leuchtenburg, *Roosevelt and the New Deal*, 296–297; and Dallek, *Roosevelt and American Foreign Policy*, 209–210. "[Ba]ttle scarred" Finland would neverthe-less resume payments with "unfailing regularity" in June 1943: "Finland Resumes World War Debt Payments to U.S.," *Chicago Daily Tribune*, 16 June 1943, 1. The logic for repayment appears to reflect what Erkki Liikanen, governor of the Bank of Finland, describes as "a conscious means to improve Finland's financial reputa-tion" following problematic debt repayments to France in the 1920s: "The country that paid its debt, became an early member of the IMF, and joined the EU." Speech at the 15th Maple Leaf and Eagle Conference, University of Helsinki, 13 May 2014.

166. For such arguments, see Dallek, *Roosevelt and American Foreign Policy*, 74; and Pratt, *A History of the United States Foreign Policy*, 325.

167. Keynes note, 2 November 1939, in Keynes, *The Collected Writings*, vol. 22, 26.

168. Kimball, "Lend-Lease and the Open Door," 240.

169. The quote occurred around April 1936. See Blum, *The Morgenthau Diaries*, vol. 1, 141.

170. Kimball, "Lend-Lease and the Open Door," 239–240.

171. Ibid.

172. FO 371/24245, Note, 29 January 1940, "War Debts, Survey of American Press and Radio, Nov. 1939–8 Jan. 1940."

173. Ibid.

174. Ibid.

175. Olson, *Those Angry Days*, 330, 333.

176. FO 371/24245, citing *Daily Express*, 6 January 1940.

177. FO 371/24245, Note from BLI, 12 January 1940.

178. FO 371/24245, Cover note, 2 February 1940, "Survey of United States Press and Radio Re-action."

179. FO 371/24245, Halifax to Beaverbrook, 16 December 1939.

180. T 160/934, Note, 7 January 1940.

181. FO 371/24245, Chancery to BLI, 10 January 1940.

182. FO 371/24245, Darvall to Cowell, 22 January 1940.

183. FO 371/24245, FO to Holmes, 21 February 1940.

184. FO 371/24245, Treasury to Balfour, 4 April 1940.

185. FO 371/24245, Note to Newton, 4 April 1940.

186. FO 371/24245, Halifax note, 26 July 1940.

187. Kimball, "Beggar My Neighbor," 758.

188. *Congressional Record*, Senate, 4 March 1940, 2286; *Congressional Record*, House, 4 March 1940, 2332; *Congressional Record*, House, 28 May 1940, 7049; *Congressional Record*, House, 28 May 1940, 7016; *Congressional Record*, House, 14 June 1940, 8295.

189. *Congressional Record*, Senate, 14 June 1940, 8228.

190. Zahniser, "Rethinking the Significance of Disaster," 253. See also J. Jackson, *The Fall of France*, 236–238.

191. Ibid., 255. Zahniser suggests that Reynaud, the minister of finance, approached Bullitt on 22 February 1939 with an offer of $10 billion in gold and certain islands as an initial payment on the war debt. See Roosevelt and Bullitt, *For the President*, 315–317.

192. Self, *War Debt Controversy*, 209.

193. The dollar drain would have been even larger without assistance from Canada. On these points, see T 247/52, "American Programme of Financial Assistance, 1940–1941."

194. Self, *War Debt Controversy*, 209. See also Sayers, *Financial Policy*, 367; and Reynolds, *The Creation of the Anglo-American Alliance*, 146–147.

195. Dobson, "The Export White Paper," 62–63.

196. Self, *War Debt Controversy*, 209.

197. FO 371/24245, Note, "British War Debts to the United States," 2 August 1940.

198. See documents within T 247/52, American programme of financial assistance, 1940–1941.

199. Britain obtained fifty destroyers in exchange for allowing the establishment of U.S. naval and air bases on ninety-nine-year rent-free leases in the Bahamas, Antigua, St. Lucia, Trinidad, Jamaica, and British Guiana. See Whitham, "Sore Thumbs and Beachcombers," 479–480.

200. CO 323/1750/10, BLI report, survey of press and radio, 1940.

201. FO 371/24245, Note, "British War Debts to the United States."

202. Ibid.

203. Ibid.

204. On these preparations, see T 247/52, especially Keynes, "Notes for USA," 27 October 1940; Keynes "Supplementary Note," 1 November 1940; and Catto, "Draft on Direct British Investments in USA," ca. November 1940.

205. FO 371/24245, Note, 7 December 1940.

206. FO 371/26209, Butler to Hull, 15 December 1940.

207. On Churchill's "high hopes," in contrast to Chamberlain's "cynicism about the U.S.A.," see Reynolds, *The Creation of the Anglo-American Alliance*, 98.

208. NAII, RG 59, Box 4968, 841.5151/1579–1899, Johnson, London Embassy to Secretary of State, 8 November 1940.

209. Quoted in Wheeler-Bennett, *King George VI*, 521.

210. Reynolds, "Lord Lothian and Anglo-American Relations," 48–53.

211. Saucier, "Mr. Kerry Goes to Washington," 374, citing K. Davis, *FDR: The War President*, 46–48; Langer and Gleason, *The Challenge to Isolation*, 521–522; Langer and Gleason, *The Undeclared War*, 216–217. See also Hull, *Memoirs*, 872.

212. Blum, *The Morgenthau Diaries*, vol. 2, 199.

213. Saucier, "Mr. Kerry Goes to Washington," 374, citing, K. Davis, *FDR: The War President*, 48; Langer and Gleason, *The Undeclared War*, 217.

214. Roosevelt remained unsure about the severity of Britain's financial situation, and the extent to which Lothian's comments were surprising to the administration remains debatable. As Hull would note, "the ambassador had stated nothing we did not know already." Nevertheless, Lothian's remarks seemingly encouraged the Roosevelt administration to act. See Saucier, "Mr. Kerry Goes to Washington," 375–376; and Kimball, "Beggar My Neighbor," 771–772.

215. Saucier, "Mr. Kerry Goes to Washington," 377.

216. Woods, *A Changing of the Guard*, 200.

217. FO 371/24245, Lothian to Washington, "British War Debts to the United States," 6 December 1940.

218. T 160/934, Note to Hopkins, 12 December 1940.

219. Steil, *The Battle of Bretton Woods*, 97–98, citing Keynes, entry for 27 October 1940, in *The Collected Writings*, vol. 13, 13–26.

220. Saucier, "Mr. Kerry Goes to Washington," 377–378, citing Reynolds, *The Creation of the Anglo-American Alliance*, 150–151; and Reynolds, "Lord Lothian and Anglo-American Relations," 44.

221. Churchill, *The Second World War*, 500–501.

222. Dallek, *Roosevelt and American Foreign Policy*, 255.

223. Roosevelt's remaining chief advisers—Stimson, Hull, and Knox—eventually came to favor these proposals. Saucier, "Mr. Kerry Goes to Washington," 400, citing Blum, *The Morgenthau Diaries*, vol. 2, 208–209; K. Davis, *FDR: The War President*, 73–74; Kimball, *The Most Unsordid Act*, 120–121; and Langer and Gleason, *The Undeclared War*, 238.

224. Hull also said, "we would have more control over process of war materials if we did not give British cash with which to bid against us for supplies in the open market." Both this quote and the one in the text appear in Hull, *Memoirs*, vol. 1, 873.

225. Blum, *The Morgenthau Diaries*, vol. 2, 208–209.

226. On the Lend-Lease speech, given on 11 March 1941, see FDRL, "Our Documents: Lend Lease," http://docs.fdrlibrary.marist.edu/odlendls.html.

227. Ibid.

228. Skidelsky, *Keynes*, 621.

229. Saucier, "Mr. Kerry Goes to Washington," 399–401, citing K. Davis, *FDR: War President*, 74–76; Langer and Gleason, *The Undeclared War*, 238–240; and Reynolds, *From Munich to Pearl Harbor*, 105–106.

230. Self, *War Debt Controversy*, 210, citing National Archives, London, Prime Minister's Office files (PREM) 3/486/1, Churchill to Roosevelt, 8 December 1940.

231. NAII, RG 59, Box 4968, 841.5151/1579–1899, Johnson, London Embassy to Secretary of State, 19 December 1940.

232. Ibid.

233. Kimball, "Lend-Lease and the Open Door."

234. Some U.S. historians were sympathetic to Britain's position and stressed the impracticality of attempting to collect war debts at that time: Frasure, *British Policy in the War* Debts. Yet such a stance remained contentious. In 1941, Clarence P. Gould reviewed Frasure's *British Policy in the War Debts* in the *Mississippi Valley Historical Review*. Gould said that the author took for granted that payment of debts and reparations would have been economically impossible: "This assumption needs reconsideration in view of recent military expenditures completely drawing the sum involved in the debts" (133).

235. Olson, *Those Angry Days*, 279, 283–284.

236. *Congressional Record*, House, 5 February 1941, 580.

237. Ibid., 639–640.

238. Ibid., 598.

239. Ibid., 622.

240. Ibid.

241. FO 371/26209, Williams note, 9 January 1941.

242. *Congressional Record*, House, 5 February 1941, 621–622; *Congressional Record*, Senate, 21 October 1939, 685–687.

243. FO 371 26209, Williams note, 9 January 1941.

244. FDRL, Official Files 48, England–Folder 1940–1941, Hearn to President, February 1941, and Early to Herne, 12 February 1941.

245. Olson, *Those Angry Days*, 285.

246. Steil, *The Battle of Bretton Woods*, 105.

247. Ibid., 105–106.

248. Burk, "American Foreign Economic Policy and Lend-Lease," 64. See also Sayers, *Financial Policy*, 408; and Ovendale, *Anglo-American Relations*, 43; and Self, *War Debt Controversy*, 210.

249. Steil, *The Battle of Bretton Woods*, 108.

250. Allen, "Mutual Aid between the U.S. and the British Empire," 276.

251. NAII, RG 59, Box 4967, 841.51/8-742–841.5151/1578A, Heatherington, Sterling Balances and Britain's External Debt, 15 November 1944. See also Kimball, *The Most Unsordid Act*, 6.

252. P. Clarke, *The Last Thousand Days of the British Empire*, x.

253. Kimball, "Lend-Lease and the Open Door," 234.

254. Acheson, *Present at the Creation*, 28.

255. HSTL, Oral History Interview with John M. Leddy, 15 June 1973, 29–31. See also HSTL, Oral History Interview with Hubert F. Havlik, 20 June 1973.

256. NAII, RG 59, Box 4967, 841.51/8-742–841.5151/1578A, Heatherington, Sterling Balances and Britain's External Debt.

257. This description is often but erroneously attributed to the Marshall Plan. On this clarification, see Geneva Overholser, "The Churchill (Mis)Quote," *Washington Post*, 8 June 1997. The seminal account remains Kimball, *The Most Unsordid Act*.

258. Churchill and Roosevelt, *Churchill and Roosevelt*, vol. 1, 139, referencing an unsent message from Churchill to Roosevelt, 1 March 1941.

259. Steil, *The Battle of Bretton Woods*, 105.

260. Olson, *Those Angry Days*, 279, 283–284.

261. Kimball, "Beggar My Neighbor," 769.

262. T 247/53, Keynes note, 6 March 1941.

263. Kimball, "Beggar My Neighbor," 771.

264. The United Kingdom only drew $390 million. University of Kentucky Library, Special Collections Research Center, Frederick Vinson Papers (FVP), Box 149, White to Brooks, 31 January 1946; Kimball, "Beggar My Neighbor," 767. Keynes had originally sought a $900 million loan but only managed to secure funding worth $425 million following months of delays. See T 247/53, Keynes to Cohen, 19 March 1941; Note by Keynes, 22 March 1941; Keynes to Morgenthau, 28 July 1941; and Morgenthau to Keynes, 8 August 1941.

265. Kimball, "Beggar My Neighbor," 769–770.

266. FO 371/26209, Washington to FO, 28 June 1941.

267. FDRL, Official File 212, Foreign Debts 1939–1945, Hull to Morgenthau, 28 May 1941.

268. On 1941 as the end of war-debt data collection, see T 385/204, Binns to Morris, "World War I Debt: 'The Balance,'" 8 February 1974.

269. FDRL, Official File 212, Foreign Debts 1939–1945, Note, 2 January 1942.

270. On the scholarly debate surrounding U.S. entry into the Second World War, and specifically the increasingly contested claim of covert escalation, see Schuessler, "The Deception Dividend," 133–165; Reiter and Schuessler, "FDR, US Entry into World War II, and Selection Effects Theory," 176–185; Reiter, "Democracy, De-

ception, and Entry into War," 594–623; Trachtenberg, "Dan Reiter and America's Road to War in 1941"; and Darnton, "Archives and Inference," 84–126.

271. Kimball, "Lend-Lease and the Open Door," 255.

272. T 247/54, Walter Lippman to Keynes, 11 December 1941.

273. Kimball, *The Juggler*, 58–59.

274. Roosevelt to Churchill, 11 February 1942, in Churchill and Roosevelt, *Churchill and Roosevelt*, vol. 1, 358.

275. *Congressional Record*, House, 10 March 1942, 2190–2191.

276. The author of the report was later identified as Isaiah Berlin. Millar to Butler, 6 July 1942, enclosed paper by Berlin, in Berlin, *Isaiah Berlin*, vol. 1, 401.

277. T 172/1983, Catto to Chancellor, 29 July 1942.

278. T 247/72, Keynes to Grant, 5 October 1942, attachment "Summary of Report on Anti-British Feeling in the United States."

279. Kimball, "Lend-Lease and the Open Door," 241. Memories of old and new war debts informed negotiations and related concessions. As Keynes put it, "If we are prepared to agree to nothing . . . we stand the risk of losing the waiving of war debts." Keynes to Catto and Hopkins, 28 August 1941, in Keynes, *The Collected Writings*, vol. 23, 206.

280. Steil, *The Battle of Bretton Woods*, 97.

281. Ibid., 105–106.

282. Kimball, "Lend-Lease and the Open Door," 242–246, 258–259. See also Rothbard, *A History of Money and Banking in the United States*, 479–480; Steil, *The Battle of Bretton Woods*, 99–124; Woods, *A Changing of the Guard*, 30.

283. Steil, *The Battle of Bretton Woods*, 97–98, citing Keynes, entry for 27 October 1940, in *The Collected Writings*, vol. 13, 13–26.

284. Kimball, "Lend-Lease and the Open Door," 248–250.

CHAPTER 5. NEW LOANS AND OLD DEBTS, 1943–1951

1. Robert Self, who has produced one of the most impressive and detailed studies of these unpaid war debts to date, concludes that the controversy was "effectively laid to rest" in May 1940 when the prime minister issued an appeal for U.S. aid and was no longer at risk of a "flare up" after the U.S. entered the war (*War Debt Controversy*, 214, 203). See also Whitham, "Sore Thumbs and Beachcombers," 466. Some historians suggest that the issue of the war debts had come to "the end" or simply "died" soon after 1934. See, for example, editorial note by Elizabeth Johnson, in Keynes, *The Collected Writings*, vol. 18, 390; and McKercher, "Our Most Dangerous Enemy," 768.

2. The extant literature suggests that states that repaid their debts in the 1930s did not always benefit from lower interest rates in the early post–Second World War period relative to those that defaulted. See, for example, Eichengreen and Portes, "Debt and Default in the 1930s," 599–640; and Lindert and Morton, "How Sovereign Debt Has Worked," 39–106. For an important account of the consequences of default on these war debts, which finds that the "economic landscape after a *final* debt reduction is characterized by higher income levels and

growth, lower debt servicing burdens and lower government debt," see Reinhart and Trebesch, "A Distant Mirror of Debt, Default, and Relief," 49–51.

3. Author's interviews and exchanges with representatives of the U.S. and British Treasuries in 2017 and 2018. Official histories also appear to share this assumption. A report on the war debts produced by the British government more than twenty years later suggests that the matter was "never reopened" following the outbreak of war, when "both the United Kingdom and United States were faced with more pressing problems" (T 312/2626, Anson to Wyatt, "First World War Debt to United States of America," 19 August 1960). Some policymakers have suggested that the history of the war debts actually ended in 1934 with "mutual ill will between the United States and her debtors" (Stimson and Bundy, *On Active Service in Peace and War*, 218).

4. See data presented in Statistical Appendices to the U.S. Treasury Department, *Annual Report* (1944–1947).

5. Ritschl, "Sustainability of High Public Debt," 179, 183. On the British government's postwar efforts to achieve sovereign debt sustainability, including the use of financial repression and partial defaults, see Hileman, "Sovereign Debt Sustainability, Financial Repression, and Monetary Innovation."

6. As David Edgerton explains, "Britain . . . was not, as it routinely alleged, bankrupt, but merely under temporary financial pressure because of the sudden end of the war in the Far East and American decisions on Lend-Lease: Britain remained easily Europe's largest economy and, second only to the United States, a massive global trading presence" (*Britain's War Machine*, 5). On the acute problem of financing purchases from the United States even from the early stages of the war, see Reynolds, *The Creation of the Anglo-American Alliance*, 146.

7. G. Herring, "The United States and British Bankruptcy," 260, 280; Alexander Cadogan, quoted in Toye, "Churchill and Britain's 'Financial Dunkirk,'" 329–360; Dobson, *The Politics of the Anglo-American Economic Special Relationship*, 78.

8. Keynes, "The Last Months of Lend Lease," in *The Collected Writings*, vol. 24, 410. Chancellor of the Exchequer Hugh Dalton also used the same phrase (*High Tide and After*, 73). Such statements benefit from wider economic context. As Edgerton explains, "It was, however, only a financial and not a commercial or industrial Dunkirk" (*Britain's War Machine*, 297).

9. Acheson, *Present at the Creation*, 28. See also G. Herring, "The United States and British Bankruptcy," 277; and Behrman, *The Most Noble Adventure*, 50.

10. As Francis Beckett put it, "The stark truth was that Britain must have a loan, and there was only one place it could come from: the USA" (*Clem Attlee*, 222). Few other viable sources of credit existed. European financial markets had been devastated during the war, and the United Kingdom had already accumulated immense sterling debts to other countries. On the rationale for seeking U.S. aid, and the need for dollars, see CAB 66/65/51, Memorandum prepared by Keynes, "Overseas Financial Policy in Stage III," 3 April 1945.

11. Ikenberry, "Rethinking the Origins of American Hegemony," 384. Viewing the United States as a more coercive hegemon, structuring the system to strengthen its own international economic position, contrasts with scholarship claiming that it instead prioritized the creation and enforcement of the essential rules of the system.

Scholars have also advanced similar arguments that the stability of the pre–First World War international political economy rested on the leadership of the United Kingdom. See, for instance, Gilpin, *War and Change in World Politics*; and Kindleberger, *The World in Depression*.

12. Burnham, "Re-evaluating the Washington Loan Agreement," 241–259.

13. It is important to recognize the lengthy persistence of imperial preference thereafter. Nor did the agreement end the sterling area. See Schenk, *Britain and the Sterling Area*.

14. On the persuasive interpretation that convertibility was a "heavy condition" that was "destined to force the United Kingdom into a speedy bankruptcy" if enacted, see H. James, *Europe Contested*. Some scholars suggest a clear connection between U.S. demands for convertibility and the crisis of 1947. See, for instance, Gannon, "The Special Relationship and the 1945 Anglo-American Loan," 1, 14. Others argue that the obligation to make sterling convertible was not strictly speaking a cause of the economic crisis. See, for instance, Gardner, *Sterling-Dollar Diplomacy*, 313–318.

15. P. Clarke, *The Last Thousand Days of the British Empire*, part 4.

16. Gardner, *Sterling-Dollar Diplomacy*, 208, 224. For more on the history of the IMF, see H. James, *International Monetary Cooperation since Bretton Woods*. On why it would prove far easier to create multilateral institutions in international monetary relations rather than trade, see Daunton, "From Bretton Woods to Havana," 47–78.

17. As files from subsequent administrations reveal, the Johnson Act never applied "to loans to foreign governments which are members both of the International Bank for Reconstruction and Development and the International Monetary Fund." White House, 13 April 1954, U.S. Declassified Documents Online, accessed 19 April 2017, Annex C, NSC 5808/1. Many scholars and government documents erroneously state that the U.S. repealed the Johnson Act when it initiated Lend-Lease. On this point, see T 381/77, Allan to Crawford, 11 May 1977, Annex A, "History of WW1 Debt, 1931–1977." Contrary to such accounts, the act still existed, albeit in a limited form. According to the NSA, "By the 1970s, the Johnson Act had been so interpreted and amended that it only applied to certain Communist countries." Gerald R. Ford Presidential Library, U.S. Policy toward East-West Economic Relations, 19 January 1977, attachment, National Security Memorandum, 18 October 1976, 66–67.

18. There exists an expansive literature concerning the motivations for transatlantic economic cooperation. Some historians do recognize a desire to avoid the mistakes of the interwar period but spare only a few words on this subject and rarely specify war debts. See, for instance, Gardner, *Sterling-Dollar Diplomacy*, 1, 4, 54–56, 84; G. Herring, *Aid to Russia*, 150, 156, 162; Eckes, *A Search for Solvency*, 181, 206; and Steil, *The Battle of Bretton Woods*, 97, 107, 180. More broadly, see Louis, *Imperialism at Bay*; R. Clarke, *Anglo-American Economic Collaboration in War and Peace*; Cohen, "The Revolution in Atlantic Economic Relations," 106–133.

19. Some scholars have noted this point. See, for example, Woods, *A Changing of the Guard*, 156, 220, 236, 265; and Dobson, *U.S. Wartime Aid to Britain*, 5, 17, 24.

20. FO 371/52957, Judson to Balfour, "Notes on the Loan," 23 May 1946.

21. For a variety of sources that support this claim, see, for instance, FO 371/52957, Judson Minute, "World War I Debts and the Loan Debate," 25 June 1946; "Loan Debate Opens in Congress," *Financial Times*, 9 July 1946; and *Congressional Record*, House, 11 July 1946, 8697, 8701–8703, 8706, 8715, 8723. On the case for including war loans as a cost to the American people, see Rockoff, *America's Economic Way of War*, 144–145.

22. Postwar economic challenges included the unprecedented size of national debt, inflation, labor strikes, reconversion, price controls, and housing shortages. On these points, see Gardner, *Sterling-Dollar Diplomacy*, 193–194; and Paterson, "Presidential Foreign-Policy, Public-Opinion, and Congress," 5–6.

23. Truman said to King George VI in 1945, "You've had a revolution." The king said, "Oh no! we don't have those here" (Dalton, *The Political Diary*, 361).

24. Woods, *A Changing of the Guard*, 301.

25. See, for instance, Gardner, *Sterling-Dollar Diplomacy*, 193–194, 202, 236–239; Grant, "Truman and the British Loan Act of 1946," 492; Toye, "Churchill and Britain's 'Financial Dunkirk,'" 351; Woods, *A Changing of the Guard*, 301; and Gannon, "The Special Relationship and the 1945 Anglo-American Loan," 14. Scholars such as Thomas Paterson have suggested that Truman was less constrained by Congress on foreign policy issues than widely assumed, due in part to the ignorance or indifference of public opinion. He concedes that most Americans followed the discussion on the Anglo-American loan, however, and that political debate did follow on this specific issue (Paterson, "Presidential Foreign-Policy, Public-Opinion, and Congress," 5–6, 10, 17).

26. See, for example, Palen, *The "Conspiracy" of Free Trade*; and Dobson, *The Politics of the Anglo-American Economic Special Relationship*.

27. On claims of timidity, see G. Herring, "The United States and British Bankruptcy," 260, 280.

28. The British government waived its interest payments on the loan six times—in 1956, 1957, 1964, 1965, 1968, and 1976—claiming that international exchange-rate conditions and foreign currency reserves made payment impractical. The U.S. did not treat these deferments as defaults, as the loan was renegotiated in 1956–1957 to allow for the UK to suspend payments of principal and interest in any year up to seven times during the remaining life of the loan. This modification was mutually agreed and approved by Congress. The British government would consider this option annually. Writing in 1993, for example, HM Treasury officials explained, "Towards the end of each calendar year we have to consider whether we exercise the option, or bisque, to defer scheduled annual principal and interest payments for the current years on the long-term North American debt." T 509/17, Crane to White, McIntyre, 8 December 1993; Bennett to Bobb, Crane, 28 September 1993; Northern (Barson) to Crane, 18 October 1993. See also Hileman, "Sovereign Debt Sustainability, Financial Repression, and Monetary Innovation"; Hileman, "Overlooked Sovereign Credit Events and Partial Defaults"; and Philip Thornton, "Britain Pays Off Final Instalment of US Loan—after 61 Years," *The Independent*, 29 December 2006.

29. In 1946, France requested a major loan from the United States to support a modernization plan and to fund a large dollar deficit. The Truman administration passed the request to the Export-Import Bank, which granted some of the required aid. Instead of the requested $3.5 billion, however, France received only $650 million. On this decision, see Casey, *Saving International Capitalism during the Early Truman Presidency*, 112–116, 121–123; and Hill, "American Efforts to Aid French Reconstruction between Lend-Lease and the Marshall Plan," 522, citing *FRUS*, 1946, Ambassador in France to Secretary of State, 15 January 1946, and Secretary of State to Caffery, 4 February 1946, 399–400, 409–411. In the same year, the Italian government also requested a loan, seeking $940 million from the Export-Import Bank to purchase essential reconstruction materials. The Export-Import Bank went on to consider credits to Italy not exceeding $100 million. On the case for these credits, see *FRUS*, 1946, The British Commonwealth, Western and Central Europe, vol. 5, Memorandum by the Staff Committee to the National Advisory Council, 15 November 1946.

30. Statement by Keynes at press conference, 12 September 1945, in Keynes, *The Collected Writings*, vol. 24, 464.

31. FVP, Box 148, Vinson to Keynes, 19 November 1945.

32. Such rough diplomacy complements persuasive claims that Bretton Woods was fundamentally a victory for the U.S. "dressed up as benign multilateralism" (H. James, "The Multiple Contexts of Bretton Woods," 411–430). On the claim that the United Kingdom was vital to U.S. postwar international monetary and trading order, see Fforde, *The Bank of England and Public Policy*, 87; and Kindleberger, *A Financial History of Western Europe*, 419.

33. FO 371/52957, Note on Loan, 23 May 1946; and Note on World War I Debt and the Loan Debate, 25 June 1946.

34. Both governments held many opposing views concerning the future of the international economic order, but war debts did not appear to play a significant or direct role in negotiations. The IMF archives, for example, provide no relevant data on this subject. On these tensions, see Daunton, "Britain and Globalisation since 1850," 1–42; and Steil, *The Battle of Bretton Woods*.

35. Thomas Zeiler's detailed study of trade negotiations makes only passing reference to this issue (*Free Trade, Free World*, 24). Policymakers and U.S. senators did occasionally raise the issue of unpaid war debts to criticize or support the European Recovery Program. See, for instance, *Congressional Record*, Senate, 25 March 1948, 3548–3549; *Congressional Record*, Senate, 13 July 1949, 9377–9378; HSTL, Oral History Interview with John W. Snyder, 20 February 1969, 1146–1148; and HSTL, Oral History Interview with J. Burke Knapp, 24 and 30 July 1975, 90.

36. Quantitative research using longer time-series analyses reveals that economists have underestimated the cost of default (Catão and Mano, "Default Premium," 91–110). On markets retaining a long memory of default, see Flandreau and Zumer, *The Making of Global Finance*, 57.

37. T 247/67, Keynes to Maynard, 15 April 1943, attachment "Forthcoming Conversations with the United States on Economic Questions," 13 April 1942.

38. "FDR Says 'No War Debts': Lend-Lease Defined," *Daily Mail*, 8 September 1943, 1.

39. *Hansard*, 12 April 1943, col. 938; NAII, RG 59, Box 4967, 841.51/8-742–841.5151/1578A, Heatherington, Sterling Balances and Britain's External Debt, 15 November 1944. On this budget in the context of those before and after, see NAII, RG 59, Box 4966, 5151.1579/1899–/1859, Winant to Secretary of State, 26 April 1944. On the economic effect of the wars more broadly, see Milward, *The Economic Effects of the Two World Wars on Britain*.

40. Hinds, "Sterling and Imperial Policy," 149. For a full list, see P.B., "The Sterling Balances," 358. Britain had also acquired a significant trade deficit during the war. Large amounts had been borrowed from the Empire and sterling area. At the end of the war, the United Kingdom's creditors would seek to claim their assets. On these points, see Killick, *The United States and European Reconstruction*, 32–34.

41. The major holders of this debt were India and Pakistan. During the 1940s and early 1950s, the United Kingdom reached a series of agreements with major holders of sterling that limited liquidity, but enforcement remained difficult and problematic. The long-term impact of the sterling "overhang" was therefore important because these debts remained a burden. See Schenk, *The Decline of Sterling*, 39, 67–68, 87–88; and Schenk, *Britain and the Sterling Area*, 20–25.

42. Edgerton, *Britain's War Machine*, 281.

43. Dobson, "The Export White Paper," 59. For broader economic context, see Middleton, "Struggling with the Impossible," 103–154.

44. NAII, RG 59, Box 4967, 841.51/8-742–841.5151/1578A, Fullerton to Wadleigh, Department of State, 10 June 1943.

45. As British exports fell, however, so too did those of its key competitors. This situation therefore posed a temporary difficulty, albeit one that would be exacerbated by the United States' sudden termination of Lend-Lease in 1945. On the argument that the United Kingdom's "stupendous relative decline in wartime was caused not by its decision to fight, but by that of the USA," see Edgerton, *Britain's War Machine*, 296–297. On the importance of contextualizing and defining decline, especially in the postwar period, see Tomlinson, "Inventing 'Decline,'" 731–757. See also Tomlinson, "The Decline of Empire and the Economic 'Decline' of Britain"; and Edgerton, "The Decline of Declinism," 201–206. On the case for absolute and relative decline, see Gamble, *Britain in Decline*.

46. *Hansard*, 12 April 1943, col. 938.

47. Ibid., col. 940. On reciprocal aid or "Reverse Lend-Lease," see D.P.E., "Lend-Lease and Reverse Lend-Lease Aid," 157–164.

48. *Hansard*, 14 April 1943, col. 1282; NAII, RG 59, Box 4966, 5151.1579/1899–/1859, 24, Gallman to Secretary of State, 15 May 1943, Attachment prepared by Egerton: "The Budget for 1934–44."

49. NAII, RG 59, Box 4966, 5151.1579/1899–/1859, Division of European Affairs, Memorandum, 16 June 1943.

50. Woods, *A Changing of the Guard*, 301.

51. By summer, the White House had decided that such a transition was politically impossible anyway. See ibid., 156–157, 301.

52. Keynes, "The Problem of Our External Finance in the Transition," quoted in Steil, *The Battle for Bretton Woods*, 190–191.

53. T 247/67, "Note to Keynes," 31 December 1943, attachment "Report on America."

54. Henry Morgenthau and Lord Cherwell discussed the necessary parameters of cooperation. For clarity, Roosevelt had refused to commit himself to the cancellation of Lend-Lease debts, especially in the wake of what he believed to be British assertions of imperial self-interest in Europe. See Steil, *The Battle of Bretton Woods*, 277–279.

55. Wilder Foote to Stettinius, 2 August 1944, Stettinius Papers, quoted in G. Herring, "The United States and British Bankruptcy," 264–265; NAII, RG 59, Box 4967, 841.51/8/742–841.5151/1578A, Fetter to Collado, Financial Policy to the U.K. at the Close of the Pacific War, 16 December 1944.

56. FDRL, PSF, Subject File, Box 175, Memorandum for the President, Handling and Financing of European Reconstruction Operations, 21 February 1944; NAII, RG59, Box 4967, 841.51/8-742–841.5151/1578A, Fetter to Collado, Financial Policy to the U.K. at the Close of the Pacific War, 16 December 1944. Dean Acheson had proposed to open the way to a new program of foreign loans via the repeal of the Johnson Act. "Shorter Notes," 775.

57. "Cancel 1918 War Debts," *Evening Telegraph*, 25 May 1945, 3.

58. For more on these points, see G. Herring, "The United States and British Bankruptcy," 271–272. Herring has discussed the 1945 hearings and debates on Lend-Lease at greater length in "Lend-Lease to Russia and the Origins of the Cold War," 93–114.

59. *Congressional Record*, House, 6 March 1945, 1824.

60. This account of the war-debts saga prompted Woodruff to raise what would become a familiar question in Congress over the following year: "Are we justified in believing our experience in this war will be greatly different, except in increased degree, than it was during and following the other one?" *Congressional Record*, House, 13 March 1945, 2141–2142.

61. See, for instance, Gardner, *Sterling-Dollar Diplomacy*, 193–194, 202, 236–239; Grant, "Truman and the British Loan Act of 1946," 492; Woods, *A Changing of the Guard*, 301; Gannon, "The Special Relationship and the 1945 Anglo-American Loan," 14; and Paterson, "Presidential Foreign-Policy, Public-Opinion, and Congress," 5–6, 10, 17.

62. Quote appears in G. Herring, "The United States and British Bankruptcy," 273–274. See also FDRL, Harold Smith Papers, Record of conference, Truman and Harold Smith, 26 April 1945; and Truman, *Memoirs*, vol. 1, 46, 97–98.

63. McCullough, *Truman*, 152, 325.

64. G. Herring, "The United States and British Bankruptcy," 272–273.

65. See, for instance, Dobson, *U.S. Wartime Aid to Britain*; and Hathaway, *Ambiguous Partnership*.

66. G. Herring, "The United States and British Bankruptcy," 274. The Churchill cable is quoted in Truman, *Memoirs*, vol. 1, 230–231. For earlier British inquiries regarding the status of the Phase II program, see Steil, *The Battle of Bretton Woods*, 280.

67. Truman, *Memoirs*, vol. 1, 231.

68. McCullough, *Truman*, 425.

69. Hennessy, *The Prime Minister*, 147–177.

70. Gardner, *Sterling-Dollar Diplomacy*, 238. The Labour government was well aware of such hostility and actively sought to manage such challenges (Anstey, "The Projection of British Socialism," 417–451).

71. Steil, *The Battle of Bretton Woods*, 291–292.

72. Mallaleiu, *British Reconstruction and American Policy*, 22.

73. J. Walker, *Prompt and Utter Destruction*, 77–91. On the use of nuclear weapons on Hiroshima and Nagasaki unfairly obscuring the importance of the Soviet intervention in the war with Japan, see W. Wilson, "The Winning Weapon?," 162–167.

74. G. Herring, "The United States and British Bankruptcy," 276.

75. Behrman, *The Most Noble Adventure*, 50.

76. Truman, *Memoirs*, vol. 1, 475–476.

77. Acheson, *Present at the Creation*, 122.

78. Such views are largely accepted within the historiography. On the unpersuasive claim that Truman's decision was a calculated act of pressure to bankrupt Britain, however, see Kolko, *The Politics of War*. For a strong rebuttal, see G. Herring, "The United States and British Bankruptcy," 279–280.

79. G. Herring, "The United States and British Bankruptcy," 277, esp. 279n57.

80. FO 115/4225, Balfour to Foreign Office, 21 August 1945, 48; T 236/437, Record of meeting, 23 August 1945.

81. Bew, *Citizen Clem*, 366.

82. The British had made intellectual contributions to the architecture of the fund and the bank, to be sure, but they would concede many of the substantive debates. On these points, see Steil, *The Battle of Bretton Woods*, 221, 228–229, 244. As Skidelsky explains, Keynes "gave the Bretton Woods Agreement its distinction not its substance" (quoted ibid., 246). As Steil puts it, "the final lawyer-laden text held only scattered traces of his thinking, and fewer of his prose" (246). The Bretton Woods agreements were also more than just a product of Anglo-American negotiations concerning Western interests but also involved large discussions about international support for the economic development of southern countries. On this valuable insight, see Helleiner, *Forgotten Foundations of Bretton Woods*.

83. Despite popular calls for the complete repeal of the Johnson Act, only countries which would become members of the proposed international institutions would enjoy the benefit of its repeal, which at least one newspaper saw as "an added inducement in their participation." "Bretton Woods in Congress," *The Times*, 19 February 1945, 7.

84. Woods, *A Changing of the Guard*, 236.

85. *Congressional Record*, House, 6 June 1945, 5656.

86. Ibid., 5650.

87. *Congressional Record*, Senate, 17 July 1945, 7599.

88. Woods, *A Changing of the Guard*, 236 (see also 237–238); Steil, *The Battle of Bretton Woods*, 255–260.

89. HSTL, Official File, 1174, Lend-Lease 1945, Edwards to Truman, 31 August 1945.

90. NAII, RG 59, Box 4967, 841.51/8-742–841.5151/1578A, Fetter to Collado, Financial Policy to the U.K. at the Close of the Pacific War, 16 December 1944. Even if this limitation did not exist, the present unused lending power of the Export-Import Bank was so small that it could not make a substantial loan to the United Kingdom.

91. NAII, RG 59, Box 5938, 841.5055/1-145–841.51/3-3145, Fales to Secretary of State, 14 February 1945, Subject: "Does Britain desire American capital?"

92. Cairncross, *Years of Recovery*, 8; Cairncross, *The British Economy since 1945*, 45–86. See also Howson, *British Monetary Policy*; Tomlinson, *Employment Policy*; and Kynaston, *Austerity Britain*. More broadly, see Milward, *The Economic Effects of the Two World Wars*; and Crafts and Woodward, *The British Economy since 1945*.

93. On the rationale for seeking U.S. aid, see CAB 66/65/51, "Overseas Financial Policy in Stage III," 3 April 1945.

94. Ibid.

95. Dalton, *High Tide and After*, 73.

96. Ibid. See also Steil, *The Battle of Bretton Woods*, 292–294.

97. CAB 66/65/51, "Overseas Financial Policy in Stage III."

98. Woods, *A Changing of the Guard*, 260; Dormael, *Bretton Woods*, 275.

99. Fforde, *The Bank of England and Public Policy*, 87. The United Kingdom was in many ways vital to the U.S. postwar international monetary and trading order. Kindleberger, *A Financial History of Western Europe*, 419. On the interesting argument that this advantage developed into a weakness as Keynes desperately sought to protect his Bretton Woods legacy against the end-of-year deadline for agreement, see Steil, *The Battle of Bretton Woods*, 296–297, 304–305.

100. Steil, *The Battle of Bretton Woods*, 296–300; Gardner, *Sterling-Dollar Diplomacy*, 205, 211–213.

101. CAB 66/65/51, "Overseas Financial Policy in Stage III."

102. Ibid.

103. Both the United States and the United Kingdom would reduce these debts not via default or restructuring but by financial repression—namely, a tax on bondholders and savers via negative or below-market real interest rates aided by inflation. See Reinhart and Sbranci, "The Liquidation of Government Debt," esp. 6–7.

104. On the postwar economy, see Rockoff, *America's Economic Way of War*, 162–173, 215–219; Gordon, *The Rise and Fall of American Growth*, 535–565; Eichengreen, *Exorbitant Privilege*, 39; Phillips, "The Long Story of U.S. Debt"; and Higgs, "Wartime Prosperity?," 41–60.

105. Truman, *Memoirs*, vol. 1, 413–415. The Truman administration believed that an alleged deficit in the British balance of payment of $3.1 billion at the end of 1946 was closer to $2.3 billion. Both governments also had different figures for gold and dollar holdings.

106. See, for example, Gardner, *Sterling-Dollar Diplomacy*, 224; and Woods, *A Changing of the Guard*, 387.

107. This point is raised briefly in Gardner, *Sterling-Dollar Diplomacy*, 4: "Almost all the documentation regarding plans for the peace drafted by the range of competing agencies charged with developing America's post-war policies were infused by historical accounts of . . . *the challenges posed by interwar indebtedness as a whole*" (emphasis added). See Clavin, "Reparations in the Long Run," 515–530, esp. 518, 520.

108. "Truman Says, 'Wipe the Slate Clean': New Lend-Lease Will Bridge the Gap," *Daily Mail*, 31 August 1945.

109. HSTL, Official File, Box 942, 212 A, 1945–49, Truman to Stewart, 9 November 1945.

110. Ibid.

111. This arrangement is recounted in FVP, Box 148, Memo for the president, n.d. [ca. early September 1945]. See also Truman, *Memoirs*, vol. 1, 409–410.

112. Casey, *Saving International Capitalism during the Early Truman Presidency*, 73–74.

113. FVP, Box 148, Memo of meeting, 3 August 1945.

114. FVP, Box 148, Pritchard to Secretary, 22 August 1945.

115. FVP, Box 148, Embassy (Winant) to Washington, 17 August 1945.

116. FVP, Box 148, Folder SS/Loan, Paraphrase of Telegram, American embassy, London to Secretary of State Washington, 17 August 1945.

117. Clayton to Hoffman, 14 May 1943, cited in Wevill, *Britain and America after World War II*, loc. 1064.

118. FVP, Box 148, Memorandum for the President, n.d. [ca. early September 1945].

119. Record of a Meeting, 23 August 1945, in Keynes, *Collected Writings*, vol. 24, 420–424.

120. Ibid.

121. Ibid.

122. Gardner, *Sterling-Dollar Diplomacy*, 189–190.

123. F. Williams, *A Prime Minister Remembers*, 132.

124. Steil, *The Battle of Bretton Woods*, 294.

125. F. Williams, *A Prime Minister Remembers*, 132–133.

126. Bew, *Citizen Clem*, 372–373.

127. Truman, *Memoirs*, vol. 1, 413–415.

128. Ibid., 413.

129. For detailed accounts of the negotiations, see Wevill, *Britain and America after World War II*, loc. 958–1987; Bullen and Pelly, *Documents on British Policy Overseas*; and Pressnell, *External Economic Policy since the War*.

130. On these divisions, see *FRUS*, 1945, vol. 6, Memorandum on Financial and Trade Discussions, Acheson to Certain American Missions, 10 September 1945, 121.

131. *FRUS*, 1945, vol. 6, Minutes of Meeting of the US-UK Combined Top Committee, 11 September 1945, 123.

132. Statement by Lord Keynes at press conference, 12 September 1945, in Keynes, *The Collected Writings*, vol. 24, 464. For a transcript of Halifax's and Keynes's opening remarks at the press conference held on 13 September 1945, see FO 371/45700.

133. Gardner, *Sterling-Dollar Diplomacy*, 201–202. Historians and biographers made little mention of these issues. See, for instance, Fossedal, *Our Finest Hour*; and Skidelsky, *Keynes*.

134. See, for instance, *Congressional Record*, House, 18 December 1931, 803–804. On Clayton and the history of the war-debts issue, see, for instance, FVP, Box-folder 389-25, December 18, 1931, Congressional speech by Vinson in opposition to Hoover's foreign-debt moratorium, 72nd Congress, 1st session.

135. HSTL, William L. Clayton Papers, Clayton to Russell, 1 October 1945.

136. Gardner, *Sterling-Dollar Diplomacy*, 193–196, 201–205.

137. P. Clarke, *The Last Thousand Days of the British Empire*, 374. "The Dining Room Is Closed," *Chicago Tribune*, August 25, 1945; "Santa Claus Dies Hard," *Chicago Tribune*, August 23, 1945. The same paper was quick to note that Keynes, who was asking for a gift or loan, had also been "an advocate of British repudiation of World War I debt." "Britain Asking 3 to 6 Billion as U.S. Gift or Loan," *Chicago Daily Tribune*, 13 September 1945, 7.

138. Minutes of Top Committee Meeting, 17 September 1945, as reproduced in Keynes, *The Collected Writings*, vol. 24, 484; and FO 371/45700, Keynes to Dalton, 21 September 1945. The British did not initially indicate the definite amount they required, offering only a figure of $3–6 billion. See HSTL, Clayton Papers, Clayton to Baruch, 15 September 1945, and Clayton to Crow, 21 September 1945.

139. FO 371/45701, Halifax to Bevin, 27 September 1945.

140. FVP, Box 148, Clayton to Vinson, 27 November 1945.

141. As Clayton put it, "I can assure you that their chances of excluding American businessmen from world trade are extremely slim." HSTL, Clayton Papers, Clayton to Sholtz, 4 October 1945.

142. HSTL, Clayton Papers, Clayton to Wood, 17 November 1945.

143. HL Deb., 18 December 1945, vol. 138, cc785.

144. Borthwick Institute for Archives, University of York, Earl of Halifax Diary, 27 September 1945.

145. Gardner, *Sterling-Dollar Diplomacy*, 201–202.

146. On the issue of convertibility, O. J. McDiarmid, chief of the Monetary Affairs Staff, recalled, "There was a lot of impatience with the British. . . . It should have been obvious, but it wasn't obvious that it was going to be a long time before sterling would be convertible, and that the same applied to other European currencies." As McDiarmid conceded, "Instead of being a four billion dollar job, it turned out to be a 16 or 20 billion dollar job." See HSTL, Oral History Interview with O. J. McDiarmid by Richard D. McKinzie, 20 June 1974.

147. Of the estimated balance of $12 billion, $4 billion would be written off; of the remaining $8 billion, 10 percent, or $800 million, would be made freely convertible for any current purposes, and the remaining $7.2 billion would be funded at no interest, to be paid off in fifty annual installments of 2 percent beginning after five years. On these details, see FO 371/45716, Minutes, 20 September 1945. On the consequences, see Dobson, *The Politics of the Anglo-American Economic Special Relationship*, 84–85; Gardner, *Sterling-Dollar Diplomacy*, 202–205; and Hinds, "Sterling and Imperial Policy," 149. The size of these debts was also important. As Keynes noted, "The very size of these sterling debts is itself a protection.

The old saying holds. Owe your banker £1,000 and you are at his mercy; owe him £1,000,000 and the position is reversed" (CAB 66/65/51, "Overseas Financial Policy in Stage III").

148. On U.S. discussions concerning the need for a waiver, and its associated difficulties, see *FRUS*, 1945, The British Commonwealth, The Far East, vol. 6, "Minutes of a Meeting," 11 October 1945. See also Kunz, *The Economic Diplomacy of the Suez Crisis*, 8.

149. Gardner, *Sterling-Dollar Diplomacy*, 205; R. Clarke, *Anglo-American Economic Collaboration in War and Peace*, 2.

150. Halifax Diary, 25 September 1945; T 247/47, Keynes to Dalton, 1 October 1945. These meetings are covered in more detail in Wevill, *Britain and America after World War II*, loc. 1413–1421.

151. *FRUS*, 1945, vol. 6, Memorandum on Progress of US-UK Negotiations, Clayton to Truman, 24 September 1945, 134. See also Wevill, *Britain and America after World War II*, loc. 1371–1396.

152. Gardner, *Sterling-Dollar Diplomacy*, 201–202.

153. Terms of Assistance Memorandum prepared by Keynes and reproduced in Keynes, *The Collected Writings*, vol. 24, 504.

154. Steil, *The Battle of Bretton Woods*, 295; Halifax Diary, 5 February 1946; Wevill, *Britain and America after World War II*, loc. 1643.

155. Steil, *The Battle of Bretton Woods*, 294–295.

156. FO 371/45702, Dalton to Halifax, 8 October 1945; Wevill, *Britain and America after World War II*, loc. 1435–1450.

157. F. Beckett, *Clem Attlee*, 225.

158. FO 371/45703, Dalton to Halifax et al., 13 October 1945.

159. Keynes to Dalton, 18 October 1945, in Keynes, *The Collected Writings*, vol. 24, 549.

160. Ibid.

161. Halifax Diary, 17 October 1945; also, for example, HSTL, Clayton Papers, Senator Moore to Clayton, 12 October 1945.

162. Sixty percent disapproved, and 13 percent had no opinion. On this data, see FO 371/44538, "Supplementary to Weekly Political Summary," 12 October 1945.

163. FO 371/45704, Keynes to Dalton, 18 October 1945; Halifax Diary, 17 October 1945.

164. Steil, *The Battle of Bretton Woods*, 295–296; Wevill, *Britain and America after World War II*, loc. 1536–1546.

165. Catto does not appear to recognize that the war debts had by now grown to $6.4 billion. As such, his proposals were less generous than he assumed. On this message, see Fforde, *The Bank of England and Public Policy*, 80; see also BE G1/18, Governor's File, G1/262, Governor's File, and G18/3, Lord Catto's Papers, Catto to Keynes, 16 October 1945.

166. Keynes to Catto, 22 October 1945, in Keynes, *The Collected Writings*, vol. 24, 564–565.

167. See Fforde, *The Bank of England and Public Policy*, 32–34 and 73–87, for their role in the course of negotiations, citing, in part, BE CBP 376.02/1–9, USA.

168. Keynes to Catto, 22 October 1945, 565–566.

169. Ibid.

170. T 247/47, "American Loan, 1944–1946."

171. Steil, *The Battle of Bretton Woods*, 297.

172. Keynes to Catto, 22 October 1945, 566.

173. The cabinet advanced two proposals. Plan A was a loan totaling $2.5 billion repayable over fifty years at 1 percent with the option of a further $2 billion interest-free to facilitate convertibility on current transactions within the sterling area. Plan B proposed borrowing on commercial terms without commitments of any kind. The British government was only willing to ratify the Bretton Woods proposals if it secured the first option. These revised offers undermined earlier commitments and threatened what progress had already been made in negotiations. Halifax and Keynes rejected Plan B, which they believed would involve more onerous terms, and put off talking to the Americans about Plan A. This period of delay provided them with time to convince the cabinet to compromise, aided in large part by a return of two delegation members to London. See Pressnell, *External Economic Policy since the War*, 295; editorial note, in Keynes, *The Collected Writings*, vol. 24, 568–569; and Dalton, *High Tide and After*, 77–78.

174. FVP, Clayton to Vinson, 5 November 1945. The ambassador in the United Kingdom had earlier informed the secretary of state that the "serious" position of the talks focused largely on "US insistence on a loan on strictly commercial lines" and "the inadequate size of suggested loan and the burden of servicing it," concluding, "Whatever happened the UK were determined not to take loan commitments which they could not meet." The ambassador's note also highlights the existence of additional international tensions. The British government was "having 'a hell of a time' with" the Australian government, which had protested the British position in commercial policy negotiations. *FRUS*, 1945, vol. 6, Winant to Secretary of State, 3 November 1945.

175. T 236/466, Dalton to Halifax and Keynes, 6 November 1945.

176. FO 371/45708, Record of Meeting, 5 November 1945, quoted in Wevill, *Britain and America after World War II*, loc. 1567–1577.

177. Toye, *The Labour Party and the Planned Economy*; Dalton, *High Tide and After*, 85.

178. Dalton, *High Tide and After*, 73.

179. K. Harris, *Attlee*, 275; and Toye, *The Labour Party and the Planned Economy*, 85.

180. F. Williams, *A Prime Minister Remembers*, 134.

181. Woods, *A Changing of the Guard*, 337.

182. T 236/456, Brand to Eady, 30 October 1945, quoted in Wevill, *Britain and America after World War II*, loc. 1567–1577.

183. Keynes to Eady, 8 November 1945, in *The Collected Writings*, vol. 24, 588n25.

184. FO 371/45716, Minutes of a meeting of the Finance Committee, 15 November 1945.

185. Wevill, *Britain and America after World War II*, loc. 1590–1601; Skidelsky, *Keynes*, 434.

186. FVP, Box 148, Vinson to Keynes, 19 November 1945.

187. Keynes to Eady, 8 November 1945, in *The Collected Writings*, vol. 24, 588.

188. T 236/441, Record of a Meeting of ministers held on 23 November 1945.

189. Editorial note, in Keynes, *The Collected Writings*, vol. 24, 595–596.

190. Wevill, *Britain and America after World War II*, loc. 1651–1671, citing FO 371/45711, Dalton to Halifax, Keynes and Brand, 29 November 1945; British Mission to Cabinet Offices, 30 November 1945; and Attlee and Dalton to Halifax, 30 November 1945.

191. Dalton, *Political Diary*, 365.

192. Editorial note, in Keynes, *The Collected Writings*, vol. 24, 604. On U.S. suspicions that "Bridges may have been sent because of dissatisfaction re Halifax, Keynes, *et al*" and Vinson subsequently going "out of his way to build up the actions of and effective negotiations by the older group," see *FRUS*, 1945, vol. 6, 187, Secretary of State to the Ambassador in the United Kingdom (Winant), 3 December 1945.

193. For an overview of the specific provisions of the Anglo-American Financial Agreement, including waivers and sterling balances, see Rosenson, "The Terms of the Anglo-American Financial Agreement," 178–187.

194. Gardner, *Sterling-Dollar Diplomacy*, 202–205, 211–213; Cairncross, *Years of Recovery*, 105; Steil, *The Battle of Bretton Woods*, 296–300. Many elements of the agreement were favorable, especially the terms concerning Lend-Lease and the rate of interest. On the former, as Steil explains, "given that total American Lend-Lease aid to Britain, net of the $5 billion of so-called Reverse Lend-Lease assistance from Britain, had amounted to $22 billion, this was, from the administration's perspective, an act of extraordinary American magnanimity" (*The Battle of Bretton Woods*, 299). On the latter, HM Treasury would long consider this debt as one of a small number of "very low-cost loans." See T 509/17, Draft reply to Hunt, December 1993.

195. FVP, Box 149, Memo for President, 3 December 1945.

196. Wevill, *Britain and America after World War II*, loc. 1684–1694.

197. Dalton to Keynes, 5 December 1945, in Keynes, *The Collected Writings*, vol. 24, 604.

198. Dalton, *High Tide and After*, 74–75.

199. The quote appears in F. Williams, *A Prime Minister Remembers*, 134.

200. Wevill, *Britain and America after World War II*, loc. 1703.

201. Fforde, *The Bank of England and Public Policy*, 86.

202. Polk and Patterson, "The British Loan," 429. See also Gardner, *Sterling-Dollar Diplomacy*, 225–236.

203. Gardner, *Sterling-Dollar Diplomacy*, 225–236.

204. For further details, and Bevin's criticisms of what he believed to be the cowardice of the opposition, see Dormael, *Bretton Woods*, 276–280.

205. HC Deb., 13 December 1945, vol. 417, cc722–723. Churchill's reference to 1931 probably refers to the Hoover moratorium and neglects the resumption of payments between 1932 and 1934. On Bevin's criticisms of this comparison, see HC Deb., 13 December 1945, vol. 417, cc731–732.

206. Steil, *The Battle for Bretton Woods*, 300–301.

207. This condition appears to have been relevant both technically and politically. Attlee had been informed in early December that he could not expect Congress to approve the loan agreement if Parliament rejected Bretton Woods. See *FRUS*, 1945, vol. 6, "Minutes of a Meeting," Winant to Secretary of State, 3 December 1945.

208. White House, 13 April 1954, U.S. Declassified Documents Online, accessed 19 April 2017, Annex C, NSC 5808/1.

209. HL Deb., 18 December 1945, in Keynes, *The Collected Writings*, vol. 24, 615–616.

210. Polk and Patterson, "The British Loan," 434.

211. HL Deb., 18 December 1945, in Keynes, *The Collected Writings*, vol. 24, 615–616.

212. Steil, *The Battle for Bretton Woods*, 301–304.

213. T 247/128, Keynes to Vinson, 20 December 1945; Keynes to White, 20 December 1945; and Keynes to Clayton, 21 December 1945.

214. See, for instance, H. Fletcher Moulton, "The American Loan," *The Times*, 14 December 1945, 5; Robert Boothby, "The American Loan," *The Times*, 15 and 20 December 1945, both 5; "The American Loan" and "Letters to Editor: The American Loan," *Birmingham Daily Post*, 13 and 17 December 145. For more positive views in the local press, see "American Loan Welcomed," *Sevenoaks Chronicle and Kentish Advertiser*, 21 December 1945.

215. "The Consequences," 897.

216. T 247/128, Vinson to Keynes, 1 January 1946; FVP, Box 149, Vinson to Keynes, 1 January 1946. Clayton, now away on holiday, also responded favorably: "Your remarks are good reading even on a vacation. I only hope we shall be able to make as able and effective a presentation before Congress." HSTL, Clayton Papers, Clayton to Keynes, 29 December 1945.

217. Truman, *Memoirs*, vol. 1, 478–480.

218. FVP, Box 149, "Editorials—British Loan, 7 December 1945." U.S. press summarized in "The American Loan," *The Times*, 21 December 1945, 3.

219. FVP, Box 149, Feltus to Vinson, 19 March 1946.

220. Quoted in Gardner, *Sterling-Dollar Diplomacy*, 240–242. See also Woods, *A Changing of the Guard*, 378.

221. Democrats lost fifty-four seats to the Republican Party in the House and eleven seats to the Republicans in the Senate. These losses had allowed Republicans to take control of both chambers. Data on Truman's job approval from the American Presidency Project, "Presidential Job Approval," http://www.preside ncy.ucsb.edu/data/popularity.php?pres=33&sort=pop&direct=DESC&Submit=DI SPLAY.

222. FVP, Box 149, "Digest of Opinions," 7 December 1945; Feltus to Vinson, 25 February 1946; Feltus to Vinson, 11 March 1946; and Note, 15 May 1946.

223. FVP, Box 149, Feltus to Vinson, 25 February 1946; and Feltus to Vinson, 19 March 1946.

224. FVP, Box 148, *Wall Street Journal*, 13 November 1945, "Ballyhoo for Britain: Top US Agencies Map Drive to Make Public Favour Loan to England," and attached note, 14 November 1945.

225. Data cited in Gannon, "The Special Relationship and the 1945 Anglo-American Loan," 12–13.

226. FVP, Box 149, "Digest of Opinions."

227. FVP, Box 149, Feltus to Vinson, 19 March 1946.

228. FO 115/4206, Makins to Butler, Brand, Lee, Record of Conversation, 14 December 1945.

229. FVP, Box 148, "Ballyhoo for Britain," and attached note. Clayton was keenly aware that "these polls nearly all report a considerable majority against a loan to Britain" and blamed people not understanding the necessity of the loan and the prejudiced framing of the question. See HSTL, Clayton Papers, Clayton to Wood, 17 November 1945.

230. Gardner, *Sterling-Dollar Diplomacy*, 248. The Savannah Conference of March 1946, which represented the inaugural meeting of the IMF and IBRD, revealed serious divisions concerning international financial policy on both sides of the Atlantic. Ibid., 242–248, 258–268.

231. "Vinson Campaigns for British Loan," *New York Times*, 9 January 1946.

232. HSTL, Acheson File, Box 27, British Loan, Radio broadcast by Vinson and Acheson, "The British Loan—What It Means to Us," 12 January 1946. See also Vinson and Acheson, *The British Loan*.

233. Radio broadcast by Vinson and Acheson, "The British Loan." See also Acheson, *Present at the Creation*, 387.

234. Acheson File, Box 27, British Loan, Vinson and Acheson, "The British Loan."

235. Ibid.

236. Ibid.

237. Ibid. See also Vinson and Acheson, *The British Loan*.

238. Acheson File, Box 27, British Loan, Interview, 3 January 1946.

239. Vinson made a similar argument in March: "The financial burden which the Agreement will place upon the Government of the United Kingdom is a much more reasonable one than that imposed after the last war, and one which it should be able to meet. For these reasons, the failure of Britain to maintain payments on the World War I debt provides no basis for believing that they will default on the proposed credit." Statement by Secretary Vinson on World War I debt of the United Kingdom to the United States, 6 March 1946, US Treasury Department, Press Releases, 15 June 1972.

240. Acheson File, Box 134, British Loan, "The Mutual Advantages of the British Loan," address by Dean Acheson before Economic Club of Detroit, 19 March 1946.

241. Ibid.

242. Gannon, "The Special Relationship and the 1945 Anglo-American Loan," 12–13; Reynolds, "A Special Relationship," 3; Gardner, *Sterling-Dollar Diplomacy*, 248.

243. T 236/2410, Keynes to Bridges, 8 February 1946.

244. Ibid. Keynes also believed that failure now, rather than in the previous year, empowered the British position by setting an important international precedent: "My judgement has always been that, if we failed to come to any agreement last

autumn, our prospects were indeed black, but that, if we had reached agreement with the Administration on lines the Administration thought to be fair and Congress rejected it, the situation would be wholly changed. We could then, without justifiable complaint from anyone, ask our friends to rally round. Moreover, a breakdown last autumn would probably have meant that the United States would woo other countries with offers of financial assurance. If, however, Congress now turns us down, that will mean that no-one can have any very high hopes of substantial financial aid."

245. T 236/2410, Note to Waley, "What happens if we do not get the U.S. loan," 12 February 1946. On some of the assumptions in this approach being too optimistic, especially with regard to gold and dollar resources, see T 236/2410, Keynes note, 12 February 1946.

246. Boyle, "British-Foreign-Office View of Soviet-American Relations," 317; Skidelsky, *Keynes*; Gannon, "The Special Relationship and the 1945 Anglo-American Loan," 13; Woods, *A Changing of the Guard*, 387. Some scholars claim that Moscow interpreted the extended debates about ratification on both sides of the Atlantic as evidence of the disintegration of the wartime alliance and consequently helped to launch the Cold War. See James and James, "Origins of the Cold War," 617–618. See also Paterson, "The Abortive American Loan to Russia," 73.

247. Gardner, *Sterling-Dollar Diplomacy*, 248–250. See also Toye, "Churchill and Britain's 'Financial Dunkirk,'" 351; Gardner, *Sterling-Dollar Diplomacy*, 238–239, 248–250, 252; and Harbutt, *The Iron Curtain*, 160, 171, 168, 191.

248. On Attlee's long-held anti-Soviet leanings, see Attlee, *As It Happened*, 91–92; and K. Harris, *Attlee*, 156–157. See also Deighton, "Britain and the Cold War," 118–122.

249. Gannon, "The Special Relationship and the 1945 Anglo-American Loan," 14.

250. Wevill, *Britain and America after World War II*, loc. 906–910.

251. PREM 8/197, "Churchill and the Loan," 14 March 1946; and Vandenberg, *Private Papers*, 11, 230.

252. T 247/47, "Random Reflections from a Visit to the USA," 4 April 1946.

253. F. Beckett, *Clem Attlee*, 225. For an account that supports congressional views and suggests that Keynes was sent to "cadge" U.S. "handouts," see Barnett, *The Lost Victory*, 41, 132, 195.

254. Dalton, *Political Diary*, 366.

255. FO 371/52593, Halifax to Dalton, 26 March 1946; T 236/461, Washington to Cabinet Office, 12 February 1946; FO 371/52953, Eady to Brand, Extract from Chancellor's speech, 11 April 1946. See also Wevill, *Britain and America after World War II*, loc. 1801–1812.

256. HC Deb., 11 April 1946, vol. 421, cc2161.

257. T 236/2410, Halifax to FO, 30 January 1946.

258. Wevill, *Britain and America after World War II*, loc. 1854–1866.

259. "U.S. Congress and Strike Control," *The Times*, 8 February 1946, 3. See also FO 115/4253, The Consideration by Congress of the Anglo-American Financial Agreement, Prepared by the Embassy.

260. On this crucial amendment—which the Truman administration believed to be "the most dangerous"—and its links to unpaid war debts, see "Senate Defeats Amendment to British Loan," *The Times*, 9 May 1946, 4.

261. Gardner, *Sterling-Dollar Diplomacy*, 252–253.

262. HSTL, Official File, Box 942, 212 A, 1945–49, Letter, 3 July 1946; and FVP, Box 149, Biemiller to Vinson, 2 April 1946.

263. HSTL, Official File, Box 942, 212 A, 1945–49, Truman to Speaker, 29 June 1946. See also HSTL, Official File, Box 942, 212 A, 1945–49, Statement by the president, 15 July 1946.

264. Wevill, *Britain and America after World War II*, loc. 1887–1888.

265. Even this thoroughly researched defense erroneously concludes that the United Kingdom stopped repayment to the United States in 1931. This document appears in FO 371/52957, "Implementation of the Financial Agreement," Report, Committee on Banking and Currency, 14 June 1946.

266. Gardner, *Sterling-Dollar Diplomacy*, 252.

267. A small number of historians raise this issue but do so only briefly. See, for instance, Grant, "Truman and the British Loan Act of 1946," 494–495.

268. "Loan Debate Opens in Congress," *Financial Times*, 9 July 1946.

269. FO 371/52957, Judson to Balfour et al., "Notes on the Loan," 23 May 1946.

270. *Congressional Record*, House, 11 July 1946, 8697.

271. Ibid., 8701–8703.

272. Ibid., 8715.

273. Ibid., 8715.

274. Ibid., 8706.

275. Ibid., 8723.

276. Ibid., 8720.

277. Ibid., 8720.

278. FO 371/52957, Judson Minute, "World War I Debts and the Loan Debate," 25 June 1946.

279. See, for example, various reports contained in FO 371/52955, FO 371/52956, and FO 371/52957.

280. FO 371/52957, Note on Loan prepared by Judson, 23 May 1946. See, for example, FVP, Box 00169, Memorandum: World War I Debt of the United Kingdom to the United States, n.d.

281. FO 371/52957, Judson Minute, "World War I Debts and the Loan Debate."

282. Ibid.

283. *Congressional Record*, House, 11 July 1946, 8679. See also comments on 8715.

284. FO 371/52957, Telegram to Inverchapel, 4 July 1946; Washington to FO, 5 July 1946; and Judson, "British Loan Debate," 2 July 1946.

285. The final payment totaled $119,403,000: FVP, Box 149, Trade and Financial Statistics, Table 11.

286. Statement by Fred. M. Vinson, Secretary of the Treasury, before the Senate Committee on Banking and Currency, 5 March 1946, in U.S. Treasury Department, Press Releases, 14 June 1972 (containing data from 1945 and 1946), 15.

287. The Canadian cabinet had avoided addressing the issue of any ongoing commitment to economic assistance after the end of the Japanese war, which meant that Mutual Aid initially stopped alongside Lend-Lease. On this point, see Library and Archives, Canada, Ottawa, Cabinet Conclusions, 26 June 1945; and Cabinet Conclusions, 28 June 1945.

288. The idea of a loan had nevertheless been proposed originally in 1944 and was eventually agreed in early 1946. On the Canadian loan, see Bryce, *Canada and the Cost of World War II*, 284, 289, 293; Bothwell and English, "Canadian Trade Policy in the Age of American Dominance and British Decline," 52–65; and Mac-Kenzie, "The Path to Temptation," 196–220.

289. Schenk, *The Decline of Sterling*, 62; Bryce, *Canada and the Cost of World War II*, 315; Gannon, "The Special Relationship and the 1945 Anglo-American Loan," 1, 14. See also Pressnell, *External Economic Policy since the War*.

290. C. Newton, "The Sterling Crisis of 1947," 391–408.

291. Schenk, *The Decline of Sterling*, 62–63; Cairncross, *Years of Recovery*, 162. The *Chicago Daily Tribune* commented that the sterling convertibility crisis facing the British government would be "the biggest international financial battle since it repudiated its debt to America after World War I." Joseph Cerutti, "Press of Time Speeds British Debt Struggle," *Chicago Daily Tribune*, 11 May 1947, A7.

292. Truman, *Memoirs*, vol. 2, 118.

293. Such a conclusion challenges more pessimistic accounts about the merits of public opinion and democratic control of foreign affairs. See, for instance, Lippmann, *The Public Philosophy*, 20. See more recently, Achen and Bartels, *Democracy for Realists*.

294. BE OV31/101, No. 4528, 18 August 1947; and No. 8436, 19 August 1947. For more detail on these events, see Hileman, "Overlooked Sovereign Credit Events and Partial Defaults," 21–22. See also Gardner, *Sterling-Dollar Diplomacy*, 322–323.

295. BE OV31/101, No. 4570, Washington to FO, 20 August 1947.

296. BE OV31/101, Cmd. 7210, 20 August 1947; Gardner, *Sterling-Dollar Diplomacy*, 323–325, 342–344. These insights originate in Hileman, "Overlooked Sovereign Credit Events and Partial Defaults," 21–24.

297. BE OV31/102, No. 117, Wilson-Smith, 1 October 1948. Hileman suggests that there were two additional instances of British default—namely, the failure to negotiate down or block a large portion of the sterling balances and the violation of article 9 of the Financial Agreement. On these points, see Hileman, "Overlooked Sovereign Credit Events and Partial Defaults," 24–25.

298. Pimlott, *Harold Wilson*, 135–137; Cairncross, *The British Economy since 1945*, 56–57; Schenk, *The Decline of Sterling*, 71–72.

299. Gavin, "The Gold Battles within the Cold War," 65–66.

300. Cairncross and Eichengreen, *Sterling in Decline*, xvii.

301. Pimlott, *Harold Wilson*, 134–136; Schenk, *The Decline of Sterling*, 100–101. The archives do not reveal any discussion of the effect of this decision on outstanding First World War debts. On the potential effect of devaluation on the sterling value of debt payments to the United States and sterling receipts from inter-allied payments, see Cairncross and Eichengreen, *Sterling in Decline*, 61.

302. Cairncross, *The British Economy since 1945*, 55; Schenk, *The Decline of Sterling*, 78.

303. Schenk, *The Decline of Sterling*, 68–79; Cairncross and Eichengreen, *Sterling in Decline*, 151–155; Bordo, "The Bretton Woods International Monetary System," 45.

304. Cairncross and Eichengreen, *Sterling in Decline*, xvii.

305. Bordo, "The Bretton Woods International Monetary System," 45; Dominguez, "The Role of International Organizations in the Bretton Woods System," 379. For an empirical investigation of the conditions leading to devaluations and external sector performance thereafter during the Bretton Woods period (1954–1971), see Edwards and Santaella, "Devaluation Controversies in the Developing Countries," 405–460.

306. S. Newton, "The 1949 Sterling Crisis," 180.

307. Gardner, *Sterling-Dollar Diplomacy*, 435; Woods, *A Changing of the Guard*, 365.

308. T 381/77, "First World War Debt," 11 May 1977, attachment titled "History of WW1 Debt, 1931–77."

309. T 312/262, Anson to Wyatt, 19 August 1960; T 385/204, Peirson note, 16 December 1971, attachment "UK Long-Term Debt to the USA."

310. On the U.S. initiative to aid western Europe, see Fossedal, *Our Finest Hour*; DeLong and Eichengreen, "The Marshall Plan"; and Steil, *The Marshall Plan*. Concerning the longer-term origins of the plan, and how events in the interwar period informed its creation, see Hogan, *The Marshall Plan*. For a challenge to popular claims that the British government "misused" Marshall Plan aid, see Tomlinson, "Correlli Barnett's History," 222–238.

311. See, for instance, *Congressional Record*, Senate, 25 March 1948, 3548–3549; *Congressional Record*, Senate, 13 July 1949, 9377–9378; HSTL, Oral History Interview with John W. Snyder, 20 February 1969, 1146–1148; and HSTL, Oral History Interview with J. Burke Knapp, 24 and 30 July 1975, 90.

312. The United States had revised the United Kingdom's Second World War debts down to $437 million, which comprised a line of credit and Lend-Lease, and would lend again via the Economic Cooperation Administration Mutual Security Agency in 1960 and in the form of Export-Import Bank loans between 1966 and 1969. See T 385/204, Peirson note, 16 December 1971, attachment "UK Long-Term Debt to the USA."

313. T 236/736, Bridges to Churchill, 11 August 1948.

314. T 236/736, "Churchill and the War Debts," 19 April 1948.

315. Ibid.; T 236/736, "War Debt Repayment," 14 June 1948. On the error, see Churchill, *The Gathering Storm*, 23. This was not the only instance of an error in his work. On the process of editing his book and other errata, see Cannadine and Quinault, *Winston Churchill in the Twenty First Century*, 122.

316. T 236/736, Haslam to Atkinson, 13 May 1947; and JGO to Clarke, 20 May 1948.

317. T 236/736, Bridges to Churchill, 11 August 1948.

318. T 236/736, Churchill to Bridges, 15 August 1948; and Bridges to Churchill, 17 August 1948.

319. T 236/736, Churchill to Bridges, 15 August 1948; and Bridges to Churchill, 17 August 1948.

320. T 236/736, "Churchill and the War Debts."

321. T 160/1411/12, Edmunds to Chadwick, 29 April 1947.

322. T 160/1411/12, Edmunds to Chadwick, 1 May 1947.

323. Australia owed £79,724,220 and New Zealand owed £26,191,108 for the First World War. On these amounts, see T 312/262, Marshall to Cox, 28 February 1963; and Cox to Marshall, 5 March 1963.

324. Schenk, *The Decline of Sterling*, 53–57, 59.

325. In March 1947, for instance, New Zealand made a gift of £10 million sterling (£12.5 million in New Zealand currency) to the United Kingdom, in respect of the fact that it had borne such a large portion of the economic as well as the military burden of the war. On this point, see J. Baker, *The Official History of New Zealand in the Second World War*, 527. On Australia and New Zealand assuming a greater burden of British Commonwealth security, and the economic elements driving these changes, see Te Rua Mahara o te Kāwanatanga, National Archives, Wellington, New Zealand, R17722423 ABHS 950 W5422 14 111 3/1, part 2, Note for Mr. Nash, 12 April 1946; and Australia, National Archives, Canberra, A5954 1800/10, Minutes of Meeting at 10 Downing Street, 22 May 1946. On the United Kingdom and Commonwealth security issues more broadly, see Robb and Gill, *Divided Allies*.

Chapter 6. A Long Shadow, 1952–2020

1. For the latest published figures, see U.S. Department of the Treasury and Office of Management and Budget, "U.S. Government Foreign Credit Exposure as of December 31, 2009, Part I: Summary Analysis" (data retrieved 2011), 33.

2. See, for example, U.S. Treasury file, Schuerch to Geithner, "Litigation Relating to World War I Debt," 3 November 1998.

3. Author's exchanges with British and U.S. Treasury officials, 2017 and 2018.

4. State of New York, Surrogate's Court, File No. P 1886/1934, 16 November 1998; and U.S. Department of the Treasury and Office of Management and Budget, "U.S. Government Foreign Credit Exposure as of December 31, 2002–2009, Part I: Summary Analysis" (2002–2009), data as of year-end, 31 December 1999–2009, n11.

5. U.S. Treasury, Schuerch to Geithner, "World War I Debt: Treasury Audit," 21 October 1998.

6. Rohrer, "What's a Little Debt between Friends?"

7. Drezner, *The System Worked*; Tooze, *Crashed*.

8. Paul Heffernan, "London Talks set on German Debts," *New York Times*, 24 February 1952, 1.

9. Galofré-Vilà et al., "The Economic Consequences of the 1953 London Debt Agreement," 1–29; Kaiser, "One Made It out of the Debt Trap."

10. The parties that were involved besides West Germany and the United Kingdom included Belgium, Canada, Denmark, France, Greece, Iran, Ireland, Italy,

Liechtenstein, Luxembourg, Norway, Pakistan, Spain, Sweden, Switzerland, South Africa, the United States, Yugoslavia, and others. The states of the Eastern Bloc were not involved.

11. Galofré-Vilà et al., "The Economic Consequences of the 1953 London Debt Agreement"; Kaiser, "One Made It out of the Debt Trap."

12. Vagts, "Sovereign Bankruptcy," 302–306.

13. Kaiser, "One Made It out of the Debt Trap."

14. Dwight D. Eisenhower Presidential Library, GF 151-E-2 Foreign Debts and Foreign Loans, Box 1202, White House Central Files, 1954–61, Message to President, 24 August 1953. See also *Congressional Record*, Senate, 1953, 8919–8948.

15. T 381/77, Allan to Crawford, 11 May 1977, Annex A, "History of WW1 Debt, 1931–1977." The pertinent reference appears in article 5(1). See also T 385/204, Peirson to Taylor, "World War One Debt," 20 June 1972; and Peirson to Lovell, "World War One Debt," 7 July 1972.

16. T 385 204, Thorp to Peirson, "World War One Debt," 25 April 1972.

17. Lyndon B. Johnson Presidential Library, Henry "Joe" Fowler Papers (HFP), International—Balance of Payments: Foreign debts, U.S. Treasury Department, Report, Gold losses and debt repayment, 12 February 1968.

18. HFP, International—Balance of Payments: Foreign debts, Memorandum, world war indebtedness, 30 June 1967, supplement, newspaper article, 18 December 1966.

19. Stockman, *The Great Deformation*; Bowie and Immerman, *Waging Peace*, 75.

20. Cairncross, *The British Economy since 1945*, 116, 118.

21. *FRUS*, 1955–57, vol. 15, Memo from Deputy Undersecretary of State for Economic Affairs to the Chairman of the Council on Foreign Economy Policy, 14 November 1956.

22. Ibid.

23. See, for instance, the renewal of the Mutual Security Act of 1951: *Congressional Record*, House, 1956, 15695. On foreign aid, see "Major Defeat for President Eisenhower," *The Times*, 15 August 1957, 7.

24. See, for example, Sir Derwent Hall Caine, "England's War Debts," *New York Times*, 10 January 1955.

25. Britain missed six interest payments in total: 1956, 1957, 1964, 1965, 1968, and 1976.

26. See Dwight D. Eisenhower Presidential Library, GF 151-E-2 Foreign Debts and Foreign Loans, Box 1202, White House Central Files, 1954–61, *Chicago Daily Tribune*, n.d. [ca. March 1957].

27. Schenk, *The Decline of Sterling*, 103–107; Cairncross and Eichengreen, *Sterling in Decline*.

28. T 312/2626, Anson to Wyatt, 19 August 1960.

29. T 312/2626, Marshall to Cox, 28 February 1963; Marshall to Cox, 28 February 1963, attachment; and Cox to Marshall, 5 March 1963. Specifically, for the 1914–1918 war, Australia owed £79,724,220 and New Zealand £26,191,108.

30. Eichengreen, "From Benign Neglect to Malignant Preoccupation," 185–242.

31. Economic and political interests drove many states to adopt the pegged system. More broadly, politics—and specifically political instability—helped to play a role in regime selection. In sum, more unstable countries were less likely to pick a pegged exchange-rate system. See Edwards, "Exchange Rates and the Political Economy of Macroeconomic Discipline," 159–163.

32. The administration chose not to adopt trade and capital controls to end the deficit and gold outflow, which would have contradicted its goals of trade and currency liberalization. These issues are covered in more detail in Gavin, "The Gold Battles within the Cold War," 67–70.

33. John F. Kennedy Presidential Library, Box 291 Balance of payments and gold: General, Cabinet committee report on balance of payments, 6 April 1963.

34. John F. Kennedy Presidential Library, Box 291, Balance of payments and gold: General, Cabinet committee on balance of payments for meeting on 18 April 1963.

35. J. Young, *The Labour Governments*, 124. See also Gavin, "The Gold Battles within the Cold War," 70, 81, 92–93; and Collins, "The Economic Crisis of 1968," 400.

36. *FRUS*, 1961–63, vol. 9, Foreign Economic Policy, document 17, Report by the Cabinet Committee on Balance of Payments to Kennedy, 27 July 1962; and document 18, memorandum from Dillon to Kennedy, 9 October 1962.

37. The offset problem would continue throughout the 1960s, as German purchases waned and further negotiated compromises emerged. Gavin, *Gold, Dollars, and Power*, 144–146, 162–164. See also Zimmermann, *Money and Security*.

38. On this argument, see Monet and Puy, "Do Old Habits Die Hard?"

39. Rockoff, *America's Economic Way of War*, 286–297.

40. On 28 May 1964, Greece reached an agreement with the U.S. providing for the refinancing of the $12,167,000 loan granted that government in 1929 as postwar financial aid. Greece agreed to an eighty-year repayment schedule at 2 percent interest. Greece remains current on this loan. Its last installment is due on 17 November 2048. See U.S. Treasury Department, *Annual Report* (1964), 104–105; and Hall and Sargent, "Complications for the United States from International Credits," 1–58.

41. Note, Office of Industrial Nations, Treasury Department, Issues related to the French balance of payments surplus, 5 November 1965, 13. Document originally located via U.S. Declassified Documents Online, http://tinyurl.galegroup.com/tinyurl/4gyeCo (accessed 19 April 2017).

42. Lyndon B. Johnson Presidential Library, Bator, Box 15, Balance of Payments, World War I debts, Memorandum for the President, 11 May 1966.

43. Ibid. See also Gavin, *Gold, Dollars, and Power*, 126–130. On French gold reserves, see Bordo, Simard, and White, "France and the Bretton Woods International Monetary System 1960 to 1968," 153–180; and Eichengreen, "Global Imbalances and the Lessons of Bretton Woods," 39–50. See also Friedman and Schwartz, *A Monetary History of the United States*.

44. HFP, International—Balance of Payments: Foreign debts, Smith, Memorandum to Secretary, 28 April 1966, "French World War I Debts."

45. Document originally located via U.S. Declassified Documents Online, http://tinyurl.galegroup.com/tinyurl/4gyMW7 (accessed 19 April 2017). See also NAII, RG 59, Bureau of European Affairs, Memorandum from Acting Secretary of State George Ball regarding Congressional inquiries concerning WWI war debts and reparations to Germany, Department of State, 15 August 1966. For examples of press attention in this period, see "French to Pay War Debt Could Be Touchy, Treasury Says," *Wall Street Journal*, 10 March 1965, 4; "1st War Debt to U.S. Reaches 21 Billions," *Chicago Tribune*, 17 December 1966, B13; and Aldo Beckman, "U.S. Already over Brink of Insolvency, Senator Warns: Says Chits Could Deplete Gold Reserve," *Chicago Tribune*, 18 September 1966, 5.

46. HL Deb., 5 May 1965, vol. 265, cc1025–1026WA (written answers, Lords), 1025WA.

47. First World War (Debts and Credits), HC Deb., 25 October 1966, vol. 734, c133W (written answers), 133W.

48. See, for example, "Washington Split on War Debts," *The Times*, 7 October 1966, 1.

49. Ibid., 1.

50. Tomlinson, *The Labour Governments*, 51–52; Cairncross, *The Wilson Years*, 71; Ponting, *Breach of Promise*, 49–50; Bale, "Dynamics of a Non-decision," 204.

51. H. Wilson, *The Labour Government*, 128–129.

52. Jones, "A Decision Delayed," 569–595; J. Young, *The Labour Governments*, 48; Peden, *Arms, Economics and British Strategy*, 331–343; and Dockrill, *Britain's Retreat from East of Suez*.

53. On the U.S. Treasury's calls for changes, see NAII, RG 59, 24/34187, Memorandum, "Treasury Request for Modification," 12 July 1966.

54. Document originally located via U.S. Declassified Documents Online, http://tinyurl.galegroup.com/tinyurl/4gyMW7 (accessed 19 April 2017). See also NAII, RG 59, Bureau of European Affairs, Memorandum from Acting Secretary of State George Ball to Fowler, regarding Congressional inquiries concerning WWI war debts and reparations to Germany, Department of State, 15 August 1966.

55. Many scholars have criticized this devaluation as unnecessarily belated. See, for example, Cairncross and Eichengreen, *Sterling in Decline*, 2, 156–217. On the devaluation as a more logical response to the changing balance of power in the international economy, see S. Newton, "The Sterling Devaluation of 1967," 912–945.

56. On the links between economics and nuclear weapons, see Gill, *Britain and the Bomb*, 145, 162. See also Gavin, *Gold, Dollars, and Power*, esp. 135–164. On the president's commitment to the existing offset agreement, see *FRUS, 1964–68*, vol. 8, International Monetary and Trade Policy, Document 88, Meeting of the Cabinet Committee on Balance of Payments, 25 March 1966; Document 90, Memorandum from Fowler to Johnson, 23 April 1966; and Document 104, Editorial note. On U.S. efforts to stem proliferation more broadly, see also Gavin, *Nuclear Statecraft*.

57. Ball to Fowler, 15 August 1966.

58. Ibid.

59. Gavin, *Gold, Dollars, and Power*, 171–173.

60. HFP, International—Balance of Payments: Foreign debts, Bowman to Fowler, 12 October 1967. See also *Congressional Record*, 11 October 1967, Appendix, A5008, citing an editorial from the *Nashville Banner*.

61. "Tax? April Fool!," 35.

62. HFP, International—Balance of Payments: Foreign debts, Smith to Secretary, 19 February 1968, Subject: State Department Views on French World War I Debts. On these rising congressional challenges and growing press interest, see Norman C. Miller, "Pressure in Congress Builds to Make France Pay Off Its War Debt," *Wall Street Journal*, 8 February 1968, 1; "The Reluctant Debtor," *Chicago Tribune*, 4 March 1968, 20; and Louis Dombrowski, "Chance Slim for U.S. Collecting WW I Debt," *Chicago Tribune*, 9 February 1968, C8.

63. HFP, International—Balance of Payments: Foreign debts, Treasury Dept. Report, Gold Losses and Debt Repayment, 12 February 1968. This pessimistic view was shared by the U.S. State Department: Dombrowski, "Chance Slim for U.S. Collecting WW I Debt."

64. Nixon achieved a significant margin of victory in the Electoral College but held a narrow lead in the popular vote. On the election, see Boy, "Popular Control of Public Policy," 429–449; and LaFeber, *The Deadly Bet*, esp. 4–18.

65. Schenk, *The Decline of Sterling*, 317.

66. Gavin, *Gold, Dollars, and Power*, 187, citing *FRUS*, 1969–72, vol. 1, Nixon to Haldeman, Ehrlichman, and Kissinger, 2 March 1970.

67. Gavin, *Gold, Dollars, and Power*, 187; Gowa, *Closing the Gold Window*; Matusow, *Nixon's Economy*.

68. Irwin, "The Nixon Shock after Forty Years," 30; and Eichengreen, "From Benign Neglect to Malignant Preoccupation," 185–242. Some scholars have argued that the ongoing U.S. balance of payments deficit was not really a problem and that the Bretton Woods System could have continued indefinitely. See Despres, Kindleberger, and Salant, "The Dollar and World Liquidity," 526–529. On the argument for merely prolonging the life of the Bretton Woods system, see Bordo and Eichengreen, "Implications of the Great Depression for the Development of the International Monetary System," 403–454. See also Bordo and Eichengreen, *A Retrospective on the Bretton Woods System*.

69. Gavin, *Gold, Dollars, and Power*, 188. As Gavin points out, U.S. trade surpluses had declined from $6.8 billion in 1964 to merely $600 million by 1968. By 1969, the overall current account deficit, which included trade, services, tourism, and government expenditure abroad, reached $1 billion.

70. As Arthur Burns noted, many of these decisions were taken by small groups with limited international economic expertise: diary entry, 26 November 1971, in *Inside the Nixon Administration*, 66.

71. Irwin, "The Nixon Shock after Forty Years," 33; Odell, *U.S. International Monetary Policy*, 263.

72. The import surcharge was lifted four months later after the Smithsonian Agreement led to new exchange-rate parities. On these points, see Irwin, "The Nixon Shock after Forty Years," 29–56.

73. Schenk, *The Decline of Sterling*, 317.

74. The Smithsonian Agreement was created by the Group of Ten (G-10), which included Belgium, Canada, France, Germany, Italy, Japan, the Netherlands, Sweden, the United Kingdom, and the United States.

75. "The Nixon Shock."

76. See, for instance, Cromwell, *The United States and the European Pillar*, 72–73; Matusow, *Nixon's Economy*, 130–133; Zimmermann, "Western Europe and the American Challenge," 127–155; Gray, "Floating the System," 295–323; and Robb, *A Strained Partnership?*, 38.

77. T 385/204, Peirson note, 16 December 1971, attachment "UK Long-Term Debt to the USA." The British press was also aware of these outstanding debts. See "US Still Owed Millions," *The Guardian*, 23 December 1971, 2.

78. Robb, *A Strained Partnership?*, 30; Cairncross, *The British Economy since 1945*, 188–189, 208–209.

79. T 385/204, Thorp to Lovell, "World War One Debt," 28 February 1972, attachment, "Statement of Hennessey," 18 February 1972.

80. Richard Nixon Presidential Library, John M. Hennessy Papers, Box 1, Chronological Files, January 1972–November 1972, Hennessy to Winn, 20 March 1972; and Hennessy to Britton, 29 February 1972. The total amount of credit utilized since the Second World War stood at $46 billion as of 31 December 1970. Of this sum, $18 billion in principal had been repaid, plus the interest due, and $28 billion of the principal remained to be collected. The total amount reported in arrears was $506 million, with 1.8 percent of the principal outstanding, most of which is contracted in nine countries.

81. T 385/204, Thorp to Lovell, "World War One Debt," 28 February 1972.

82. Ibid.

83. T 385/204, Peirson to Taylor, "World War One Debt," 9 March 1972. More broadly, see Robb, "The 'Limit of What Is Tolerable,'" 321–337.

84. NAII, RG 59, 24/34187, Memorandum, "Treasury Request for Modification," 12 July 1966; and memorandum from Solomon, n.d. [ca. 12 July 1966].

85. T 385/204, Peirson to Taylor, "World War One Debt," 9 March 1972. Prime Minister Edward Heath had signed the Treaty of Accession in January 1972, but the United Kingdom's membership of the EC only came into effect on 1 January 1973.

86. T 385/204, Peirson to Thorp, "World War One Debt," 29 March 1972.

87. On Anglo-American tensions in the early 1970s, see Robb, *A Strained Partnership?*, 24–72.

88. T 385/204, Thorp to Peirson, "World War One Debt," 25 April 1972.

89. Ibid. On the history and challenges of monetary reform, see Needham, *Monetary Policy from Devaluation to Thatcher*.

90. T 385/204, Peirson to Lovell, "World War One Debt," 29 March 1972. See also T 312/3360, Note from Foggarty, 6 April 1972. A similar issue had aroused attention in 1965 concerning 1838 Mississippi Union bonds (referred to as "state of Mississippi bonds"): T 312/3360, Young to Mews, 3 March 1965; Pitchew to Young, 10 March 1965; and Extract from Minute by Watts, 8 April 1965.

91. T 385/204, Peirson to Taylor, "World War One Debt," 20 June 1972. Furthermore, article 2 of the Pecuniary Claims Convention of 1910 or article 5 of the Anglo-U.S. Convention of 1853 for the Settlement of Outstanding Claims by a

Mixed Commission "probably bars HMG from bringing up the question of these debts in the form of a claim against the US government, though the legal opinion was not certain." On this point, see T 385/204, Peirson to Lovell, "World War One Debt," 7 July 1972.

92. T 312/3360, Peirson to Lovall, Foggary, "World War One Debt," 7 July 1972; T 385/204, Peirson to Taylor, "World War One Debt," 20 June 1972; and T 312/3360, Memorandum respecting repudiated debts of the Southern States of the United States of America, 1932.

93. T 385/204, Peirson to Lovell, "World War One Debt," 7 July 1972.

94. HM Treasury could be seen to have embraced elements of what some social scientists have termed alternative analysis or "red-teaming," albeit focusing on an economic competitor rather than a military threat. See Zenko, *Red Team*.

95. T 385/204, Fogarty to Rawlinson, "World War 1 Debts," 11 July 1972.

96. Ibid.

97. T 385/204, Thorp to Peirson, "World War I Debts," 21 July 1972.

98. Ibid.

99. Ibid.

100. T 385/204, Thorp to Morris, "World War I Debts," 29 August 1972.

101. T 385/204, Thorp to Morris, 8 February 1973.

102. Ibid.

103. T 385/204, Thorp to Morris, 9 March 1973.

104. *Congressional Record*, House, 11 April 1973, 11817. See also the supportive comments on 11818–11819.

105. Lester L. Wolff, interview with the author, January 2018.

106. T 385/204, Thorp to Morris, 23 April 1973.

107. Nixon was probably aware of the war-debts problem. In addition to senior members of his own staff dealing with the issue, it remained politically relevant. In a letter addressed to the president on 18 July 1973 and retained in the White House Correspondence Files, a community-college teacher offered Nixon a "drastic" solution to "our economic problems" that suggested the president "demand our European allies to pay their debts to the United States, which occurred from World War I, and on, especially World War II." See Richard Nixon Presidential Library, White House Correspondence Files: FO (Foreign Affairs), Box 44, GEN FO 4, 1/1/73–8/9/74, Sherf to Nixon (10–12), 18 July 1973.

108. T 385/204, Thorp to Morris, 13 November 1973.

109. Flandreau and Zumer, *The Making of Global Finance*, 57.

110. Ibid.

111. T 385/204, Delinquent foreign debts and claims owed to the United States, Tenth report, 5 December 1973.

112. T 381/77, Allan to Walker, 4 February 1977, attachment, "World War One Debts—the Bertram Estate."

113. T 381/77, Allan to Crawford, 11 May 1977, Annex A, "History of WW1 Debt, 1931–1977."

114. Wolff interview.

115. T 385/204, Fenton to Harrop, 22 July 1975.

116. Ibid.

117. This counterfactual raises important but challenging questions about U.S. perceptions regarding the value of the debts relative to the difficulty of their collection. See Bunzl, "Counterfactual History," 845–858; and Tetlock and Belkin, "Counterfactual Thought Experiments in World Politics," 1–38.

118. Ball to Fowler, 15 August 1966.

119. T 381/77, Allan to Crawford, 11 May 1977, Annex A.

120. Gerald R. Ford Presidential Library, Ron Nessen Papers, Box 39, "Reagan-Nationwide TV Address, 3/31/76"; and Box C29, folder: "Presidential Handwriting, 10/15/1975," Memorandum for the president, from Walker to President, 7 October 1975, and attached document, "New York City: Part II." On parallels between U.S. policy toward New York in the 1970s and Germany in the 1930s, specifically concerning nonintervention in financial crisis, see H. James, *The Reichsbank and Public Finance in Germany*, 271.

121. U.S. Treasury Department, *Annual Report* (1976), 583.

122. "Good News from Finns on World War I Debt," *New York Times*, July 30, 1975.

123. Gerald R. Ford Presidential Library, President's Speeches and Statements, Box 37, "8/3/76, Remarks during a Toast in Honor of President Urho Kekkonen of Finland at a State Dinner."

124. See U.S. Treasury Department, *Annual Report* (1977), 164; and Hall and Sargent, "Complications for the United States," 43n77.

125. Statistical Appendix to U.S. Treasury Department, *Annual Report* (1976).

126. On this decision, see Callaghan, *Time and Chance*, 413–450; Healey, *The Time of My Life*, 427–432; Burk and Cairncross, "*Good-Bye, Great Britain*," 14–15; C. Rogers, "Economic Policy and the Problem of Sterling," 353–354; Burk, *Old World, New World*, 628; Schenk, *The Decline of Sterling*, 368–378. On the broader weaknesses and instabilities of the British economy, see Schenk, *International Economic Relations*, ch. 4; Ziegler, *Edward Heath*, 401–427; and Clark, *The Tories*, 350–353. For a helpful overview of the crisis, see Ludlam, "The Gnomes of Washington," 713–727.

127. Burk and Cairncross, "*Good-Bye, Great Britain*"; Wass, *Decline to Fall*; Hickson, *The IMF Crisis of 1976*; Schenk, *The Decline of Sterling*, 357–358; A. Beckett, *When the Lights Went Out*, ch. 7. See also Coopey and Woodward, *Britain in the 1970s*. Some observers feared a potential sovereign default. In 1976, fears that the United Kingdom might withdraw from IMF negotiations deeply concerned Ed Yeo III, undersecretary for monetary affairs at the U.S. Treasury: "We feared that if a country like Britain blew up, defaulted on its loans, and froze convertibility, we could have a real world depression." Quoted in H. James, *International Monetary Cooperation since Bretton Woods*, 280–281.

128. BE 7A174/2, Couzens to PPS, 16 September 1977, attached, "Debt Repayment."

129. This subject is covered in greater detail in Gill, "Rating the United Kingdom," 1016–1037.

130. T 381/50 (titled "First World War Debt"), Walker to Hosker, 6 May 1977; Allan to Crawford, 11 May 1977; Walker to Quinn, 6 May 1977; Allan to Crawford, 11 May 1977; Walker, 17 June 1977; Smeeton to Allan, "Credit

Rating," 8 July 1977; George to Gill, "New York Borrowing Operation," 15 July 1977.

131. T 381/77, Walker to Hosker, 6 May 1977.

132. T 381/77, Alexander to Long, 6 October 1977.

133. T 381/77, Gill, Note for the Record, 23 January 1978.

134. The final payments were used to finance cultural exchanges between the two countries. See U.S. Treasury Department, *Annual Report* (1977), 164; and Hall and Sargent, "Complications for the United States," 43n77.

135. T 381/51, 390, Note from Barratt, 24 January 1978; and Gill to Hancock, "Submission," 26 January 1978.

136. T 370/471, "HMG's Application," 9 March 1978; Note from Gill, 15 March 1978; T 381/52, and Jones to Hancock, "HMG's Application," 10 March 1978; T 381/51, Economic view from Britain, 18 January 1978; T 381/53, Note, 22 March 1978; and T 381/52, Note, 14 March 1978.

137. BE 2A50/1, "British Budget," *New York Times*, 1 April 1978; *Hansard*, HC Deb., 11 April 1978, vol. 947, cc1185–1186; Gill, "Rating the United Kingdom," 1016–1037.

138. Lake, "Rightful Rules," 605. On the economic determinants driving banks' lending behavior in this period, which share some similarities with the rating agencies', see Edwards, "LDCs' Foreign Borrowing and Default Risk," 726–734.

139. See Cantor and Packer, "Determinants and Impact of Sovereign Credit Ratings," 37–54; Bissoondoyal-Bheenick, "An Analysis of the Determinants of Sovereign Ratings," 279; and Gaillard, *A Century of Sovereign Ratings*, 73. See also Gill and Gill, "The Great Ratings Game."

140. Gill, "Rating the United Kingdom," 1016–1037.

141. The notion of a "psychological statute of limitations" emerged in author's interview with Wolff, January 2018.

142. Robb, *Jimmy Carter and the Anglo-American Special Relationship*.

143. *The Economist*, 24 September 1977; Wiseley, "Paying Debts," 6.

144. U.S. Treasury Department, *Annual Report* (1979), 89.

145. Statistical Appendix to U.S. Treasury Department, *Annual Report* (1980).

146. The U.S. Treasury paid these T-bills after a short delay but only grudgingly agreed to provide additional interest covering the period of delay following legal challenges. See Zivney and Marcus, "The Day the United States Defaulted on Treasury Bills," 475–489; and Austin, "Has the U.S. Government Ever 'Defaulted'?"

147. Bertram was a native citizen of Scotland and a resident alien of the United States from 1913 until his death in 1934. Surrogate's Court of New York, Westchester County, 89 Misc. 2d 55, 389 N.Y.S. 2d 999 (14 December 1976), 3.

148. Ibid.

149. T 385/204, Alexander to Crew, 13 December 1972.

150. "Court Backs 1927 Bequest on War Debt," *New York Times*, 10 April 2000.

151. Surrogate's Court of New York, Westchester County, 89 Misc. 2d 55, 389 N.Y.S. 2d 999, 5.

152. T 385/204, Morris to Hedley-Miller, 31 January 1973. The chancellor of the exchequer and senior officials within HM Treasury identified the possible

risks in the 1930s. See, for example, T 233/2169, Treasury solicitor, 25 November 1936.

153. T 385/204, Morris to Hedley-Miller, 31 January 1973.

154. T 381/77, Allan to Walker, 4 February 1977, attachment, "World War One Debts—the Bertram Estate."

155. T 381/77, Allan to Walker, 9 February 1977.

156. T 381/77, Allan to Crawford, 11 May 1977; and Annex A, "History of WW1 Debt, 1931–1977."

157. For a full schedule of payments between 1923 and 1984, see Moulton and Pasvolsky, *War Debts and World Prosperity*, 440.

158. U.S. Treasury file, Littler to Sprinkel, June 1984. See also Schuerch to Geithner, "Litigation Relating to World War I Debt," 3 November 1998.

159. The war debts do not appear to have played any significant role in Lawson's wider thinking in the 1980s. Yet large unpaid debts could have held some broader relevance to the controversial "Lawson Doctrine," whereby the chancellor had argued that there was no reason to be concerned about large current account deficits if the imbalances were the result of private-sector decisions. In sum, successive current account deficits can result in large debt accumulation. If this large accumulation of unsustainable debt ends up with a large devaluation, however, there could potentially be serious consequences for public debt. On the Lawson Doctrine, see Blanchard, "Current Account Deficits in Rich Countries," 191–219; and Edwards, "Exchange Rate Puzzles and Dilemmas," 146.

160. U.S. Treasury file, Sprinkel to Chancellor of the Exchequer, n.d. [ca. June 1984].

161. The limited availability of relevant archival materials from this period makes it difficult to explain this policy shift. It is possible that attitudes about long-term debts were changing. Only two years later, the British government resigned itself to some of its own historical losses, accepting limited compensation from the Soviet Union regarding the Bolshevik government's earlier repudiation. The United States also began discussing the issue with the Soviet Union on similar terms. On these points, see Schuker, *American "Reparations" to Germany*, 8–9n1, citing *New York Times*, 16 July 1986.

162. See, for instance, HL Deb., 23 October 2002, vol. 639, cc103–104WA (written answers, Lords), 103WA.

163. Schuerch to Geithner, "Litigation Relating to World War I Debt," 3 November 1998.

164. Ibid.

165. Ibid.

166. Ibid.

167. Ibid.

168. State of New York, Surrogate's Court, File No. P 1886/1934, 16 November 1998.

169. "Court Backs 1927 Bequest on War Debt."

170. U.S. Department of the Treasury and Office of Management and Budget, "U.S. Government Foreign Credit Exposure as of December 31, 2002–2009, Part I: Summary Analysis" (2002–2009), data as of year-end, 31 December 1999–2009.

171. U.S. Treasury file, Schuerch to Geithner, "World War I Debt: Treasury Audit," 21 October 1998.

172. Ibid.

173. Ibid.

174. Ibid.

175. Ibid.

176. Ibid.

177. Toussaint, *The Debt System*, 183, 204.

178. Uli Schmetzer, "Russia to Pay Off Old Bonds," *Chicago Tribune*, 28 November 1996.

179. Suddath, "Why Did World War I Just End?"; Roger Boyes, "For Fritz, the War Really Is Over—but It Has Taken 91 Years to Pay the Winners," *The Times*, 2 October 2010, 48.

180. Suddath, "Why Did World War I Just End?"

181. A resolution of the problem of government debt claims against Germany arising from the First World War had been deferred "until a final general settlement of this matter" by the 1953 London agreement on German external debts, which was ratified by the U.S. Senate and has the status of a treaty. See U.S. Treasury Department, *Annual Report* (1980), 98. See also U.S. House of Representatives, *Hearings before the Committee on Appropriations, House of Representatives, Nineteenth Congress, Second Session* (Washington, DC: U.S. Government Printing Office, 1968), 133.

182. T 509/17, Dixon to Doig, Treasury enquiry, war debts, 28 February 1995. Another relevant file may also help future research in this area. In 2021, I used a Freedom of Information request to secure access to T 509/31. Nevertheless, "owing to measures in place in response to the COVID-19 pandemic," HM Treasury was understandably unable to process this request, as all staff were working remotely and consequently unable to physically access paper file records.

183. "A Debtor Remembers," *Los Angeles Times*, 25 January 1995.

184. T 509/17, Dixon to Doig, 28 February 1995.

185. Ibid. The note nevertheless recognized that "much of Germany's WWI reparations bill was never paid and in strict theory remained an issue to be resolved with a reunified Germany," but it made clear, "it never crossed our mind here to resurrect the topic, hence our astonishment at this whiff of grapeshot—and I do not think, moreover, that we had any ideas what our supposed debt to the US was." On the relevant portion of the London Debt Agreement, see article 5(1).

186. Conny Lotze, "France Seeking War Reparation from Germany," UPI, 22 December 1990, https://www.upi.com/Archives/1990/12/22/France-seeking-war-reparation-from-Germany/6463661842000/. See also "Germans Honour Prewar Debt," *The Guardian*, 31 August 1991, 10.

187. Gordon Brown does not appear to have commented publicly on the issue of British war debts. In his memoirs, he does express his commitment to "widespread relief of [international] debt" but also the importance of "fiscal discipline" (*My Life, Our Times*, ch. 6).

188. HC Deb., 28 February 2002, vol. 380, cc1439–1441W (written answers), 1439W.

189. HL Deb., 17 July 2002, vol. 637, cc158–159WA (written answers, Lords), 158WA; HL Deb., 30 July 2002, vol. 638, c161WA (written answers, Lords), 161WA.

190. HL Deb., 23 October 2002, vol. 639, cc103–104WA (written answers, Lords), 103WA.

191. HL Deb., 20 January 2003, vol. 643, cc72–73WA (written answers, Lords), 73WA; HL Deb., 11 July 2003, vol. 651, c66WA (written answers, Lords), 66WA; HL Deb., 16 September 2003, vol. 652, c170WA (written answers) 170WA; and HL Deb., 19 January 2005, vol. 668, cc110–111WA (written answers, Lords), 110WA.

192. Philip Thornton, "Britain Pays Off Final Instalment of US Loan—after 61 Years," *The Independent*, 29 December 2006.

193. T 509/17, Draft reply to Hunt, December 1993. On discussions about early repayment of amounts owed to Canada to provide funds for academic exchanges between the two states and HM Treasury's resistance to forgoing "a favourable rate of interest," see T 509/17, Macdonald to Major, 3 November 1994; Note, n.d. [ca. November 1994]; No. 10 to Macdonald, 25 November 1994; Crane to Cunliffe, 26 April 1995; Pellew to Hook, 26 May 1995; Crane to Allan, 15 June 1995; and Budd to Allan, 15 June 1995.

194. See, for instance, Thornton, "Britain Pays Off Final Instalment"; and Rohrer, "What's a Little Debt between Friends?"

195. Rohrer, "What's a Little Debt between Friends?"

196. Ibid.

197. Tooze, *Crashed*.

198. Drezner, *The System Worked*.

199. See, for instance, David Woolner, "How War Debts, High Tariffs, and Competitive Devaluation Led to War," *Business Insider*, 8 October 2010, https://www.businessinsider.com/how-war-debts-high-tariffs-and-competitive-devaluation-led-to-war-2010-10?r=US&IR=T.

200. Ritschl, "Reparations, Deficits, and Debt Default," 110–139. On Germany as the largest debt defaulter of the twentieth century and the need for an orderly resolution of the Greek debt crisis, see Ritschl, "Calling Germany on Its Hypocrisy in the Eurozone Debt Crisis."

201. Clift, "The UK Macroeconomic Policy Debate and the British Growth Crisis," 151–173. More broadly, see Tomlinson, "Britain since the 1970s," 181–198.

202. James Hurley, "Britain's Credit Rating Downgraded from AAA to Aa1," *The Telegraph*, 22 February 2013.

203. Patrick Hennessy, "George Osborne: No Let Up in Plan to Cut Deficit after AAA Downgrade," *The Telegraph*, 22 February 2013.

204. Peter Hitchens, "Britain's Vast Unpaid Debt to the USA," *MailOnline*, 2 August 2014, http://hitchensblog.co.uk/2014/08/britains-vast-unpaid-debt-to-the-usa.html.

205. See, for instance, H. James, "International Order after the Financial Crisis," 525–537; and Eichengreen, *Hall of Mirrors*.

206. U.S. Department of the Treasury and Office of Management and Budget, "U.S. Government Foreign Credit Exposure as of December 31, 2009, Part I: Summary Analysis," 32–33.

Conclusion

1. See, for instance, Reinhart and Rogoff, *This Time Is Different*, 96; and Jeremy Warner, "Britain Would Be Unwise to Ruin Its Perfect Record on Sovereign Debt by Defaulting on the EU Divorce Bill," *The Telegraph*, 11 June 2019.

2. Edwards, *American Default*, xiv.

3. Leith-Ross, *Money Talks*, 178–179. On the rewards of default for Germany, for instance, exceeding what it paid in reparations, see Norbert, *Hitler's Magician*, 212–214.

4. Frieden, "Winners and Losers in the Latin America Debt Crisis," 23–37; Frieden, *Debt, Development, and Democracy*; Tomz and Wright, "Empirical Research on Sovereign Debt and Default," 247–272.

5. On the heterogeneous effects of default across societies, see DiGiuseppe and Shea, "The Devil's Haircut," 1889–1922.

6. Roos, *Why Not Default?*, 48, 173, 213–218, 307–308. Potential examples such as Argentina in 2001 and Ecuador in 2008 are debatable. On the complexity of assessing these kinds of cases, especially over the longer term, see Datz and Corcoran, "Deviant Debt," 300–313; and Gill, "Review Essay: Rethinking Sovereign Default." On debt restructurings as sometimes being attractive deals for both debtors and some of their creditors, see Datz, "What Life after Default?," 456–484. See also Edwards, "Sovereign Default, Debt Restructuring, and Recovery Rates."

7. Edwards, *American Default*, 186–200.

8. Edwards, Longstaff, and Garcia Marin, "The U.S. Debt Restructuring of 1933."

9. For a detailed account, see the National Archives, London, Cabinet file 23/79/7, May 30, 1934.

10. Stannage, *Baldwin Thwarts the Opposition*.

11. Gardner, *Sterling-Dollar Diplomacy*; Kimball, *The Most Unsordid Act*.

12. Dallek, *Roosevelt and American Foreign Policy*, 74; and P. Kennedy, *The Rise and Fall of the Great Powers*, 330.

13. Cole and Kehoe, "The Role of Institutions in Reputation Models of Sovereign Debt," 45–64; Fuentes and Saravia, "Sovereign Defaulters," 336–347; Rose and Spiegel, "Noneconomic Engagement and International Exchange," 337–363; Tomz and Wright, "Sovereign Theft," 69–110.

14. Shea, "Financing Victory," 771–795; Allen and DiGiuseppe, "Tightening the Belt," 647–659; Flores-Macías and Kreps, "Borrowing Support for War," 997–1020; DiGiuseppe, "The Fiscal Autonomy of Deciders," 317–338; Shea and Poast, "War and Default," 1876–1904. On the rise of external financing for war, see Zielinski, *How States Pay for Wars*, 109.

15. Catão and Mano, "Default Premium," 91–110; and Cruces and Trebesch, "Sovereign Defaults," 85–117.

16. Flandreau and Zumer, *The Making of Global Finance*, 57.

17. U.S. Treasury file, Schuerch to Geithner, "World War I Debt: Treasury Audit," 21 October 1998.

Epilogue

1. Ben Wright, "UK Government to 'Pay Back' All World War One Debt," *The Telegraph*, 3 December 2014. Few outlets noted the Britain government's unpaid international loans following World War I. For a rare exception, see Stephen Castle, "That Debt from 1720? Britain's Payment Is Coming," *New York Times*, 27 December 2014.

2. Author's interviews, 2017–2018.

3. H. James, "Deep Red," 333.

4. U.S. Treasury file, Schuerch to Geithner, "Litigation Relating to World War I Debt," 3 November 1998; and Schuerch to Geithner, "World War I Debt: Treasury Audit," 21 October 1998.

5. For a recent example, see HC Deb., 28 February 2002, vol. 380, cc1439–1441W, 1439W.

6. Rohrer, "What's a Little Debt between Friends?"; see also HL Deb., 23 October 2002, vol. 639, cc103–104WA (written answers, Lords), 103WA.

7. Neither the U.S. Treasury nor HM Treasury has provided an official position on the matter more recently, but there is no available evidence to suggest that the U.S. or British government position has changed.

8. Keynes to Catto, 22 October 1945, in Keynes, *The Collected Writings*, vol. 24, 564–565.

9. On "muddling through" as a recurring theme in British politics, see Hennessy, *Muddling Through*.

10. I. Fisher, *The Money Illusion*.

11. On the "political triumph of paying for the first world war," albeit focused on smaller domestic war loans, see James Mackintosh, "Why Britain Should Pay Off War Loans," *Financial Times*, 19 January 2012.

12. Adam Forrest, "UK Debt Now Bigger than Size of Whole Economy," *The Independent*, 19 June 2020.

13. On suggestions that the British government might be willing to pay off a decades-old debt to improve diplomatic relations with Iran, see Karl McDonald, "Why Britain Owes Iran £450m—and Why It Might Finally Pay It Back," *i*, 16 November 2017, updated 17 July 2020, inews.co.uk/news/world/britain-owes-iran-450m-might-finally-pay-back-104060; and "Iran Claims UK Was Open to Paying £400m in Owed Money to Free Nazanin Zaghari-Ratcliffe," *The Telegraph*, 23 September 2019.

Bibliography

ARCHIVES

United Kingdom

Bank of England Archive, London
Borthwick Institute for Archives, University of York
Cambridge University Library
Churchill College Archives, Cambridge
National Archives, Public Records Office, London
Seeley Library, Cambridge

United States of America

Bancroft Library, University of California, Berkeley, California
Carter, Jimmy, Presidential Library, Atlanta, Georgia
Eisenhower, Dwight D., Presidential Library, Abilene, Kansas
Federal Reserve Bank of New York Archive, New York
Ford, Gerald R., Presidential Library, Ann Arbor, Michigan
Hoover, Herbert, Presidential Library, West Branch, Iowa
International Monetary Fund Archives, Washington, DC
Johnson, Lyndon B., Presidential Library, Austin, Texas
Kennedy, John F., Presidential Library, Columbia Point, Boston
National Archives, College Park, Maryland

Nixon, Richard, Presidential Library, Yorba Linda, California
Roosevelt, Franklin D., Presidential Library, Hyde Park, New York
Special Collections Research Center, University of Kentucky Library, Lexington, Kentucky
Truman, Harry S., Presidential Library, Independence, Missouri
Yale University Library, Manuscripts and Archives, New Haven, Connecticut

AUTHOR INTERVIEWS

Interviews with HM Treasury officials, 2017, 2018
Interviews with U.S. Treasury officials, 2018
Interview with Lester L. Wolff, 2018

GOVERNMENT PUBLICATIONS

Annual Report of the Secretary of the Treasury on the State of the Finances, including Statistical Appendices (Washington, DC: Government Printing Office)
Command Papers (His/Her Majesty's Stationery Office), various
Congressional Record
Foreign Relations of the United States
Hansard
U.S. Government Foreign Credit Exposure reports, 1999–2009

NEWSPAPERS AND NEWS WEBSITES

BBC News Magazine
Birmingham Daily Post
Business Insider
Chicago Tribune
Daily Herald
Daily Mail
Daily Mirror
Daily Telegraph
Edinburgh Evening News
Evening Telegraph
Financial Times
The Guardian
Helena Daily Independent
i
The Independent
Kentish Advertiser

Lancashire Evening Post
MailOnline
New York Herald Tribune
New York Times
Saturday Evening Post
The Scotsman
Sevenoaks Chronicle
The Times
UPI
Vox
Wall Street Journal
Washington Post
Western Gazette
Western Morning News

BOOKS, ARTICLES, AND OTHER SOURCES

Achen, Christopher H., and Larry M. Bartels. *Democracy for Realists: Why Elections Do Not Produce Responsive Government*. Princeton, NJ: Princeton University Press, 2016.

Acheson, Dean. *Present at the Creation: My Years in the State Department*. New York: Norton, 1969.

Adams, R. J. Q. *Bonar Law*. London: John Murray, 1999.

Adamson, Michael R. "The Failure of the Foreign Bondholders Protective Council Experiment, 1934–1940." *Business History Review* 76, no. 3 (2002): 479–514.

———. "'Must We Overlook All Impairment of Our Interests?': Debating the Foreign Aid Role of the Export-Import Bank, 1934–41." *Diplomatic History* 29, no. 4 (2005): 589–623.

Adelman, Jeremy, and Jonathan Levy. "The Fall and Rise of Economic History." *Chronicle Review*, 1 December 2014. https://www.chronicle.com/article/the-fall-and-rise-of-economic-history/.

Ahamed, Liaquat. *Lords of Finance: 1929, The Great Depression, and the Bankers Who Broke the World*. London: Random House/Windmill Books, 2010. epub version 1.0.

Alichi, Ali. "A Model of Sovereign Debt in Democracies." IMF Working Paper 08/152. International Monetary Fund, Washington, DC, 2008.

Allen, Matthew, and Matthew DiGiuseppe. "Tightening the Belt: Sovereign Debt and Alliance Formation." *International Studies Quarterly* 57, no. 4 (2014): 647–659.

Allen, R. G. D. "Mutual Aid between the U.S. and the British Empire, 1941–45." *Journal of the Royal Statistical Society* 109, no. 3 (1946): 243–277.

Allport, Alan. *Britain at Bay: The Epic Story of the Second World War: 1938–1941*. London: Profile Books, 2020.

Alstyne, Richard W. Van. "American Loans to the Allies, 1914–1916." *Pacific Historical Review* 2, no. 2 (1933): 180–193.

Álvarez-Nogal, Carlos, and Christophe Chamley. "Debt Policy under Constraints: Philip II, the Cortes, and Genoese Bankers." *Economic History Review* 67, no. 1 (2014): 192–213.

Ams, Julianne, Reza Baqir, Anna Gelpern, and Christoph Trebesch. "Sovereign Default." Chapter 7 in *Sovereign Debt: A Guide for Economists and Practitioners*, edited by S. Ali Abbas, Alex Pienkowski, and Kenneth Rogoff. Oxford: Oxford University Press, 2019.

Anson, Michael, Norma Cohen, Alastair Owens, and Daniel Todman. "Your Country Needs Funds: The Extraordinary Story of Britain's Early Efforts to Finance the First World War." *Bank Underground*, 8 August 2017. https://bankunderground.co.uk/2017/08/08/your-country-needs-funds-the-extraordinary-story-of-britains-early-efforts-to-finance-the-first-world-war/.

Anstey, Caroline. "The Projection of British Socialism: Foreign Office Publicity and American Opinion, 1945–50." *Journal of Contemporary History* 19, no. 3 (1984): 417–451.

Armus, Seth D. *French Anti-Americanism, 1930–1948: Critical Moments in a Complex History*. Plymouth, UK: Lexington, 2007.

Artaud, Denise. *La reconstruction de l'Europe, 1919–1929*. Paris: Champion, 1973.

———. "Reparations and War Debts: The Restoration of French Financial Power, 1919–1929." In *French Foreign and Defence Policy, 1918–1940: The Decline and Fall of a Great Power*, edited by Robert Boyce, 94–100. London: Routledge, 1998.

Astore, Marianna, and Michele Fratianni. "'We Can't Pay': How Italy Dealt with War Debts after World War I." *Financial History Review* 26, no. 2 (2019): 197–222.

Atkin, John. "Official Regulation of British Overseas Investment, 1914–1931." *Economic History Review* 23, no. 2 (1970): 324–335.

Attlee, Clement. *As It Happened*. London: Heinemann, 1954.

Auld, George P. "The British War Debt: Retrospect and Prospect." *Foreign Affairs* 16, no. 4 (1938): 640–650.

Austin, D. Andrew. "Has the U.S. Government Ever 'Defaulted'?" Congressional Research Service, R44704, 8 December 2016.

Baker, J. V. T. *The Official History of New Zealand in the Second World War, 1939–1945: War Economy*. Wellington, New Zealand: Historical Publications Branch, 1965.

Baker, Ray Stannard. *Woodrow Wilson and the World Settlement: Written from His Unpublished and Personal Material.* 3 vols. New York: Doubleday, 1923.

Bale, Tim. "Dynamics of a Non-decision: The 'Failure' to Devalue the Pound, 1964–7." *Twentieth Century British History* 10, no. 2 (1999): 192–217.

Ballard-Rosa, Cameron. *Democracy, Dictatorship, and Default: Urban-Rural Bias and Economic Crises across Regimes.* Cambridge: Cambridge University Press, 2020.

———. "Hungry for Change: Urban Bias and Autocratic Sovereign Default." *International Organization* 70, no. 2 (2016): 313–346.

Baptiste, Fitzroy Andre. "The British Grant of Air and Naval Facilities to the United States in Trinidad, St. Lucia and Bermuda in 1939." *Caribbean Studies* 16, no. 2 (1976): 5–43.

Barber, William J. *Designs within Disorder: Franklin D. Roosevelt, the Economists, and the Shaping of American Economic Policy, 1933–45.* Cambridge: Cambridge University Press, 1996.

Barnett, Correlli. *The Lost Victory: British Dreams, British Realties, 1945–50.* London: Faber and Faber, 1995.

Barta, Zsófia. *In the Red: The Politics of Public Debt Accumulation in Developed Countries.* Ann Arbor: University of Michigan Press, 2021.

Beckett, Andy. *When the Lights Went Out: What Really Happened to Britain in the Seventies.* London: Faber and Faber, 2010.

Beckett, Francis. *Clem Attlee.* London: Richard Cohen Books, 1997.

Behrman, Greg. *The Most Noble Adventure: The Marshall Plan and the Time When America Helped Save Europe.* New York: Free Press, 2007.

Bennett, Edward W. *Germany and the Diplomacy of the Financial Crisis of 1931.* Cambridge, MA: Harvard University Press, 1971.

Bernanke, Ben, and Harold James. "The Gold Standard, Deflation and Financial Crisis in the Great Depression: An International Comparison." In *Financial Markets and Financial Crises*, edited by R. Glenn Hubbard, 33–68. Chicago: University of Chicago Press, 1991.

Berlin, Isaiah. *Isaiah Berlin.* Vol. 1, *Letters, 1928–1946.* Edited by Henry Hard. Cambridge: Cambridge University Press, 2004.

Bernstein, Michael A. *The Great Depression: Delayed Recovery and Economic Change in America, 1929–1939.* 1987. Reprint, Cambridge: Cambridge University Press, 1997.

Bew, John. *Citizen Clem: A Biography of Attlee.* London: Riverrun, 2016.

Bidwell, Percy W., and Arthur R. Upgren. "Trade Policy for National Defense." *Foreign Affairs* 19, no. 2 (1941): 282–296.

Bissoondoyal-Bheenick, Emawtee. "An Analysis of the Determinants of Sovereign Ratings." *Global Finance Journal* 15, no. 3 (2005): 251–280.

Blake, Robert. *The Unknown Prime Minister: The Life and Times of Andrew Bonar Law, 1858–1923*. London: Eyre and Spottiswoode, 1955.

Blanchard, Oliver. "Current Account Deficits in Rich Countries." *IMF Staff Papers* 54, no. 2 (2007): 191–219.

Blum, John Morton. *From the Morgenthau Diaries*. Vol. 1, *Years of Crisis, 1928–1938*. Boston: Houghton Mifflin, 1959.

———. *From the Morgenthau Diaries*. Vol. 2, *Years of Urgency, 1938–1941*. Boston: Houghton Mifflin, 1965.

Bogdanor, Vernon. *The Coalition and the Constitution*. London: Hart, 2011.

———. *The People and the Party System: The Referendum and Electoral Reform in British Politics*. Cambridge: Cambridge University Press, 1981.

Boller, Paul F., and John H. George. *They Never Said It: A Book of Fake Quotes, Misquotes, and Misleading Attributions*. Oxford: Oxford University Press, 1989.

Bordo, Michael D. "The Bretton Woods International Monetary System: A Historical Overview." In *A Retrospective on the Bretton Woods System: Lessons for International Monetary Reform*, edited by Michael D. Bordo and Barry Eichengreen, 3–108. Chicago: University of Chicago Press 1993.

Bordo, Michael D., and Barry Eichengreen. "Implications of the Great Depression for the Development of the International Monetary System." In *The Defining Moment: The Great Depression and the American Economy in the Twentieth Century*, edited by Michael D. Bordo, Claudia Goldin, and Eugene N. White, 403–454. Chicago: University of Chicago Press, 1998.

———, eds. *A Retrospective on the Bretton Woods System: Lessons for International Monetary Reform*. Chicago: University of Chicago Press, 1993.

Bordo, Michael D., Dominique Simard, and Eugene N. White. "France and the Bretton Woods International Monetary System 1960 to 1968." In *International Monetary Systems in Historical Perspective*, edited by J. Reis, 153–180. London: Palgrave Macmillan, 1995.

Borensztein, Eduardo, and Ugo Panizza. "The Costs of Sovereign Default." *IMF Economic Review* 56, no. 4 (2009): 683–741.

Bothwell, Robert, and John English. "Canadian Trade Policy in the Age of American Dominance and British Decline, 1943–1947." *Canadian Review of American Studies* 8, no. 1 (1977): 52–65.

Bowie, Robert R., and Richard H. Immerman. *Waging Peace*. Oxford: Oxford University Press 1997.

Boy, Richard W. "Popular Control of Public Policy: A Normal Vote Analysis of the 1968 Election." *American Political Science Review* 66, no. 2 (1972): 429–449.

Boyce, Robert. "Business as Usual: The Limits of French Economy Diplomacy, 1926–33." In *French Foreign and Defence Policy, 1918–1940: The Decline and Fall of a Great Power*, edited by Robert Boyce, 106–130. London: Routledge, 1998.

Boyden, Roland W. "Relation between Reparations and the Interallied Debts." *Proceedings of the Academy of Political Science* 12, no. 4 (1928): 21–28.

Boyer, George R., and Timothy J. Hatton. "New Estimates of British Unemployment, 1870–1913." *Journal of Economic History* 62, no. 3 (2002): 643–675.

Boyle, P. G. "British-Foreign-Office View of Soviet-American Relations, 1945–1946." *Diplomatic History* 3, no. 3 (1979): 307–320.

Braumoeller, Bear F. "The Myth of American Isolationism." *Foreign Policy Analysis* 6, no. 4 (2010): 349–371.

Broadberry, Stephen N. *The British Economy between the Wars: A Macroeconomic Survey*. Oxford, UK: Basil Blackwell, 1986.

Broadberry, Stephen N., and Nicholas Crafts. "UK Productivity Performance from 1950 to 1979: A Restatement of the Broadberry-Crafts View." *Economic History Review* 56 (2003): 718–735.

Broadberry, Stephen N., and Peter Howlett. "The United Kingdom: 'Victory at All Costs.'" In *The Economics of World War II: Six Great Powers in International Comparison*, edited by Mark Harrison, 43–80. Cambridge: Cambridge University Press, 1998.

Bromhead, Alan de, Alan Fernihough, Markus Lampe, and Kevin Hjortshøj O'Rourke. "When Britain Turned Inward: The Impact of Interwar British Protection." *American Economic Review* 109, no. 2 (2019): 325–352.

Brooks, Sarah M., Raphael Cunha, and Layna Mosley. "Categories, Creditworthiness, and Contagion: How Investors' Shortcuts Affect Sovereign Debt Markets." *International Studies Quarterly* 59, no. 3 (2015): 587–601.

Brown, Gordon. *My Life, Our Times*. London: Bodley Head, 2017.

Bryce, Robert, *Canada and the Cost of World War II: The International Operations of Canada's Department of Finance, 1939–1946*. Montreal: McGill-Queens University Press, 2005.

Buch, Claudia, and R. P. Heinrich. "Twin Crises and the Intermediary Role of Banks." *International Journal of Finance and Economics* 4, no. 4 (1999): 313–323.

Buiter, Willem, and Ebrahim Rahbari. "Why Governments Default." Chapter 19 in *Sovereign Debt Management*, edited by Rosa Lastra and Lee Buchheit, 257–286. Oxford: Oxford University Press, 2014.

Bullen, Roger, and M. E. Pelly, eds. *Documents on British Policy Overseas*. Series 1, vol. 3, *Britain and America: Negotiation of the United States Loan, 3 August–7 December 1945*. London: Her Majesty's Stationery Office, 1986.

Bulow, Jeremy, and Kenneth Rogoff. "A Constant Recontracting Model of Sovereign Debt." *Journal of Political Economy* 97, no. 1 (1989): 155–178.

———. "Sovereign Debt: Is to Forgive to Forget?" *American Economic Review* 79, no. 1 (1989): 43–50.

Bunte, Jonas. *Raise the Debt: How Developing Countries Choose Their Creditors*. Oxford: Oxford University Press, 2019.

Bunzl, Martin, "Counterfactual History: A User's Guide." *American Historical Review* 109, no. 3 (2004): 845–858.

Burk, Kathleen. "American Foreign Economic Policy and Lend-Lease." In *The Rise and Fall of the Grand Alliance, 1941–45*, edited by Ann Lane and Howard Temperley, 43–68. New York: St Martin's, 1995.

———. *Britain, America and the Sinews of War*. Oxford: Oxford University Press, 1989.

———. "A Merchant Bank at War: The House of Morgan, 1914–1918." In *Money and Power: Essays in Honour of L. S. Pressnell*, edited by P. L. Cottrell and D. E. Moggridge, 155–172. London: Palgrave, 1988.

———. *Old World, New World: The Story of Britain and America*. London: Abacus, 2009.

Burk, Kathleen, and Alec Cairncross. *"Good-Bye, Great Britain": The 1976 IMF Crisis*. New Haven, CT: Yale University Press, 1992.

Burnham, Peter. "Re-evaluating the Washington Loan Agreement: A Revisionist View of the Limits of Postwar American Power." *Review of International Studies* 18, no. 3 (1992): 241–259.

Burnet, Gilbert. *History of His Own Time: Autobiography*. London: Phoenix, 1986.

Burns, James MacGregor. *Roosevelt: The Lion and the Fox*. New York: Harcourt, Brace and World, 1956.

Caballero, Ricardo J., Emmanuel Farhi, and Pierre-Olivier Gourinchas. "The Safe Assets Shortage Conundrum." *Journal of Economic Perspectives* 31, no. 3 (2017): 29–46.

Cairncross, Alec. *The British Economy since 1945*. London: Blackwell, 1995.

———. *The Wilson Years: A Treasury Diary, 1961–1969*. London: Historian's Press, 1997.

————. *Years of Recovery: British Economic Policy, 1945–1951*. London: Methuen, 1985.

Cairncross, Alec, and Barry Eichengreen. *Sterling in Decline: The Devaluations of 1931, 1949 and 1967*. 2nd ed. Basingstoke, UK: Palgrave, 2003.

Callaghan, James. *Time and Chance*. Glasgow: William Collins Sons, 1988.

Cannadine, David. *Mellon: An American Life*. New York: Knopf, 2006.

Cannadine, David, and Roland Quinault, eds. *Winston Churchill in the Twenty First Century*. Cambridge: Cambridge University Press, 2004.

Cantor, Richard, and Frank Packer. "Determinants and Impact of Sovereign Credit Ratings." *FRBNY Economic Policy Review* 1996:37–54.

Capie, Forrest H., Terry C. Mills, and Geoffrey E. Wood. "Debt Management and Interest Rates: The British Stock Conversion of 1932." *Applied Economics* 18, no. 10 (1986): 1111–1126.

Carcasson, Martin. "Herbert Hoover and the Presidential Campaign of 1932: The Failure of Apologia." *Presidential Studies Quarterly* 28, no. 2 (1998): 349–365.

Casey, Kevin M. *Saving International Capitalism during the Early Truman Presidency: The National Advisory Council on International Monetary and Financial Problems*. London: Routledge, 2001.

Cassel, Gustav. *The Downfall of the Gold Standard*. Oxford, UK: Clarendon, 1936.

Catão, Luis A. V., and Rui C. Mano. "Default Premium." *Journal of International Economics* 107 (2017): 91–110.

Cater, Susan B., Scott Sigmund Gartner, Michael R. Haines, Alan L. Olmstead, Richard Sutch, and Gavin Wright, eds. *Historical Statistics of the United States, Millennium Edition*. Vol. 2, part B, *Work and Welfare*. New York: Cambridge University Press, 2006.

Chamberlain, Neville. *The Neville Chamberlain Diary Letters*. Vol. 3, *Heir-Apparent, 1928–1933*. Edited by Robert Self. Aldershot, UK: Ashgate, 2002.

————. *The Neville Chamberlain Diary Letters*. Vol. 4, *The Downing Street Years, 1934–1940*. Edited by Robert Self. Aldershot, UK: Ashgate, 2005.

Churchill, Winston. *The Gathering Storm*. Vol. 1 of *The Second World War*. Boston: Houghton Mifflin, 1985.

Churchill, Winston, and Franklin D. Roosevelt. *Churchill and Roosevelt: The Complete Correspondence*. Vol. 1, *Alliance Emerging, October 1933–November 1942*. Edited by Warren F. Kimball. Princeton, NJ: Princeton University Press, 1984.

———. *Churchill and Roosevelt: The Complete Correspondence.* Vol. 2, *Alliance Forged, November 1942–February 1944.* Edited by Warren F. Kimball. Princeton, NJ: Princeton University Press, 1984.

Clark, Alan. *The Tories: Conservatives and the Nation State, 1922–1997.* London: Phoenix, 1998.

Clarke, Peter. *The Last Thousand Days of the British Empire: The Demise of a Superpower, 1944–47.* London: Penguin, 2007.

Clarke, Richard. *Anglo-American Economic Collaboration in War and Peace, 1942–1949.* Oxford: Oxford University Press, 1982.

Clarke, Stephen V. *Exchange-Rate Stabilization in Mid-1930s: Negotiating the Tripartite Agreement.* Princeton Studies in International Finance 41. Princeton, NJ: Princeton University Press, 1977.

———. "The Reconstruction of the International Monetary System: The Attempts of 1922 and 1933." Princeton Studies in International Finance 33, 1973.

Clavin, Patricia. "Explaining the Failure of the World Economic Conference." In *The Interwar Depression in an International Context*, edited by Harold James, 77–99. Munich: Oldenbourg Wissenschaftsverlag, 2002.

———. *Failure of Economic Diplomacy: Britain, Germany, France and the US, 1931–1936.* London: Palgrave, 1995.

———. "The Fetishes of So-Called International Bankers: Central Bank Co-operation for the World Economic Conference, 1932–3." *Contemporary European History* 1, no. 3 (1992): 281–311.

———. "Reparations in the Long Run." *Diplomacy & Statecraft* 16, no. 3 (2005): 515–530.

Clement, Piet, "'The Touchstone of German Credit': Nazi Germany and the Service of the Dawes and Young Loans." *Financial History Review* 11, no. 1 (2004): 33–50.

Clift, Ben. "The UK Macroeconomic Policy Debate and the British Growth Crisis: Debt and Deficit Discourse in the Great Recession." In *The British Growth Crisis: Building a Sustainable Political Recovery*, edited by J. Green, C. Hay, and P. Taylor-Gooby, 151–173. London: Palgrave Macmillan, 2015.

Cohen, Benjamin J. "The Revolution in Atlantic Economic Relations: A Bargain Comes Unstuck." In *The United States and Western Europe: Political, Economic and Strategic Perspectives*, edited by W. Hanreider, 106–133. Cambridge, MA: Winthrop, 1974.

Cohrs, Patrick. *The Unfinished Peace after World War I: America, Britain and the Stabilisation of Europe, 1919–1932.* Cambridge: Cambridge University Press, 2006.

Colby, Bainbridge. "Should War Debts Be Cancelled?" *Proceedings of the Academy of Political Science* 15, no. 1 (1932): 65–72.

Cole, Harold L., and Patrick Kehoe. "The Role of Institutions in Reputation Models of Sovereign Debt." *Journal of Monetary Economics* 35, no. 1 (1995): 45–64.

Cole, Harold L., and Timothy Kehoe. "Self-Fulfilling Debt Crises." *Review of Economic Studies* 67, no. 1 (2000): 91–116.

Cole, Wayne S. *Roosevelt and the Isolationists, 1932–45.* Lincoln: University of Nebraska Press, 1983.

Collier, David. "Understanding Process Tracing." *PS: Political Science and Politics* 44, no. 4 (2011): 823–830.

Collins, Robert M. "The Economic Crisis of 1968 and the Waning of the 'American Century.'" *American Historical Review* 101, no. 2 (1996): 396–422.

Conn, Stetson, Rose C. Engelman, and Byron Fairchild. *The Western Hemisphere: Guarding the United States and Its Outposts, United States Army in World War II.* Washington, DC: United States Government, 1964.

Conn, Stetson, and Byron Fairchild. *The Framework of Hemisphere Defense.* Washington, DC: Center of Military History United States Army, 1989.

"Consequences, The." *The Economist*, 22 December 1945.

Coolidge, Calvin. *The Autobiography of Calvin Coolidge.* New York: Cosmopolitan, 1929.

Cooper, John Milton, Jr. "The Command of Gold Reversed: American Loans to Britain, 1915–1917." *Pacific Historical Review* 45, no. 2 (1976): 209–230.

Cooper, Richard N. "Fettered to Gold? Economic Policy in the Interwar Period." *Journal of Economic Literature* 30, no. 4 (1992): 2120–2128.

Coopey, Richard, and Nicholas Woodward, eds. *Britain in the 1970s: The Troubled Economy.* Abingdon, UK: Routledge, 1996.

Costigliola, Frank. "Anglo-American Financial Rivalry in the 1920s." *Journal of Economic History* 37, no. 4 (1977): 911–934.

———. *Awkward Dominion: American Political, Economic, and Cultural Relations with Europe, 1919–1933.* Ithaca, NY: Cornell University Press, 1988.

———. "The Other Side of Isolation: The Establishment of the First World Bank, 1929–1930." *Journal of American History* 59, no. 3 (1972): 602–620.

———. "The United States and the Reconstruction of Germany in the 1920s." *Business History Review* 50, no. 4 (1976): 485–494.

C.R. "Economic History Is Dead; Long Live Economic History?" *The Economist*, 7 April 2015.

Crafts, N. F. R. "Long-Term Unemployment in Britain in the 1930s." *Economic History Review* 40, no. 3 (1987): 418–432.

Crafts, N. F. R., and Nicholas C. Woodward, eds. *The British Economy since 1945*. Oxford: Oxford University Press, 1991.

Crafts, Nicholas, and Peter Fearon. "Lessons from the 1930s Great Depression." *Oxford Review of Economic Policy* 26, no. 3 (2010): 285–317.

Craig, F. W. S. *British Parliamentary Election Results, 1918–49*. Basingstoke, UK: Palgrave Macmillan, 1977.

Cromwell, William C. *The United States and the European Pillar: The Strained Alliance*. Basingstoke, UK: Macmillan, 1992.

Crosby, Alfred W. *America's Forgotten Pandemic: The Influenza of 1918*. Cambridge: Cambridge University Press, 1989.

Crowther, Samuel. *America Self-Contained*. New York: Doubleday, Doran, 1933.

Cruces, Juan, and Christoph Trebesch. "Sovereign Defaults: The Price of Haircuts." *American Economic Journal: Macroeconomics* 5, no. 3 (2013): 85–117.

Curtis, K. Amber, Joseph Jupille, and David Leblang. "Iceland on the Rocks: The Mass Political Economy of Sovereign Debt Resettlement." *International Organization* 68, no. 3 (2014): 721–740.

Dallek, Robert. *Franklin D. Roosevelt and American Foreign Policy*. 1979. Reprint, Oxford: Oxford University Press, 1995.

Dalton, Hugh. *High Tide and After: Memoirs*. London: Muller, 1962.

———. *The Political Diary of Hugh Dalton, 1918–40, 1945–60*. Edited by Ben Pimlott. London: Jonathan Cape, 1987.

Darnton, Christopher. "Archives and Inference: Documentary Evidence in Case Study Research and the Debate over US Entry into World War II." *International Security* 42, no. 3 (2018): 84–126.

Datz, Giselle. "What Life after Default? Time Horizons and the Outcome of the Argentine Debt Restructuring Deal." *Review of International Political Economy* 16, no. 3 (2009): 456–484.

Datz, Giselle, and Katharine Corcoran. "Deviant Debt: Reputation, Litigation, and Outlier Effects in Argentina's Debt Restructuring Saga." *New Political Economy* 25, no. 2 (2020): 300–313.

Daunton, Martin J. "Britain and Globalisation since 1850: III. Creating the World of Bretton Woods, 1939–1958." *Transactions of the Royal Historical Society Presidential Address* 18 (2008): 1–42.

———. "From Bretton Woods to Havana: Multilateral Deadlocks in Historical Perspective." In *Deadlocks in Multilateral Negotiations: Causes and Solutions*, edited by Amrita Narlikar, 47–78. Cambridge: Cambridge University Press, 2010.

———. "How to Pay for the War: State, Society and Taxation in Britain, 1917–24." *English Historical Review* 111, no. 443 (1996): 882–919.

———. *Just Taxes: The Politics of Taxation in Britain, 1914–1979*. Cambridge: Cambridge University Press, 2002.

———. *Wealth and Welfare: An Economic and Social History of Britain, 1851–1951*. Oxford: Oxford University Press, 2007.

Davis, Kenneth. *FDR: The War President, 1940–1943*. New York: Random House, 2000.

Dayer, Roberta Allbert. "The British War Debts to the United States and the Anglo-Japanese Alliance, 1920–1923." *Pacific Historical Review* 45, no. 4 (1976): 569–595.

———. *Finance and Empire: Sir Charles Addis, 1861–1945*. New York: Palgrave Macmillan, 1988.

———. "Strange Bedfellows: J. P. Morgan & Co., Whitehall and the Wilson Administration during World War I." *Business History* 18, no. 2 (1976): 127–151.

"Debt Finale, The." *The Economist* 116, no. 4686 (17 June 1933).

DeConde, Alexander. *A History of American Foreign Policy*. New York: Scribner, 1963.

Deighton, Anne. "Britain and the Cold War, 1945–1955." In *The Cambridge History of the Cold War*, vol. 1, *Origins*, edited by Melvyn P. Leffler and Odd Arne Westad, 112–132. Cambridge: Cambridge University Press, 2010.

DeLong, J. Bradford, and Barry Eichengreen. "The Marshall Plan: History's Most Successful Structural Adjustment Program." NBER Working Paper 3899, National Bureau of Economic Research, 1991.

Denman, James, and Paul McDonald. "Unemployment Statistics from 1881 to the Present Day." *Labour Market Trends*, January 1996, 5–18.

Despres, Emil, Charles Kindleberger, and William Salant. "The Dollar and World Liquidity: A Minority View." *The Economist*, 5 February 1996, 526–529.

DeWitt, Howard Arthur. "Hiram Johnson and Early New Deal Diplomacy, 1933–1934." *California Historical Quarterly* 53, no. 4 (1974): 377–386.

———. "Hiram W. Johnson and American Foreign Policy, 1917–1941." PhD diss., University of Arizona, 1972.

DiGiuseppe, Matthew. "The Fiscal Autonomy of Deciders: Creditworthiness and Conflict Initiation." *Foreign Policy Analysis* 11, no. 3 (2015): 317–338.

DiGiuseppe, Matthew, and Patrick Shea. "The Devil's Haircut: Investor-State Disputes over Debt Restructuring." *Journal of Conflict Resolution* 63, no. 8 (2019): 1889–1922.

Dimsdale, N. H. "British Monetary Policy and the Exchange Rate, 1920–1938." *Oxford Economic Papers* 33, no. 2 (1981): 306–349.

Divine, Robert. *The Illusion of Neutrality*. Chicago: Chicago University Press, 1966.

———. *Roosevelt and World War II*. Baltimore: Johns Hopkins University Press, 1969.

Dobson, Alan P. "The Export White Paper, 10 September 1941." *Economic History Review* 39, no. 1 (1986): 59–76.

———. *The Politics of the Anglo-American Economic Special Relationship, 1940–1987*. Sussex, UK: Wheatsheaf Books, 1988.

———. *U.S. Wartime Aid to Britain, 1940–1946*. London: Croom Helm, 1986.

Dockrill, Saki. *Britain's Retreat from East of Suez: The Choice between Europe and the World?* Basingstoke, UK: Palgrave Macmillan 2002.

Dominguez, Kathryn M. E. "The Role of International Organizations in the Bretton Woods System." In *A Retrospective on the Bretton Woods System: Lessons for International Monetary Reform*, edited by Michael D. Bordo and Barry Eichengreen, 357–404. Chicago: University of Chicago Press 1993.

Dormael, Arman van. *Bretton Woods: Birth of a Monetary System*. Basingstoke, UK: Palgrave, 1978.

D.P.E. "Lend-Lease and Reverse Lend-Lease Aid: Part II." *Bulletin of International News* 22, no. 4 (1945): 157–164.

Drelichman, Mauricio, and Hans-Joachim Voth. "Duplication without Constraints: Álvarez-Nogal and Chamley's Analysis of Debt Policy under Philip II." *Economic History Review* 69, no. 3 (2016): 999–1006.

———. *Lending to the Borrower from Hell: Debt, Taxes, and Default in the Age of Philip II*. Princeton, NJ: Princeton University Press, 2014.

Drezner, Daniel. *The System Worked: How the World Stopped Another Great Depression*. Oxford: Oxford University Press, 2016.

Drummond, Ian M. *The Floating Pound and the Sterling Area, 1931–1939*. Cambridge: Cambridge University Press, 1981.

DuBoff, Richard B. *Accumulation and Power: Economic History of the United States*. London: Routledge, 1989.

Dutton, David. *Simon: A Political Biography*. London: Aurum, 1992.

Dyson, Kenneth. "Morality of Debt: A History of Financial Saints and Sinners." *Foreign Affairs*, 3 May 2015. https://www.foreignaffairs.com/articles/2015-05-03/morality-debt.

———. *States, Debt, and Power: "Saints" and "Sinners" in European History and Integration*. Oxford: Oxford University Press, 2014.

Eckes, Alfred E., Jr. *A Search for Solvency: Bretton Woods and the International Monetary System, 1941–1971*. Austin: University of Texas Press, 1975.

Edgerton, David. *Britain's War Machine: Weapons, Resources and Experts in the Second World War*. London: Penguin, 2012.

———. "The Decline of Declinism." *Business History Review* 71, no. 2 (1997): 201–206.

———. *Warfare State: Britain, 1920–1970*. Cambridge: Cambridge University Press, 2005.

Edwards, Sebastian. *American Default: The Untold Story of FDR, the Supreme Court, and the Battle over Gold*. Princeton, NJ: Princeton University Press, 2018.

———. *Crisis and Reform in Latin America: From Despair to Hope*. Oxford: Oxford University Press for the World Bank, 1995.

———. "Exchange Rate Puzzles and Dilemmas." In *The Price, Real and Financial Effects of Exchange Rates*, 144–147. BIS 96, Bank of International Settlements, 2002.

———. "Exchange Rates and the Political Economy of Macroeconomic Discipline." *American Economic Review* 86, no. 2 (1996): 159–163.

———. "Gold, the Brains Trust and Roosevelt." *History of Political Economy* 49, no. 1 (2017): 209–238.

———. "Keynes and the Dollar in 1933." *Financial History Review* 24, no. 3 (2017): 209–238.

———. "LDCs' Foreign Borrowing and Default Risk: An Empirical Investigation, 1976–1980." *American Economic Review* 74, no. 4 (1984): 726–734.

———. "The London Monetary and Economic Conference of 1933 and the End of the Great Depression." *Open Economies Review* 28, no. 3 (2017): 431–459.

———. "Sovereign Default, Debt Restructuring, and Recovery Rates: Was the Argentinean 'Haircut' Excessive?" *Open Economies Review* 26, no. 5 (2015): 1–29.

Edwards, Sebastian, F. A. Longstaff, and A. G. Garcia Marin. "The U.S. Debt Restructuring of 1933: Consequences and Lessons." NBER w21694, National Bureau of Economic Research, November 2015.

Edwards, Sebastian, and Julio Santaella. "Devaluation Controversies in the Developing Countries: Lessons from the Bretton Woods Era." In *A Retrospective on the Bretton Woods System: Lessons for International Monetary Reform*, edited by Michael D. Bordo and Barry Eichengreen, 405–460. Chicago: University of Chicago Press, 1991.

Eggerston, Gauti B. "Great Expectations at the End of the Depression." *American Economic Review* 98, no. 4 (2008): 1476–1516.

Eichengreen, Barry. "The Bank of France and the Sterilization of Gold, 1926–1932." *Explorations in Economic History* 23, no. 1 (1986): 56–84.

———. *Exorbitant Privilege: The Rise and Fall of the Dollar*. Oxford: Oxford University Press, 2011.

———. "From Benign Neglect to Malignant Preoccupation: US Balance of Payments Policy in the 1960s." In *Economic Events, Ideas, and Policy: The 1960s and After*, edited by George Perry and James Tobin, 185–242. Washington, DC: Brookings Institution Press, 2000.

———. "Global Imbalances and the Lessons of Bretton Woods." *Economie Internationale* 100, no. 4 (2004): 39–50.

———. *Golden Fetters: The Gold Standard and the Great Depression, 1919–39*. Oxford: Oxford University Press, 1992.

———. *Hall of Mirrors: The Great Depression, The Great Recession, and the Uses—and Misuses—of History*. Oxford: Oxford University Press, 2015.

———. "Historical Research on International Lending and Debt." *Journal of Economic Perspectives* 5, no. 2 (1991): 149–169.

———. "The Origins and Nature of the Great Slump Revisited." *Economic History Review* 45, no. 2 (1992): 213–239.

———. "Restructuring Sovereign Debt." *Journal of Economic Perspectives* 17, no. 4 (2003): 75–98.

———. *Sterling and the Tariff, 1929–32*. Princeton Studies in International Finance 48. Princeton, NJ: Princeton University Press, 1981.

———. "The U.S. Capital Market and Foreign Lending, 1920–1955." In *Developing Country Debt and the World Economy*, edited by Jeffrey D. Sachs, 237–248. National Bureau of Economic Research. Chicago: University of Chicago Press, 1989.

Eichengreen, Barry, and Richard Portes. "Debt and Default in the 1930s: Causes and Consequences." *European Economic Review* 30, no. 3 (1986): 599–640.

———. "The Interwar Debt Crisis and Its Aftermath." *World Bank Research Observer* 5, no. 1 (1990): 69–94.

Eichengreen, Barry, and Jeffrey Sachs. "Exchange Rates and Economic Recovery in the 1930s." *Journal of Economic History* 45, no. 4 (1985): 925–946.

Eichengreen, Barry, and Peter Temin, "Fetters of Gold and Paper." *Oxford Review of Economic Policy* 26, no. 3 (2010): 370–384.

Einzig, Paul. *Germany's Default: The Economics of Hitlerism*. London: Macmillan, 1934.

Ellis, Ethan. *Republican Foreign Policy, 1921–33*. New Brunswick, NJ: Rutgers University Press, 1968.

English, William B. "Understanding the Costs of Sovereign Default: American State Debts in the 1840's." *American Economic Review* 86, no. 1 (1996): 259–275.

Evans, Richard J., *Altered Pasts: Counterfactuals in History*. Boston: Little, Brown 2014.

Fairfield, Tasha. "Going Where the Money Is: Strategies for Taxing Economic Elites in Unequal Democracies." *World Development* 47, no. 1 (2012): 42–57.

Feiling, Keith. *The Life of Neville Chamberlain*. London: Macmillan, 1946.

Feis, Herbert. *1933: Characters in Crisis*. Boston: Little, Brown, 1966.

Feldman, Gerald D. "Political Disputes about the Role of Banks." In *The Role of Banks in the Inter-war Economy*, edited by Harold James, Hakan Lindgren, and Alice Teichova, 13–18. Cambridge: Cambridge University Press, 1991.

Ferguson, Niall. *The Ascent of Money*. London: Allen Lane, 2008.

———. *The Pity of War*. London: Penguin, 2009.

———. "Political Risk and the International Bond Market between the 1848 Revolution and the Outbreak of the First World War." *Economic History Review* 59, no. 1 (2006): 70–112.

———, ed. *Virtual History: Alternatives and Counterfactuals*. London: Penguin, 2014.

Ferrell, Robert H. *American Diplomacy in the Great Depression: Hoover-Stimson Foreign Policy, 1929–1933*. New Haven, CT: Yale University Press, 1957.

———, ed. *Inside the Nixon Administration: The Secret Diary of Arthur Burns, 1969–1974*. Lawrence: University Press of Kansas, 2010.

———. *The Presidency of Calvin Coolidge*. Lawrence: University Press of Kansas, 1998.

Ferris, John Robert. *Men, Money, and Diplomacy: The Evolution of British Strategic Policy, 1919–26*. Ithaca, NY: Cornell University Press, 1989.

Fforde, John. *The Bank of England and Public Policy, 1941–1958*. Cambridge: Cambridge University Press, 1992.

Field, Alexander J. *A Great Leap Forward: 1930s Depression and U.S. Economic Growth*. New Haven, CT: Yale University Press, 2012.

Findlay, Ronald, and Kevin H. O'Rourke. *Power and Plenty: Trade, War, and the World Economy in the Second Millennium*. Princeton, NJ: Princeton University Press, 2009.

Finn, Margot C. *The Character of Credit: Personal Debt in English Culture, 1740–1914*. Cambridge: Cambridge University Press, 2008.

Finnemore, Martha, and Kathryn Sikkink. "International Norm Dynamics and Political Change." *International Organization* 52, no. 4 (1998): 887–917.

Fisher, David Hackett. *Historian's Fallacies: Toward a Logic of Historical Thought*. London: Harper, 1970.

Fisher, Irving. "Cancelation of the War Debts." Southwest Foreign Trade Conference Address, 2 July 1931.

——. "A Compensated Dollar." *Quarterly Journal of Economics* 27 (1913): 385–397.

——. *The Money Illusion.* New York: Adelphi, 1928.

——. *The Purchasing Power of Money.* New York: Macmillan, 1911.

Fishlow, Albert. "Lessons from the Past: Capital Markets during the 19th Century and the Interwar Period." *International Organization* 39, no. 3 (1985): 383–439.

Flandreau, Marc, Norbert Gaillard, and Frank Packer. "To Err Is Human: Rating Agencies and the Interwar Foreign Government Debt Crisis." BIS Working Paper 335, Bank of International Settlements, 2010.

Flandreau, Marc, and Frédéric Zumer. *The Making of Global Finance, 1880–1913.* Paris and Washington, DC: Organisation for Economic Co-operation and Development, 2004.

Fleming, Anne. *City of Debtors: A Century of Fringe Finance.* Cambridge, MA: Harvard University Press, 2018.

Flores-Macías, Gustavo, and Sarah Kreps. "Borrowing Support for War." *Journal of Conflict Resolution* 61, no. 5 (2017): 997–1020.

Floud, Roderick, Jane Humphries, and Paul Johnson, eds. *The Cambridge Economic History of Modern Britain.* Vol. 2, *1870 to the Present.* 2nd ed. Cambridge: Cambridge University Press, 2012.

Fogel, Robert William, and G. R. Elton. *Which Road to the Past? Two Views of History.* New Haven, CT: Yale University Press, 1983.

Foley-Fisher, Nathan, and Eoin McLaughlin. "State Dissolution, Sovereign Debt and Default: Lessons from the UK and Ireland, 1920–1938." *European Economic Review* 87 (2016): 272–286.

Forbes, Neil. *Doing Business with the Nazis: Britain's Economic and Financial Relations with Germany, 1931–1939.* London: Frank Cass, 2000.

Fossedal, Gregory A. *Our Finest Hour: Will Clayton, the Marshall Plan, and the Triumph of Democracy.* Stanford, CA: Hoover Institution Press, 1993.

Frasure, Carl M. *British Policy in the War Debts and Reparations.* Philadelphia: Doreince, 1940.

Frieden, Jeffry. *Debt, Development, and Democracy: Modern Political Economy and Latin America, 1965–1985.* Princeton, NJ: Princeton University Press, 1991.

——. "Winners and Losers in the Latin America Debt Crisis: The Political Implications." In *Debt and Democracy in Latin America*, edited by B. Stallings and R. Kaufman, 23–37. Boulder, CO: Westview, 1989.

Friedman, Milton, and Anna J. Schwartz. *A Monetary History of the United States, 1867–1960*. Princeton, NJ: Princeton University Press, 1963.

Fry, Geoffrey K. "A Reconsideration of the British General Election of 1935 and the Electoral Revolution of 1945." *History* 76, no. 246 (1991): 43–55.

Fuentes, Michael, and Diego Saravia. "Are Sovereign Defaulters Punished?" In *Sovereign Debt: From Safety to Default*, edited by Robert W. Kolb, 149–154. Hoboken, NJ: Wiley, 2011.

———. "Sovereign Defaulters: Do International Capital Markets Punish Them?" *Journal of Development Economics* 91, no. 2 (2010): 336–347.

Fuller, Edward W., and Robert C. Whitten. "Keynes and the First World War." *Libertarian Papers* 9, no. 1 (2017): 1–39.

Fuller, Robert Lynn. *Phantom of Fear: The Banking Panic of 1933*. Jefferson, NC: McFarland, 2011.

Gaillard, Norbert. *A Century of Sovereign Ratings*. London: Springer, 2011.

Galofré-Vilà, Gregori, Christopher M. Meissner, Martin McKee, and David Stuckler. "The Economic Consequences of the 1953 London Debt Agreement." *European Review of Economic History* 23, no. 1 (2019): 1–29.

Gamble, Andrew. *Britain in Decline*. 4th ed. London: Macmillan, 1994.

Gannon, Philip. "The Special Relationship and the 1945 Anglo-American Loan." *Journal of Transatlantic Studies* 12, no. 1 (2014): 1–17.

Gardner, Richard N. *Sterling-Dollar Diplomacy: The Origins and Prospects of Our International Order*. 1956. Reprint, New York: McGraw-Hill, 1969.

Gavin, Francis J. "The Gold Battles within the Cold War: American Monetary Policy and the Defense of Europe, 1960–1963." *Diplomatic History* 26, no. 1 (2002): 61–94.

———. *Gold, Dollars, and Power: The Politics of International Monetary Relations, 1958–1971*. Chapel Hill: University of North Carolina Press, 2004.

———. *Nuclear Statecraft: History and Strategy in America's Atomic Age*. Ithaca, NY: Cornell University Press, 2012.

Gay, Edwin F. "War Loans or Subsidies." *Foreign Affairs* 4, no. 3 (1926): 394–405.

George, Alexander, and Andrew Bennett. *Case Studies and Theory Development in the Social Sciences*. Cambridge MA: MIT Press, 2005.

Gerwarth, Robert. *The Vanquished: Why the First World War Failed to End, 1917–1923*. London: Penguin, 2016.

Gerwarth, Robert, and Erez Manela. *Empires at War, 1911–1923*. Oxford: Oxford University Press, 2014.

Gill, David James. *Britain and the Bomb: Nuclear Diplomacy*. Stanford, CA: Stanford University Press, 2014.

———. "Rating the United Kingdom: The British Government's Sovereign Credit Ratings, 1976–1978." *Economic History Review* 68, no. 3 (2015): 1016–1037.

———. "Review Essay: Rethinking Sovereign Default." *Review of International Political Economy* 28, no. 6 (2021): 1751–1770.

Gill, David James, and Michael J. Gill. "The Great Ratings Game: How Countries Become Creditworthy." *Foreign Affairs*, 21 January 2015. https://www.foreignaffairs.com/articles/united-states/2015-01-21/great-ratings-game.

Gill, Michael J., David James Gill, and Thomas J. Roulet. "Constructing Trustworthy Historical Narratives: Criteria, Principles and Techniques." *British Journal of Management* 29, no. 1 (2018): 191–205.

Gilman, Martin. *No Precedent, No Plan: Inside Russia's 1998 Default*. Cambridge, MA: MIT Press, 2010.

Gilpin, Robert. *War and Change in World Politics*. New York: Cambridge University Press, 1981.

Gilsinan, Kathy. "65 Words Just Caused Argentina's $29-Billion Default." *The Atlantic*, 31 July 2014. https://www.theatlantic.com/international/archive/2014/07/65-words-just-caused-argentinas-29-billion-default/375368/.

Goldin, Claudia. "Cliometrics and the Nobel." *Journal of Economic Perspectives* 9, no. 2 (1995): 191–208.

Goodman, David. "The Bank of England, 1914 War Loans and a Patriotic Cover-Up." *Bloomberg Markets*, 8 August 2017. https://www.bloomberg.com/news/articles/2017-08-08/the-bank-of-england-1914-war-loans-and-a-patriotic-cover-up.

Gordon, Robert. *The Rise and Fall of American Growth: The U.S. Standard of Living since the Civil War*. Princeton, NJ: Princeton University Press, 2014.

Gould, Clarence P. "Review: Carl M. Frasure, *British Policy in the War Debts and Reparations*." *Mississippi Valley Historical Review* 28, no. 1 (1941): 133–134.

Gowa, Joanne. *Closing the Gold Window: Domestic Politics and the End of Bretton Woods*. Ithaca, NY: Cornell University Press, 1983.

Grant, Philip A., Jr. "President Harry S. Truman and the British Loan Act of 1946." *Presidential Studies Quarterly* 25, no. 3 (1995): 494–495.

———. "President Warren G. Harding and the British War Debt Question, 1921–23." *Presidential Studies Quarterly* 25, no. 3 (1995): 479–487.

Gray, William Glenn. "Floating the System: Germany, the United States, and the Breakdown of Bretton Woods, 1969–1973." *Diplomatic History* 31, no. 2 (2007): 295–323.

Grigg, P. J. *Prejudice and Judgement*. London: Jonathan Cape, 1948.

Grossman, Herschel I., and John B. Van Huyck. "Sovereign Debt as a Contingent Claim: Excusable Default, Repudiation, and Reputation." *American Economic Review* 78, no. 5 (1988): 1088–1097.

Guzman, Martin, José Antonio Ocampo, and Joseph E. Stiglitz, eds. *Too Little, Too Late: The Quest to Resolve Sovereign Debt Crises*. New York: Columbia University Press, 2016.

Hachey, Thomas E., and R. C. Lindsay. "Winning Friends and Influencing Policy: British Strategy to Woo America in 1937." *Wisconsin Magazine of History* 55, no. 2 (1971–1972): 120–129.

Hale, David. "The Newfoundland Lesson." *International Economy*, 22 June 2003, 51–61.

Hall, George J., and Thomas J. Sargent. "Complications for the United States from International Credits: 1913–1940." Chapter 1 in *Debt and Entanglements: Between the Wars*, edited by Era Dabla-Norris, 1–58. International Monetary Fund, 2019.

Harbutt, Fraser J. *The Iron Curtain: Churchill, America, and the Origins of the Cold War*. Oxford: Oxford University Press, 1989.

Hargreaves, E. L. *The National Debt*. Abingdon, UK: Routledge 2006.

Harris, Kenneth. *Attlee*. London: Weidenfeld and Nicolson, 1995.

Harris, Max. *Monetary War and Peace: London, Washington, Paris, and the Tripartite Agreement of 1936*. Cambridge: Cambridge University Press, 2021.

Hathaway, Robert M. *Ambiguous Partnership: Britain and America, 1944–47*. New York: Columbia University Press, 1981.

Hattersley, Roy. *David Lloyd George: The Great Outsider*. Boston: Little, Brown, 2010.

Hawthorn, Geoffrey. *Plausible Worlds: Possibility and Understanding in History and the Social Sciences*. Cambridge: Cambridge University Press, 1991.

Hayford, Marc, and Carl Pasurka Jr. "The Political Economy of the Fordney-McCumber and Smoot-Hawley Tariff Acts." *Explorations in Economic History* 29, no. 1 (1992): 30–50.

Healey, Denis. *The Time of My Life*. London: Michael Joseph, 1989.

Helleiner, Eric. *Forgotten Foundations of Bretton Woods: International Development and the Making of the Postwar Order*. Ithaca, NY: Cornell University Press, 2014.

Henderson, Hubert D. *The Inter-war Years and Other Papers: A Selection from the Writings of Hubert Douglas Henderson*. Oxford, UK: Clarendon, 1955.

Hennessy, Peter. *Muddling Through: Power, Politics and the Quality of Government in Postwar Britain*. London: Victor Gollancz, 1996.

———. *The Prime Minister: The Office and Its Holders since 1945*. London: Allen Lane, 2000.

Herring, George C., Jr. *Aid to Russia, 1941–1946: Strategy, Diplomacy, the Origins of the Cold War*. New York: Columbia University Press, 1973.

———. "Lend-Lease to Russia and the Origins of the Cold War, 1944–1945." *Journal of American History* 56 (1969): 93–114.

———. "The United States and British Bankruptcy, 1944–1945: Responsibilities Deferred." *Political Science Quarterly* 86, no. 2 (1971): 260–280.

Herriot, Edouard. *Jadis*. Vol. 2. Paris: Flammarion, 1948.

Hickson, Kevin. *The IMF Crisis of 1976 and British Politics*. London: I. B. Tauris, 2005.

Higgs, Robert. "Wartime Prosperity? A Reassessment of the U.S. Economy in the 1940s." *Journal of Economic History* 52, no. 1 (1992): 41–60.

Hileman, Garrick. "Overlooked Sovereign Credit Events and Partial Defaults: British Debt Sustainability in the Post–Second World War Period." SSRN, 2017.

———. "Sovereign Debt Sustainability, Financial Repression, and Monetary Innovation: Britain and Currency Black Markets in the Mid-20th century." PhD diss., London School of Economics and Political Science, 2015.

Hill, John S. "American Efforts to Aid French Reconstruction between Lend-Lease and the Marshall Plan." *Journal of Modern History* 64, no. 3 (1992): 500–524.

Hilt, Eric, and Wendy M. Rahn. "Financial Asset Ownership and Political Partisanship: Liberty Bonds and Republican Electoral Success in the 1920s." NBER Working Paper 24719, National Bureau of Economic Research, 2018.

Hinds, Allister E. "Sterling and Imperial Policy, 1945–1951." *Journal of Imperial and Commonwealth History*, 15, no. 2 (1987): 148–169.

Hirst, Francis W. *The Consequences of the War to Great Britain*. London: Humphrey Milford, 1934.

Hogan, Michael J. *Informal Entente: The Private Structure of Cooperation in Anglo-American Economic Diplomacy, 1918–28*. Columbia: University of Missouri Press, 1977.

———. *The Marshall Plan: America, Britain and the Reconstruction of Western Europe, 1947–1952*. Cambridge: Cambridge University Press, 1987.

Hoover, Herbert. *The Memoirs of Herbert Hoover*. Vol. 2, *The Cabinet and Presidency, 1920–1933*. New York: Macmillan, 1952.

———. *The Memoirs of Herbert Hoover*. Vol. 3, *The Great Depression*. New York: Macmillan, 1952.

Horn, Martin. *Britain, France, and the Financing of the First World War*. Montreal: McGill-Queens University Press, 1992.

———. "J. P. Morgan & Co., the House of Morgan and Europe 1933–1939." *Contemporary European History* 14, no. 4 (2005): 519–538.

———. "A Private Bank at War: J. P. Morgan & Co. and France, 1914–1918." *Business History Review* 74, no. 1 (2000), 85–112.

Howson, Susan. *British Monetary Policy, 1945–51*. Oxford: Oxford University Press, 1991.

———. *Domestic Monetary Management in Britain, 1919–38*. Cambridge: Cambridge University Press, 1975.

———. "The Management of Sterling, 1932–1939." *Journal of Economic History* 40, no. 1 (1980): 53–60.

———. *Sterling's Managed Float: The Operations of the Exchange Equalisation Account, 1932–39*. Princeton, NJ: Princeton University Press, 1980.

Hull, Cordell. *The Memoirs of Cordell Hull*. 2 vols. New York: Macmillan, 1948.

Hunt, Edwin S. *The Medieval Super-companies: A Study of the Peruzzi Company of Florence*. Cambridge: Cambridge University Press, 1994.

Ikenberry, G. John. "Rethinking the Origins of American Hegemony." *Political Science Quarterly* 104, no. 3 (1989): 375–400.

Irwin, Douglas A. "Did France Cause the Great Depression?" NBER Working Paper 16350, National Bureau of Economic Research, 2010.

———. "The Nixon Shock after Forty Years: The Import Surcharge Revisited." *World Trade Review* 12, no. 1 (2013): 29–56.

———. *Peddling Protectionism: Smoot-Hawley and the Great Depression*. Princeton, NJ: Princeton University Press, 2011.

———. "The Smoot-Hawley Tariff: A Quantitative Assessment." *Review of Economics and Statistics* 80, no. 2 (1998): 326–334.

Jackson, Julian. *The Fall of France: The Nazi Invasion of 1940*. Oxford: Oxford University Press, 2001.

Jackson, Peter. "Post-war Politics and the Historiography of French Strategy and Diplomacy Before the Second World War." *History Compass* 4–5 (2006): 870–905.

Jacob, Philip E. "Influences of World Events on U.S. 'Neutrality' Opinion." *Public Opinion Quarterly* 4, no. 1 (1940): 48–65.

Jacobson, Jon. "Is There a New International History of the 1920s?" *American Historical Review* 88, no. 3 (1983): 617–645.

James, Harold. "The Causes of the German Banking Crisis of 1931." *Economic History Review* 37, no. 1 (1984): 68–87.

———. "The Central European Banking Crisis Revisited." In *Business in the Age of Extremes: Essays in Modern German and Austrians Economic History*, edited by Hartmut Berghoff, Jurgen Kocka, and Dieter Ziegler, 119–130. Cambridge: Cambridge University Press, 2013.

———. *The Creation and Destruction of Value: The Globalization Cycle.* Cambridge, MA: Harvard University Press, 2009.

———. "Deep Red: The International Debt Crisis and Its Historical Precedents." *American Scholar* 56, no. 3 (1987): 331–341.

———. *The End of Globalization: Lessons from the Great Depression.* Cambridge, MA: Harvard University Press, 2001.

———. *Europe Contested: From the Kaiser to Brexit.* Abingdon, UK: Routledge, 2019.

———. *Europe Reborn: A History 1914–2000.* 2003. Reprint, Abingdon, UK: Routledge, 2015.

———. "Financial Flows across Frontiers during the Interwar Depression." *Economic History Review* 45, no. 3 (1992): 594–613.

———. *The German Slump: Politics and Economics, 1924–1936.* Oxford, UK: Clarendon, 1986.

———. "The Great Depression and the Great Recession." *Journal of Modern European History* 11, no. 3 (2013): 308–314.

———. "International Capital Movements and the Global Order." In *The Cambridge History of Capitalism*, vol. 2, edited by Larry Neal and Jeffrey G. Williamson, 264–300. Cambridge: Cambridge University Press, 2014.

———. *International Monetary Cooperation since Bretton Woods.* Oxford: Oxford University Press, 1996.

———. "International Order after the Financial Crisis." *International Affairs* 87, no. 3 (2011): 525–537.

———. Introduction to *The Interwar Depression in an International Context*, edited by Harold James, vii–xv. Munich: Oldenbourg Wissenschaftsverlag, 2002.

———. Introduction to *The Role of Banks in the Interwar Economy*, edited by Harold James, Hakan Lindgren, and Alice Teichova, 1–12. Cambridge: Cambridge University Press, 1991.

———. "The Multiple Contexts of Bretton Woods." *Oxford Review of Economic Policy* 28, no. 3 (2012): 411–430.

———. "1929: The New York Stock Market Crash." *Representations* 110, no. 1 (2010): 129–144.

———. *The Reichsbank and Public Finance in Germany, 1924–1933: A Study in the Politics of Economics During the Great Depression.* Frankfurt am Main: F. Knapp, 1985.

James, Harold, and Marzenna James. "Origins of the Cold War: Some New Documents." *Historical Journal* 37, no. 3 (1994): 615–622.

Jeansonne, Glen. *The Life of Herbert Hoover: Fighting Quaker, 1928–33.* Basingstoke, UK: Palgrave Macmillan, 2012.

Jervis, Robert. "The Future of World Politics: Will It Resemble the Past?" *International Security* 16, no. 3 (1991–1992): 39–73.

———. *Perception and Misperception in International Politics.* Princeton, NJ: Princeton University Press, 1976.

Johnson, Lyndon Baines. *The Vantage Point: Perspectives of the Presidency: 1961–1960.* London: Weidenfeld and Nicolson, 1971.

Johnson, Niall. *Britain and the 1918–19 Influenza Pandemic: A Dark Epilogue.* Abingdon, UK: Routledge 2006.

"Johnson Act, The: Extension of Credit to a Government in Default." *Columbia Law Review* 35, no. 1 (1935): 102–104.

Jones, Daniel, Stuart Bremer, and David Singer. "Militarized Interstate Disputes, 1816–1992: Rationale, Coding Rules, and Empirical Patterns." *Conflict Management and Peace Science* 15 (1996): 163–213.

Jones, Matthew. "A Decision Delayed: Britain's Withdrawal from South East Asia Reconsidered, 1961–68." *English Historical Review* 117, no. 472 (2002): 569–595.

Kaiser, Jürgen. "One Made It out of the Debt Trap: Lessons from the London Debt Agreement of 1953 for Current Debt Crises." Friedrich Ebert Stiftung, Berlin, 2013.

Kang, Sung Won, and Hugh Rockoff. "Capitalizing Patriotism: The Liberty Loans of World War I." NBER Working Paper 11919, National Bureau of Economic Research, January 2006.

Keiger, John F. V. "Raymond Poincaré and the Ruhr Crisis." In *French Foreign and Defence Policy, 1918–1940: The Decline and Fall of a Great Power*, edited by Robert Boyce, 49–70. London: Routledge, 1998.

Kennedy, Paul. *The Rise and Fall of the Great Powers.* New York: Random House, 1987.

———. *Strategy and Diplomacy, 1870–1945.* London: Fontana, 1989.

Kennedy, Susan E. *The Banking Crisis of 1933.* Lexington: University Press of Kentucky, 1973.

Kent, Bruce. *The Spoils of War: The Politics, Economics, and Diplomacy of Reparations 1918–1932.* Oxford, UK: Clarendon, 1991.

Keynes, John Maynard. *The Collected Writings of John Maynard Keynes.* Vol. 2, *The Economic Consequences of the Peace.* Edited by Elizabeth Johnson and Donald Moggridge. 1978. Reprint, Cambridge: Cambridge University Press for the Royal Economic Society, 2012.

———. *The Collected Writings of John Maynard Keynes.* Vol. 13, *The "General Theory" and After: Part 1. Preparation.* Edited by Elizabeth Johnson and Donald Moggridge. 1978. Reprint, Cambridge: Cambridge University Press for the Royal Economic Society, 2012.

———. *The Collected Writings of John Maynard Keynes.* Vol. 16, *Activities 1914–1919: The Treasury and Versailles.* Edited by Elizabeth Johnson. 1977. Reprint, Cambridge: Cambridge University Press for the Royal Economic Society, 2013.

———. *The Collected Writings of John Maynard Keynes.* Vol. 18, *Activities 1922–1932: The End of Reparations.* Edited by Elizabeth Johnson. 1978. Reprint, Cambridge: Cambridge University Press for the Royal Economic Society, 2013.

———. *The Collected Writings of John Maynard Keynes.* Vol. 22, *Activities 1939–1945: Internal War Finance.* Edited by Donald Moggridge. 1978. Reprint, Cambridge: Cambridge University Press for the Royal Economic Society, 2013.

———. *The Collected Writings of John Maynard Keynes.* Vol. 23, *Activities 1940–43: External War Finance.* Edited by Donald Moggridge. 1979. Reprint, Cambridge: Cambridge University Press for the Royal Economic Society, 2013.

———. *The Collected Writings of John Maynard Keynes.* Vol. 24, *Activities 1922–1932: The Transition to Peace.* Edited by Donald Moggridge. 1979. Reprint, Cambridge: Cambridge University Press for the Royal Economic Society, 2013.

———. *The Economic Consequences of the Peace.* New York: Harcourt Brace, 1920.

———. *A Revision of the Treaty, Being a Sequel to the Economic Consequences of the Peace.* New York: Harcourt, Brace, 1922.

Killick, John. *The United States and European Reconstruction 1945–1960.* London: Routledge, 2013.

Kimball, Warren F. "'Beggar My Neighbor': America and the British Interim Finance Crisis, 1940–1941." *Journal of Economic History* 29, no. 4 (1969): 758–772.

———. *The Juggler: Franklin Roosevelt as Wartime Statesman.* Princeton, NJ: Princeton University Press, 1991.

———. "Lend-Lease and the Open Door: The Temptation of British Opulence, 1937–1942." *Political Science Quarterly* 86, no. 2 (1971): 232–259.

———. *The Most Unsordid Act: Lend-Lease, 1939–1941.* Baltimore: Johns Hopkins University Press, 1969.

Kindersley, Robert M. "British Overseas Investments in 1932 and 1933." *Economic Journal* 44, no. 175 (1934): 365–379.

———. "British Overseas Investments in 1934 and 1935." *Economic Journal* 46, no. 184 (1936): 645–661.

———. "British Oversea Investments in 1935 and 1936." *Economic Journal* 47, no. 188 (1937): 643–662.

Kindleberger, Charles P. *A Financial History of Western Europe*. 1984. Reprint, Oxford: Oxford University Press, 1993.

———. *The World in Depression, 1929–1939*. 1978. Reprint, Berkeley: University of California Press, 2013.

Kohlscheen, Emanuel. "Sovereign Risk: Constitutions Rule." *Oxford Economic Papers* 62, no. 1 (2010): 62–85.

Kolb, Robert W. "Sovereign Debt." In *Sovereign Debt: From Safety to Default*, edited by Robert W. Kolb, 4–7. Hoboken, NJ: Wiley, 2011.

Kolko, Gabrile. *The Politics of War: The World and United States Foreign Policy, 1943–1945*. New York: Random House, 1968.

Krishner, Jonathan. *Appeasing Bankers: Financial Caution on the Road to War*. Princeton, NJ: Princeton University Press, 2007.

Krugman, Paul. *The Return of Depression Economics*. London: Allen Lane, 1999.

Kunz, Diane B. "American Bankers and Britain's Fall from Gold." In *The Role of Banks in the Interwar Economy*, edited by Harold James, Hakan Lindgren, and Alice Teichova, 35–48. Cambridge: Cambridge University Press, 1991.

———. *The Economic Diplomacy of the Suez Crisis*. Chapel Hill: University of North Carolina Press, 1991.

Kynaston, David. *Austerity Britain 1945–51*. London: Bloomsbury, 2007.

LaFeber, Walter. *The Deadly Bet: LBJ, Vietnam, and the 1968 Election*. Lanham, MD: Rowman and Littlefield, 2005.

Lake, David A. "Rightful Rules: Authority, Order, and the Foundations of Global Governance." *International Studies Quarterly* 54, no. 3 (2010): 587–613.

Langer, William L., and S. Everett Gleason. *The Challenge to Isolation, 1939–1940*. New York: Harper, 1952.

———. *The Undeclared War, 1940–1941: The World Crisis and American Foreign Policy*. New York: Harper, 1953.

Leaviss, Jim. "What Happened the Last Time the UK Defaulted?" *Bond Vigilantes*, February 2, 2010. https://www.bondvigilantes.com/insights/2010/02/what-happened-the-last-time-the-uk-defaulted.

Lebow, Richard Ned. *Forbidden Fruit: Counterfactuals and International Relations*. Princeton, NJ: Princeton University Press, 2010.

Leffler, Melvyn P. "American Policy Making and European Stability, 1921–1933." *Pacific Historical Review* 46, no. 2 (1977): 207–228.

———. *The Elusive Quest: America's Pursuit of European Stability and French Security, 1919–1933*. Chapel Hill: University of North Carolina Press, 1979.

———. "The Origins of Republican War Debt Policy, 1921–23: A Case Study in the Applicability of the Open Door Interpretation." *Journal of American History* 59 (1972): 585–601.

Leith-Ross, Frederick. *Money Talks: Fifty Years of International Finance: The Autobiography of Sir Frederick Leith-Ross*. London: Hutchinson, 1968.

Leuchtenburg, William E. *Franklin D. Roosevelt and the New Deal, 1932–1940*. New York: Harper, 1963.

Levy, Jonathan. *Freaks of Fortune: The Emerging World of Capitalism and Risk in America*. Cambridge, MA: Harvard University Press, 2012.

Lienau, Odette. "The Longer-Term Consequences of Sovereign Debt Restricting." Chapter 7 in *Sovereign Debt Management*, edited by Rosa Lastra and Lee Buchheit. Oxford: Oxford University Press, 2014.

———. *Rethinking Sovereign Debt: Politics, Reputation, and Legitimacy in Modern Finance*. Cambridge, MA: Harvard University Press, 2014.

Lindert, Peter, and Peter Morton. "How Sovereign Debt Has Worked." In *Developing Country Debt and Economic Performance*, vol. 1, edited by Jeffrey Sachs, 39–106. Chicago: University of Chicago Press, 1989.

Lipartito, Keith. "Review Essay: Reassembling the Economic." *American Historical Review* 121, no. 1 (2016): 101–139.

Lippmann, Walter. *The Public Philosophy*. Boston: Little, Brown, 1955.

Lipson, Charles. "Bankers' Dilemmas: Private Cooperation in Rescheduling Sovereign Debts." *World Politics* 38, no. 1 (1985): 200–225.

Louis, Wm. Roger. *Imperialism at Bay: The United States and the Decolonization of the British Empire, 1941–1945*. Oxford, UK: Clarendon, 1977.

Lloyd George, David. "Address to the American Club." London, 12 April 1917. Accessed at FirstWorldWar.com, https://www.firstworldwar.com/source/usawar_lloydgeorge.htm.

———. *The Truth about Reparations and War Debts*. London: Heinemann, 1932.

———. *War Memoirs of David Lloyd George: 1917*. Boston: Little, Brown, 1934.

Ludlam, Steve. "The Gnomes of Washington: Four Myths of the 1976 IMF Crisis." *Political Studies* 40, no. 4 (1992): 713–727.

Macdonald, James. *A Free Nation Deep in Debt: The Financial Roots of Democracy*. Princeton, NJ: Princeton University Press, 2006.

MacKenzie, Hector. "The Path to Temptation: The Negotiation of Canada's Reconstruction Loan to Britain in 1946." *Historical Papers* 17, no. 1 (1982): 196–220.

Macleod, Iain. *Neville Chamberlain*. London: Frederick Muller, 1961.

MacMillan, Margaret. *Peace Makers: The Paris Conference of 1919 and Its Attempt to End the War*. London: John Murray, 2001.

Mallaleiu, William C. *British Reconstruction and American Policy, 1945–1955*. New York: Scarecrow, 1956.

Malone, Samuel W. "Sovereign Debt Problems and Policy Gambles." In *Sovereign Debt: From Safety to Default*, edited by Robert W. Kolb, 43–50. Hoboken, NJ: Wiley, 2011.

Mantoux, Étienne. *The Carthaginian Peace; or, The Economic Consequences of Mr Keynes*. Oxford: Oxford University Press, 1946.

Margo, Robert. "Employment and Unemployment in the 1930s." *Journal of Economic Perspectives* 7, no. 2 (1993): 41–59.

Marks, Sally. "The Myths of Reparations." *Central European History* 11, no. 3 (1978): 231–255.

Marquand, David. *Ramsay MacDonald*. London: Jonathan Cape, 1977.

Matusow, Allen. *Nixon's Economy: Boom, Busts, Dollars and Votes*. Lawrence: University Press of Kansas, 1998.

Maurer, Noel. *The Empire Trap: The Rise and Fall of U.S. Intervention to Protect American Property Overseas, 1893–2013*. Princeton, NJ: Princeton University Press, 2013.

McAdoo, William G. *Crowded Years: The Reminiscences of William G. McAdoo*. Boston: Houghton Mifflin, 1931.

McCullough, David. *Truman*. New York: Simon and Schuster, 1993.

McDonald, Andrew. "The Geddes Committee and the Formulation of Public Expenditure Policy, 1921–1922." *Historical Journal* 32, no. 3 (1989): 644–674.

McKercher, Brian J. C. "'Our Most Dangerous Enemy': Great Britain Pre-eminent in the 1930s." *International History Review* 13, no. 4 (1991): 751–783.

———. *Transition of Power: Britain's Loss of Global Pre-eminence to the United States, 1930–1945*. Cambridge: Cambridge University Press, 1999.

McVey, Frank. *The Financial History of Great Britain, 1914–1918*. Oxford: Oxford University Press, 1918.

Meyer, Lorenzo. "The Expropriation and Great Britain." Translated by Lidia Lozano. In *The Mexican Petroleum Industry in the Twentieth Century*, edited by Jonathan C. Brown and Alan Knight, 154–172. Austin: University of Texas Press, 1992.

Middlemas, Keith, and John Barnes. *Baldwin: A Biography*. London: Weidenfeld and Nicolson, 1969.

Middleton, Roger. "British Monetary and Fiscal Policy in the 1930s." *Oxford Review of Economic Policy* 26, no. 3 (2010): 414–441.

―――. "Struggling with the Impossible: Sterling, the Balance of Payments and British Economic Policy, 1949–72." In *The Open Economy Macromodel: Past, Present and Future*, edited by Arie Arnon and Warren Young, 103–154. London: Springer, 2002.

Mills, Ogden L. "Our Foreign Policy: A Republican View." *Foreign Affairs* 6, no. 4 (1928): 555–572.

Milward, Alan S. *The Economic Effects of the Two World Wars on Britain.* London: Palgrave Macmillan, 1970.

Mitchener, Kris James, Kirsten Wandschneider, Kevin Hjortshøj O'Rourke. "The Smoot-Hawley Trade War." CESifo Working Paper 8966, 2021.

Moggridge, Donald. *British Monetary Policy: The Norman Conquest of $4.86.* Cambridge: Cambridge University Press, 1972.

Moley, Raymond. *After Seven Years.* New York: Harper, 1939.

―――. *The First New Deal.* San Diego: Harcourt, Brace and World, 1966.

Monet, Eric, and Damien Puy. "Do Old Habits Die Hard? Central Banks and the Bretton Woods Puzzle." IMF Working Paper WP/19/161, July 2019.

More, Charles. *Black Gold: Britain and Oil in the Twentieth Century.* London: Continuum, 2009.

Morrison, James Ashley. "Shocking Intellectual Austerity: The Role of Ideas in the Demise of the Gold Standard." *International Organization* 70, no. 1 (2015): 175–207.

Mortimer, Ian. *The Perfect King: The Life of Edward III, Father of the English Nation.* London: Vintage 2008.

Mosley, Layna. *Global Capital and National Governments.* Cambridge: Cambridge University Press, 2003.

Moulton, Harold, and Leo Pasvolsky. *War Debts and World Prosperity.* Washington, DC: Brookings Institution Press, 1932.

―――. *World War Debt Settlements.* New York: Macmillan, 1926.

Mouré, Kenneth. *The Gold Standard Illusion: France, the Bank of France, and the International Gold Standard, 1914–1939.* Oxford: Oxford University Press, 2002.

―――. *Managing the Franc Poincaré: Economic Understanding and Political Constraint.* Cambridge: Cambridge University Press, 1991.

―――. "'Une Eventualité Absolument Exclue': French Reluctance to Devalue, 1933–1936." *French Historical Studies* 15, no. 3 (1988): 479–505.

Murray, Robert K. *The Harding Era: Warren G. Harding and His Administration.* Oxford: Oxford University Press, 1969.

Nasar, Sylvia. *Grand Pursuit: The Story of the People Who Made Modern Economics.* London: Fourth Estate, 2012.

Needham, Duncan. *Monetary Policy from Devaluation to Thatcher, 1967–1982.* Basingstoke, UK: Palgrave, 2014.

Nelson, Stephen C., and David A Steinberg. "Default Positions: What Shapes Public Attitudes about International Debt Disputes?" *International Studies Quarterly* 62, no. 3 (2018): 520–533.

Nevins, Allan. *The New Deal and World Affairs: A Chronicle of International Affairs, 1933–1945.* New Haven, CT: Yale University Press, 1950.

Newton, C. C. S. "The Sterling Crisis of 1947 and the British Response to the Marshall Plan." *Economic History Review* 37, no. 3 (1984): 391–408.

Newton, Scott. "The 1949 Sterling Crisis and British Policy towards European Integration." *Review of International Studies* 11, no. 3 (1985): 169–182.

———. "The Sterling Devaluation of 1967, the International Economy and Post-war Social Democracy." *English Historical Review* 125, no. 515 (2010): 912–945.

Nicolson, Harold. *Harold Nicolson: Diaries and Letters, 1930–1939.* Edited by Nigel Nicolson. London: Collins, 1966.

"Nixon Shock, The." *Treasury Today,* September 2011. http://treasurytoday.com/2011/09/the-nixon-shock.

Norbert, Muhlen. *Hitler's Magician: Schacht.* London: Routledge, 1938.

North, Douglass C., and Barry R. Weingast. "Constitutions and Commitment: The Evolution of Institutions Governing Public Choice in Seventeenth-Century England." *Journal of Economic History* 49, no. 4 (1989): 803–832.

Oatley, Thomas. 2011. "The Reductionist Gamble: Open Economy Politics in the Global Economy." *International Organization* 65, no. 2 (2011): 311–341.

O'Brien, Patrick. "The Economic Effects of the Great War." *History Today* 44, no. 12 (1994). https://www.historytoday.com/archive/economic-effects-great-war.

Odell, John S. *U.S. International Monetary Policy: Markets, Power, and Ideas as a Source of Change.* Princeton, NJ: Princeton University Press, 1982.

Officer, Lawrence H. *Between the Dollar-Sterling Gold Points.* Cambridge: Cambridge University Press, 1996.

———. "Exchange Rates between the United States Dollar and Forty-One Currencies." MeasuringWorth, 2021. http://www.measuringworth.com/exchangeglobal/.

Olson, Lynne. *Those Angry Days: Roosevelt, Lindbergh, and America's Fight over World War II, 1939–1941.* New York: Random House, 2013.

Oosterlinck, Kim. *Hope Springs Eternal: French Bondholders and the Repudiation of Russian Sovereign Debt*. Translated by Anthony Bulger. New Haven, CT: Yale University Press, 2014.

———. "Sovereign Debt Defaults: Insights from History." *Oxford Review of Economic Policy* 29, no. 4 (2013): 697–714.

Orde, Anne. *British Policy and European Reconstruction after the First World War*. Cambridge: Cambridge University Press, 2001.

O'Riordan, Elspeth. *Britain and the Ruhr Crisis*. Basingstoke, UK: Palgrave, 2001.

Ovendale, Ritchie. *Anglo-American Relations in the Twentieth Century*. Basingstoke, UK: Palgrave, 1998.

Oye, Kenneth A. "The Sterling-Dollar-Franc Triangle: Monetary Diplomacy 1929–1937." In *Cooperation under Anarchy*, edited by Kenneth A. Oye, 182–208. Princeton, NJ: Princeton University Press, 1988.

Özler, Sule. "Have Commercial Banks Ignored History?" *American Economic Review* 83, no. 3 (1993): 608–620.

Palen, Marc-William. *The "Conspiracy" of Free Trade: The Anglo-American Struggle over Empire and Economic Globalisation, 1846–1896*. Cambridge: Cambridge University Press, 2017.

Panizza, Ugo, Federico Sturzenegger, and Jeromin Zettelmeyer. "The Economics and Law of Sovereign Debt and Default." *Journal of Economic Literature* 47, no. 3 (2009): 651–698.

Papadia, Andrea. "Sovereign Defaults during the Great Depression: The Role of Fiscal Fragility." Economic History Working Papers 68943, London School of Economics and Political Science, Department of Economic History, 2017.

Parker, R. A. C. *Chamberlain and Appeasement: British Policy and the Coming of the Second World War*. London: Macmillan, 1993.

Parrini, Carl. *Heir to Empire: United States Economic Diplomacy, 1916–23*. Pittsburgh: University of Pittsburgh Press, 1969.

Paterson, Thomas G. "The Abortive American Loan to Russia and the Origins of the Cold War, 1943–1946." *Journal of American History* 56, no. 1 (1969): 70–92.

———. "Presidential Foreign-Policy, Public-Opinion, and Congress: The Truman Years." *Diplomatic History* 3, no. 1 (1979): 1–18.

Pavanelli, Giovanni. "The Great Depression in Irving Fisher's Work." *History of Economic Ideas* 11, no. 1 (2003): 151–167.

P.B. "The Sterling Balances: Britain's Debts to the Sterling Area Countries." *World Today* 2, no. 8 (1946): 353–362.

Peden, George C. *Arms, Economics and British Strategy: From Dreadnoughts to Hydrogen Bombs*. Cambridge: Cambridge University Press, 2007.

———. *British Rearmament and the Treasury*. Edinburgh: Scottish Academic Press, 1979.

———. "A Matter of Timing: The Economic Background to British Foreign Policy, 1937–1939." *History* 69, no. 225 (1984): 15–28.

———. *The Treasury and British Public Policy, 1906–1959*. Oxford: Oxford University Press, 2000.

Phillips, Matt. "The Long Story of U.S. Debt, from 1790 to 2011." *Atlantic*, 13 November 2012.

Pimlott, Ben. *Harold Wilson*. London: BCA, 1992.

Plesur, Milton. "The Republican Congressional Comeback of 1938." *Review of Politics* 24, no. 4 (1962): 525–562.

Polk, Judd, and Gardner Patterson. "The British Loan." *Foreign Affairs* 24, no. 3 (1946): 429–440.

Ponting, Clive. *Breach of Promise: Labour in Power, 1964–1970*. London: Hamish Hamilton, 1989.

Pratt, Julius W. *A History of the United States Foreign Policy*. 3rd ed. Englewood Cliffs, NJ: Prentice-Hall, 1972.

Pressnell, L. S. *External Economic Policy since the War*. Vol. 1, *The Postwar Financial Settlement*. London: Her Majesty's Stationery Office, 1987.

Rappleye, Charles. *Herbert Hoover in the White House: The Ordeal of the Presidency*. New York: Simon and Schuster, 2016.

Rathbone, Albert. "Making War Loans to the Allies." *Foreign Affairs*, April 1925, 371–398.

Rauchway, Eric. *The Money Makers: How Roosevelt and Keynes Ended the Depression, Defeated Fascism, and Secured a Prosperous Peace*. New York: Basic Books, 2015.

———. *Winter War: Hoover, Roosevelt, and the First Clash over the New Deal*. New York, Basic Books, 2018.

Reid, Leonard J. *Britain and the War Debts*. London: Jenkins, 1933.

Reinhart, Carmen M. "This Time Is Different Chartbook: Country Histories on Debt, Default, and Financial Crises." NBER Working Paper 15815, National Bureau of Economic Research, 2010.

Reinhart, Carmen M., and Kenneth S. Rogoff. *This Time Is Different: Centuries of Financial Folly*. Princeton, NJ: Princeton University Press, 2011.

Reinhart, Carmen M., and M. Belen Sbranci. "The Liquidation of Government Debt." IMF Working Paper 15/7, 2015.

Reinhart, Carmen M., and Christoph Trebesch. "A Distant Mirror of Debt, Default, and Relief." Munich Discussion Paper 2014-49, 2014.

Reiter, Dan. "Democracy, Deception, and Entry into War." *Security Studies* 21, no. 4 (2012): 594–623.

Reiter, Dan, and John M. Schuessler. "FDR, US Entry into World War II, and Selection Effects Theory." *International Security* 35, no. 2 (2010), 176–185.

Renshaw, Patrick. "Black Friday, 1921." *History Today* 21, no. 6 (1971). https://www.historytoday.com/archive/black-friday-1921.

Reynolds, David. *The Creation of the Anglo-American Alliance, 1937–41: A Study in Competitive Cooperation.* Chapel Hill: University of North Carolina Press, 1988.

———. *From Munich to Pearl Harbor: Roosevelt's America and the Origins of the Second World War.* Chicago: Ivan R. Dee, 2002.

———. *The Long Shadow: The Great War and the Twentieth Century.* London: Simon and Schuster, 2014.

———. "Lord Lothian and Anglo-American Relations, 1939–1940." *Transactions of the American Philosophical Society* 73, no. 2 (1983): 1–65.

———. "A Special Relationship—America, Britain and the International Order since the World War II." *International Affairs* 62, no. 1 (1985–1986): 1–20.

Rhodes, Benjamin D. "Herbert Hoover and the War Debts, 1919–33." *Prologue* 6, no. 2 (1974): 130–144.

———. "Reassessing 'Uncle Shylock': The United States and the French War Debt, 1917–1929." *Journal of American History* 55, no. 4 (1969): 787–803.

———. *United States Foreign Policy in the Interwar Period, 1918–1941: The Golden Age of American and Diplomatic Complacency.* Westport, CT: Praeger, 2001.

Richardson, J. Henry. *British Economic Foreign Policy.* 1936. Reprint, New York: Routledge, 2018.

Rieffel, Alexis. *Restructuring Sovereign Debt: The Case for Ad Hoc Machinery.* Washington, DC: Brookings Institution Press, 2003.

Ripsman, Norrin M., and Jack S. Levy. "Wishful Thinking or Buying Time? The Logic of British Appeasement in the 1930s." *International Security* 33, no. 2 (2008): 148–181.

Ritschl, Albrecht. "Calling Germany on Its Hypocrisy in the Eurozone Debt Crisis." Research Impact Case Study, London School of Economics, 2014. http://www.lse.ac.uk/Research/research-impact-case-studies/calling-germany-on-its-hypocrisy-in-the-eurozone-debt-crisis.

———. "'Dancing on a Volcano': The Economic Recovery and Collapse of Weimar Germany, 1924–33." In *The World Economy and National Economies in the Interwar Slump*, edited by Theo Balderston, 105–142. Basingstoke, UK: Palgrave, 2003.

———. "The German Transfer Problem, 1920–33: A Sovereign-Debt Perspective." *European Review of History* 19, no. 6 (2012): 943–964.

———. "Reparations, Deficits, and Debt Default: The Great Depression in Germany." In *The Great Depression of the 1930s: Lessons for Today*, edited by Nicholas Crafts and Peter Fearon, 110–139. Oxford: Oxford University Press, 2013.

———. "Sustainability of High Public Debt: What the Historical Record Shows." *Swedish Economic Policy Review* 3, no. 1 (1996): 175–198.

Robb, Thomas K. *Jimmy Carter and the Anglo-American Special Relationship*. Edinburgh: Edinburgh University Press, 2016.

———. "The 'Limit of What Is Tolerable': British Defence Cuts and the 'Special Relationship,' 1974–1976." *Diplomacy and Statecraft* 22, no. 2 (2011): 321–337.

———. *A Strained Partnership? US-UK Relations in the Era of Détente*. Manchester: Manchester University Press, 2013.

Robb, Thomas K., and David James Gill. *Divided Allies: Strategic Cooperation against the Communist Threat in the Asia-Pacific during the Early Cold War*. Ithaca, NY: Cornell University Press, 2019.

Roberts, Priscilla. "Lord Lothian and the Atlantic World." *Historian* 66, no. 1 (2004): 97–127.

Robertson, James C. "The British General Election of 1935." *Journal of Contemporary History* 9, no. 1 (1974): 149–164.

Rockoff, Hugh. *America's Economic Way of War*. Cambridge: Cambridge University Press, 2012.

Rogers, Chris. "Economic Policy and the Problem of Sterling under Harold Wilson and James Callaghan." *Contemporary British History* 25, no. 3 (2011): 339–363.

Rogers, James Harvey. *America Weighs Her Gold*. New Haven, CT: Yale University Press, 1931.

Rohrer, Finlo. "What's a Little Debt between Friends?" *BBC News Magazine*, 10 May 2006. http://news.bbc.co.uk/2/hi/uk_news/magazine/4757181.stm.

Roos, Jerome. *Why Not Default? The Political Economy of Sovereign Debt*. Princeton, NJ: Princeton University Press, 2019.

Roosevelt, Franklin D. *Franklin D. Roosevelt and Foreign Affairs, January 1933–January 1937*. Vol. 1. Edited by Edgar B. Nixon. Cambridge, MA: Harvard University Press, 1969.

———. "Our Foreign Policy: A Democratic View." *Foreign Affairs* 6, no. 4 (1928): 573–586.

Roosevelt, Franklin D., and William C. Bullitt. *For the President Personal and Secret: Correspondence between Franklin D. Roosevelt and*

William C. Bullitt. Edited by Orville H. Bullitt. Boston: Houghton Mifflin, 1972.

Rose, Andrew K., and Mark M. Spiegel. "Noneconomic Engagement and International Exchange: The Case of Environmental Treaties." *Journal of Money, Credit, and Banking* 41, nos. 2–3 (2009): 337–363.

Rosenson, Alex. "The Terms of the Anglo-American Financial Agreement." *American Economic Review* 37, no. 1 (1947): 178–187.

Roth, Tim. *British Protectionism and the International Economy: Overseas Commercial Policy in the 1930s*. Cambridge: Cambridge University Press, 1992.

Rothbard, Murray N. *A History of Money and Banking in the United States*. Auburn, AL: Ludwig von Mises Institute, 1976.

Saiegh, Sebastian. "Coalition Governments and Sovereign Debt Crises." *Economics & Politics* 21, no. 2 (2009): 232–254.

Sandleris, Guido. "The Costs of Sovereign Default: Theory and Empirical Evidence." *Economía* 16, no. 2 (2016): 1–27.

Sargent, Thomas J., George Hall, Martin Ellison, Andrew Scott, Harold James, Era Dabla-Norris, Mark De Broeck, Nicolas End, and Marina Marinkov. *Debt and Entanglements between the Wars*. Washington, DC: International Monetary Fund, 2019.

Saucier, Craig Edward. "Mr. Kerry Goes to Washington: Lord Lothian and the Genesis of the Anglo-American Alliance, 1939–1940." PhD diss., Louisiana State University, 2008.

Sayers, R. S. *The Bank of England, 1891–1944*. Cambridge: Cambridge University Press, 1976.

———. *Financial Policy, 1939–45*. London: HMSO / Longmans, Green, 1956.

Schatz, Arthur W. "The Anglo-American Trade Agreement and Cordell Hull's Search for Peace 1936–1938." *Journal of American History* 57, no. 1 (1970): 85–103.

Schenk, Catherine. *Britain and the Sterling Area: From Devaluation to Convertibility in the 1950s*. Abingdon, UK: Routledge, 1994.

———. *The Decline of Sterling: Managing the Retreat of an International Currency, 1945–1992*. Cambridge: Cambridge University Press, 2013.

———. *International Economic Relations*. London: Routledge, 2011.

Schlesinger, Arthur M. *The Age of Roosevelt: The Crisis of the Old Order, 1919–1933*. Boston: Houghton Mifflin, 1956.

———. *The Coming of the New Deal*. Boston: Houghton Mifflin, 1959.

Schnabel, Isabel. "The Twin German Crisis of 1931." *Journal of Economic History* 64, no. 3 (2004): 822–871.

Schrecker, Ellen. *The Hired Money: The French Debt to the United States 1917–29*. New York: Arno, 1978.

Schuessler, John M. "The Deception Dividend: FDR's Undeclared War." *International Security* 34, no. 4 (2010): 133–165.

Schuker, Stephen A. *American "Reparations" to Germany, 1919–33: Implications for the Third-World Debt Crisis*. Studies in Finance 61. Princeton, NJ: Princeton University Press, 1988.

———. *The End of French Predominance in Europe: The Financial Crisis of 1924 and the Adoption of the Dawes Plan*. Chapel Hill: University of North Carolina Press, 1976.

———. "The Gold Exchange Standard." In *International Financial History in the Twentieth Century: System and Anarchy*, edited by Marc Flandreau, Carl-Ludwig Holtfrerich, and Harold James, 77–94. Cambridge: Cambridge University Press, 2003.

———. "J. M. Keynes and the Personal Politics of Reparations: Part 1." *Diplomacy & Statecraft* 25, no. 3 (2014): 453–471.

Schumacher, Julian, Christoph Trebesch, and Henrik Enderlein. "Sovereign Defaults in Court." *Journal of International Economics* 131 (2021): art. 103388.

Schwartz, Jordan A. *Interregnum of Despair: Hoover, Congress and the Depression*. Urbana: University of Illinois Press, 1970.

Self, Robert. *Britain, America, and the War Debt Controversy: The Economic Diplomacy of an Unspecial Relationship*. London: Routledge, 2006.

———. *Neville Chamberlain: A Biography*. Aldershot, UK: Ashgate, 2006.

———. "Perception and Posture in Anglo-American Relations: The War Debt Controversy in the 'Official Mind,' 1919–1940." *International History Review* 29, no. 2 (2007): 282–312.

Shamir, Haim. *Economic Crisis and French Foreign Policy: 1930–1936*. New York: Brill, 1989.

Shay, Paul. *British Rearmament in the Thirties: Politics and Profits*. Princeton, NJ: Princeton University Press, 1979.

Shea, Patrick. "Borrowing Trouble: Sovereign Credit, Military Regimes, and Conflict." *International Interactions* 42, no. 3 (2016): 401–428.

———. "Financing Victory: Sovereign Credit, Democracy, and War." *Journal of Conflict Resolution* 58, no. 5 (2014): 771–795.

Shea, Patrick, and Paul Poast. "War and Default." *Journal of Conflict Resolution* 62, no. 9 (2018): 1876–1904.

"Shorter Notes." *The Economist*, 9 December 1944.

Simon, Viscount. *Retrospect*. London: Hutchinson, 1952.

Skålnes, Lars S. "Grand Strategy and Foreign Economic Policy: British Grand Strategy in the 1930s." *World Politics* 50, no. 4 (1998): 582–616.

Skidelsky, Robert. *John Maynard Keynes, 1883–1946: Economist, Philosopher, Statesman*. London: Macmillan, 2000.

Slater, Martin. *The National Debt: A Short History*. Oxford: Oxford University Press, 2018. Ebook.

Sobel, Robert. *Coolidge: An American Enigma*. 1998. Reprint, Washington, DC: Regnery, 2015.

Stannage, Tom. *Baldwin Thwarts the Opposition: The British General Election of 1935*. London: Croom Helm, 1980.

Stasavage, David. "Private Investment and Political Institutions." *Economics & Politics* 14, no. 1 (2003): 41–63.

———. *Public Debt and the Birth of the Democratic State: France and Great Britain, 1688–1789*. Cambridge: Cambridge University Press, 2003.

Steil, Benn. *The Battle of Bretton Woods: John Maynard Keynes, Harry Dexter White, and the Making of a New World Order*. Princeton, NJ: Princeton University Press, 2013.

———. *The Marshall Plan: Dawn of the Cold War*. New York: Simon and Schuster, 2018.

Stevenson, David. *1914–1918: The History of the First World War*. London: Allen Lane, 2004.

Stevenson, John, and Chris Cook. *The Slump: Society and Politics during the Depression*. London: Jonathan Cape, 1977.

Stimson, Henry Lewis. *The Politics of Integrity: The Diaries of Henry L. Stimson: 1931 to 1945*. New York: McGraw-Hill, 1976.

Stimson, Henry Lewis, and McGeorge Bundy. *On Active Service in Peace and War*. New York: Harper, 1947.

Stockman, David A. *The Great Deformation: The Corruption of Capitalism in America*. New York: Public Affairs, 2013.

Strachan, Hew. *Financing the First World War*. Oxford: Oxford University Press, 2004.

———. *The First World War: A New History*. New York: Simon and Schuster, 2014.

Strange, Susan. "Debt and Default in the International Political Economy." In *Debt and the Less Developed Countries*, edited by Jonathan David Aronson, 7–26. Boulder, CO: Westview, 1979.

Straumann, Tobias. *1931: Debt, Crisis, and the Rise of Hitler*. Oxford: Oxford University Press, 2019.

Striner, Richard. *Woodrow Wilson and World War I: A Burden Too Great to Bear*. Lanham, MD: Rowman and Littlefield, 2016.

Stubbings, Matthew. "Free Trade Empire to Commonwealth of Nations: India, Britain and Imperial Preference, 1903–1932." *International History Review* 41, no. 2 (2019): 323–344.

Sturzenegger, Federico, and Jeromin Zettelmeyer. *Debt Defaults and Lessons from a Decade of Crises.* Cambridge, MA: MIT Press, 2007.

———. "Haircuts: Estimating Investor Losses in Sovereign Debt Restructurings, 1998–2005." *Journal of International Money and Finance* 27, no. 5 (2008): 780–805.

Suddath, Claire. "Why Did World War I Just End?" *Time*, 4 October 2010.

Tannenwald, Nina. *The Nuclear Taboo: The United States and the Non-Use of Nuclear Weapons since 1945.* Cambridge: Cambridge University Press, 2007.

"Tax? April Fool!" *The Economist*, 6 April 1968.

Temin, Peter. "The Rise and Fall of Economic History at MIT." MIT Department of Economics Working Paper 13-11, 2013.

Temin, Peter, and David Vines. *The Leaderless Economy: Why the World Economic System Fell Apart and How to Fix It.* Princeton, NJ: Princeton University Press, 2013.

Tetlock, Philip E., and Aaron Belkin. "Counterfactual Thought Experiments in World Politics." In *Counterfactual Thought Experiments in World Politics: Logical, Methodological, and Psychological Perspectives*, edited by Philip E. Tetlock and Aaron Belkin, 1–38. Princeton, NJ: Princeton University Press, 1996.

Thomas, Gordon, and Max Morgan-Witts. *The Day the Bubble Burst: A Social History of the Wall Street Crash of 1929.* London: Penguin, 1980.

Thorpe, Andrew. *The British General Election of 1931.* Oxford: Oxford University Press, 1991.

Tomlinson, Jim. "Britain since the 1970s: A Transition to Neoliberalism?" In *Money and Markets: Essays in Honour of Martin Daunton*, edited by Julian Hoppit, Duncan Needham, and Adrian Leonard, 181–198. Suffolk, UK: Boydell and Brewer, 2019.

———. "Correlli Barnett's History: The Case of Marshall Aid." *Twentieth Century British History* 8, no. 2 (1997): 222–238.

———. "The Decline of Empire and the Economic 'Decline' of Britain." *Twentieth Century British History* 14, no. 3 (2003): 201–221.

———. *Employment Policy: The Crucial Years 1939–55.* Oxford: Oxford University Press, 1987.

———. "Inventing 'Decline': The Falling Behind of the British Economy in the Postwar Years." *Economic History Review* 49, no. 4 (1996): 731–757.

———. *The Labour Governments, 1964–1970.* Vol. 3, *Economic Policy.* Manchester: Manchester University Press, 2004.

Tomz, Michael. *Reputation and International Cooperation: Sovereign Debt across Three Centuries.* Princeton, NJ: Princeton University Press, 2007.

Tomz, Michael, and Mark L. J. Wright. "Do Countries Default in Bad Times?" *Journal of the European Economic Association* 5, nos. 2–3 (2007): 352–360.

———. "Empirical Research on Sovereign Debt and Default." *Annual Review of Economics* 5, no. 1 (2013): 247–272.

———. "Sovereign Theft: Theory and Evidence about Sovereign Default and Expropriation." In *The Natural Resources Trap: Private Investment without Public Commitment*, edited by William Hogan and Federico Sturzenegger, 69–110. Cambridge, MA: MIT Press, 2010.

Tooze, Adam. *Crashed: How a Decade of Financial Crises Changed the World*. London: Allen Lane, 2018.

———. *The Deluge: The Great War and the Remaking of Global Order, 1916–1931*. London: Penguin, 2015.

———. *Wages of Destruction: The Making and Breaking of the Nazi Economy*. London: Penguin, 2007.

Toussaint, Eric. *The Debt System: A History of Sovereign Debts and Their Repudiation*. Chicago: Haymarket Books, 2018.

Toye, Richard. "Churchill and Britain's 'Financial Dunkirk.'" *Twentieth Century British History* 15, no. 4 (2004): 329–360.

———. *The Labour Party and the Planned Economy, 1931–1951*. Suffolk, UK: Boydell, 2003.

———. "The New Commanding Height: Labour Party Policy on North Sea Oil and Gas, 1964–74." *Contemporary British History* 16, no. 1 (2002): 89–118.

Trachtenberg, Marc. "Dan Reiter and America's Road to War in 1941." In "Democracy, Deception, and Entry into War," H-Diplo/ISSF Roundtable 5-4, H-Net, 17 May 2013.

———. "My Story." H-Diplo Essay 313, Essay Series on Learning the Scholar's Craft: Reflections of Historians and International Relations Scholars, 16 February 2021. https://hdiplo.org/to/E313.

———. "Reparation at the Paris Peace Conference." *Journal of Modern History* 51, no. 1 (1979): 24–55.

———. *Reparations in World Politics: France and European Economic Diplomacy, 1916–1923*. New York: Columbia University Press, 1980.

Trentmann, Frank. *Free Trade Nation: Commerce, Consumption, and Civil Society in Modern Britain*. Oxford: Oxford University Press, 2009.

Truman, Harry. *Memoirs by Harry S. Truman*. Vol. 1, *1945: Year of Decisions*. New York: Doubleday 1955.

———. *Memoirs of Harry S. Truman*. Vol. 2, *Years of Trial and Hope, 1946–53*. New York: Hodder, 1956.

Tugwell, Rexford. *The Brains Trust*. New York: Viking, 1968.

————. *In Search of Roosevelt*. Cambridge, MA: Harvard University Press, 1972.

Turner, Arthur. *The Cost of War: British Policy on French War Debts*. Brighton, UK: Sussex Academic Press, 1998.

Turner, John. *British Politics and the Great War: Coalition and Conflict, 1915–1918*. New Haven, CT: Yale University Press, 1992.

Vagts, Detlev F. "Sovereign Bankruptcy: In re Germany (1953): In re Iraq (2004)." *American Journal of International Law* 98, no. 2 (2004): 302–306.

Vandenberg, Arthur, Jr. *The Private Papers of Senator Vandenberg*. London: Victor Gollanz, 1953.

Vansittart, Robert. *The Mist Procession*. London: Hutchinson, 1958.

Viner, Jacob. "Reviewed Work: *The Carthaginian Peace—or the Economic Consequences of Mr. Keynes* by Étienne Mantoux." *Journal of Modern History* 19, no. 1 (1947): 69–70.

Vinson, Fred M., and Dean Acheson. *The British Loan—What It Means to Us*. U.S. Department of State. Washington, DC: Government Printing Office, 1946.

Vinson, J. C. "War Debts and Peace Legislation: The Johnson Act of 1934." *Mid-America: An Historical Review* 50 (1968): 206–222.

Walker, J. Samuel. *Prompt and Utter Destruction: Truman and the Use of Atomic Bombs against Japan*. Chapel Hill: University of North Carolina Press, 2004.

Wapshott, Nicholas. *Keynes Hayek: The Clash that Defined Modern Economics*. New York: Norton, 2012.

"War Debts, The." *The Economist*, 21 April 1934.

"War Debt Palaver." *The Economist* 117, no. 4706 (4 November 1933).

"War Debts—A Postscript." *The Economist* 115, no. 4660 (17 December 1932).

Wass, Douglas. *Decline to Fall: The Making of British Macro-economic Policy and the 1976 IMF Crisis*. Oxford: Oxford University Pres, 2008.

Watt, D. Cameron. *Succeeding John Bull: America in Britain's Place, 1900–1975*. Cambridge: Cambridge University Press, 1984.

Weldon, Duncan. *Two Hundred Years of Muddling Through: The Surprising Story of the British Economy*. Boston: Little, Brown, 2021.

Wevill, Richard. *Britain and America after World War II: Bilateral Relations and the Beginnings of the Cold War*. London: I. B. Tauris, 2012. Ebook.

Wheeler-Bennett, John W. *King George VI: His Life and Reign*. London: Macmillan, 1958.

Whitham, Charlie. "Seeing the Wood for the Trees: The British Foreign Office and the Anglo-American Trade Agreement of 1938." *Twentieth Century British History* 16, no. 1 (2005): 29–51.

———. "Sore Thumbs and Beachcombers: Britain, the War Debt, and the Cession of the British West Indies, July 1938–May 1940." *Journal of Imperial and Commonwealth History* 25, no. 3 (1997): 466–488.

Williams, Francis. *A Prime Minister Remembers.* London: Heinemann, 1960.

Williamson, Philip. *National Crisis and National Government: British Politics, the Economy and Empire, 1926–1932.* Cambridge: Cambridge University Press, 1992.

Williamson, Samuel H. "Seven Ways to Compute the Relative Value of a U.S. Dollar Amount, 1790 to Present." MeasuringWorth, 2021. https://www.measuringworth.com/calculators/uscompare/.

Wilson, Harold. *The Labour Government, 1964–1970: A Personal Record.* London: Weidenfeld and Nicolson and Michael Joseph, 1971.

Wilson, Joan Hoff. *American Business and Foreign Policy, 1920–1933.* Lexington: University Press of Kentucky, 1971.

Wilson, Ward. "The Winning Weapon? Rethinking Nuclear Weapons in Light of Hiroshima." *International Security* 31, no. 4 (2007): 162–179.

Wiltz, John Edward. "The Nye Committee Revisited." *Historian* 23, no. 2 (1961): 211–233.

Wiseley, William. "Paying Debts." *The Economist*, 24 September 1977.

Wolcott, Susan. "Keynes versus Churchill: Revaluation and British Unemployment in the 1920s." *Journal of Economic History* 53, no. 3 (1993): 601–628.

Woods, Randall Bennett. *A Changing of the Guard: Anglo-American Relations, 1941–1946.* Chapel Hill: University of North Carolina Press, 1990.

Wormell, Jeremy. *The Management of the National Debt of the UK, 1900–1932.* London: Routledge, 1999.

W.O.S. "Britain's Budget Surpluses and War Debt." *Foreign Affairs* 14, no. 1 (1935): 163–164.

Young, G. M. *Stanley Baldwin.* London: Hart-Davis, 1952.

Young, John W. *The Labour Governments, 1964–1970.* Vol. 2, *International Policy.* Manchester: Manchester University Press, 2003.

Young, Lowell. "Franklin D. Roosevelt and America's Islets: Acquisition of Territory in the Caribbean and in the Pacific." *Historian* 35, no. 2 (1973): 205–220.

Zahniser, Marvin R. "Rethinking the Significance of Disaster: The United States and the Fall of France in 1940." *International History Review* 14, no. 2 (1992): 252–276.

Zeiler, Thomas. *Free Trade, Free World: The Advent of GATT.* Chapel Hill: University of North Carolina Press, 1999.

Zenko, Micah. *Red Team: How to Succeed by Thinking like the Enemy.* New York: Basic Books, 2015.

Ziegler, Philip. *Edward Heath: The Authorised Biography*. New York: Harper, 2011.

Zielinski, Rosella. *How States Pay for Wars*. Ithaca, NY: Cornell University Press, 2018.

Zimmermann, Hubert. *Money and Security: Troops, Monetary Policy, and West Germany's Relations with the United States and Britain, 1950–1971*. Cambridge: Cambridge University Press, 2002.

———. "Western Europe and the American Challenge: Conflict and Cooperation in Technology and Monetary Policy, 1965–1973." In *Between Empire and Alliance: America and Europe during the Cold War*, edited by Marc Trachtenberg, 127–155. Lanham, MD: Rowman and Littlefield, 2003.

Zivney, Terry L., and Richard D. Marcus. "The Day the United States Defaulted on Treasury Bills." *Financial Review* 24, no. 3 (1989): 475–489.

Index